A NEW DEAL FOR BLACKS

v. 1

A NEW DEAL FOR BLACKS

The Emergence of Civil Rights
as a National Issue
Volume I: The Depression Decade

WITHDRAWN

HARVARD SITKOFF

New York
OXFORD UNIVERSITY PRESS
1978

Copyright © 1978 by Oxford University Press, Inc.

Library of Congress Cataloging in Publication Data

Sitkoff, Harvard.
   A new deal for blacks.
   Includes bibliographical references and index.
    1. Afro-Americans—Civil rights.   2. Afro-Americans
—History—1877–1964. I. Title.
E185.61.S546   323.42'3'0973   78–2633
ISBN 0-19-502418-4

The excerpt from the play "Don't You Want to Be Free" by Langston
Hughes is reprinted by permission of Harold Ober Associates Incorporated.
Copyright © 1938 by Langston Hughes. Renewed.

The lines from the poem "Reverie on the Harlem River" are taken from the
volume *Selected Poems* by Langston Hughes. Copyright © by Langston
Hughes. Reprinted by permission of Alfred A. Knopf, Inc.

Printed in the United States of America

To My Mother and
the Memory of My Father

probable. I have concentrated on the occurrences that ultimately led to significant racial reforms—but did not do so in the 1930s. For civil rights, the depression decade proved to be a time of planting, not harvesting. It was an era of rising black expectations and decreasing Negro powerlessness, an age of diminishing white indifference to the plight of Afro-Americans. As such, the New Deal years are a turning point in race relations trends. They constitute a watershed of developments whose outgrowth was a broad-based social movement aimed at bringing about a fuller participation of blacks in American society. The complex cause of that transformation is the subject of *A New Deal For Blacks*. The title is not meant to convey that the struggle for racial equality either began or achieved fulfillment in the 1930s. It does not mean that blacks received their proper due from the government programs we refer to as the New Deal. Nor should the titled be construed to signify that Franklin D. Roosevelt and the New Deal were the sole or primary determinants of the emergence of civil rights as a national issue. Governmental action, I have tried to make clear, was but one of the interrelated reasons for that phenomenon. Rather, *A New Deal for Blacks* is an abbreviated indication both of the subject and era covered in this volume and of my thesis that a variety of fundamental changes in the status of race relations occurred in the 1930s, setting it apart from the preceding decades.

Given the focus of my study, and the publisher's insistence on brevity, much had to be omitted. I am acutely aware of what has been overlooked, of all the books I have not written. Any one of the chapters could easily have been expanded to a book-length treatment. Moreover, because I have concentrated on national developments furthering the cause of racial justice my research has been admittedly selective. What follows is far from the whole picture; it is more an overview of a dozen diverse transformations than an in-depth analysis of any single one. Consequently, much work remains to be done in the manuscript and archival collections I have researched. I hope this book provokes the interest that leads others to pursue the paths I have not taken.

Those who follow, I trust, will understand that I tried to be not merely as accurate as I could in my research and writing but also as objective as possible in my judgments. I sought to keep my biases out of this study; I know that aim is beyond possibility. Much of my understanding of the dynamics of civil rights, as well as the inspiration for this project, flowed from my own involvement in the movement for racial justice. I believe again in that struggle. That should be borne in mind by the reader.

It has often been emphasized that research and writing are lonely enterprises. Yet, during the many years I pursued this topic I have been the recipient of generous assistance and encouragement. To mention all who helped would require almost as many pages of acknowledgement as there are text. Special thanks, however, are due to the cordial guidance of library staffs across the country. I am especially grateful to the archivists at Atlanta, Dillard, and Duke universities, the Labor History Archives of Wayne State University, the Library of Congress, the Michigan Historical Collection of the University of Michigan, the National Archives, the Oral History Collection of Columbia University, the Franklin D. Roosevelt Library, the Schomburg Branch of the New York Public Library, and the Southern Historical Collection of the University of North Carolina. I also wish to single out for thanks the Eleanor Roosevelt Institute for a research grant; the Starobin family for providing me with a wonderful home in which to write; Sheldon Meyer, Parke Puterbaugh, and Susan Rabiner for their acumen; and my colleagues at the University of New Hampshire for being supportive in all the ways that count.

The aid of fellow scholars has been inestimable. Even a cursory glance at my notes would indicate this. Publishing costs, moreover, forced me to abbreviate, quite drastically, these notes. The original footnotes and bibliography, which more accurately suggest my intellectual indebtedness, appear in my doctoral disserta-

tion at Columbia University. Although hopelessly inadequate re-
payment for all the ideas and information I received from them, I
principally wish to acknowledge how much I owe to the scholarship of Lerone Bennett, Jr., Barton J. Bernstein, Dan T. Carter,
Leslie H. Fishel, Jr., John B. Kirby, Thomas A. Kreuger, James T.
Patterson, George B. Tindall, Raymond Wolters and Robert L.
Zangrando. Their works were my constant companions in this effort. An extra special debt of gratitude is owed to Henry Berger,
Richard Dalfiume, and August Meier. The insights and knowledge
I received from their writings and their critiques of my manuscript suffuse this volume. At Columbia University, Sigmund
Diamond and Charles V. Hamilton provided wise counsel on how
to improve my dissertation, and Kenneth T. Jackson gave unselfishly at the roughest moments. His astuteness and kindness
were appreciated far more than I ever expressed at the time. And
special thanks to Regina Morantz for her shrewd criticisms and
invaluable reassurances, and to Bill Chafe for all of the above and
so much else. Suffice to say, the assistance of those named has
contributed mightily to the strengths of this book; I alone am responsible for its weaknesses.

Primarily, there is William E. Leuchtenburg. All the possible
good that could be said of a mentor and model has already been
expressed by those who have been fortunate enough to work with
him. I will only gladly add my amen to the paeans of praise for
his unfailing goodness, patience, selflessness, skill, and judgment.
As only I can truly know, whatever merits this book possesses are
due to this wise and wonderful teacher.

Lastly, for what my wife Evelyn has given to me and to this
project, words are inadequate. She and I understand; that is
enough.

Durham, New Hampshire
June 1978   HARVARD SITKOFF

Contents

A NEW DEAL FOR BLACKS

1

"The Dusk of Dawn"

Following the election of 1876, the civil rights issue imperceptibly ebbed from the mainstream of American life and thought. Unmistakably, although never all at once or fully so, the leading voices of Northern liberalism increasingly voiced indifference to the plight of blacks, disenchantment with Radical reconstruction, and opposition to their former goal of a racially equalitarian nation. The Republican party replaced its bloody shirt with the garb of sectional—white—reconciliation, and the Reconstruction rhetoric of antislavery veterans, emphasizing the inalienable national rights of all men, metamorphosed into shibboleths of white supremacy and assertions that the white South knew best how to handle the "Negro problem." "Wendell Phillips and William Lloyd Garrison are not exactly extinct forces in American politics," noted the New York *Times* in 1876, "but they represent ideas in regard to the South which the great majority of the Republican party have outgrown."[1]

The Congress certainly proved the New York *Times* correct. After acting to provide the Afro-American with freedom, equality, and the vote, it permitted the white South to reduce him to a state of peonage, to disregard his rights, and to disenfranchise

him by force, intimidation, and statute. In 1878 Congress forbade
the use of the Army to protect black voters. In ensuing years
Congress twice refused to pass the needed Federal Elections Bill.
In 1894 it cut off all appropriations for special federal marshalls
and supervisors assigned to Southern polling places. No effort
was made to intervene in "Southern affairs." No action was taken
to protect Negro rights. Legislators in the 1890s no longer submitted civil rights bills even perfunctorily. By the turn of the
century, an advocate of total disfranchisement of Negroes in
Alabama could point to Congress and assert confidently that "we
have now the sympathy of thoughtful men in the North to an
extent that never before existed." In 1901 the last black representative left Congress; it would be three decades before another
would take his place. No hope (or apprehension) remained that
Congress would insist on the enforcement of its Reconstruction
legislation.[2]

The Supreme Court trod the same path. It too refused to con-
summate the changes in Negro-white relations promised by the
Fourteenth and Fifteenth amendments and a score of supporting
statutes. As early as 1873, in the *Slaughter-House Cases,* which
did not involve blacks at all, the high court sounded retreat by
signaling its intention to let the white South settle its own racial
affairs without undue judicial interference. Although the aim of
the framers of the Fourteenth Amendment had been to protect
the legal and political rights of the Afro-American against arbi-
trary state action, exemplified by the Black Codes, a five-man
majority on the Court now asserted that it was *not* the purpose
of the amendment "to transfer the security and protection of . . .
civil rights . . . from the states to the federal government."
Three years later the retreat from the concept of federally
guaranteed civil rights turned into a rout. In the *Cruikshank* and
Reese cases, the Supreme Court denied blacks the protection of
the Fourteenth Amendment in all cases except those of official
state discrimination, and affirmed the power of the individual
states to control suffrage requirements, thereby opening the door

to all manner of racial discrimination and disfranchisement schemes.[3]

The cruelest blows were still to come. By votes of eight-to-one the Supreme Court nullified the Civil Rights Act of 1875, which denied Congress the power to prohibit the practice of discrimination by individuals, and approved state-imposed segregation as consonant with the supreme law of the land. Writing into the Constitution their own beliefs in the inferiority of blacks, the late nineteenth-century justices tightened every possible shackle confining the ex-slaves. With impunity the Court struck down a state law forbidding segregation on public carriers as an undue burden on interstate commerce and then turned around to uphold the constitutionality of a state law requiring segregation on such carriers. Indeed, in a wide-ranging series of opinions that established precedents for all other courts to follow and articulated the norms of national belief and values, the Supreme Court legitimized the right of states to exclude blacks from jury service; to prohibit intermarriage; to segregate school children; to deny blacks equality in public accommodations; to permit the disfranchisement of Negroes; and finally to bar all interracial contact, however selective or voluntary. A legal counter-revolution had occurred. Insofar as they protected the civil rights of blacks, the Reconstruction amendments and legislation were dead.[4]

Few American scholars mourned. Many had performed yeoman duty for the legislators and justices, preaching the folly of governmental tampering with local folkways and placing their imprimatur on the doctrine of inherent and irremediable racial differences. Their notions thus provided the intellectual rationalizations for the demise of civil rights. A generation of editors, clergymen, and educators followed suit. They vied to justify white supremacy by appeals to Darwinism; by affirmation of the gospel of Anglo-Saxonism enunciated by Columbia University's eminent political scientist John W. Burgess; by utilizing the historical truths propounded by that university's leading student of the Reconstruction era, William H. Dunning; by extending the then current arguments favoring immigration restriction or American expansionism in the Pacific and Caribbean; by selective citations of scriptural and scientific evidence; and most of all by endlessly repeating the exhortations of Yale's leading luminary, William Graham Sumner, that one could not alter prejudice by stateways, that changing "the system" was like "making a man of sixty into something else than what his life has made him," and that however a "man may curse his fate because he is born of an inferior race," heaven will never answer his "imprecations."[5]

The rediscovery of the Mendelian laws of heredity, which sparked new interest in the genetic transmission of racial characteristics, bolstered such beliefs. By 1900 the eugenics movement was in full bloom. It thrived in a climate of racism. Led by Charles B. Davenport, a biologist who was even ready to ascribe prostitution to an inherited predisposition to hypereroticism rather than to environmental causes, the eugenicists claimed that nature, not nurture, accounted for the superiority of white over black. They also asserted a unilinear vertical progression of the races with Negroes biologically the most inferior and Caucasians the most exalted. Given this combination of congenital racial traits and the Nordic monopolization of desirable characteristics, the eugenics movement publicly advocated whatever they thought necessary to preserve the racial purity of white Americans. Usually this meant either segregation or sterilization of the "lower" races to prevent the pollution of those more "civilized."[6]

Not surprisingly, most white Americans at the beginning of the twentieth century believed that, for the good of all, the naturally superior whites should rule over the baser races. They heard or read little to the contrary. Even most humanitarian reformers still concerned with racial injustice counseled gradualism rather than immediacy. They talked of the necessity of preparing the freedmen for citizenship, emphasizing the long-term gains to be derived from education, religion, and economic uplift while denigrating strategies predicated on agitation, force or political activity.[7]

The Southern Way had become the American Way. "Agitation of the Negro question," observed Charles Beard, had become "bad form in the North." Ray Stannard Baker reported that the "place" of Negroes had been defined and settled, "and the less they are talked about the better." But white Americans sang popular songs about blacks with such titles as "If the Man in the Moon Were a Coon" and "All Coons Look Alike to Me." They watched early Thomas Edison movies like "Colored Boy Eating Watermelons" and "Chicken Thieves," or the highly popular silent films "Rastus in Zululand" and "Coon Town Suffragettes." They read Charles Carroll's *The Negro a Beast* and Robert W. Shufeldt's *The Negro: A Menace to American Civilization.* Their short stories featured Negro characters with such mocking names as Lady Adelia Chimpanzee and Abraham Lincum. And their most prestigious journals—*Nation, Harper's Weekly,* and *Independent*—all once militantly equalitarian in their racial attitudes, now regularly demeaned "the darky" and portrayed Afro-Americans as not ready to possess the full rights and responsibilities of citizenship in a white man's government. "Northern men," the New York *Times* opined in 1900, "no longer denounce the suppression of the Negro vote in the South as it used to be denounced in Reconstruction days. The necessity of it under the supreme law of self-preservation is candidly recognized."[8]

Such total acquiescence by Northern liberals and government officials gave the white South all the permission it needed to institutionalize its white supremacist beliefs. First came disfranchisement. Accomplished in the 1880s mainly through fraud, force, and intimidation, all the Southern states felt emboldened enough in the next decade to follow the lead of the 1890 Mississippi state constitutional convention in officially adopting such disfranchising measures as the poll tax, the "understanding" and "good character" tests, the white primary, and the "grandfather clause." State Senator Carter Glass proclaimed the intent of these measures to his Old Dominion colleagues: "Discrimination!" Glass expounded at his state's constitutional convention in 1901. "Why,

that is precisely what we propose; that, exactly, is what this convention was elected for—to discriminate to the very extremity of
permissible action under the limitations of the Federal Constitution, with a view to the elimination of every Negro voter who can
be gotten rid of, legally, without materially impairing the numerical strength of the white electorate.[9]

Glass and his counterparts throughout the South succeeded
completely. In Louisiana over 130,000 blacks had gone to the
polls in 1896. They were a voting majority in twenty-six parishes.
In 1900, two years after the adoption of a new state constitution
modeled on Mississippi's, Negro voter registration dropped 96
percent. A bare 5000 blacks now voted in Louisiana; in not a single parish could their votes carry an election. In Alabama, a state
with an adult Negro population of nearly 300,000, the number of
blacks permitted to vote in the new century hovered around
3500. In Georgia some 10,000 out of an adult population of
370,000 blacks now voted. In Virginia it was about 15,000 out of
a possible 250,000. Less than 1000 blacks voted in Mississippi;
some 300,000 were by white standards qualified to vote.[10]

Moreover, the adoption of the white primary by every Southern
state, barring blacks from the nominating process—the only elections that mattered in a solidly one-party region—made even the
tiny handful of Negro votes cast in the general elections meaningless. Politically the color line had been fully drawn. "I am just as
much opposed to Booker Washington as a voter, with all his
Anglo-Saxon reenforcements," declared Senator J. K. Vardaman
of Mississippi, "as I am to the cocoanut-headed, chocolate-cov-
ered, typical little coon, Andy Dotson, who blacks my shoes every
morning. Neither is fit to perform the supreme function of citizenship."[11]

Political impotency bore on every aspect of Afro-American life.
Unable to participate in the enactment or enforcement of the
law, Southern blacks became increasingly vulnerable to physical
assault and oppression. "You understand," a prominent white
citizen of Tuskegee, Alabama, told a Negro educator, "that we

have the legislature, we make the laws, we have the judges, the sheriffs, the jails. We have the hardware stores and the arms." And daily violence, or the threat of it, created an atmosphere of ever-present fear for blacks. They could never assume the safety of their persons or property. Petty brutality, lynchings and pogroms against the Negro section of towns occurred so frequently in the first decade of the twentieth century that they appeared commonplace, hardly newsworthy. Negro organizations recorded over a thousand lynchings of Southern blacks between 1900 and 1915. How many went uncounted no one can tell. No one today can even begin to estimate the number of blacks beaten, tortured, or killed by whites in those years. Nor can one describe adequately the terror of living with a constant fear of barbarity, of having your security subject to the whim of those who despise you, of having no recourse to police or courts.[12]

In addition, the Southern states adopted a host of statutes methodically outlawing everything "interracial." These new segregation laws expressed the white South's all-encompassing belief in the inequality of blacks. Most Southern states now formally required Negroes and whites to be born separately in segregated hospitals; to live their lives as separately as possible in segregated schools, public accommodations, and places of work and recreation; and, presumably, to dwell in the next life separately in segregated funeral homes and cemeteries. The rapid proliferation of Jim Crow laws inspired an irrational competition among Southern legislators to erect ever more and higher barriers between the races. "White" and "colored" signs sprouted everywhere and on everything. Atlanta mandated Jim Crow Bibles in its courtrooms. Alabama forbade Negroes to play checkers with whites. New Orleans segregated its prostitutes, and Oklahoma, its telephone booths. The lawmakers of Florida and North Carolina saw to it that white students would never touch textbooks used by blacks. Such edicts could not but demean the spirit of Afro-Americans, branding them with an indelible mark of inferiority. Furthermore, Jim Crow easily led to gross inequities in the distribution of pub-

lic monies for education and civic services. In 1910 the eleven
Southern states spent an average of $9.45 per white public school
student, and $2.90 per black child. Six years later the average was
$10.32 per white student, but only $2.89 per Negro pupil. By the
1920s there was one hospital bed available for every 139 American whites, but only one for every 1941 blacks. But that was not
all. Southern state and local governments also joined to deny
blacks legal justice, to victimize them by bestial convict-leasing
and chain-gang practices, and to confine them to a bare subsistence serfdom on the lowest rung of the economic ladder. "What
positive gain has the operation of the Fourteenth Amendment
been to the Negro race?" a white scholar asked in 1912. "We can
point to nothing."[13]

And blacks could do little to alter the situation or even to protest it. More than 90 percent of the Afro-Americans in 1910
lived in the South, three-quarters of them in rural areas. Theirs
was a closed society, one designed to thwart their advancement
and encourage their subservience. Southern Negroes, bereft of
white allies or governmental concern, daily faced grinding poverty, physical helplessness, and all the banal cruelties of existence under an open, professed, and boasting discrimination. All
political and economic power remained vested in whites determined to maintain the status quo, however many black lives it
took. Segregation and discrimination now seemed so permanent,
so immutable, so much an inevitable condition of life. Fatalism
spawned hopelessness, and the majority of Southern blacks succumbed to the new racial order.[14]

But not all. Some voted with their feet by migrating. Between
1890 and 1910, nearly 200,000 Southern blacks fled to the North.
Others dreamt of returning to Africa and some even attempted
the journey. Still others tried to establish autonomous black communities in the West. A few, mostly members of the tiny, Northern black elite, continued the civil rights protest movement they
had inherited from the abolitionists and Radical Republicans.
They spoke out for racial equality and justice in the Afro-Ameri-

can Council, Monroe Trotter's National Equal Rights League, Ida B. Wells's Antilynching League, the Boston Suffrage League, the Niagara Movement and John Milholland's Constitution League. Few blacks, however, heard their pleas; fewer whites heeded their demands. The civil rights organizations of the early twentieth century lacked adequate finances, political leverage, the support of most blacks, influential white allies, and access to the major institutions shaping public opinion and policy. Without some combination of these, they could not alter the course of American life and thought.[15]

In 1895, the year of Frederick Douglass's death, Booker T. Washington delivered an address at the Atlanta Exposition. His speech articulated the predominant themes of Negro advancement for the next third of a century. Emphasizing the necessity of conciliation, gradualism, and accommodation, Washington deprecated political and protest activity aimed at the immediate attainment of civil rights for blacks. "Brains, property, and character for the Negro," he hoped, "will settle the question of civil rights." Yet publicly he informed whites: "We are trying to instill into the Negro mind that if education does not make the Negro humble, simple, and of service to the community, then it will not be encouraged." And time and again he would tell blacks that "the best course to pursue in regard to civil rights . . . is to let it alone; let it alone and it will settle itself." Shortly before he died in 1915 Washington still insisted that "no law of Congress or of the State Legislature can help us as much" as the accumulation of wealth and education.[16]

Privately, however, Washington attempted to maneuver in another direction. He covertly spent thousands of his own dollars to finance test cases against the disfranchisement provisions of the Alabama and Louisiana constitutions. When the Georgia legislature took up a bill to exclude blacks from voting, he hurried to Atlanta to lobby against the measure. Moreover, Washington surreptitiously fought Jim Crow laws in Tennessee and Virginia, and assisted in several court battles against the exclusion of Negroes from juries. Washington's hopes and goals, apparently, were much the same as those of Frederick Douglass and his followers. His differences with the proponents of civil rights resided more in geography than in ideology. While others plotted utopias, Washington sought piecemeal advantages for the mass of blacks in the white supremacist South.[17]

Unfortunately, his words spoke louder than his actions. While few knew or remembered either Washington's covert activities or his eventual goals, the opponents of civil rights kept citing the soothing statements that had emanated from Tuskegee. His writings and speeches were used to fashion a myth of the Southern Negro being content with the conditions of life. Like the earlier myth of the happy slave, this new Southern myth portrayed blacks as not the equals of whites, at least not yet; as not being ready for the rights and duties of citizenship; as not wanting to associate with whites; as preferring separation of the races; and as being satisfied, even happy, with the status quo. The myth haunted the embryonic civil rights movement.[18]

The handful of blacks fighting for racial justice thus needed to shout about their dissatisfaction, to dissent from the myth Washington had helped forge. They made their primary task countering the false impression given by the man from Tuskegee that "the Negro-American assents to inferiority, is submissive under oppression, and apologetic before insult." None did so more consistently and emphatically than William Edward Burghardt Du Bois.[19]

A scholar and propagandist, Du Bois kindled the campaign for the Negro's civil rights for over half a century. After receiving an education at Fisk and Harvard universities, as well as the University of Berlin, the aloof, aristocratic professor of economics and sociology came to the fore as a neo-abolitionist spokesman with the publication in 1903 of his *The Souls of Black Folk*. It "had a greater effect upon and within the Negro race than any single book published in the country since *Uncle Tom's Cabin*," recalled James Weldon Johnson, a supporter of Washington who later followed Du Bois to the National Association for the Advancement of Colored People. No chapter of the book created greater controversy than "Of Mr. Booker T. Washington and Others." After praising the Tuskegeean for preaching "Thrift, Patience, and Industrial Training for the masses," the prodigy of the black elite then subjected Washington to a withering attack for "apologizing for injustices, North or South." He accused the Negro leader of "practically accepting the alleged inferiority of the Negro," of belittling "the emasculating effects of caste distinctions," of proposing a "submission to prejudice," of increasing the blight of segregation by failing to assail it, and of hastening disfranchisement by not "rightly valu[ing] the privilege and duty of voting." Du Bois demanded an end to accommodation. He called for a new age of agitation. "We have no right to sit silently by while the inevitable seeds are sown for a harvest of disaster to our children, black and white."[20]

Two years later Du Bois and a handful of black comrades who opposed Booker T. Washington issued a call for a new organization of men of "determined and aggressive action . . . who believe in Negro freedom and growth." In July they established the Niagara Movement. "We do not hesitate to complain," trumpeted its Declaration of Principles, "and to complain loudly and insistently. To ignore, overlook, or apologize for these wrongs is to prove ourselves unworthy of freedom. Persistent manly agitation is the way to liberty."[21]

Meeting at Harper's Ferry the following year, Du Bois hammered out the militant demands of the young movement. "We will not be satisfied to take one jot or tittle less than our full manhood rights. We claim for ourselves every single right that belongs to a freeborn American. . . . We want full manhood suffrage and we want it now. . . . We want discrimination in public accommodation to cease. . . . We want the Constitution of the country enforced." Confident that the Negro's vigorous quest for civil rights would insure its fruition, Du Bois concluded, "We are men! We will be treated as men. And We shall win!"[22]

Neither confidence nor rhetoric, however, either improved the Negro's status or weakened Washington's power in the first decade of the century. The Tuskegeean isolated the Niagara Movement from white liberals and the mass of blacks. Du Bois succeeded in reaching only a small coterie of urban, Northern college-educated Negroes. By 1910 the Niagara Movement had ceased to function. It had failed to achieve any of its stated demands. Yet it revived the abolitionist tradition of agitation and its program mapped out an alternative course to Washington's that would be followed in later years by a burgeoning corps of Afro-American and white leaders: enfranchisement and equality of opportunity for blacks, and an end to racial discrimination and segregation.[23]

But it would not happen in the Progressive era. Indeed, as white reformers articulated their vision of social justice, anti-Negro sentiment and legislation reached their zenith. Despite all the progressive talk of humanitarianism, most white reformers, like their Mugwump predecessors, either ignored the race problem or repeated the litany of Booker T. Washington. Many believed white racism a proper corollary of immigration restriction and dollar diplomacy. Others accepted black disfranchisement as the price of clean government. Some defended racial exclusionism as indispensable to a healthy labor union movement. And so it went. Few white reformers considered progressivism in any light that would benefit blacks.[24]

Even the progressive environmentalists' explanation for human shortcomings stopped at the color line. Although all manner of white misbehavior could best be understood as the consequence of poverty, family disorganization, or the lack of education, only inherent racial inferiority explained Negro failings. The voluminous literature of the biological and social sciences in the Progressive era described in meticulous detail all instances of Afro-American immorality, illegality, and even unemployment as the product of immutable racial characteristics. Quite typical of the reform mentality was John R. Commons's assertion in 1907 that the degraded status of blacks had nothing to do with white attitudes or practices. The Negro, Commons claimed, had been given opportunities "not only on equal terms, but actually on terms of preference over the whites." That they had failed to advance themselves "is recognized even by their partisans as something that was inevitable in the nature of the race at that stage of its development."[25]

So spoke reformers. Those less inclined toward change still heard clergymen preaching about the "curse of Canaan" and "God's plan for segregation." Both the fiction and the works of history they read invariably depicted blacks as slaves, and slaves as singing, shuffling, dancing, happy-go-lucky "darkies" willingly serving the good, gentle "Marse" in the big white house. And songs and films continued to advance a stereotype of the Negro as an innately inferior, immoral buffoon. Thus when the muckraking journalist Ray Stannard Baker set out in 1906 to investigate the "Negro problem," he found virtually no differences in white racial attitudes and practices anywhere in the country. North and South, in thought and behavior, the color line held taut.[26]

Certainly racial violence plagued blacks as viciously in the North as in the South. Whites lynched Negroes in almost every major city above the Mason-Dixon line in the Progressive era. White mobs rioted against Afro-Americans in Indiana, New York, Ohio, and Pennsylvania. Following the claim of a white woman in Springfield, Illinois, in 1908 that she had been raped by a black man, a crowd of whites surged through the Negro section chanting, "Lincoln freed you, we'll show you your place." For two days the whites openly burned Negro-owned buildings, flogged some fifty blacks, and lynched two hapless Afro-Americans. No Springfield whites were punished. But the news of the carnage shocked other whites to action.[27]

William English Walling, a Southern white Socialist, expressed his outrage in an article, "Race War in the North." Horrified that such a spectacle would occur in the year of the one hundredth

anniversary of the birth of Abraham Lincoln and within sight of
the grave of the Great Emancipator, Walling vividly described
the sadism of Springfield's whites and then called for a revival
of "the true spirit of the abolitionists, of Lincoln and Lovejoy
. . . to treat the Negro on a plane of absolute political and social
equality." Shortly after, two white settlement house workers,
Mary White Ovington and Dr. Henry Moskowitz, discussed the
matter with Walling and then prevailed upon Oswald Garrison
Villard, editor of the New York *Evening Post* and grandson of the
abolitionist leader, to issue a call "for the discussion of present
evils, the voicing of protests and the renewal of the struggle for
civil and political liberty."[28]

With all deliberate symbolism, Villard published his appeal on
Lincoln's Birthday in 1909. *The Call* depicted eloquently the
record of black disfranchisement and discrimination in education
and employment. It emphasized accounts of mob violence
against Afro-Americans and the inability of the victims to obtain
justice in the courts. It concluded with a ringing plea for all believers in democracy to end their silence and to remonstrate for
Negro rights. Villard's call for liberals to protest and to petition
led to a meeting in New York on May 31 and June 1. An assemblage predominated by white educators, social workers, and clergymen observed an anthropologist and a zoologist trying to prove
the equality of the races and listened to some of the militants of
the Niagara Movement argue for a new biracial organization to
oppose the persecution of blacks. Then the conferees passed several vague resolutions and agreed to meet again in a year to take
action.[29]

In 1910 the conference decided to establish a permanent organization and to adopt as its name the National Association for
the Advancement of Colored People. Formally incorporated in
the state of New York, the NAACP declared its purposes to be
"to promote equality of rights and eradicate caste or race prejudice . . . to advance the interests of colored citizens; to secure
for them impartial suffrage; and to increase their opportunities

Negro troops and some whites in Brownsville, Texas. The paucity of evidence against the Afro-American soldiers could not justify Roosevelt's draconian action. But he would not budge. He insisted on the blacks' collective guilt and denied the troops even the benefit of a court-martial.[32]

The GOP's reputation as the protector of Negro rights yearly grew more hollow and mocking. William Howard Taft accelerated Roosevelt's scheme to build a lily-white Southern GOP by further decreasing the number of federal appointments to blacks and by promising in his inaugural address to select no local officials whose appointment would cause regional opposition. Taft also publicly endorsed Washington's philosophy that Negroes should eschew politics, commenting in 1908 that Afro-Americans were "political children, not having the mental status of manhood."[33]

The Democrats promised yet less and threatened worse. Still the foremost party of the South, they stood forth proudly as the watchmen on the color line, the sentinels of white supremacy who neither slept nor wavered. They howled the loudest when Roosevelt invited Washington to lunch and succored the President when Republicans criticized his handling of the Brownsville affair. The Democrats, moreover, prodded the opposing party in power to begin segregating federal employees. The Lost Cause had not lost its champion. While carrying the banner of democracy, perennial presidential candidate William Jennings Bryan defended Negro disfranchisement "on the grounds that civilization has a right to preserve itself."[34]

Nor could blacks turn with hope to the Socialists. Jack London wrote often of Negro inferiority, claiming he was "first of all a white man and only then a Socialist." Victor Berger, insisting "that the Negroes and mulattoes constitute a lower race," employed themes of white supremacy to win the votes of white workers. Most Socialists, however, just looked away when facing a race issue, desiring to avoid the onus of "black" being added to the stigma of "red" they already had. Officially the Socialist party maintained a discreet silence on Negro rights. It contended that all racial problems would wither away after the overthrow of capitalism. Until that day, Eugene Debs announced, "we have nothing special to offer the Negro, and we cannot make separate appeals to all the races."[35]

Not a single national political party wooed the Negro vote in 1912, the highpoint of progressivism. The GOP, for the first time since 1868, shied from adding even a splinter of a civil rights plank to its party platform. Teddy Roosevelt's Bull Moosers pledged to battle for the Lord and social justice, but not for blacks. Roosevelt rudely rebuffed the NAACP's request to include a statement opposing unfair discriminatory and disfranchising laws in the Progressive platform. He also refused to permit the seating of Negro delegates from Southern states. Roosevelt clearly acted on the premise that support for Negro rights would cost more politically than could possibly be gained. So did every other party. Not a single word about civil rights appeared in the Democratic, Progressive, Republican, Prohibition, Socialist, or Socialist-Labor platforms. Too few blacks voted. Too few whites cared.[36]

The election of Woodrow Wilson led to the most Southern-dominated, anti-Negro, national administration since the 1850s. Dixie Democrats held sway, from the Virginian in the White House to the new Chief Justice, Edward D. White of Louisiana, to the leadership of both House and Senate. In 1913 and 1914 democratic representatives introduced more racist legislation than had ever been submitted to any previous Congress. The Executive Branch pushed the segregation of federal workers. It dismissed or downgraded hundreds of black civil servants. And President Wilson, claiming nothing could be done to improve the status of blacks, opposed all proposals for a national commission to study the race question; refused to appear at a Negro school or black conference; would not publicly denounce lynching; and pronounced the appointment of black officials in the South "a social blunder of the worst kind." At the height of Wilson's New Freedom, D. W. Griffith released his rabidly racist movie, "The Birth of a Nation," and whites masked in sheets burned a cross atop Stone Mountain in Georgia to mark the resurrection of the Ku Klux Klan.[37]

Wilson's wartime administration proved as disastrous for Afro-Americans as had his reform administration. The Army retired Colonel Charles Young, the highest ranking Negro officer, on the spurious ground of ill health to avoid promoting him. The great mass of black soldiers were confined to non-combatant labor battalions. When pressed to explain this policy, Army officials responded that Afro-Americans lacked the natural attributes to fight courageously. The Navy, moreover, accepted Negroes only as messboys, and the Marine Corps excluded them completely. Worse still to Negro leaders, the War Department did little to stop violence against blacks in uniform in the South. To forestall possible retaliation by the Negroes in the Fifteenth New York Infantry against the whites of Spartanburg, South Carolina, who had beaten up a black soldier, the War Department peremptorily shipped the Afro-American regiment overseas to face the German armies. When Negroes in the Twenty-fourth Infantry rioted against Houston whites to protest police brutality and harassment, the Army tried and sentenced thirteen blacks to hang for murder and mutiny, summarily carrying out the executions before the cases could reach the judge advocate general for review. In other trials fifteen more Negro soldiers received death sentences and fifty-three were imprisoned for life. Overseas, the military requested French troops not to "spoil" Afro-Americans by treating them as equals. It might, Army officials intimated, lead to mass rapes of whites by the Negro soldiers. And in Kansas a general ordered his black troops not to press to gain admission to local theatres or restaurants that discriminated against them, despite state laws to the contrary. "White men had made the Division," the commander scolded the blacks in his charge, "and they can break it just as easily if it becomes a trouble maker."[38]

Another white official cautioning black soldiers predicted:

"You niggers are wondering how you are going to be treated after the war. Well, I'll tell you, you are going to be treated exactly like you were before the war; this is a white man's country and we expect to rule it." His assessment proved correct. Afro-American servicemen came home in 1919 to find their reward a bloody summer of race riots. Throughout the country whites mobilized to roll back the economic gains made by Negroes during the war, to restore the racial *status quo ante bellum,* and to stifle the competition of blacks for housing and jobs, both in short supply in 1919. Some twenty-five race riots broke out that year, and at least seventy Negroes were lynched, some of them still wearing their military uniforms.[39]

Afro-Americans responded in diverse ways. Particularly in the North, some Negroes exhibited an increasing readiness to fight and die in their own defense. Retaliatory violence by blacks kept the blood flowing in the "Red Summer" of 1919. Negro editors aggressively urged the "New Negro" to battle for his rights and crush white oppression. "We return fighting," Du Bois proclaimed in *The Crisis.* "Make way for Democracy! We saved it in France, and by the Great Jehovah, we will save it in the United States of America, or know the reason why." Others turned to economic radicalism, trusting the solution of the race problem to united action by white and black workers against the capitalist class. Some hoped that Negro entry into the trade union movement would result in the collapse of the caste system. And still others, updating Booker T. Washington's strategies, counseled Afro-Americans to take "advantage of the disadvantages" inherent in segregation and build the ghetto into a Black Metropolis.[40]

The ideology with the greatest appeal to the black masses following the First World War came from a Jamaican, Marcus Moziah Garvey. Founded in 1914, the Universal Negro Improvement Association (UNIA) sought the liberation of both Africans and Afro-Americans through the colonization of the motherland by American blacks. Decrying the futility of the Negro struggle for freedom in the United States, Garvey mocked the NAACP's campaigns against lynching and disfranchisement. He urged Afro-Americans to abstain from politics and to invest their funds in the UNIA's Black Star Steamship Line and other all-Negro business enterprises. Preaching race pride, he glorified separatism, declared all programs promoting interracialism to be plots against blacks, and labeled Du Bois and the NAACP worse enemies of the Afro-American than the KKK. "I believe in a pure black race," Garvey gloated, "just as all self-respecting whites believe in a pure white race."[41]

Although diametrically opposed to Garveyism, neither the Department of Race Relations of the Federal Council of Churches of Christ in America nor the Commission on Interracial Cooperation (CIC) fared better than the UNIA in diminishing the oppression of Afro-Americans. Organized in 1921, the Federal Council's agency sought to promote Negro rights by distributing educational materials on the race issue and by instituting "Race Relations Sunday" and "Interracial Brotherhood Month." But to no avail. The member churches of the Federal Council, even in the North, did little to echo the liberal pronouncements of the Department of Race Relations and even less to practice what it preached. The CIC, working exclusively in the South, hoped that good works rather than pious rhetoric would abrade racial discrimination. But it settled for the appearance of racial peace. Begun by inheritors of the Tuskegee machine and Southern white liberals in 1919 "to quench, if possible, the fires of racial antagonism which were flaming at that time with such deadly menace," the CIC shunned controversy at all costs. It avoided direct contact with the NAACP and other Northern-based "meddlers." It refused to back the campaign for the federal anti-lynching bill introduced by Congressman L. C. Dyer of St. Louis in 1922. And it temporized on even its program of research and education to propitiate the Southern ruling classes. The price it paid in calming the apprehensions of whites brought nothing in return for Negro rights.[42]

The same fate doomed the work of the National Urban League

(NUL) in the North. Established in 1911 as the National League
on Urban Conditions by an interracial group ideologically close
to Booker T. Washington, it sought initially to find jobs and housing for black migrants to the city. It tried to assist Negroes in
adjusting to urban life, but when the massive migration during
the war revealed the paucity of the Urban League's resources
and the magnitude of the problems Afro-Americans faced, it
turned to an emphasis upon the professional training of black
social workers. Then in the mid-1920s, the NUL switched to
conducting investigations of conditions among Negroes in cities,
aligning itself with the National Conference of Social Work. Yet
whatever tack it tried, the Urban League could not achieve its
goals: equality of opportunity and the inclusion of blacks into all
aspects of American society.[43]

Seeking to avoid the stigma of radicalism tainting the NAACP,
the Urban League shunned politics and agitation. It neither campaigned for civil rights legislation nor challenged Jim Crow
practices. With most of its budget coming from the Altman,
Carnegie, Rosenwald, and Rockefeller philanthropies, the NUL
placed its stock in conciliation and private negotiations. It eschewed public protest in favor of friendly appeals to the goodwill of the white community, especially employers. *Opportunity,*
its monthly journal, founded in 1923, showcased Negro cultural
contributions. Not until 1928, when Elmer Carter succeeded
Charles S. Johnson as editor, did *Opportunity* change its focus
and begin to highlight the economic and political plight of Afro-
Americans. In sum, whether stressing adjustment or advancement, pursuing interracial diplomacy or publishing fact-crammed
surveys, the Urban League produced few tangible successes. The
ghettoization of the North did not abate. It swelled. The American Federation of Labor (AFL) remained impervious to all pleas
to cease discrimination. In 1927 it reaffirmed its refusal to accept
Negroes. The Afro-American continued to receive more alms than
opportunities.[44]

No Negro leader or strategy or tactic could stem the tide of

discrimination and segregation. In vain the NAACP kept protesting. But through most of the decade it appeared to be marking
time, and struggling to do that. Under the leadership of James
Weldon Johnson—an artist more suited for the theatre and poetry
than the arena of politics and agitation—the membership of the
NAACP slipped from a high of over ninety thousand in 1919 to
about twenty thousand in 1929. Association expenditures for staff,
publicity, and programs fell proportionately. Still, it kept aloft
the banners of racial justice, valiantly if not effectively. It did
much to publicize the hostility of organized labor to blacks, but
could not dent the racial exclusivity of the AFL. Union leaders
refused to even meet with NAACP officials to discuss the matter.
When the decade ended, Negroes comprised less than 2 percent
of all union workers, half of whom were in the all-black Brotherhood of Sleeping Car Porters, a nearly extinct union in 1929
ignored by the federal government, the Pullman Company, and
the AFL alike. Similarly, the NAACP railed against disfranchisement but could not add blacks to Southern voting rolls. All of
the association's demands that the Republican administration in
Washington secure the franchise for Negroes came to naught.
So did their appeals to Congress for an anti-lynching bill. Only
eight Northern Democrats broke party regularity to vote for the
measure, and the Republicans meekly capitulated to the threat
of a Southern filibuster in the Senate. GOP leaders fully acqui-
esced to Dixie's demand that the bill be shelved indefinitely. The
NAACP could do little but speculate on the Negro leaving the
party of Lincoln.[45]

Defeat bred disillusionment; powerlessness fostered frustration.
Acrimony abounded. The NAACP lashed out at its black critics,
and black criticism of the NAACP grew more brazen. Du Bois
assailed Garvey as, "without doubt, the most dangerous enemy of
the Negro race in America and the world. . . . He is either a lu-
natic or a traitor." Garvey countered by "expelling" Du Bois from
the black race and pummeling the association for being ashamed
of blackness. Such radical trade union organizers as Chandler

Owen, A. Philip Randolph, and Hubert H. Harrison attacked
Garvey, the NAACP, and the Urban League for focusing on race
rather than class and for hindering the development of an interracial labor or socialistic movement. And while the great bulk of
Afro-American editors, educators, and clergymen—still loyal to
the philosophy of Booker T. Washington—criticized the association for too much agitation, militants like Monroe Trotter accused
the NAACP of not decrying Jim Crow vigorously enough. "Where
in heaven's name do we Negroes stand?" Du Bois retorted:

> If we organize separately for anything—"Jim Crow!" scream all
> the Disconsolate; if we organize with white people—"Traitors!
> Pressure! They're betraying us!" yell all the Suspicious. If, un-
> able to get the whole loaf we seize half to ward off starvation—
> "Compromise!" yell all the Scared. If we let the half loaf go
> and starve—"Why don't you *do* something?" yell those same
> critics, dancing about on their toes.

Regardless of what the Disconsolate, the Suspicious, or the
Scared yelled, or what the NAACP or any other Negro betterment group proposed, the basic problem remained the inability
of Afro-Americans to compel necessary alterations in their status
and the absence of a compelling rationale for whites to modify
their treatment of blacks. White indifference and black weakness
stymied the hope for any viable program of Negro advancement
in the twenties.[46]

Politicians acted accordingly. Too few Negroes voted; most
legislators saw no reason to buck the opposition or apathy of their
mainly white constituencies on racial issues. During the twenties,
the Republicans did not need the votes of Afro-Americans to
elect presidents or control Congress, and the Democrats did not
even bother to compete for the Negro vote nationally. The GOP
found it more profitable to appeal to Southern whites than to
support civil rights. It still yearned to build a lily-white Southern
Republican party. It kept trying. When the NAACP mailed a
questionnaire in 1920 to seventeen men considered possible Republican presidential candidates, asking for their views on civil

rights, only three bothered to respond. Not one of them, however, would commit himself. Questionnaires sent out in 1924 and 1928 drew similarly dismal responses.[47]

Genial Warren Harding took no action offensive to the most virulent white supremacist, refusing to endorse any of the proposals being pressed by civil rights advocates. The Republican President continued Wilson's policy of decreasing the number of federal appointments going to blacks. Rather than curtailing segregation in executive departments, Harding permitted it to increase. His Justice Department declined to investigate either lynchings or the Ku Klux Klan. He opposed the establishment of an interracial commission to study the race issue. Nothing was done to thwart the spread of peonage or to decrease the size of the American force occupying Haiti. And Harding would not interfere with the Republican decision in the Senate to surrender to Dixie's demand to kill the Dyer anti-lynching bill. The President had his eyes on the white vote in the South. "Normalcy" on matters of race meant the continuation of the lily-white Republican movement nurtured by Roosevelt and Taft. Speaking at Woodrow Wilson Park in Birmingham, Alabama, in 1921, Harding emphasized the "fundamental, eternal, and inescapable differences" dividing the races. He called upon Negroes and whites to "stand uncompromisingly against every suggestion of social equality. . . . Racial amalgamation there cannot be."[48]

Calvin Coolidge followed the racial policies of his predecessor, albeit coolly and silently. Not believing that Washington should interfere in any way in local race matters, or that he should exert himself on such national issues as lynching, disfranchisement, or discrimination in federal employment, Coolidge did absolutely nothing to assist blacks. But he did appoint as his personal secretary and chief adviser on Southern patronage, Bascom C. Slemp, a former Virginia congressman widely heralded as a key architect of lily-white Republicanism in the South. Yet no better alternatives to the GOP existed for Negroes in 1924. The Democrats seemed as offensive as ever, defeating an anti-Klan plank at their national convention and, once again, not permitting a single Afro-American delegate to participate in the party's proceedings. Briefly, Negro leaders looked wistfully at the third party movement led by Senator Robert M. La Follette of Wisconsin. The NAACP pleaded with the Progressives to take "enlightened and far-sighted steps against race and color discrimination." They would not. Both the platform of the Conference for Progressive Political Action and La Follette's personal statement on the issues of the day failed to even mention the Negro. The most liberal party platform ever written to that date said nothing about the Klan, lynching, disfranchisement, or discrimination. Those Negroes voting went nearly 90 percent for Coolidge.[49]

Then came Herbert Hoover and the zenith of Republican efforts to build a lily-white GOP in the South. Chief Justice William Howard Taft confided in 1928 that Hoover aimed "to break up the solid south and to drive the negroes out of Republican politics." The Republican candidate only partly succeeded, but not for want of trying. Following the bolt away from Al Smith that year by Florida, North Carolina, Tennessee, Texas, and Virginia—the first crack in the Democratic Solid South since Reconstruction—Hoover acted to prove that the party of Lincoln no longer cared to give even lip service to the ideals of racial justice. He appointed almost no blacks to federal office, closed down the Negro division of the Republican National Committee, and made fewer public statements on race than any other President in the century. Black workers were excluded from federal construction jobs on the Boulder Dam. The President's Commission on Law Enforcement rudely rebuffed the NAACP's plea that it investigate lynching, peonage, disfranchisement, and discrimination in public accommodations. His National Advisory Committee on Education overwhelmingly voted down a proposal that federal grants to states for education be spent equitably for black as well as white schooling. And for his first appointment to the Supreme Court, Hoover nominated John J. Parker, a Southern white Republican on record in opposition to Negro enfranchisement.[50]

And so it went in the 1920s. Culturally the Afro-American remained largely either invisible or an object of disdain. If not publicizing Negro "crime waves," most of the white press ignored blacks. Hardly a news story appeared on Negro accomplishments or an editorial on the agony of being black in white America. Few newspapers even dignified the spelling of Negro with a capital "N." Amusement park signs still urged whites to "Hit the Coon and Get a Cigar." On the motion picture screen, blacks invariably acted comical or criminal, and slow-witted. Of the Negro roles in movies reviewed by *Variety* between 1920 and 1930, fully 80 percent were maids and butlers. No black entertainer performed regularly on network radio. White listeners usually heard Negroes only as a stereotyped "Tom" or "Mammy," reinforcing the image of blacks as lazy, inept, and stupid. Syndicated in 1928, the *Amos 'n' Andy* radio show fittingly climaxed a decade of anti-Negro sketches and "coon" and "darky" jokes on the airwaves.[51]

Much of the scholarship on race similarly perpetuated a conception of the Negro as an inferior being. Although Franz Boas and his disciples protested against the doctrine of race as the crucial determinant of all history, civilization, and culture, and riddled the pseudo-scientific evidence purporting to demonstrate the Negro's inferiority, their efforts made slow headway outside the university. Discourse in the twenties continued to be dominated by Theodore Lothrop Stoddard's polemic, *The Rising Tide of Color Against White Supremacy*, a harrowing view of the threat posed by "colored" peoples, and by the warnings of Henry Pratt Fairchild, president of the American Sociological Society, that America's stability rested upon the necessity of discriminating against the innately inferior Afro-Americans. Biologists contributed their due by propagating notions of the inadequate cranial capacity of Negroes, their ape-like physical characteristics, and the horrors resulting from race crossing or intermixture. And historians of American slavery stressed the beneficence of that institution in civilizing the African savage. All these notions found their way into the encyclopedias and textbooks of the era, gaining an ever-increasing audience and further legitimacy.[52]

Racism, moreover, gained its greatest intellectual support from the newest vogue science of the twenties, psychology. Psychologists interpreted the intelligence tests used in the First World War as incontrovertible proof of the intellectual superiority of white over black. The I.Q. results, concluded Dr. Robert M. Yerkes, chairman of the psychological committee established by the Army to determine the abilities and aptitude of volunteers and draftees, "brought into clear relief . . . the intellectual inferiority of the negro. Quite apart from educational status, which is utterly unsatisfactory, the negro soldier is of relatively low grade intelligence." The tests' findings, Yerkes proclaimed, proved that even improved education "will not place the negro race on a par with its Caucasian competitors." Princeton psychologist Carl C. Brigham, who directed the Army's testing program, similarly asserted in his much-cited *A Study of American Intelligence* that education would not lift the lowly Negro intellect to the high level of the Nordics. Both scientists downplayed the fact that Northern blacks did better than Southern whites on the tests, and both barely considered the relationship between intelligence and environment. Yet their views held sway in the twenties. Their assertions became psychological dogma.[53]

Though less manifest, certain harbingers of change nonetheless appeared. Most stemmed from the mass migration of blacks to the cities and to the North. This escape from the shadow of the plantation would profoundly affect the course of civil rights. Between 1910 and 1920 the "Great Migration" brought more than half a million blacks northward, and some three-quarters of a million Negroes left the South in the 1920s. The percentage of blacks living in cities jumped from 22 percent in 1900 to 34 percent in 1920, and then to 40 percent in 1930. That year, not one of the five cities with the largest Negro populations was in the South. Indeed, while the Afro-American population in the South increased by 5 percent in the twenties, the black population in the North mushroomed by 63 percent. Few who followed the North Star found the Promised Land. Most found squalor, discrimination by labor unions and employees, decayed housing milked by white slumlords, enmity between white policemen and the black community, and liquor and narcotics the only escape from despair. Yet for millions of Afro-Americans, the Northern urban ghetto also meant surcease from permanent tenantry, poverty, disease, and ignorance. The death rate per thousand Negroes dropped from 25 in 1900 to 16.3 in 1930. Between 1915 and 1930 the infant mortality rate per 1000 live Negro births was almost halved—181.2 to 99.9. Black expectation of life span at birth increased from 33 in 1900 to 48 by 1930. Similarly, Afro-American illiteracy decreased from some 45 percent of the adult population in 1900 to 16.4 percent in 1930. By then New York blacks had a lower illiteracy rate than the whites of Alabama, Georgia, Louisiana, Mississippi, South Carolina, Virginia, or Kentucky. Over 98 percent of Afro-Americans aged seven to thirteen in New York, Ohio, and Illinois attended school in the twenties, compared to less than 65 percent of their counterparts in Louisiana, Georgia, and Alabama. Overall, the percentage of Negro youth enrolled in school doubled in the years from 1900 to 1930; the number of public high schools for blacks increased from 91 in 1915 to nearly 1000 in 1930; and total Negro college enrollment rose from less than 2000 in 1915 to about 14,000 at the start of the Great Depression.[54]

Northern Negroes, unlike their Southern brethren, could also vote. In 1928, for the first time in the century, an Afro-American was elected to Congress. Other blacks won local offices in Chicago, Cleveland, Detroit, New York City, and Philadelphia, and Negro votes in those cities became an important factor in determining election results. Politically, the Negro slowly began to command attention. The bonds of hopelessness of the rigid caste system of the Black Belt less and less characterized all of black America.[55]

Hope sprouted also from the seeds of spiritual emancipation

planted by the literary movement of the 1920s that Afro-Americans labeled the "Harlem Renaissance," the "Black Renaissance," and the "New Negro Movement." Whether celebrating the racial chauvinism of blacks, the identification of Afro-Americans with Africa, or decrying lynchings and discrimination, Negro poets and novelists sought to free themselves from white symbols and images and to write in their own idiom. "We younger Negro artists who create now intend to express our individual dark-skinned selves without fear or shame," declared Langston Hughes. "If white people are pleased we are glad. If they are not, it doesn't matter. We know we are beautiful. And ugly, too. . . . We build our temple for tomorrow, strong as we know how, and we stand on top of the mountain, free within ourselves." By focusing white America's attention on the Negro, by awakening the pride of Afro-Americans in their race and folk tradition, and by militant protests and demands for civil rights, the New Negro articulated the consciousness of the possibility of change brought about by migration, urbanization, and education.[56]

So did Marcus Garvey. Despite his opposition to civil rights organizations, Garvey did more than any previous Negro leader to convince blacks to believe in their ability to shape their destiny. A master showman, Garvey dramatized the extreme plight of Afro-Americans and the desperate necessity of change. An intuitive psychologist, he radicalized the powerless by instilling in them a sense of their potential power. And a persuasive teacher, the Jamaican leader convinced masses of Negroes that white racism and not black failings explained their lowly status. Years after his deportation in 1927, some of Garvey's most bitter black enemies would be utilizing this legacy to forge a powerful campaign for civil rights.[57]

But this would not happen immediately. That year, the dean of Howard University lamented, "The Young American Negro is practically asleep." The impact following the trek of blacks out of the rural South would not be fully felt until the 1930s. A mood of complacency, of callousness, of suspicion of reform, still hovered over the land in the twenties, affecting the mass of Negroes and whites alike. It was not a time of concern, of caring about the downtrodden. Few looked to the government to protect the rights of the forgotten. Negro organizations remained too weak to reward friends and punish enemies. Most whites either considered Jim Crow a boon or knew little of the black plight. Symptomatic of the age, at the dedication of the Lincoln Memorial in the mid-twenties, far from the gaze of the Emancipator, Negroes were roped off in a segregated section across the road from all whites. Several years later, the Hoover Administration segregated Afro-American Gold Star Mothers from whites on their voyage to France. "Surely there was no time in the history of our country," *The Nation* observed, "when segregation was less necessary and more cruel." It was a fitting epitaph.[58]

2

An Old Deal, A Raw Deal

Neither the Great Depression nor the New Deal initially innervated the struggle for black rights. The continuity of racism in American life and thought early in the 1930s overshadowed any portents of change. The plight of Afro-Americans, however, did change—for the worse. The depression dealt a staggering blow to blacks. It magnified all their traditional economic liabilities. It created newer and harsher ones. No group could less afford the precipitous decline that followed the stock market crash of 1929. None suffered more from it. "I couldn't imagine such financial disaster touching my small world; it surely concerned only the rich," Gordon Parks, who would later gain fame as a photographer and film director, remembered in his autobiography. His boyhood in St. Paul, Minnesota, had been relatively secure up until the fall of 1929.

> But by the first week of November I too knew differently; along with millions of others across the nation, I was without a job. All that next week I searched for any kind of work that would prevent my leaving school. Again it was, "We're firing, not hiring." "Sorry, Sonny, nothing doing here." Finally, on the seventh of November I went to school and cleaned out my

locker, knowing it was impossible to stay on. A piercing chill was in the air as I walked back to the rooming house. The hawk had come. I could already feel his wings shadowing me.

By 1933 most blacks could neither find jobs of any kind nor contracts for their crop at any price. Although only a small minority of Afro-Americans had tasted the fruits of prosperity in the twenties, the great majority of blacks now experienced extreme privation and the concomitant ravages of malnutrition, disease, overcrowding, and family disintegration. "At no time in the history of the Negro since slavery," concluded T. Arnold Hill of the Urban League, "has his economic and social outlook seemed so discouraging." On the eve of the New Deal, a specter of starvation haunted black America.[1]

The heaviest toll came in the rural South. Over half the Negroes in the United States lived there in 1930, and few went unaffected by the drop in cotton prices from eighteen cents per pound in 1929 to less than six cents per pound at the start of 1933. Some two million black farmers long used to subsistence living were devastated. Cotton farming had been depressed and overpopulated prior to 1929; after the crash, the earnings of Negro landowners, cash tenants, sharecroppers, and wage laborers all spiraled steeply downward. Over two-thirds of the Negroes cultivating cotton in the early thirties received no profits from the crop, either breaking even or going deeper in debt. With little or no provision for rural relief, most grew what they could, hunted, scavenged, and begged to stay alive. Some left. Even without the lure of jobs, the city beckoned.[2]

Those rural blacks who migrated to the urban South did little to help the situation for the Afro-Americans already residing there. Even before the Great Depression, these city blacks had been hurt by a growing Negro population and a loss of jobs to whites and to mechanization. Then the crash erased the category known as "Negro jobs." Unemployed whites scrambled for the menial jobs traditionally reserved for Afro-Americans, particularly street cleaning, garbage collecting, and domestic service.

Negro maids, cooks, and housekeepers—the hardest hit by white displacement—constituted nearly half the urban black unemployed in the South. But no job was safe for Negroes. White girls replaced black men as restaurant and hotel employees and elevator operators. The more the depression worsened, the more whites demanded that blacks be dismissed. Desperate whites in Atlanta organized the Black Shirts in 1930 around the slogan "No Jobs for Niggers Until Every White Man Has a Job!" Similar organizations in other cities chanted: "Niggers, back to the cotton fields— city jobs are for white folks." In Mississippi white railroadmen desiring the jobs of black firemen unleashed a region of terror and violence. That was the way they dealt with the unemployment problem, wrote Hilton Butler in the *New Republic.* "Dust had been blown from the shotgun, the whip, and the noose, and Ku Klux practices were being resumed in the certainty that dead men not only tell no tales but create vacancies." By 1931, one-third of the Afro-Americans in Southern cities could find no employment. During the next year, the percentage rose to over one-half.[3]

Indigents in Southern cities, unlike their rural counterparts, could at least receive public relief on occasion. But rampant discrimination kept Afro-Americans barely above starvation level. Negroes suffered both as Southerners and as blacks. First, Southern states granted the lowest unemployment benefits in the country. Blacks were hurt far more than whites by this because of their relatively greater need for assistance and their disproportionate numbers on relief rolls. In Mississippi, over half Negro, less than 9 percent of the Afro-Americans received any relief in 1932, compared to over 14 percent of the whites. Southern officials knew the score. Yet they steadfastly refused to increase welfare allotments. They rationalized the disparity in benefits paid by their region vis-à-vis the rest of the nation on the basis of the lower cost of living in the South, although the gap in prices never approximated the chasm in payments. Second, the Afro-Americans received less than Southern whites because of racial exclusion and differentials. Many religious and charitable organizations refused to feed Negroes in their soup kitchens or extend any other aid to the black needy. Cities and states set harsher standards for blacks than whites to qualify for public assistance, and paid Afro-Americans less per month than they did whites on relief.[4]

The more than two million blacks living outside the South in 1930 faced less discrimination in the administration of relief but an equally dismal employment situation. A study of some two thousand families in Harlem indicated that the median income of skilled workers had dropped from $1955 in 1929 to $1003 in 1932, a decline of 48.7 percent. The wages of Harlem professionals and clerical job holders similarly plummeted. Unemployment among blacks in 1932 ran between 40 and 50 percent in Harlem and topped 56 percent in Philadelphia, while both Chicago and Detroit reported that over 40 percent of male Afro-Americans and 55 percent of Negro females could find no work. The white jobless rate in these four cities was 23 percent for men and 14 percent for women. In Gary, Indiana, half the Negro population was on full relief and another 30 percent on partial relief. Surveying the cities of the nation at the end of 1932, Kelly Miller, a Negro sociologist at Howard University, reported that "fully a third of the race is unemployed and another third under-employed." The Afro-American, Miller observed, was "the surplus man, the last to be hired and the first to be fired."[5]

Many of the same causes that led to the firing of blacks in the urban South operated nationally. More than four out of every five male Negro non-agricultural workers were semi-skilled or unskilled laborers, while this was true of only two out of every five white males. Hard times had their severest impact on the least skilled. They were the workers who first received wage cuts and then pink slips. Moreover, blacks constituted the bulk of domestic workers, whose employment depended on the prosperity of others in the community. In 1934 domestics accounted for 43 percent of the urban blacks on relief in the North.[6]

Outright discrimination by employers and unions added to the burdens borne by black workers. According to the Mayor's commission that investigated the economic conditions responsible for the Harlem riot in 1935, two-thirds of the hotels in Manhattan employed no blacks. Gimbel's department store refused to hire Negroes. So did the Metropolitan Life Insurance Company, despite its more than a hundred thousand Afro-American policy holders. The Interborough Rapid Transit Company counted only about five hundred blacks in its work force of over sixteen thousand, all as cleaners and porters; the Consolidated Gas Company employed less than two hundred Negroes among its ten thousand workers, all as hallmen or messengers; and the New York Edison Company hired even fewer Afro-Americans while employing even more men. It too confined its handful of black workers to the lowest-paying, least secure, most menial tasks. The Newspaper Printing Pressmen and Assistants' union, moreover, had no blacks in a membership of nearly three thousand. Neither did the Teamster local of Railway Express Employees, with over two thousand unionists, nor the Manhattan local of the International Brotherhood of Electrical Workers, representing more than six thousand workers. The combined building trades unions, over forty thousand strong, had less than a thousand Negroes.[7]

Despite such discrimination and the total absence of new employment opportunities, Southern blacks migrated northward. About four hundred thousand Negroes left the South in the thirties, half the number that had migrated in the preceding decade but still a large enough influx to increase the Negro population of the North by roughly 25 percent. Only one Northern city had a Negro population of more than a hundred thousand in 1930; by 1935 there were eleven. Yet the number of jobs in the North declined. Public relief inevitably became the major instrument of the Afro-American's struggle for survival.

The inability of cities and states to shoulder the relief burden without federal assistance wreaked havoc in the Negro community in the early years of the depression. Two million blacks, half the urban Afro-American population, were on the relief rolls. By the start of 1933 Philadelphia could not provide its recipients with a health-sustaining diet. Detroit allowed fifteen cents a day per individual and then ran out of funds altogether. Everywhere breadlines lengthened, apple vendors multiplied, pawnshops swelled with used clothing and furniture, and the rate of rent eviction cases zoomed upward. Describing the situation in Harlem in her autobiography, social worker Anna Arnold Hedgeman wrote that following the financial collapse in 1929

> a large mass of Negroes were faced with the reality of starvation and they turned sadly to public relief. A few chanted optimistically, "Jesus will lead me and the Welfare will feed me," but others said it was a delusion, for the Home Relief Bureau allowed only eight cents a meal for food. Meanwhile, men, women and children combed the streets and searched in garbage cans for food, foraging with dogs and cats . . .
>
> Many families had been reduced to living below street level. It was estimated that more than ten thousand Negroes lived in cellars and basements which had been converted into makeshift flats. Packed in damp, ratridden dungeons, they existed in squalor not too different from that of Arkansas sharecroppers.

The Negro, long used to living hand-to-mouth, was now, according to the Urban League, "hanging on by the barest thread."[8]

Nonetheless, most blacks who could vote in 1932 rallied around the slogan "who but Hoover." The GOP still appeared the lesser evil. Despite the severity of the Great Depression, despite Hoover's belief that the federal government had no business aiding the millions of indigents, despite the President's disbanding the black Tenth Cavalry and its members being dispersed to menial jobs, despite his refusal to be photographed with Negro leaders, despite the percentage of blacks at the 1932 Republican convention being the smallest of any GOP convention in the century, and despite the meaningless Negro plank adopted by the Republicans for their platform that year—a plank labeled mere "flapdoodle" by Walter White of the NAACP, a "catchpenny device to get the votes from the unthinking"—the great majority of black newspapers and magazines stayed Republican.

An article in *The Crisis,* entitled "Why the Negro Should Vote for
Mr. Hoover," warned that a vote for Franklin Delano Roosevelt
was a vote to extend segregation. White, the new executive secretary of the NAACP, condemned the New York governor's civil
rights record and "overtures to the Southern Bourbons." The election of Roosevelt, predicted Roscoe Conkling Simmons, the head
of the Negro Republican Speakers' Committee, would "put the
Negro again into virtual slavery." Following Frederick Douglass,
the majority of Afro-Americans continued to view the GOP as a
ship compared to the Democrats' stormy sea. "The future of the
black man," the Chicago *Defender* pointed out in a manner
representative of the Negro press in 1932, "so far as his civil
rights are concerned, is at least safe in the hands of the Republican Party."[9]

Prior to his presidency Roosevelt certainly did not deserve better press. He had never championed the Negro's cause. He had
shown no concern for racial problems. His political career had
been a model of deference to the white South on racial issues.
He knew what was required of a Northern Democrat with national ambitions and he did it, apparently without compunction.
Roosevelt participated in the Jim-Crowing of the Navy as Assistant Secretary of that department under President Woodrow Wilson, never uttering, privately or publicly, a single word of protest.
He boasted of singlehandedly writing black Haiti's constitution
during the American intervention of 1915. After the 1919 race
riot in Washington, he wrote to a friend in Little Rock: "With
your experience in handling Africans in Arkansas, I think you had
better come up here and take charge of the Police Force." Pointedly, Roosevelt proclaimed himself an adopted son of Georgia
after purchasing property in Warm Springs. He never commented
on the segregated folkways of the state or the racial restrictive
covenant on his land. Time and again he referred to his happiness
in being a Georgian as well as a New Yorker. Roosevelt, in short,
was a loyal Democrat, a Northern politician in a party that was
overwhelmingly Southern. As late as 1929, he made a public point

of denying that he had lunched with Afro-Americans. And, as many Negro leaders correctly claimed in the 1932 campaign, the New York governor had ignored blacks in appointments and legislation.[10]

Roosevelt showed no sign of diminishing his solicitude for the white South during the 1932 campaign. He was silent on the rights of Afro-Americans. At the Democratic national convention in Chicago, his aides openly courted Southern backing for his nomination, spurned the NAACP's request that Roosevelt endorse a civil right plank for the platform, and supported as his running mate a Texan anathema to Negro right organizations. The Democratic nominee, in fact, had been the leading candidate of Dixie on the first and on all succeeding ballots. Refusing all suggestions that he appeal openly for the Negro vote, Roosevelt remained true to his backers throughout the fall. The small number of registered blacks in the North could not compete in Roosevelt's calculations with his desire to re-solidify the Solid South. Without benefit of explanation or excuse, the Democratic candidate mailed back unanswered the questionnaire sent out by the NAACP soliciting his views on Negro matters.[11]

The black electorate agreed with the Negro leadership's negative reaction to Roosevelt. The Great Depression enabled Roosevelt to sweep 42 of the 48 states by 472 electoral votes to Hoover's 59, but he trailed Al Smith in attracting Negroes to the Democratic fold. Although black unemployment hovered around 50 percent, over two-thirds of those Afro-Americans voting went Republican, an even higher proportion than had voted for Hoover in 1928. The Democrat carried but four of the fifteen most populous Negro wards in the North. He won black majorities only in New York and Kansas City, where the Tammany and Pendergast machines assiduously cultivated Afro-Americans with political favors. Better than two-thirds of the black vote in New Haven, Columbus, Wilmington, Philadelphia, and Detroit went Republican. "The 1932 election showed less of a defection among Negroes than among other groups of Republican voters," wrote Samuel

Lubell. "In both Chicago and Cleveland nearly a third of all Negro males were jobless, yet Hoover drew more than three-fourths of the vote in the heaviest Negro wards."[12]

Afro-Americans had no cause for optimism in 1933. Their vote having gone so solidly for the losing party, they had no claim on the new president. While civil rights spokesmen at the time of the inauguration publicly expressed hope that a "liberal in politics and economics might well be expected to be a liberal in race relations," they privately anticipated little assistance from the Roosevelt Administration. His need to work harmoniously with a largely Southern-controlled Congress and Southern-staffed federal bureaucracy augured poorly for Negro rights. So did the fact that the number two man in the government, Vice-President John Nance Garner, who was still highly influential in Congress, strongly opposed anti-lynching legislation and other measures to promote civil rights. Both Garner and Roosevelt believed that party unity necessitated placating Democrats from Dixie on all issues of race. Throughout their careers this had been the first rule of national Democratic politics. It was the *quid* upon which Southern votes for the *quo* depended. Both accepted as a touch-stone of Democratic loyalty the assertion that the federal govern-ment had no right to meddle in a state's conduct of racial affairs. Accordingly, the President and Vice-President viewed civil rights as the one subject to be most avoided lest it wound the party.[13]

Most of those closest to Roosevelt in 1933 shared this belief. His key political advisors, Louis Howe and James A. Farley, warned the President to avoid any acts or public statements likely to antagonize the white South. They sought to protect the Boss from what they regarded as the folly of the civil rights issue. White House aides constantly screened press releases and presi-dential messages to make sure no offending word to the South slipped through. They particularly viewed Eleanor Roosevelt's early activities on behalf of the Negro with trepidation. Often they beseeched the President to limit what his wife said and did.[14]

The palace guard of Press Secretary Stephen Early and Appointments Secretary Marvin McIntyre played a major role in shielding the President on matters pertaining to blacks. Both men endeavored quite openly to diminish Eleanor Roosevelt's influence on racial policy and to frustrate her efforts to get the administration interested in the Negro's plight. Early and McIntyre conspired against the First Lady's wishes to have a Negro reporter admitted to White House press conferences and to permit black delegations to confer with the President. NAACP leaders could not even make it beyond the waiting room to see Roosevelt in 1933. "What do you *boys* want?" his assistants had sneered.[15]

On those occasions when Early and McIntyre lost out to Mrs. Roosevelt's persistence, they schemed to turn the rest of the White House staff against the First Lady. In one memorandum to Eleanor Roosevelt's secretary, Early contrived to prove the President's wife responsible for the abuse heaped on Roosevelt by civil rights organizations. He viciously denounced Walter White "as one of the worst and most continuous of troublemakers." Early complained that White, a friend of Eleanor's, had the audacity to bombard the Chief Executive with "voluminous" and "insulting" letters. White, he went on, had the gall to imply that the government countenanced discrimination. "There was no use in my trying to explain," Eleanor Roosevelt later wrote about Early and McIntyre, "because our basic values were very different."[16]

With the exception of Secretary of the Interior Harold L. Ickes, Roosevelt's first Cabinet shared the apprehension about Negro rights prevalent in the White House. Black leaders considered the heads of the military departments obsessed by a mania to uphold Jim Crow in the armed services, and termed Cordell Hull of Tennessee, the secretary of state, an "impregnable fortress" of hostility to Negroes. Attorney General Homer S. Cummings, a former chairman of the Democratic National Committee, struck these leaders as a poor choice for the top post in the Justice Department because of his excessive partisanship. They did not want the department to calculate its position on lynching and disfranchise-

ment solely on the basis of whether the Democrats stood to gain
or lose political advantages. Henry Wallace, according to civil
rights spokesmen, especially feared antagonizing Southerners on
the race issue. No other department was as controlled by white
supremacists both in the bureaucracy and in Congress as was the
Department of Agriculture. It had the smallest percentage of
black employees and was the last to appoint a Negro adviser.
"You didn't dare take a Negro to lunch at Agriculture," recalled
Dr. Will Alexander, one of the few supporters of civil rights working on New Deal farm programs. Wallace not only ducked action
on Negro rights but complained to Alexander: "Will, don't you
think the New Deal is undertaking to do too much for Negroes."
And Secretary of Labor Frances Perkins and Harry Hopkins,
head of the Federal Emergency Relief Administration, both of
whom had been sympathetic to the civil rights cause as social
workers in New York, initially shied away from acting on their
convictions. Like virtually every other official in the Executive
Branch, they too feared provoking Southern opposition in Congress to the New Deal.[17]

However, far more than the personnel selected by Roosevelt
and his own lack of distress regarding the special problems of
blacks limited progress on civil rights. Hard times set the contours
of New Deal policy. The continuation of massive unemployment
affecting millions of Americans defined Roosevelt's mandate and
limited the uses to which his power could be put. The electorate
wanted relief and recovery. All else had to wait. For Roosevelt
and the preponderance of Americans economic reconstruction
had the highest priority in the 1930s. "First things come first,"
the President emphasized repeatedly, "and I can't alienate certain
votes I need for measures that are more important at the moment
by pushing any measures that would entail a fight." Roosevelt
would not defy Congress on racial matters. To do so jeopardized
the bills and appropriations needed to battle the joblessness,
privation, and misery that the nation considered its most vital
immediate concern.[18]

The domination of Congress by Southern Democrats increased Roosevelt's disinclination to make civil rights a priority item. Throughout the thirties, the representatives of Dixie remained entrenched in the most powerful seats in Congress. Southerners controlled over half the committee chairmanships and a majority of leadership positions in every New Deal Congress. The combination of a seniority rule determining access to congressional influence, a one-party political tradition below the Mason-Dixon line, and Democratic weakness outside the South prior to 1930 resulted in legislative hegemony for the advocates of white supremacy. Roosevelt had no alternative but to cooperate with the Southerners who ran Congress. Their extensive experience on Capitol Hill and disproportionate power in the congressional "inner club" doomed all possibility of securing legislation they opposed vehemently. Even as minor a matter as the invitation of a Negro to the Senate restaurant in 1934 resulted in Southern Democrats howling their rage and threatening to cut off appropriations. The very threat of a filibuster in the Senate or obstruction by the House Committee on Rules weighed heavily on Roosevelt.[19]

The political reality of Southern control of Congress could not be wished away. The key to congressional approval was held by the committee chairmen and a small group of "influentials" led by Garner, Joseph Robinson of Arkansas, Mississippi's Byron "Pat" Harrison, and James Byrnes of South Carolina in the Senate, and their counterparts in the House, Tennessee's Joseph T. Byrns, William Bankhead of Alabama, Sam Rayburn of Texas, and North Carolina's Robert L. "Muley" Doughton. They would brook no presidential interference in racial matters, and they controlled enough votes to back their threat. Roosevelt needed their support. Even if he had evidenced a desire to fight for civil rights, which he did not, this fact would have stopped him. "Politics is the art of the possible," he lectured to one New Dealer while elucidating his reasons for not advocating a bill to abolish the poll tax. "I do not believe in attempting something for the purpose of

one's image. I believe you should never undertake anything unless you have evidence that you have at least a 50-50 chance of
winning."[20]

"I did not choose the tools with which I must work," Roosevelt
explained to Walter White on another occasion. This time he was
declining to press for anti-lynching legislation.

> Had I been permitted to choose them I would have selected
> quite different ones. But I've got to get legislation passed by
> Congress to save America. The Southerners by reason of the
> seniority rule in Congress are chairman or occupy strategic
> places on most of the Senate and House committees. If I come
> out for the anti-lynching bill now, they will block every bill I
> ask Congress to pass to keep America from collapsing. I just
> can't take that risk.[21]

The workings of the broker state further hindered New Deal
involvement in civil rights. The pluralistic politics practiced by
Roosevelt worked to the disadvantage of the poor and unorgan-
ized black community. Weak Negro rights organizations inevitably fared meagerly in a system assigning privileges on the
strength of the groups demanding them. As Henry Lee Moon of
the NAACP later analyzed it:

> The public interest, democratic principles, justice, ethics, or
> even the law are seldom the bases upon which conflicts are
> resolved. Faced with the necessity of resolving a conflict, ad-
> ministration invariably yields to that group which can bring the
> greatest pressure to bear, illustrating anew that government in
> a democracy is government by compromise. Too frequently this
> compromise is characterized by the forced yielding on the part
> of the weaker to the stronger of two contending groups. . . . It
> is obvious that under such conditions, the claims of the Negro,
> however sound, just and legal, are seldom granted when they
> appear to conflict with the claims of a white group.

Afro-Americans simply lacked the resources to reward their
friends and punish their enemies. The opponents of Negro rights
possessed that power.[22]

Time and again, New Dealers committed to civil rights succumbed to a stronger force. No one in the government battled harder or longer for the Afro-American than Ickes. Yet he gained few victories in his many bouts. He succeeded in getting Roosevelt to establish an interdepartmental committee on Negro affairs in 1933, but the combined opposition of the National Recovery Administration (NRA), Civilian Conservation Corps (CCC), and the War, Labor, and Agriculture departments aborted its promise. It would not persevere to guarantee equity to blacks. The efforts of Ickes and his assistants were stifled by other government officials who feared antagonizing local interests and Southern congressmen. Economic recovery came first, they maintained; the New Deal needed all the powerful allies it could muster, they insisted. Roosevelt agreed. Opposition to black workers on Public Works Administration projects by Southern contractors, building trades unions, and congressmen, for example, forced Ickes to compromise his non-discrimination order in such cities as Atlanta, Memphis, and Montgomery. Ickes also had to yield to the demands of the Navy and white tourist interests that he relent from aiding the NAACP's campaign to end segregation in the Virgin Islands.[23]

The consequences of Negro powerlessness revealed themselves most starkly in the treatment of blacks in the initial agricultural and industrial recovery programs. Afro-Americans could do nothing to counter the control over the early New Deal exercised by Southern congressmen in alliance with well-financed industrial associations, local unions, and farm lobbies. Negroes lacked the wherewithal to compete with those desiring them to remain the mudsill. Not a single Negro organization sent a spokesman to testify at the congressional hearings considering farm and industrial legislation. The major associations promoting Negro rights did not even establish a watchdog operation to press the interests of blacks in the New Deal until October 1933. Moreover, although some twenty groups officially sponsored the Joint Committee on National Recovery, it operated with a working staff of two and an annual budget of less than $5000. All it could do was issue press releases and prepare reports. It failed to modify government policies and practices. Unimpeded by a countervailing power, the NRA did not protect blacks from employers who discriminated against them and the AAA Cotton Section did nothing to prevent landowners from cheating Negro tenants and share-croppers out of their fair share of payment benefits.[24]

Lastly, a decentralized administration thwarted proponents of equality for Afro-Americans. Local control usually resulted in decisions inimical to blacks, however garbed in fancy phrases such as Tennessee Valley Authority director David Lilienthal's "grassroots democracy" or Henry Wallace's "hierarchy of New England town meetings." In the North racist employers, trade unions, and city officials flagrantly disregarded non-discriminatory rules promulgated in Washington. Worse yet for blacks, the day-to-day management of the New Deal in the South, where three-quarters of the Negroes still lived, remained in the hands of the hierarchy that had traditionally oppressed Afro-Americans and still stood to profit by discriminating against blacks. Because the most powerful whites in the South kept the records and wrote the reports that determined the activities of the AAA, the Resettlement Administration, and the Farm Credit Administration in their region, blacks never shared equitably in the benefits from these programs. New Dealers desiring to counter racial discrimination thus fought for greater federal control and less decentralization. As one proponent of Negro rights argued, the "greater the area of government, the less it will be influenced by local prejudices." However, Southern politicians well understood this and usually prevailed in limiting federal control. When the President's Commission on Tenancy wrote into its recommendations that the funds should be administered by civil servants free from local political domination (Roosevelt asked Congress to include this provision in its law), Southerners, however, mustered enough votes to override the provision on three separate occasions. The House and Senate leadership did not want a distribution of benefits based on need, but one that would do the most political good and assist blacks least.[25]

Those same desires governed the distribution of relief funds. Again the result was an inequitable share of assistance for blacks from the Works Progress Administration (WPA) and Federal Emergency Relief Administration (FERA). Executive orders to the contrary, local officials persisted in discriminating against Negroes in both direct relief and work relief programs. All efforts by Roosevelt and Hopkins to shift greater control over relief operations to Washington failed. Democratic politicians jealously guarded WPA patronage in their own bailiwicks. They therefore determined which groups would benefit most and which least. Of the more than ten thousand WPA supervisors operating in the South, eleven were Negro.[26]

Throughout the South, Afro-Americans in need had far greater difficulty in obtaining public assistance than did whites in the same economic circumstances. Those blacks who did get relief generally received smaller benefits than whites. "There will be no Negroes pushing wheelbarrows and boys driving trucks getting forty cents an hour when the good white men and white women, working on the fields alongside these roads, can hardly earn forty cents a day," announced a Georgia official. Governor Eugene Talmadge flatly refused to follow government guidelines on equal relief pay for blacks and whites. Atlanta distributed average monthly relief checks of $32.66 to whites and $19.29 to blacks. Some Southern politicians defended the discrepancy with the argument that Afro-Americans had always had less than whites, that they required less to live. Others claimed that the relief levels set by Washington made Negroes "uppity" and hard to hire for dirty work at substandard wages. Many a Dixie Democrat simply thought it a waste to give relief funds to disfranchised recipients who could not vote their appreciation. Whatever the explanation, the federal government usually gave in. *Opportunity* could only wonder: "Does this presage the end of that heralded concern for the Forgotten Man?"[27]

It certainly seemed so during the first New Deal. Because local unions and contractors regulated the labor supply, Negroes never received their equal share of employment in the work undertaken by the Corps of Engineers. Southern congressional insistence that the expenditure of federal funds for education be determined by local school boards forced the Office of Education to acquiesce in the denial of equality to Afro-Americans. The Federal Housing Administration (FHA) encouraged residential segregation. Established by the National Housing Act of 1934 as a shot in the arm for the sickly construction industry, the FHA wrote into its *Underwriting Manual* the warning that property values deteriorate when Negroes move into predominantly white neighborhoods. The FHA also refused to guarantee mortgages on homes purchased by blacks in white communities, augmenting the trend toward residential segregation. It answered the protests of civil rights organizations by acknowledging that it depended upon powerful Southern congressmen for authorization and appropriations and upon the cooperation of local real estate agents in stimulating the building and purchase of new homes, its primary purpose. The desire for economic recovery, not racial reform, guided its policies. Similarly, the Federal Subsistence Homesteads Corporation announced that it would approve only "projects which take the existing economic and social pattern to be found in the locality." During its two years in operation, it began work on thirty-one communities. Not one was racially integrated. Not one was solely for Negroes.[28]

Vociferous opposition by the local white majority in the Tennessee Valley also dashed Negro hopes for equal treatment by the TVA. After an inspection trip to Norris, Tennessee, and Muscle Shoals, Alabama, for the NAACP in July 1933, John P. Davis and Charles H. Houston announced: "In TVA the South is in the saddle." They reported seeing not a single Negro in clerical or office positions. There was not one black foreman. Afro-Americans received less than one percent of the TVA payroll. They were excluded from living in the new model town of Norris. A year later the situation remained much the same. Norris was still all-white. Other TVA sites Jim Crow-ed blacks in housing and recreational facilities. TVA local officials denied blacks their proportionate share of jobs and relegated them to the least skilled, lowest paying tasks. At Wheeler Dam not one of the more than three hundred carpenters employed by the TVA was black. Those in charge also refused to admit Negroes to TVA vocational schools or to training sessions in foremanship. "There is no glimmer of hope for the Negro population," Davis concluded in 1935.[29]

Rampant discrimination in the Civilian Conservation Corps deepened Davis' pessimism. Negroes constituted only 5 percent of those enrolled by the CCC in 1933, and only 6 percent a year later. Despite an unemployment rate for young black males twice that of their white counterparts, the local officials who selected the CCC enrollees repeatedly gave preference to whites. "The benefits of the Civilian Conservation Corps," wrote Arthur Raper of the Black Belt, "have been limited almost wholly to whites. . . . The CCC has remained a white institution, with no more coloring than landownership, which tolerates the possession of one acre in twenty by Negroes." In Dallas County, Alabama, with a population more than three-quarters black, the whites chosen for the CCC outnumbered Negroes by more than two to one. Clarke and Washington Counties in Georgia, 60 percent Negro, had no blacks in the CCC. Mississippi, over half black, permitted but 1.7 percent of its CCC allotment to go to Afro-Americans.[30]

Despite persistent appeals by civil rights groups, the forces opposed to a new deal for blacks could not be slowed in the first Roosevelt Administration. Economic reconstruction took precedence over all other concerns. Congress held the power of the purse, and the South held power in Congress. The traditions of the Democratic party and of decentralized administration bolstered local control in racial matters. Not even the analogue of war emboldened the Roosevelt Administration to supplant the determination of racial practices by city and county officials. Racism remained sovereign. The proponents of Negro rights

were too weak; those content with the existing status of blacks
had enough power to do what they willed. Afro-Americans could
do little more than protest. The great majority of New Dealers
accepted discrimination against blacks as an inevitable cost of
economic recovery and relief. And the great majority of blacks
suffered.[31]

No group needed social security more than Negroes, and none
got less of it. The Wagner-Lewis social security bill excluded
farmers and domestics, 65 percent of all Afro-American workers.
In addition Negroes had to bear the double burden of being
Southern and black. The decentralized system permitted the
South to pay the lowest old-age assistance benefits, roughly half
that of Northern states. Local administration of the programs to
aid dependent children and the blind meant that Afro-Americans
in the South received less than whites, and much less than the
extent of their need. Senator Wagner agreed with the Negroes
who cried foul, but added that he was powerless to do anything
about it.[32]

Nor could Wagner do much to protect Afro-Americans from
being excluded from the labor union movement. He wanted to,
but wanted passage of his National Labor Relations Act in 1935
more. Consequently, he conceded to the hue and cry of the American Federation of Labor and the representatives of the white
South to gain the votes he needed. "Much against his will," stated
Wagner's aide Leon Keyserling, the senator "had to consent to the
elimination" of a clause prohibiting union discrimination and exclusion of blacks "in order to prevent scuttling of the entire bill."
The strongest force prevailed. The civil rights groups pressing
for the anti-discrimination amendment could not match the influence of those opposed to it.[33]

So it went in the first Roosevelt Administration. The federal
government countenanced discrimination and its Negro critics
howled. The cornerstones of the early New Deal, the AAA and
NRA, elicited the greatest volume of criticism. Virtually everything done by the Agricultural Adjustment Administration, civil

rights spokesmen proclaimed, had made the plight of the black farmer even more desperate. In particular, black critics of the New Deal excoriated the AAA Cotton Section for perpetrating a mass eviction of the black peasantry. Estimates of the number of Negroes driven out of cotton production by the 40 percent reduction in crop acreage ran as high as half a million, one-third of the total number of Afro-Americans engaged in agriculture in 1933. Such charges grossly overestimated the damage done by the AAA. According to the 1940 census figures, the number of Negro farmers declined in the 1930s by 67,000 or 4.5 percent, considerably less than the 15 percent drop between 1910 and 1920 or the 8.6 percent decline in the 1920s. Moreover, no clear correlation existed between AAA practices and the black exodus from the cotton counties. More Afro-Americans left the rural South in the period from 1931 to 1933 than in the first two years of the New Deal. More Negroes quit farming toward the end of the thirties, after AAA procedures had been modified to give black tenants a larger share of the benefits, than in the early years of the New Deal when all the cards were stacked in favor of the white landlord. Regardless of the facts, the claim of Negroes that the AAA drove hundreds of thousands of blacks from the land persisted in the thirties. It gained currency because so much of the first New Deal was in fact discriminatory against blacks.[34]

Certainly the AAA did nothing to lift the Afro-American from the lowest rungs on the agricultural ladder or to insist that black farmers be treated equally with whites. Not a single Negro served on an AAA county committee throughout the South. Yet every Negro farm operator had to abide by their decisions. The rare black farmer who owned the land he tilled suffered most from the compulsory crop reduction policy agreed upon by the large landowners because it lowered drastically his already minimal income. Many owners had to become tenants. Because AAA committees usually ignored the rights of tenants, many Negro tenants descended to sharecropping. Discrimination by the AAA left blacks without the payment benefits due them and bereft of a fair

committee to appeal to for equity. Some left to join the ranks of
the urban unemployed. Others labored for white farmers for a
few dir es a day. In 1934 Raper estimated the average annual
salary ol Negro cotton farmers at less than $200. Woofter's study
of over six hundred cotton counties in other areas of the South
pinpointed the consequences of the discrimination by the AAA:
a mean net income of $295 per year for Negro sharecroppers
compared to $417 for white croppers and $175 per year for the
black wage hand against $232 for whites. No New Deal program,
Davis concluded, "has used cruder methods in enforcing poverty
on the Negro farm population." The AAA was no new deal for
blacks; it was a continuation of the same old raw deal.[35]

Black leaders felt the same about the NRA. In a time of worsening mass black poverty and well-founded suspicions that the
New Deal would do nothing special to aid blacks, most Negro
spokesmen lamented the coming of the Blue Eagle for legitimat-
ing wage differentials for the South, excluding the bulk of black
labor from NRA provisions and failing to reduce Afro-American
joblessness. Over a hundred NRA codes permitted Southern employers to pay their workers a lower minimum wage than that
allowed in the rest of the nation. Occupational classifications,
moreover, denied many blacks in industries under the Blue Eagle
even the same minimal wage paid to whites. Eleven thousand of
the thirteen thousand Negroes in Southern cotton mills were
classified so as to exclude them from all NRA benefits. The NRA
never even promulgated codes to cover the bulk of domestic and
unskilled Negro labor. They remained as poor and as unpro-
tected by the government as ever. Ironically, the enforcement of
NRA codes without regard to race also aggravated the plight of
Afro-Americans. Many an employer required by the NRA to pay
Negro workers the same salary as whites fired the blacks. If they
had to pay equal wages they preferred labor of their own race.
Other white employers under NRA orders to raise the wage scale
of their Negro menial workers replaced Afro-Americans with machines. Indeed, few blacks gained much more than a raise in their

cost of living from the NRA. They paid in higher prices the cost of increasing the wages of whites. With justification the Negro press referred to the NRA with scorn as "Negro Run Around," "Negroes Ruined Again," "Negro Rarely Allowed," "Negro Removal Act," "Negro Robbed Again," and "No Roosevelt Again." No black editorial mourned its demise in 1935. The Blue Eagle had long since been categorized, as the Norfolk *Journal and Guide* designated it, "a predatory bird instead of a feathered messenger of happiness."[36]

Afro-Americans, in sum, received no new deal from the first Roosevelt Administration. The cards remained stacked against them, and black spokesmen bitterly mocked the nature of the game. The pages of the Negro press and civil rights journals bristled with attacks on the New Deal. *Opportunity* and *The Crisis*, hardly the most vociferous of Roosevelt's black critics, published exposé after exposé with such titles as "What Price National Recovery?" "NRA Codifies Wage Slavery," "A Wage Differential Based on Race," "What Hope for the Rural Negro?" "TVA: Lily-White Reconstruction," "The Plight of the Negro in the Tennessee Valley," "Black Wages for Black Men," and "Lily-White Social Security." John P. Davis, the head of the Joint Committee on National Recovery and the most frequent commentator on the New Deal in the Negro press, set the tone most Negro leaders echoed. He lambasted Roosevelt's programs for their "vicious discrimination." In the same manner in which he had denounced the AAA, Davis concluded that the NRA too had created a "greater hardship to Negro labor than that to which it was subjected before the plan was put into effect." He saw all the alphabet agencies as blatantly racist, embodying the New Deal's "well-defined philosophy that Negroes must be left to develop in a ghetto of their own quite apart from the white population." "On every hand," he summarized his inventory of the relief and recovery programs, "the New Deal has used slogans for the same raw deal."[37]

This opprobrium reached its apogee in a conference on "The

Position of the Negro in the Present Economic Crisis" held in Washington in 1935. Convoked by John P. Davis and Ralph Bunche, chairman of the Department of Political Science at Howard University, the meeting damned every New Deal program as inimical to the black masses. Davis's keynote address focused on capitalism as the root of the problem and on the necessity of discarding the existing economic system to give blacks a truly new deal. A. Philip Randolph complained that Roosevelt could never adequately assist Negroes as long as he perpetuated the profit system. Bunche asserted that the President's "state capitalism," like that of fascist Italy and Germany, "can at best only fix the disadvantages, the differentials, the discriminations, under which the Negro population has labored all along." The NAACP's Du Bois and Abram Harris also claimed the failure of the New Deal to aid blacks to be inherent in the failure of capitalism. Members of the Communist, Socialist, and Socialist Workers' parties joined the chorus of criticism. Although few Negroes, or their leaders, accepted such leftist analyses and prescriptions, far fewer disagreed with the overall conclusion that discrimination ran rampant through the New Deal.[38]

Even those least sympathetic to the Left at the conference emphasized the New Deal's neglect of Afro-American needs. Speeches by T. Arnold Hill of the Urban League on "The Plight of the Negro Industrial Worker" and by the prominent sociologist E. Franklin Frazier on "The Effects of the New Deal Farm Program upon the Negro" drove home the inescapable point that Negroes had not received the assistance they needed from the Roosevelt Administration. The conferees agreed that the New Deal "has utterly failed to relieve the exploitation" of Afro-Americans; that "black labor finds itself comparatively in a worse position than it occupied at the beginning of the depression"; and that "the will of those who have kept Negroes in economic disfranchisement has been permitted to prevail, and the government has looked on in silence and at times with approval. Consequently, the Negro worker has good reason to feel that his government has betrayed him under the New Deal." Such was the dominant view of the Negro leadership in 1935. Reporting on the conference for the *Defender,* Dean Kelly Miller of Howard University pinpointed the black mood: "The New Deal was criticized, denounced, and condemned." He concluded: "Nothing good was found in it."[39]

3

The Start of a New Deal

Such denunciations of the New Deal by blacks, so common between 1933 and 1935, soon stilled and then turned to praise. Especially in the second term, new forces, both in and outside the Roosevelt Administration, began to push the federal government in directions favorable to blacks. Tentatively and often with misgivings, the creators of the second New Deal began laying the foundations for the postwar advances in civil rights that C. Vann Woodward termed the Second Reconstruction. The changes seen by the average Afro-American in the thirties, however, were limited. Continuity appeared far greater in everyday black life. No one could gainsay the fact that Negroes remained in 1941, as they had in 1933, on the lowest rung of the socioeconomic ladder. Throughout the New Deal they were first-fired and last-hired. The Roosevelt Administration perpetuated more of the discrimination and segregation inherited from previous decades than it ended.

Yet all revolutions, like the mightiest rivers, begin with a trickle. During the thirties significant developments first occurred to reduce Negro powerlessness, to increase Afro-American expectations, and to alter white attitudes toward race relations. The

New Deal initiated few of these changes. But it played its part by substantively and symbolically assisting blacks to an unprecedented extent, by making explicit as never before the federal government's recognition of and responsibility for the plight of Afro-Americans, and by creating a reform atmosphere that made possible a major campaign for civil rights. These actions, asserted Gunnar Myrdal in *An American Dilemma,* "changed the whole configuration of the Negro problem." When "looked upon from the practical and political viewpoints," he opined shortly after the United States entered the Second World War, "the contrast between the present situation and the one prior to the New Deal is striking."[1]

No single individual, organization, event, or development caused the New Deal to change. In part, outside forces influenced the Roosevelt Administration. Negro voters, Southern liberals, Northern radicals, egalitarian unionists, anti-fascist scholars, and civil rights partisans all played a role, as did the transformation of Southern agriculture, the shock of Hitlerism, and the nationalization of American culture. Time and again the government acted in the interest of blacks because of the cumulative impact of these interrelated forces. The New Deal also changed in part because of the commitment to racial equality of many of those close to Roosevelt and because of the internal dynamic of its own philosophy—its concern for the dispossessed and for the underdog. The New Deal's arousal of sympathy for the forgotten man generated reform impulses that would revolutionize the black freedom struggle.

Certainly no individual did more to alter the relationship between the New Deal and the cause of civil rights than Mrs. Franklin Delano Roosevelt. Like her husband, she entered the White House with neither much knowledge of nor empathy for the problems of blacks. Despite her involvement with Afro-Americans in New York's Rivington Street settlement house during the Progressive era, it came as "quite a shock" to her in 1933 to discover that anybody would make a fuss over her lunching with a black woman in Florida. The only sign of concern for the Negro publicly shown by Eleanor Roosevelt that year, observed *The Crisis,* was her arrangement for a concert at the White House by the glee club of the Hampton Institute.[2]

That changed. Her friendship with Walter White of the NAACP and Mary McLeod Bethune, President of the National Council of Negro Women, began to resemble a crash course on the struggle of blacks against oppression. As a consequence of their frequent visits to Hyde Park and the White House, Eleanor Roosevelt became a skilled partisan of their cause. With them the First Lady also began to confer regularly with other civil rights leaders. Talking long into the evening with her Negro guests, she helped devise strategies that might gain Afro-Americans better opportunities in the New Deal. Not until 1934, however, did she either press her views on civil rights within the administration or speak them in public. Like other liberals who initially viewed the race problem as essentially economic, to be solved by New Deal antipoverty measures, Mrs. Roosevelt only gradually came to the realization that such specific matters as discrimination, lynching, and disfranchisement had to be faced directly.[3]

Mrs. Roosevelt boosted the civil rights movement in three vital ways: by playing the role of unofficial ombudsman for the Negro; by influencing the views of her husband and other New Dealers; and by prominently associating herself with Negro organizations, leaders, and issues. She goaded the President into increasing appropriations for Howard University and the Freedmen's Hospital in the capital, and pleaded with congressmen to rehabilitate the black alley slums of Washington. Her constant prodding wore down the resistance of many bureaucrats, resulting in gains for blacks in federal appointments and a diminution of government-tolerated discrimination. She particularly had success in influencing WPA chief Harry Hopkins and his assistant, Aubrey Williams, to lessen inequality in federal relief projects. In addition, Eleanor Roosevelt opened channels of communication between the administration and the civil rights movement. Few members of the President's official family initially knew much about the leading Negro rights spokesmen and organizations. Mrs. Roosevelt's persistence altered that. The Afro-American leaders who in 1933 could not get appointments to see the President found themselves frequently in the White House by 1936.[4]

Her precise impact on her husband is difficult to measure. She destroyed much of the correspondence between them, leaving historians forever in the dark. But most of those close to the President agree that she exercised a considerable influence on his outlook. "It was not unusual," Roosevelt's personal secretary remembered, "to hear him predicate an entire line of reasoning upon the statement that 'my Missus told me so and so.'" Robert Sherwood dubbed her "the keeper of and constant spokesman for her husband's conscience." Because of the President's respect for her observations, the Washington columnist Raymond Clapper listed her among "The Ten Most Powerful People in Washington." To Clapper she was "a cabinet member without portfolio." Most New Deal historians view her the same way. Frank Freidel described her as a power in both the Democratic party and the New Deal, managing her own staff, holding her own press conferences, uttering her own pronouncements on matters large and small, and chatting privately with her husband more frequently than any other politician of the thirties. "Her qualities of compassion and sensitivity," James MacGregor Burns wrote, "added a new dimension to Franklin's outlook." He judged her "of incalculable influence" on the President. According to William Leuchtenburg, "she was the good fairy who saw to it that in a world of pressure groups and partisan decisions, the President did not neglect people and causes that had no other voices in places of power." This same point has been the theme of the most recent analyses of Eleanor Roosevelt by Joseph Lash and Tamara Hareven.[5]

Civil rights spokesmen in the thirties never seemed to doubt her persuasiveness with the President. No one in the White House received more mail from them; much of this correspondence con-

tained specific requests that she talk to Franklin about this or
that matter. She was their conduit to the higher circles of the
New Deal and Democratic party. Their later writings all credit
Mrs. Roosevelt with a critical role in changing the administration's outlook on racial affairs. Those most opposed to civil rights
in the 1930s sounded the same theme. The vehemence of the battle they waged against her remains the most eloquent testimony
to her authority and prestige.[6]

Eleanor Roosevelt's importuning, bolstered by political pressure from diverse sources, gradually showed in the actions taken
by the President. He publicly promised a Negro journalist that
blacks would be included, "absolutely and impartially," in all relief and recovery programs. In an address at Howard University
he announced that, "as far as it was humanly possible," the government's policies would be predicated upon the premise "that
among American citizens there should be no forgotten men and
no forgotten races." Hesitatingly, Roosevelt eschewed the caution
of his palace guard. He permitted himself to be photographed
with Negro leaders, to confer with civil rights delegations, and to
send messages to Afro-American organizations. He also withdrew
American troops from Haiti, emphasizing the need for good
neighborly relations with the black island republic. White House
publicists, meanwhile, began to play up the President's personal
concern with the economic troubles of Afro-Americans. As token
as these steps were, they marked a break with the past procedures of both the Democratic party and Franklin Roosevelt.[7]

Moreover, acceding to his wife's pleas, Roosevelt speaking to a
conference of the Churches of Christ in America proclaimed over
a nation-wide radio network: "Lynch law is murder, a deliberate
and definite disobedience of the high command, 'Thou Shalt not
kill.' We do not excuse those in high places or low who condone
lynch law." It was not much. But Du Bois immediately noted in
The Crisis that, despite the President's "dependence upon the
bourbon and reactionary South for his political salvation," Roose-

velt was not aping his racist supporters. "It took war, riot and up-
heaval to make Wilson say one small word," Du Bois continued.
"Nothing ever induced Herbert Hoover to say anything on the
subject worth the saying. Even Harding was virtually dumb."
Only Franklin Roosevelt, concluded *The Crisis*'s editor, "has declared frankly that lynching is murder. We all knew it, but it is
unusual to have a President of the United States admit it. These
things give us hope."[8]

Eleanor Roosevelt's public deeds swelled that hope. Because of
the prominence of her position everything she officially did made
news. The repute associated with the presidency enveloped her
activities. The media reported her many speeches to Negro colleges and Afro-American organizations, as well as her pleas to
whites for "fair play and equal opportunity for Negro citizens."
NBC broadcast her address to a conference on Negro education,
enabling millions of Americans, many for the first time, to learn
of the inequities of black schooling in the South. The radio audience then heard the First Lady exhort all Americans "to work together, all of us regardless of race, creed or color," to "wipe out
the feelings of intolerance whenever we find it." In one of her
many "My Day" columns devoted to racial problems, entitled
"Do We Really Live in 'Land of the Free?'" Mrs. Roosevelt
asked: "Are you free if you cannot vote, if you cannot be sure
that the same justice will be meted out to you as to your neighbor; if you are expected to live on a lower level than your neighbor and to work for lower wages; if you are barred from certain
places and from certain opportunities?" She answered, in a *Ladies'
Home Journal* column, by asserting that the federal government
must act to promote racial equality. "There must be equality before the law, equality of education, equal opportunity to obtain a
job according to one's ability and training, and equality of participation in self-government." To a nation accustomed to hearing
the White House echo its racial prejudices, Eleanor Roosevelt's
pronouncements undoubtedly shocked. They probably influenced

some Americans to concern themselves with racial affairs for the first time. At the least, they augmented the new public dialogue on civil rights.[9]

Opportunity hailed her as "unparalleled in the history of America." *The Crisis* followed suit. Her pictures and words became a commonplace in the Negro press. Afro-Americans pointed with pride to her as the conscience of the New Deal. If no one else would, Mrs. Roosevelt had proved she could be counted on to say publicly what needed to be said, to welcome blacks to the White House, and to put in a confidential word for Negro rights with the President. To Negroes, the Urban League proclaimed, she was "the First Lady indeed!"[10]

After the 1936 election Eleanor Roosevelt moved rapidly from a public position in favor of equality of opportunity to one of endorsing specific civil rights measures. Boldly, she joined the campaign to abolish the poll tax and spoke in favor of a federal antilynching law. The more vehemently Southern Democrats objected to her interference in racial issues, the more wholeheartedly she committed herself to the cause. She identified herself with the movement by attending its conventions and special conferences, by addressing major gatherings of the NAACP, the National Negro Congress, and the Southern Conference for Human Welfare, and by accepting awards for contributions to the fight for racial justice. In 1937 Mrs. Roosevelt publicly helped raise money to continue publication of *The Crisis.* Increasingly, she showed her disdain for the whole complex of Jim Crow attitudes and activities current in the thirties. The press duly reported her traveling, eating, and socially mingling with blacks. At the opening session of the SCHW in Birmingham, Alabama, in 1939, Mrs. Roosevelt defied the local segregation ordinance by refusing to be seated on the white-only side of the hall. It might seem like a minor gesture to later generations accustomed to affirmative actions by the White House for Negro rights, yet the radical National Conference of Negro Youth, meeting soon after Eleanor Roosevelt's exploit, altered its agenda to pass a unanimous resolution acclaiming the First Lady for her brave and inspiring act.[11]

Following an address by Mrs. Roosevelt, the head of the National Negro Congress in Philadelphia wrote:

> The value of Mrs. Roosevelt's presence in Philadelphia lies in the inspiration she has given us and the extra courage and confidence her interest arouses. Now we know that when we raise our voices for more and better jobs, cheaper and more adequate housing, civil liberties and protection from the lynch mob, we have a staunch ally in the First Lady of the Land.[12]

Equally important, her public championing of civil rights emboldened other New Dealers to work for racial equality and justice. Actively encouraged by Mrs. Roosevelt, W. Frank Persons of the Labor Department took the lead in insisting upon an equitable share of CCC enrollees for Negroes. Harry Hopkins and Aubrey Williams capitalized on her support to break new ground in appointing blacks to positions of authority and in treating Negroes on relief with dignity. Other New Dealers close to Mrs. Roosevelt, including Hallie Flanagan of the Federal Theatre Project, Nathan Straus of the United States Housing Authority, John M. Carmody of the Rural Electrification Administration, and Will Alexander and Rexford G. Tugwell of the Farm Security Administration all made special efforts to provide Afro-Americans with a new deal. Some of them had been concerned with Negro rights prior to the 1930s; all felt freer to express their commitment because of Mrs. Roosevelt's backing. Their activities on behalf of blacks regularly gained the plaudits of the Negro press and civil rights organizations.[13]

So did most of President Roosevelt's appointments to the federal bench. Black leaders of every persuasion proclaimed the selection of the first Negro federal judge in American history, William Hastie of the NAACP, as an epochal act by the Chief Executive. They were also delighted by the appointment of Wil-

liam Houston, NAACP attorney Charles Houston's father, as a
United States assistant attorney general. The choices of the markedly liberal William O. Douglas and Felix Frankfurter, once an
NAACP official, for the Supreme Court further buoyed the hopes
of those involved in the movement for Negro rights. And the des-
ignation of Frank Murphy, first as attorney general and then as a
justice of the High Court, raised the expectations of the black
leadership yet higher. Murphy came to Washington with a distinguished record as a partisan of civil rights. In one of his first
acts as attorney general, Murphy, a close associate of Walter
White and a former member of the NAACP Board of Directors,
created the Civil Rights Section of the Justice Department. Its
purpose, said Murphy, was "the aggressive protection of fundamental rights inherent in a free people." "For the first time in our
history," he reported to the President, "the full weight of the Department will be thrown behind the effort" to enforce the civil
rights statutes, to conduct "an inquiry into the need for additional legislation on the subject," and to invigorate "the federal
government's endeavors to protect fundamental rights." It represented quite a turnabout from Roosevelt's first attorney general, Homer Cummings. The importance of the change was recognized at once. Writing to Walter White, Hastie could not
conceal his glee. "The worst fears of the unregenerate south are
being realized," he confided to the NAACP chieftain. "It seems,"
the Negro judge concluded after surveying the new Roosevelt
men staffing the Executive Branch and Supreme Court, "that the
U.S. Senate is the last stronghold of the Confederacy."[14]

Hastie, once an aide to the secretary of the interior, punctili-
ously lauded the racial advances prompted by Harold Ickes. A
former president of the NAACP chapter in Chicago, Ickes ended
segregation in the department's cafeterias and restrooms in 1933.
Other cabinet members and agency heads quietly followed his
precedent. Ickes also "let it be known officially that segregation
in Interior was a thing of the past." He refused positions to sub-
ordinates who would not work with blacks; he insisted that the

Public Works Administration (PWA) construction projects hire Afro-Americans as skilled as well as unskilled laborers. The PWA's enabling legislation had said nothing about discrimination. Yet Ickes boldly proceeded on the presumption "that Congress intended this program to be carried out without discrimination as to race, color or creed of the unemployed to be relieved." The secretary, moreover, stipulated that all PWA contracts include a clause specifying that the number of blacks hired and their percentage of the project payroll be equal to the proportion of Negroes in the 1930 occupational census. Although sometimes disregarded by local officials and contractors, it nevertheless resulted in unprecedented wages for many black laborers and led to the admission of hundreds of Negroes into previously lily-white Southern construction trade unions. In addition, it later led to similar quota systems to assist blacks by the U.S. Housing Authority (USHA), the Federal Works Agency, and the President's Committee on Fair Employment Practices.[15]

Because of Ickes, Negroes occupied at least one-third of all the housing units built by the PWA. Of the 48 low-rent projects completed by the Housing Division of the PWA prior to 1938, 14 were solely for Afro-Americans and 15 for joint Negro-white occupancy. The selection of sites for public housing at times furthered patterns of residential segregation, but in the 1930s what most impressed Negro leaders was that federal authorities for the first time were working to provide decent shelter for poor and middle-class Afro-Americans. The USHA gave blacks an even better housing deal. About 41,000 of the 122,000 dwelling units built by the Housing Authority between 1937 and 1942 went to Negroes. Afro-Americans predominantly occupied 118 of the nearly 400 projects completed and shared with whites some 40 others. Again segregation increased, yet civil rights spokesmen lavished tributes on the USHA because it charged Afro-Americans a lower average monthly rent than it did whites and because it permitted black families to enter the projects with higher incomes than it did whites. Such measures were seen as evidence of the USHA's determination to assist blacks. Myrdal, in fact, singled out the white officials of the USHA for their active fight against discrimination.[16]

Ickes's PWA also aided Afro-Americans through its massive construction program. It insisted, often in vain, that the percentage of federal funds spent on Negro facilities match their percentage of the population. Few officials in the South complied. Negro schools in the South, for example, received less than 10 percent of the construction funds allocated to the South by the PWA. But the totality of money spent on blacks by the PWA represented a quantum leap in expenditures for Negroes in comparison with anything previously appropriated by public or private agencies. Over $45 million went to the building and repairing of Negro schools, hospitals, and recreational facilities. The nearly $5 million granted for new buildings at Southern Negro colleges increased their total plant value by more than 25 percent. In addition, PWA loaned municipalities and states more than $20 million to construct 225 schools for blacks, to improve or alter 118 others, and to erect 64 gymnasiums, auditoriums, and dormitories for Negroes.[17]

As in public housing, Negro labor had an equal share of the PWA's construction payroll. Blacks received about 31 percent of the total wages paid by the PWA in 1936, including 15.8 percent of the skilled labor payroll, 21 percent of the semi-skilled, and 64 percent of the unskilled. Local practices varied widely. Particularly in the South, officials often disregarded PWA directives from Washington. In Chicago and Washington, D.C., the proportion of Negroes in the various categories of the 1930 employment census usually equalled the percentages of PWA pay given blacks. Detroit, Philadelphia, and Cincinnati for the most part adhered to the PWA's order to hire and pay blacks on the same basis as whites. And some cities, like Indianapolis, paid Negroes a higher percentage of the PWA payroll than required by the occupational census.[18]

To at least a minimum extent, Ickes had proved that anti-discrimination orders and racial quotas could work. His actions pointed to the direction Washington could take to give blacks a new deal. Irascible as he often was, Ickes proceeded patiently enough to avoid congressional retaliation on matters ranging from his hiring of Negro professionals to his start of desegregating National Parks in the South to his institution of integrated housing projects in the North. His success stimulated other New Deal administrators to dare to be more progressive in race relations. Indeed, by the end of the decade T.R.B. noted in the *New Republic:* "The New Dealers—to their honor, particularly Mrs. Roosevelt and Secretary Ickes—have gone a long way toward extending social equality to Negroes." Their actions also pricked the conscience and political calculations of many a Northern Democratic congressman. They wrote into more than twenty New Deal statutes the proviso: "There shall be no discrimination on account of race, creed or color." These laws, in some cases, defined discrimination as a felony punishable by a fine of up to two thousand dollars or two years in jail. They did not end discrimination by government. They did not even alter in minute ways the behavior of most local officials in the South. But the half century-long tradition of congressional indifference to white racism in the administration of federal programs had begun to end.[19]

In the administration of public relief, Ickes's precedents had an immediate, if limited, discernible impact. In May 1935 President Roosevelt issued Executive Order 7046, mandating that in the newly established WPA all those "qualified by training and experience to be assigned to work projects shall not be discriminated against on any grounds whatsoever." Hopkins reiterated the President's stricture against racial discrimination in two administrative orders of his own, sent out in the summer of 1936, and Congress joined the refrain in February 1939 by amending the Emergency Relief Act to make it unlawful for any relief official to discriminate "on account of race, creed, or color." It did not quite work this way, particularly in the South. Negroes found it more difficult than whites to get on relief rolls; they usually received less for the work relief they performed than did whites. When local officials did not overtly disregard the federal law, discrimination came guised as geographic wage differentials and occupational classifications. Negroes, like whites, never received what their needs warranted. Still, both the number of Afro-Americans on relief and the funds they earned increased steadily during Roosevelt's second term. This trend as much reflected the New Deal's determination to administer relief with more concern for need than color as it did the movement of whites from the ranks of the jobless to the employed. By 1939 the WPA provided basic earnings for one million black families. Overall, Robert Weaver concluded, the WPA was "a godsend" for blacks. *The Crisis* gave it credit for the "great gains for the race in areas which heretofore have set their faces steadfastly against decent relief for Negroes." Three decades later, an Afro-American recalled to interviewer Studs Terkel that the WPA had given blacks their first sense of being a part of things, of really being included: "It made us feel like there was something we could do in the scheme of things."[20]

Significantly, the Negro journals, which regularly scored the relief program from 1933 to 1936, did not print a single anti-WPA article during the second Roosevelt Administration. Numerous essays in *Opportunity, The Crisis,* and the Negro press lavished praise on Hopkins for the changes made in the administration of relief after 1935. The reasons why are not mysterious. The millions of dollars spent by the WPA in Afro-American communities meant survival, when even that had been previously in doubt. After 1936 the proportion of black WPA workers varied from 15 to 20 percent. In many cities the percentage of Negroes in the WPA ran as high as three to five times their percentage in the population, a testament both to the acute effect of the depression on blacks and to the readiness of the New Deal to come to their rescue. Moreover, according to Richard Sterner, who conducted the most exhaustive study of the subject, the majority of Negroes received their proper job classification from the WPA, earned the equal wages they were entitled to, and received at least their due in the special projects. Indeed, many Afro-Americans on WPA made considerably more than they could have in private employment. The Works Progress Administration, in fact, provided an economic floor for the whole black community in the 1930s, rivaling both agriculture and domestic service as the chief source of Negro income.[21]

Hopkins's insistence that the WPA treat blacks equitably went beyond economics. Over five thousand Negroes were employed as teachers and supervisors in the WPA Education Program, where nearly a quarter of a million Afro-Americans learned to read and write. Tens of thousands were trained for skilled jobs. Harlem alone had thirty-four WPA adult education centers and a higher enrollment than any other section of New York City. The Federal Music Project gave performances in all sections of the country of works by contemporary black composers; featured all-Negro casts in several of its operas; made a special effort to preserve, record, and publish Negro folk music; conducted music instruction classes for blacks in at least a dozen states; and sponsored Negro concert bands in a score of cities. Holger Cahill, head of the Federal Art Project, employed several hundred Negroes, even agreeing to the demand of the Harlem Artists' Guild that compensatory quotas be established for Afro-Americans because their suffering had been so great. Jacob Lawrence and Samuel Brown were but two of the most renowned black artists to gain training and a livelihood in the FAP. And many thousands of Afro-Americans attended art classes funded by the Project in the South Side Community Art Center in Chicago and the Harlem Art Center, whose opening ceremonies in December 1937 featured an address by Mrs. Roosevelt. Hallie Flanagan, director of the Federal Theatre Project (FTP), also made numerous special efforts to assist Negroes. She established a Negro Unit, which employed some five hundred blacks in New York in mid-1936 and brought dramas that dealt with Nat Turner, Harriet Tubman, Pierre Toussaint, and African folktales into many Negro communities for the first time. The FTP's Living Newspapers broached such controversial topics as lynching, the chain gang, the poll tax, and the invasion of Ethiopia.[22]

Congressman Martin Dies of Texas tried to use Flanagan's concern for racial equality as proof of Communist subversive activity in the Theatre Project. Dies claimed, during the hearings of the House Un-American Activities Committee in 1938, that the FTP's very lack of discrimination conformed to Communist teachings and doctrines. The same charges were hurled at the Federal Writers' Project (FWP), headed by two crusading liberals from Columbia University, Henry G. Alsberg and Reed Harris. Over two hundred black authors joined the FWP, and Alsberg, working closely with Walter White, repeatedly put pressure on state directors in the South to hire additional Negroes. FWP researchers produced the material that led to St. Clair Drake's and Horace Cayton's *Black Metropolis* and to Roi Ottley's *The Negro in New York*, as well as to numerous Negro bibliographies, directories, and state studies. The project also collected hundreds of interviews with ex-slaves and first published such Negro authors as Ralph Ellison and Richard Wright. For these reasons many Negro spokesmen acknowledged their gratitude to the WPA and the Roosevelt Administration. They credited the relief program with not merely reducing Afro-American privation but with doing so in a manner that encouraged black dignity and hope. *Opportunity* in 1939 wrote:

> It is to the eternal credit of the administrative officers of the WPA that discrimination on various projects because of race has been kept to a minimum and that in almost every community Negroes have been given a chance to participate in the work program. . . . In the northern communities, particularly the urban centers, the Negro has been afforded his first real opportunity for employment in white-collar occupations.

Hopkins had shown, despite white bureaucratic control at the local level, that the federal government desired to help blacks.[23]

So did Aubrey Willis Williams, Harry Hopkins's Deputy Works

Progress Administrator from 1935 to 1938, and the head of the National Youth Administration (NYA) until its demise in 1943. Widely attacked by white supremacists as a "nigger lover" and traitor to his region, the young Alabamian viewed progress in the Negro's educational and economic status as one of his top priorities. The NYA directly aided approximately three hundred thousand black youths. Forbidding either geographical or racial differentials, it paid exactly the same wages to Negroes as to whites. Nearly every one of the one hundred and twenty Negro colleges participated in the student aid program. Afro-Americans constituted at least 10 percent of all students helped by the NYA. An even higher percentage of Negro youth enrolled in the out-of-school work program. Half the blacks employed, moreover, worked at tasks on a professional or semi-professional level related to their future occupational interests. At Williams's insistence, the NYA fully included Afro-Americans in all its skilled manpower training programs. He was determined that Negro youth be prepared for more than the traditional black jobs of maids and janitors. Repeatedly, Williams issued directives to his state officials to be fair to Negroes. His persistence, Ira DeA. Reid reported to the American Council on Education, "has done much to offset racial discrimination in the relief administration of many southern states."[24]

Yet another white Southern proponent of civil rights, Will Alexander, directed the Farm Security Administration. Established in 1937 to aid the family farmer, the FSA valiantly, although often in vain, tried determinedly to assist black tenants and sharecroppers. Overall, the minimal amount of funds appropriated to the FSA and the need to avoid poor credit risks to keep the program self-liquidating obviated any hope to make much of a dent in rural poverty. But Alexander's desire to end racial discrimination in a program locally administered by committees of white farmers shone as a symbol of the best side of the New Deal. He fought as hard as anyone in Washington to give blacks a fair deal, and largely succeeded. Alexander appointed vigorous race relations advisors, not token window dressing as did some administrators, and the FSA employed a higher percentage of Negro supervisors than any other New Deal agency. The percentage of FSA loans given to Afro-Americans exactly equalled the percentage of Negro farm operators—even in the South. So did the cash amount of the loans. In June 1940 the fourteen hundred Negro families living on FSA homestead projects constituted 25 percent of all such families; over half the families on FSA rental cooperatives were black. Alexander's policies, especially the desegregation of some FSA projects in the South, raised the ire of many a white supremacist and large landowner. Their representatives in Congress prevented the FSA from accomplishing much. Still the glaring differences between the FSA's treatment of blacks and that of the earlier Resettlement Administration and Subsistence Homesteads Corporation epitomized the new direction taken by the New Deal after 1935.[25]

That shift in direction could also be seen in the changes in the administration of the social security system and the Civilian Conservation Corps during Roosevelt's second term. The Negroes receiving old-age assistance benefits exceeded their proportion of the elderly in the population. So did the percentage of black recipients of aid to blind and dependent children. Prior to 1936 Afro-Americans had constituted less than 6 percent of the youths in the CCC. That year their percentage shot up to 9.9 percent, and up further to 11 percent in 1938, where it hovered until Congress terminated the corps in 1942. All told, about a quarter of a million Negroes served in the CCC, nearly one-tenth of them in integrated camps. Over thirty thousand Afro-Americans who had entered the CCC as illiterates learned to read and write. Discrimination did not cease. The Army officials who ran the camps continued to ignore blacks when it came to hiring educators and professionals. They usually kept Negroes out of training programs that would lead to their advancement. Strict segregation was adhered to in the South. Yet the combined efforts of Ickes and Perkins also bore fruit in the rising percentage of blacks in the

CCC, the gradual increase in the number of Afro-Americans in supervisory positions, the attention given to educational programs for Negroes, and the adherence to an official policy of equal wages for black and white.[26]

Overall, despite the continuation of much discrimination and segregation, the New Deal's massive relief program meant relatively more to blacks than to whites. The cumulative effect of this assistance, particularly after 1935, dramatically accelerated the pace of progress in Negro education, health, and economic well-being. A million Afro-Americans took part in the literacy classes offered by a score of federal government education projects. Negro illiteracy dropped 10 percent in the thirties. The number of instructional facilities and salaries for teachers and the length of school term for Negroes all rose significantly in the late 1930s. By 1940, two-thirds of all blacks between the ages of six and twenty-five were in school, 20 percent more than in 1910. The gap in Southern public expenditures per Negro pupil rose from 29 percent of the white average in 1931 to 44 percent in 1941. The salaries of Negro teachers increased from about one-third of those for whites in 1931 to more than one-half at the end of the decade. In addition, both the number of Negro college students and Negro college graduates more than doubled during the New Deal. Almost two hundred Afro-Americans received doctorates in the 1930s, and another one hundred and twenty-eight between 1940 and 1943, compared to but forty-five in the first three decades of the century. Federal funding had started to make a real difference to Afro-Americans.[27]

Yet much remained undone. In both qualitative and quantitative measures, Negro education remained malevolently deficient. Here discrimination persisted. Over half the white Southerners polled in 1940 expressed their opposition to educational equality for blacks, and their state legislators appropriated accordingly. In much the same way, New Deal relief programs stimulated advances in public health for Afro-Americans but left blacks in a less than equal position. Between 1930 and 1940 the death rate

ısand population decreased from 10.8 to 10.4 for whites
n 16.5 to 13.9 for Negroes. The infant mortality rate per
l live births dropped from 60 to 43 for whites and from
over 100 to 73 for Afro-Americans. The best single measure of the
general level of health—life expectancy at birth—improved more
than twice as much for blacks as for whites during the New Deal
decade. Life expectancy increased from 60 to 62 for white males,
63 to 67 for white females, 47 to 52 for black males, and 49 to 55
for black females. The gaps had narrowed; absolutely and relatively, Negroes had improved their health to a greater extent than
whites, yet the differences remained a cruel reminder of the toll
exacted by racism.[28]

The very elephantine growth of the federal government boosted
the Negro's economic status. In 1941 the civil service listed over
one hundred and fifty thousand black federal employees. Less
than fifty thousand had worked for the government when Hoover
left office. The proportion of Afro-Americans in the government
work force had more than doubled to just over 10 percent, slightly
higher than the proportion of Negroes in the population. The
New Deal, perhaps most important, opened up professional opportunities on a grand scale for blacks in the federal government.
Past presidents had given only a handful of honorific posts to Negroes; Roosevelt appointed over one hundred Afro-Americans to
administrative positions, most of them directly relating to the
pressing problems of blacks. Below the administrative rank, thousands of Negroes worked in the New Deal as architects, econo-
mists, engineers, lawyers, librarians, office managers, and statisti-
cians. Tens of thousands gained employment in the government
as clerks, secretaries, and trained stenographers. Still, they were
a minority of all Negro federal employees. Most continued to toil
in the lowest general service ranks. Yet the tripling of blacks in
the civil service and their representation at unprecedented levels
impressed observers at the time. "They are the first significant
step," wrote Myrdal, "toward the participation of Negroes in federal government activity." A black columnist in the *Courier* noted

that one could not "help being convinced that the 'New Deal' is really a new deal for the Negro in Federal employment." And Ralph Bunche concluded that the "[black] positions held under the New Deal represented a radical break with the past." Few civil rights leaders failed to herald these advances as indicative of a new departure by Washington.[29]

Negro leaders also viewed the emergence of the Black Cabinet in the mid-1930s as yet another step by the New Deal in the right direction. In part a symbol of the changes in the New Deal after 1935, and in part a cause of those very changes, the federal government's race relations advisers continually pushed for more Negroes in policy-making positions, for equality in the relief and recovery programs, and for greater concern by the Roosevelt Administration on all issues of Negro rights. At the least, wrote historian George B. Tindall, "the Black Cabinet signified an interest shown by no other administration within memory."[30]

President Roosevelt had no such intentions at first. When Will Alexander and Edwin Embree of the Julius Rosenwald Fund appealed to the President early in 1933 to establish a government position for someone to look out for the Afro-American's interest in the recovery program, he demurred, fearing a clash with the Southern Democrats controlling Congress. Not until Ickes had volunteered to accept such an appointee in his department and the Rosenwald Fund had offered to pay for the salary, enabling Roosevelt to bypass Congress, did the Chief Executive approve the new position of a special assistant on the economic status of Negroes. In tune with the times, Ickes chose a white man, Clark Foreman, a young, religiously-oriented Southerner who had gained his experience in race relations as secretary of the Georgia Commission for Interracial Cooperation and as an assistant director of the Phelps-Stokes Fund. The Negro press howled at the announcement of a white being picked to represent black interests. Roy Wilkins, Walter White's new assistant in the NAACP, wrote Ickes that Afro-Americans "bitterly resent having a white man designated by the government to advise them of their welfare." Such criticism might have doomed the project in the past. But Ickes chose to compromise. He agreed to add a Negro to work with Foreman. The Rosenwald Fund put up the money for an additional official, as well as a Negro secretary. Robert Weaver, just out of Harvard with a doctorate in economics, was picked to team up with Foreman. The ball started to roll.[31]

On their own, Ickes and his two youthful assistants decided "to function generally throughout the Administration" to insure equitable treatment for blacks. About all they could accomplish initially was the recruitment of other race relations advisers. And many of them functioned primarily as public relations boosters for the administration. Often chosen for their pro-Roosevelt position in the 1932 campaign, they did little as watchdogs for the Negro's welfare. Early in 1934, however, Ickes won Roosevelt's approval for a special interdepartmental committee on Negro affairs. Ickes, Foreman, and Weaver, as well as such blacks as Robert L. Vann of the Justice Department, Harry Hunt of the Farm Credit Administration, Forrester B. Washington of FERA, and Eugene Kinckle Jones of the Commerce Department, regularly met with white representatives of the NRA, the CCC, the Agriculture Department, and the military services and regularly clashed with them. Henry Wallace, reflecting the dominant view of the early New Dealers, warned the Afro-Americans to go slow and not make trouble. In less than half a year, the Interdepartmental Group Concerned with the Special Problems of Negroes ceased to convene. Nothing had been done.[32]

The race relations advisers failed to budge most other administration officers in the first term, but their numbers grew and they privately began to confer together. By mid-1935, about forty-five blacks had taken posts in most of the cabinet departments and New Deal agencies. They included a score of young talented Afro-Americans fresh out of college, such as James C. Evans, Frank S. Horne, Rayford Logan, William J. Trent, Jr., and Ralph Bunche. The Urban League's Eugene K. Jones, William Pickens of the NAACP, and a dozen other seasoned veterans of the civil rights movement augmented their strength. In 1936 they designated themselves the Federal Council on Negro Affairs. The press usually referred to them as the Black Cabinet or Black Brain Trust.[33]

Meeting most Friday evenings at the home of Mary McLeod Bethune, the Black Cabinet forged a critical link between the New Deal and the civil rights movement. During the 1936 campaign Negro rights leaders and the race relations advisers formally came together to share information and coordinate strategy. The habit stuck. During the second Roosevelt Administration, such civil rights spokesmen as Walter White, Channing Tobias, John P. Davis, and A. Philip Randolph conferred often with the Black Cabinet. They corresponded with its members to keep apprised of governmental developments and often jointly arranged protest actions against recalcitrant New Deal officials. Never before had civil rights organizations had so inside a view of a national administration. Never before had black government employees had such outside leverage at their disposal.[34]

The Black Cabinet's very existence focused government attention on civil rights. It made the bureaucracy self-conscious of Negro matters, a necessary first step toward action by federal officials. At the least it acted as a brake, preventing the kinds of overt racial indignities previously accepted as routine. No longer could New Dealers feel free to interlard their speeches with "darky" and "coon" stories, as had Percy Wilson of the FHA before being stopped by the Black Cabinet. In addition, the Federal Council on Negro Affairs stimulated Afro-American interest in political issues. The extensive publicity afforded its activities by the Negro press to its one and one-half million readers increased black awareness of the federal issues affecting Afro-Americans. Most immediately the Black Brain Trust helped to expand the number of government jobs available to blacks by leaking to the Negro press the career positions soon to be open, by schooling blacks in the maze of civil service organizations, and by forcing an end to discriminatory hiring by various agencies.[35]

Mrs. Mary McLeod Bethune's career exemplified the meaning of the New Deal to blacks and their influence in the Roosevelt Administration. The daughter of an illiterate sharecropper, the only one of seventeen children to go to school, Mary Bethune worked her way through the Moody Bible Institute in Chicago, singlehandedly founded a Negro primary school in Florida, and then built it into Bethune-Cookman College. A follower of Booker T. Washington, she avoided racial controversy and became a leading Afro-American clubwoman in the twenties. The winds of change blown by the Great Depression, however, altered her direction. She organized the National Council of Negro Women, considering the Federation of Colored Womens' Clubs too non-political and removed from the needs of the black masses. Mrs. Bethune then began to educate Eleanor Roosevelt on the plight of the Negro. In 1934 upon the advice of the President's wife, Harry Hopkins appointed Bethune to the advisory committee of the NYA. Her forceful representation of black interests impressed Aubrey Williams. Shortly after he asked her to head the NYA's Office of Minority Affairs.[36]

From 1935 onward, Mrs. Bethune's influence in the New Deal expanded steadily. She remained close to the First Lady and a favorite of the President. Party officials sought her out on patronage matters. Federal bureaucrats sometimes heeded her word. Other black leaders deferred to her because of what she symbolized and because of her control over the tens of thousands of NYA dollars going to Afro-American communities. All who knew her remained a bit in awe of her. None doubted the iron fist inside the velvet glove. Members of the Black Cabinet liked to tell the story, apocryphal or not, of Mary Bethune's first trip to the White House to meet with the President. As she crossed the lawn, a white gardener called out to her: "Hey, there, Auntie, where y'all think your goin'?" Mrs. Bethune whirled around sharply, strode over to the gardener, and peered intently at his face. "For a moment I didn't recognize you," Bethune remarked. "Which one of my sister's children are you?" The dumbstruck gardener retreated, never again attempting to stop Bethune. Neither did some powerful New Dealers.[37]

The civil rights movement had good reason to consider Bethune one of its major assets in the thirties. The highest ranking Afro-American in the New Deal, Bethune lent her prestige to most battles for Negro rights. She helped persuade the CIC to organize the Association of Southern Women for the Prevention of Lynching, and she helped establish the Southern Conference on Human Welfare. Hardly a major NAACP conference or protest meeting failed to feature a speech or message from her. As a member of the New Negro Alliance in Washington, she boycotted and picketed stores refusing to hire blacks. Time and again she marched, orated, and signed manifestos for the release of the Scottsboro Boys, the rights of black sharecroppers, and the demand for federal anti-poll tax and anti-lynching legislation. Within the government she fought for the same causes, masking her militancy with homespun homilies and appeals to those in power based on a sense of fair play for all. Simultaneous with these activities, Bethune, the "mother superior" of the Black Cabinet, marshalled its resources to support the civil rights movement. Not surprisingly, Roi Ottley called her the "First Lady of the Struggle" in his "The Big Ten Who Rule Negro America." Not the least of her accomplishments, Bethune skillfully utilized her powers to exploit the government's facilities and auspices for a notable series of conferences on the oppression of Afro-Americans.[38]

These Washington conferences turned the national spotlight on the Negro's problems. They gained a volume of radio and newspaper coverage never bestowed on other meetings of Afro-Americans. In addition, the federal government's imprimatur gave the proceedings a legitimacy no meeting convened by the civil rights movement could equal. Yet these conferences aired and endorsed all the current demands of the Urban League, NAACP, and National Negro Congress. What Bethune began, moreover, other government officials continued. One conference after another was held in Washington in the late 1930s to focus on the needs of Afro-Americans. No administration had ever devoted as much public attention to the Negro. Scores of government-sponsored studies also criticized New Deal shortcomings and recommended increased governmental support for Negro rights. Words were certainly no substitute for action. Yet even the rhetoric represented another indicator of change in the New Deal after 1935.[39]

That a three-day National Conference on Problems of the Negro and Negro Youth would be held in Washington in 1937, sponsored by the government for the purpose of improving federal programs for blacks, and addressed by no less than four Cabinet members, six agency heads, and the President's wife, would have been inconceivable in any prior administration or even a few years earlier. It was so no longer. "This is the first time in the history of our race," Mrs. Bethune indicated in her opening remarks, "that the Negroes of America have felt free to reduce to writing their problems and plans for meeting them with the expectancy of sympathetic understanding and interpretation."[40]

A revolution in expectations had commenced. A revolution in confidence had begun. "It is impossible, really, to overestimate the importance of the New Deal to Negro Americans," wrote black historian Lerone Bennett, Jr. "The New Deal marked a major turning point in Negro fortunes." What had changed was indeed limited, but the presence of change could not be gainsaid. The economic assistance rendered the Negro community by the federal government, according to Myrdal, gave blacks a "broader and more variegated front to defend and from which to push forward." The outspoken advocacy of civil rights by prominent New Dealers helped make that issue a central item in the liberal agenda. And even Ralph Bunche, perhaps Roosevelt's severest black critic in the 1930s, admitted that the New Deal unprecedentedly granted "broad recognition to the existence of the Negro as a national problem and undertook to give specific consideration to this fact in many ways." These changes gave blacks hope. They believed that the government now really intended to

The first came at the start of the thirties when President Hoover nominated John J. Parker to the Supreme Court. When Parker ran for governor of North Carolina in 1920, he described the "participation of the Negro in politics" as "a source of evil and danger to both races," desired by neither blacks nor the GOP. During the campaign, he further proclaimed that "the Negro has not yet reached that stage in his development when he can share the burdens and responsibilities of government." Ten years later the candidacy of a Southern Republican opposed to Negro enfranchisement for the highest court in the land struck NAACP leaders as an insult that could not be ignored. The association's board of directors authorized Walter White to fight the Parker nomination and announced plans for a major campaign to block confirmation. White testified before the Senate Judiciary Committee and telegrams of protest to homestate Senators poured in from every NAACP branch. In May, for the first time since 1894, the Senate rejected a presidential recommendation for the Supreme Court. Negro leaders shouted their joy. The NAACP ballyhooed its role in the North Carolinian's defeat. The *Christian Science Monitor* certified it: "The first national demonstration of the Negro's power since Reconstruction days." Actually, blacks had little to do with the decision. Hoover's nominee had lost because of a combination of Democratic partisanship, the fierce opposition of the labor movement to Judge Parker's pro-"yellow dog" contract decisions on the Fourth Circuit Court, and the fears of Southern Senators that the elevation of a North Carolina Republican to the high court might further widen the split in the formerly solid Democratic South. Robert Wagner of New York, in fact, was the only opponent of Parker to allude to Negro rights during the Senate debate. Nevertheless, the confirmation battle had a marked effect on Afro-American spokesmen. It gave them their first taste of wielding political power at the national level, and it whetted their appetite to punish the party of Lincoln for no longer even giving lip service to the ideals of racial equality. "Negroes have delivered an effective blow against the Republican party's lily white policy," stated Walter White. They "have had a striking object lesson in the use of organized effort to defend their fundamental rights. They will not forget the lesson. . . . This victory is only the beginning."[2]

The next step, Du Bois wrote, must be "the unflinching determination of Negroes to defeat the Senators who defied their vote and supported Parker. Nothing else will convince the United States that our gesture was not mere braggadocio and bluff." The NAACP concentrated its campaign against pro-Parker Senators in 1930 on Republicans Henry J. Allen of Kansas, Jesse H. Metcalf of Rhode Island, Daniel O. Hastings of Delaware, and Roscoe McCulloch of Ohio, described by White "as a symbol of the growing disregard by the Republican Party of the Negro's interest." Allen and McCulloch lost. The depression undoubtedly was the primary reason, but in those two contests, unlike most other elections in 1930, Negro voters deserted the GOP in droves. In fact, Arthur Capper, also running for reelection to the Senate as a Kansas Republican, but with the strong backing of the NAACP, handily defeated his Democratic opponent. Publicly the association was ecstatic. It attributed the Republicans' losses "in large measure" to "the implacable and effective opposition of Negro voters." NAACP leaders now talked of the "political emancipation of colored voters." They announced as their slogan for the coming year: "The NAACP Comes of Age." In part, it did. That year the association fought Senator David Baird, Jr., in his campaign for the governorship of New Jersey, supporting Democratic nominee A. Harry Moore. He won. White claimed that blacks had cast more than 80 percent of their vote against the pro-Parker Republican. Similarly, in 1932 black voters in Pennsylvania helped the Democrats defeat Felix Grundy's bid to return to the Senate.[3]

The NAACP's feelings of political power continued to grow, despite the fact that most black voters in 1932 stayed loyal to Hoover. The association was buoyed by the changes that had occurred and that presaged a fundamental break with the past.

The Republicans had included a Negro rights plank in their platform for the first time since 1908. Its vagueness displeased the
NAACP, yet it signified the GOP's new concern about what it had
previously taken for granted. The combination of the Great Depression and the NAACP campaign against pro-Parker Senators
had forced the Republican party to begin to emphasize civil
rights issues as a means of holding the allegiance of blacks. This
appeared even more clearly on the state level. Various GOP
organizations attempted to counter the economic appeals by
Democratic candidates by drafting state party platforms opposed
to lynching, in favor of civil rights statutes, and vindicating the
right of Afro-Americans to a full and equal share of all state
benefits.[4]

In addition, many of the most prominent Negro newspapers
and spokesmen in 1932, as never before, insisted that the black
voter act independently and forsake traditional party loyalty. No
longer, they reiterated in press and pulpit, should Afro-Americans
blindly cast their ballots for Abraham Lincoln and against Jefferson Davis. "My friends, go turn Lincoln's picture to the wall,"
exhorted Robert L. Vann, publisher of the *Courier,* the nation's
largest-selling Negro newspaper. "That debt has been paid in
full." Bishop Reverdy C. Ransom of the African Methodist Episcopal Church asserted the need for blacks to unshackle themselves from the GOP, to cease being slaves to the past. "An upris-
ing of Negro voters against M. Hoover and his party," he
counseled, "would free our spirits equally as much as Mr. Lincoln's
Proclamation freed our bodies." Lester Walton, a popular black
columnist, also sounded the theme of Afro-Americans no longer
having to express their historical gratitude at the polls. The time
had come, he insisted, for blacks to support candidates and parties
only on the basis of present needs. That imperative, in fact, became the major motif of the NAACP and the Urban League during the campaign. It impressed the New York *Times* political reporter Arthur Krock as a striking turn in black political thought.
Most blacks, however, did not vote with their leaders. Only in

Detroit and Manhattan did blacks defect from the Republican party in significant numbers in 1932.[5]

Most Negro voters first deserted the GOP in 1934. That year congressional Democrats made their first concentrated attempt to woo Afro-Americans. Democratic incumbents from the North filled the *Congressional Record* with tributes to the New Deal for benefitting blacks, and they made sure their local Negro newspapers received reprints. For the first time, some Democrats campaigned in black neighborhoods. Their efforts were aided by the increasing numbers of blacks on New Deal relief projects and by the cultivation of Negro leaders by Democratic urban machines. Following the Democratic victory in the St. Louis mayoralty contest in 1933, the Dickmann organization proceeded to appoint three times as many Afro-Americans to political office than had the Republicans. On the other side of the state, the Pendergast machine did the same for Kansas City blacks. In New York City, meanwhile, Tammany Hall followed up its selection of the first two Negro judges for Harlem in 1930 with the choice in 1934 of Herbert Bruce as the first Negro district leader. By 1936 Tammany had also installed blacks as two state legislators, two aldermen, two assistant district attorneys, and a civil service commissioner. The Kelly-Nash machine in Chicago, which came to power in 1933, followed suit by finding seven prestigious state jobs and scores of clerkships for deserving Negro Democrats. The Democratic sachems in Chicago also made William Dawson their committeeman of the Second Ward and broke precedent by running a Negro to oppose the black Republican congressman, Oscar De Priest. Campaigning on a "Forward with Roosevelt" slogan, Arthur Mitchell won. The first Negro Democrat in Congress, Mitchell, like Dawson, had been a Republican stalwart as late as 1932.[6]

The Democrats also gained from Republican errors. Taking the vote of Philadelphia black for granted, the Pennsylvania GOP denied Negro Republican committeemen a fair share of political jobs. In 1932 Marshall Shepard, a Negro clergyman, and other black Republicans met with GOP boss William Vare to request

Negro representation on the Republican ticket that year. "Never! Never!" Vare thundered. "The people of Philadelphia would never stand it." So Shepard enlisted in the Democratic party and made his church the site of the first meeting in Philadelphia to support Franklin Roosevelt's candidacy. The following year Philadelphia Democrats joined with Shepard to register black voters in earnest. Throughout the North, in fact, the Negro's abandonment of the Grand Old Party quickened. In 1934, for the first time in history, a majority of Afro-American voters went Democratic. Once a Republican loyalist, but now an exponent of independent black voting, Kelly Miller exulted, "The Negro is no longer a wheelhorse of the Republican Party."[7]

The growing numbers of blacks voting in the thirties, as well as their break from the GOP, lent credence to the balance of power argument. The New Deal itself spurred Negro politicization. Many blacks who were voting for the first time in their lives in AAA and NLRB elections kept the habit. The concern demonstrated by Mrs. Eleanor Roosevelt and the Black Cabinet attracted others to the polls. The score of New Deal programs that reduced Negro illiteracy from 16.4 percent in 1930 to 11.5 percent a decade later swelled the potential size of the Negro vote, as did the many measures increasing the income, educational level, and self-image of blacks. The New Deal's very expansion into areas never before broached by the federal government made the whole concept of political participation less abstract. For millions of Americans previously apathetic about what happened in Washington, the 1930s became a decade of political involvement. Negro voting and public discussion of political affairs soared. Afro-American voter registration drives, once a rarity, now seemed commonplace in the North. They also occurred in the urban South. Students of Negro voting behavior in the thirties, moreover, noted a marked upsurge in the number of Afro-Americans who actually registered and cast ballots. In Philadelphia, for example, black registration rose from 69,214 in 1932 to 134,677 in 1940, although the Negro population in the city increased by less than 15 percent during the thirties. In Detroit the proportion of registered blacks

who voted leaped from less than thirty percent in 1930 to sixty-six
percent in 1938. Chicago recorded an even higher rate of black
voter participation than white during the depression decade.[8]

Most important, the black population in the states rich with
electoral votes continued to grow in the 1930s. Over 400,000
blacks migrated from the South during the depression, boosting
the Negro population of Illinois, Michigan, Missouri, New York,
Ohio, and Pennsylvania by one-third. These migrants joined the
2,000,000 blacks who had previously abandoned the plantations
of the South, and like them they began to develop urban attitudes,
traits, and values. Blacks in the city became less patient and more
political, less docile and more demanding, less religious and more
rebellious. And the more blacks there were in the city, the
more true this became. By 1940 the census classified 6,200,000
blacks—48 percent of the total Negro population—as urban. In Philadelphia the black population increased from 84,459 in 1910—5.5
percent of the city total—to 134,229 in 1920. By 1930 the black
population totalled 219,599—some 11 percent of Philadelphia's
population, and by 1940 it had reached 252,757—over 13 percent
of the city's total population. The number and percentage of
blacks in St. Louis climbed from 43,960 and 6.4 percent in 1910
to 109,254 and 13.5 percent in 1940. Detroit, which had only some
5000 blacks in 1910, had 40,000 in 1920, 120,000 in 1930, and
over 150,000 in 1940—nearly 10 percent of the city total. Similarly,
the number of blacks and their percentage of the total population
for seven major U.S. cities in 1940 are given below.

City	Number of blacks	Percentage of total
Kansas City	41,832	10.5
Newark	46,226	10.8
Indianapolis	51,217	13.2
Cincinnati	55,757	12.2
Pittsburgh	62,423	9.3
Cleveland	84,919	9.7
Los Angeles	97,847	5.5

Between 1910 and 1940, moreover, the black populations of Baltimore and Washington, D.C., doubled, to 165,843 and 187,266
respectively. Finally, the two cities with the largest number of
blacks, Chicago and New York City, had increases of 15 and 30
percent during the thirties in their Negro population. Chicago,
2 percent black in 1910, had a total of 282,244 Negroes in 1940,
8.3 percent of the city's population. And in New York City, the
black population rose from 91,709 in 1910—1.9 percent of the
total—to 152,467 in 1920; 327,706 in 1930; and 477,494—6.4 percent of the total—in 1940. Because of such numbers, and because
those blacks who had migrated in earlier decades gradually
emancipated themselves from their former Southern patterns of
behavior and thought, the Negro now had political power in the
North. "In no national election since 1860," *Time* observed, "have
politicians been so Negro-minded as in 1936."[9]

"In Missouri, Illinois, Indiana, Ohio, Michigan, West Virginia,
Pennsylvania, New Jersey, and New York," *Time* continued, "live
some 2,500,000 Negroes, of whom over 1,000,000 are prospective
voters this year. Moreover, in these same nine states the Roose-
velt-Landon battle will be waged especially hard, with the result
in each perhaps turning in favor of the party which can bag the
largest Black vote." Civil rights publicists went even further.
They claimed the Negro vote to be the definitive balance of
power in a close election in seventeen states with a total of nearly
three hundred electoral votes, more than twice that of the Solid
South. Throughout 1936 they emphasized the size, independence,
and strategic importance of the Afro-American vote. In articles,
conferences, editorials, speeches, and correspondence with major
politicians, civil rights spokesmen repeated over and again the
necessity of garnering black ballots in order to win. The NAACP
underscored the importance of a candidate's position on Negro
rights in winning these votes by aiding in the defeat of William
Borah in several Republican primaries that spring. The senator
from Idaho aroused the wrath of the NAACP by endorsing a
Southern filibuster against anti-lynching legislation the year be-

fore. Walter White retaliated by making the blocking of Borah's quest for the Republican nomination in 1936 a top priority. He succeeded. "Lincoln, flag-waving and mammy stories have lost their power to charm voters into the ballot boxes," *The Crisis* pointedly reminded both Democrats and Republicans, adding a postscript that blacks would cast their ballots on the basis of a candidate's present civil rights record. The Baltimore *Afro-American* compressed the warning: "Abraham Lincoln Is Not A Candidate In The Present Campaign."[10]

The GOP, eager to regain the black votes it had lost in 1934, tried to trumpet its commitment to civil rights. The party took pains to write a progressive civil rights plank into its platform, and at every opportunity denounced Roosevelt's raw deal for Afro-Americans. Unwilling to out-promise the Democrats on bread-and-butter issues, the party of Emancipation instead raised the banners of Abraham Lincoln and Frederick Douglass. Republican orators pointed to the President's dependence on race-baiting demagogues from the South and to the fact that the Democratic party label in Alabama bore the imprint "white supremacy" on its masthead. Believing they needed the Northern Negro vote to win, the GOP widely publicized its stands against lynching and discrimination and the Democrats' refusal to adopt a civil rights plank.[11]

Republican publicists pictured nominee Alfred M. Landon as a spiritual descendant of John Brown. One GOP pamphlet claimed credit for the Grand Old Party for saving the Scottsboro Boys; another, coupling pictures of Landon and Lincoln on the cover, repeated every known statement of Frederick Douglass and other black heroes on why Afro-Americans must shun the perfidious Democrats. Landon came out strongly for a federal anti-lynching law and arrogated to himself responsibility for Kansas's abolition of the poll tax. "I am unalterably opposed to lawlessness in all forms," he declared, "and, of course, this includes lynching which is a blot on our American civilization." In several speeches the GOP nominee highlighted the differences between his civil rights record and that of the Southern-dominated Democratic party. Landon also assured blacks that he would strive to see them "re-employed and integrated into the great productive life of our country." Shortly before the election he pledged in a radio address that "if ever in this country there is an attempt to persecute any minority on grounds of race, religion, or class, I will take my stand by the side of the minority."[12]

To impress the Afro-American voter further, Republican National Chairman John Hamilton beefed up the party's Negro division. He downgraded veterans from the South mainly concerned with their own sinecures, who had become symbols of political obeisance to many blacks, and elevated to power such young civil rights activists as New York Assemblyman Francis E. Rivers and the Reverend Lacey Kirk Williams of Chicago's Mt. Olive Baptist Church. The division extensively publicized the GOP's pronouncements on Negro rights. It also distributed short pro-Landon films to Negro theatres across the country and financed a tour by Jesse Owens, the recently returned hero of the Berlin Olympics, to urge Afro-Americans to stay loyal to the party of Lincoln.[13]

To match this impressive effort, the Democrats responded with a series of precedent-shattering "firsts." Some thirty black delegates from twelve states attended the 1936 Democratic national convention. Never before had the Democrats selected a single Afro-American as a delegate. Not until 1924, in fact, had they allowed a black alternate. Four years later, in 1928, at the convention in Houston, the few Negro alternates had been segregated from whites by a chicken wire screen. That was the past. The Democrats now wanted the growing Northern Negro vote. To demonstrate that change, Roosevelt in 1936 chose a Negro minister to offer the convention invocation and picked black Congressman Arthur Mitchell to deliver the welcoming address. When the Afro-American preacher began his prayer, Senator Ellison "Cotton Ed" Smith of South Carolina walked out of the session: "By God, he's as black as melted midnight! Get outa my way. This mongrel meeting ain't no place for a white man!" Smith bolted again when Mitchell started to speak, informing reporters that he absolutely refused to support "any political organization that looks upon the Negro and caters to him as a political and social equal." The Democratic National Committee supplied Negro newspapers with the details of these episodes and also played up the fact that Afro-American reporters had been seated in the convention press box for the first time.[14]

"For the first time in history," *Time* reported during the campaign, "Democrats are making a serious bid for the Negro vote." New Dealers particularly emphasized the economic assistance given blacks by the Roosevelt Administration. Democratic spokesmen never tired of pointing to the tens of thousands of black youths given work by the CCC and NYA, the many new Negro appointees and federal employees, the scores of government-sponsored educational programs for Afro-Americans, and the millions of dollars spent to construct housing, hospitals, and schools for Negroes. Most of all, they stressed that relief and work relief had literally saved Afro-Americans from hunger. "Let Jesus lead you and Roosevelt feed you" was the way one Negro preacher put it to his flock. Many black communities featured Democratic billboards proclaiming: "Do not bite the hand that feeds you." Few Afro-Americans probably needed such reminders. "Every Negro I have registered so far has said he would vote for President Roosevelt," a registrar in South Carolina reported. "They say Roosevelt saved them from starvation, gave them aid when they were all in distress."[15]

Roosevelt, however, appealed to blacks on more than just the basis of the beneficence of the New Deal. Democratic National Chairman James Farley picked as his Negro campaign managers Chicago's popular Congressman Arthur Mitchell and the Boston lawyer, Julian D. Rainey, son of the last Reconstruction congressman from South Carolina. Both pictured the President as a supporter of Negro rights and spent much time differentiating his views from those of Southern Democrats. The Negro Division dis-

tributed a million photographs of Mrs. Eleanor Roosevelt talking
with a group of black professors at Howard University. The First
Lady, moreover, played a major role in the campaign, recruiting
civil rights leaders to speak for the President, arranging for New
Dealers to address Negro gatherings, welcoming Afro-American
delegations to the White House, and attending Negro right conventions. With Stanley High, a former editor of the *Christian
Herald,* she organized a Good Neighbor League to attract Republicans to the New Deal standard. The President insisted that it
concentrate on blacks. Headed by Adam Clayton Powell, Sr.,
pastor of Harlem's Abyssinian Baptist Church and Bishop R. R.
Wright, Jr., of Philadelphia, the league's literature appealed to
blacks "to stop voting for Lincoln and vote for Roosevelt instead."
On the anniversary of the Emancipation Proclamation the league
sponsored a mass rally for the President in New York's Madison
Square Garden. Negro leaders and prominent New Dealers joined
to hail Roosevelt's policies for blacks, and Senator Wagner
termed the President a second "Emancipator" for Afro-Americans
during the proceedings, which were broadcast to more than sixty
cities. It was quite a new approach for Roosevelt and the Democrats.[16]

It paid off handsomely. According to George Gallup, an as-
tounding 76 percent of the Northern Negroes voted for Roosevelt,
a figure exceeding the proportion of Afro-American ballots cast
for Democratic local and congressional candidates. In every
Northern city but Chicago blacks voted at least 60 percent for
Roosevelt, and even in the Windy City the President more than
doubled his support from Negroes, moving from 23 to 49 percent
between 1932 and 1936. No other voting bloc shifted so perceptibly. Harlem went four to one for FDR, a 20 percent increase
over 1932. The President carried Indianapolis's black wards by
75 percent and Pittsburgh's Negro Third Ward by almost ten to
one. In Ohio's black wards in Cincinnati, Cleveland, and Columbus, where the Democrats won less than one-third of the Negro
vote in 1932, Roosevelt outdistanced all other statewide candi-

dates in garnering over two-thirds of the black vote in 1936. The same situation occurred in St. Louis and Kansas City, where FDR carried all but one of the forty Negro precincts. Similarly, in Philadelphia, where the Negro wards had voted 30 percent Democrat in 1932 (compared to the city's average of 43 percent), Roosevelt took 64 percent of the black vote in 1936, 4 percent more than the city average. Afro-Americans had indeed proved themselves an effective voting bloc. They had demonstrated their readiness to switch parties, as well as their ability to register and turn out at the polls in significant numbers. And they had done so in the states with the largest total of electoral votes.[17]

Why did the Negro vote switch so decisively? No one knows for sure. Given the absence of in-depth interviewing at the time and the scarcity of evidence indicating differences in the preferences of lower-, middle-, or upper-class Afro-Americans, all conclusions remain speculative. Extant studies of Chicago, Detroit, Philadelphia, and New York show no significant correlation between black support for Roosevelt and blacks on relief. Yet it would be foolhardy to deny that Negroes voted to continue the economic assistance they associated with Roosevelt. Likewise, changes in the attitudes of local Democratic machines toward Afro-Americans cannot be discounted. Nor can the identification of key New Dealers with the cause of civil rights.[18]

Throughout the campaign, black leaders and the Negro press mainly emphasized civil rights issues. Economic matters were secondary in their endorsements of Roosevelt. Afro-American spokesmen in 1936 talked mostly of FDR's promise at Howard University that there would be "no forgotten men and no forgotten races" in his administration, of his wife's advocacy of Negro rights, of the portent of the Black Cabinet, and of the concern for racial equality exhibited by such New Dealers as Harry Hopkins, Harold Ickes, and Will Alexander. Joel E. Spingarn, the president of the NAACP, pointed to these developments as the reason for his breaking a twenty year silence on political candidates to back Roosevelt publicly. The President had no race prejudice of any kind, Spingarn declared, and he could be trusted to do whatever he could for Afro-Americans. Spingarn also hinted at great advances for Negro rights if Roosevelt won a second term. The NAACP president campaigned for Roosevelt's reelection in a tour of eight major Northern cities. Following the election, *The Crisis* noted that Negroes voted "for Roosevelt *in spite of* the Democratic Party" and because of more than "their concern for immediate relief, either in jobs or direct assistance." They went Democratic, observed *The Crisis*, because of "a feeling that Mr. Roosevelt represented a kind of philosophy of government which will mean much to their race."[19]

Whatever the reasons for the switch, the election persuaded many a civil rights leader and white politician that the Negro vote had become a balance of power in national elections. "As long as the so-called Negro vote was part and parcel of one party, the race was politically frozen," wrote Earl Brown, the chief Negro political analyst. "It was impossible for it to be accepted on an equal basis with the rest of the electorate." That ended in 1936. "The race has finally become an integral part of both major parties, and thereby it has gained in political stature and importance." The Republicans will have to offer more to regain the black vote, and the Democrats will have to keep pace to retain the allegiance of Afro-Americans, or risk defeat in the key industrial states, Brown concluded. So did Robert L. Vann. Proposing what he called "loose leaf politics," the publisher of the *Courier* called upon blacks to bargain their vitally needed votes for advances in civil rights from both major parties. After two-thirds of a century, Stanley High observed, the Afro-American voter had become a "free lance" and would now have to be competed for by Republicans and Democrats. The Negro vote, he summed up, could control elections in Northern states totaling 157 electoral votes, 31 more than the electoral total of all the Southern states. Such observations, understandably, caused apprehension among Southern leaders. Arguing that the South must vote independently in the electoral college to protect white supremacy, the Charlestown *News and Courier* pointed with alarm to the Northern "'pivotal states' in which the negroes in the cities have the balance of power in elections."[20]

Moreover, the New Deal even stirred blacks in the South to political activity. "This AAA voting is giving them ideas that they can become regular voters," fumed the sheriff of Dallas County, Alabama. "I think it's dangerous." In Georgia the registrar of Macon County saw an increase in black voting "since Roosevelt became Santa Claus." "You ask any nigger on the street who's the greatest man in the world," exclaimed the head of the Greene County, Georgia, Democratic committee. "Nine out of ten will tell you Franklin D. Roosevelt. . . . That's why I think he is so dangerous." Few blacks actually voted in the South. The poll tax, the maze of registration requirements, the all-white primary and oppressive fear kept all but the most determined Southern blacks away from the voting booth. When Ralph Bunche and his assistants interviewed Southern officials on the political status of blacks late in 1939 for Gunnar Myrdal's comprehensive study of the Negro in the United States, they received such replies as: "No sir! No niggers vote in any primaries in *this* county," said an official of the Pickens County, South Carolina, Democratic committee; "Niggers have been ruled out. It's our private affair, and we don't invite them in, and that's that," answered the head of the Hall County, Georgia, Democratic committee; and the registrar of Marengo County, Alabama, stated bluntly, "There ain't a fuckin' nigger in this end of the country who'd so much as go near a ballot box." Statistics bore him out. In 1940 only about two hundred and fifty thousand blacks, five percent of the voting-age Negroes, cast ballots in the eleven states of the ex-Confederacy. Almost all of these votes came from the cities in Tennessee, Texas, and North Carolina. Less than one-half of one percent of the blacks aged twenty-one and over voted in Alabama, Louisiana, Mississippi, and South Carolina.[21]

Yet, as never before since Reconstruction, blacks in the South organized, attended mass meetings, sang freedom songs, and formed study groups in their campaigns for voter registration. Raleigh blacks formed a Negro Voters' League in 1931 to fight for the franchise. By 1935 the *News and Observer* placed the Negro vote at about 20 percent of the city total and considered it a balance of power in local elections. Early in 1936 Durham blacks followed suit, organizing their own Committee on Negro Affairs and setting up branches in Charlotte, Greensboro, and Winston-Salem. Together they held a pro-Roosevelt voting rally before the 1936 election.[22]

Established at a mass meeting on Lincoln's Birthday that year, the Atlanta Civic and Political League doubled the number of registered blacks from 1936 to 1939. In Savannah the Young Men's Civic Club organized in 1938 for the same purpose. Florida blacks, following the repeal of the poll tax in 1938, also showed a surge of political activity. In Tampa, where fewer than 100 blacks voted throughout most of the 1930s, a campaign led by the NAACP registered 1330 Negroes in 1939 and some 2500 blacks in 1940. The number of black Miami registrants leaped from about 50 throughout the twenty years prior to 1940 to nearly 2000 that year. Virginia blacks in the 1930s set up a Portsmouth Civic and Welfare Club, a Petersburg League of Negro Voters, a Hampton County Civic League, and a Newport News Young Men's Democratic Club, among others, to urge payment of poll taxes and to stimulate interest in voting. In Portsmouth two blacks even ran for the city council in 1936. No black had done so since 1891.[23]

"We've had a lot of trouble about niggers registering," complained the chairman of the Greenville County, South Carolina, board of registrars as civil rights organizations sparked registration campaigns in the deepest South in the late thirties. His counterpart in Charlestown explained that more blacks were seeking to vote because "the churches and preachers and the schools and all kinds of organizations are after them about their rights." In Greenville the NAACP, the Workers' Alliance, and the Textile

Workers Union of America cooperated in getting blacks registered and out on election day. Arthur Raper of the Interracial
Commission came to town to decry the white primary and the
poll tax. Mary Bethune urged a mass rally to "get representation."
Aided by the United Mine Workers, the NAACP also led the fight
to register Negro voters in Birmingham in 1938 and 1939. "The
significance of this movement, and of such events as a turnout of
5,000 Negroes to hear Negro Congressman Mitchell of Illinois,"
commented a writer for the *New Republic* on the black voter
drive in Birmingham, "is that it indicates a revival of a desire for
political rights by Negro people themselves which they have not
shown in such emphatic form since political power was restored
to the plantation owners in the 1870's."[24]

Such developments barely caused a basic change in the Afro-
American's day-to-day struggle for existence in the North or
South. The growth of Negro political power in the 1930s brought
mainly meager rewards at the local and state levels—usually
token appointments, gradual increases in the number of blacks
holding political jobs, and slight improvements in municipal
services. A number of states, including Pennsylvania and Ohio,
passed bills prohibiting racial discrimination in public accommodations and on public works but did little to enforce them.
Much the same occurred at the national level. Most of the barriers to Negro progress remained intact. Roosevelt still considered
battling the depression his overwhelming priority and that fact
continued to necessitate his accommodating the white Southerners who dominated Congress and controlled the operation of
the New Deal at the state and local levels.[25]

But the days of solicitude for the white South by Northern politicians grew short. Numerous entries in Ickes's diary recorded the
increasing concern of Democrats wanting to hold the Negro vote.
Correspondence to and from the Republican National Committee
reflected its desire to regain that vote. Senators from both parties
now vied for endorsements by the NAACP and the National
Negro Congress. Members on each side of the House aisle re-

quested Afro-American spokesmen to praise their civil rights record at election time. The Negro vote could no longer be ignored. It would, the editors of *The Nation* proclaimed, "have to be reckoned with increasingly in American life."[26]

5

A Rift in the Coalition

An interrelated series of developments in Southern politics, provoked by the New Deal, further strengthened the civil rights cause. The black struggle for equality gained new allies and prominence from the rift in the Democratic party during Roosevelt's second term, just as the defenders of white supremacy lost ground because of their internecine opposition to the New Deal. The conflict between liberals and Southern conservatives initially had little to do with race. It evolved from the apprehension of certain Southern leaders that the New Deal might jeopardize their hegemony over economic and political affairs. The leadership elites in Dixie looked askance at new federal programs that reduced dependency and paternalism in their domains, raised wages, aided the labor movement, skirted local government, and extended the New Deal to those indigents previously unassisted. Southern conservatives especially feared the threat to their dominance posed by the erosion of states' rights, the growth of executive power, and their own relative decline in importance within the Democratic party. To fight back, they cried "Nigger," exploiting the racial issue in the South to justify their opposition to New Deal measures and to counter the challenge of Southern liberals.

In the process, however, they also tinged the banner of white supremacy with the colors of extreme economic conservatism and even fascism, broke apart the white South's solidity on racial matters, and transformed measures dear to New Dealers into issues of Negro rights.

As early as 1932, Senator Carter Glass of Virginia had commented after the election: "The victory Tuesday was almost too overwhelming to be safe." Few Southern Democrats then shared his apprehension. Most relished the power and patronage that would once again be theirs after twenty years of Republican rule. They delighted also in the attention Roosevelt lavished on them. In his inimitable manner, FDR ingratiated himself with Southern leaders by flattery, royal dinners at the White House, special honors, and delightful, intimate conversations. No discordant notes were sounded at first. As the votes and speeches of Southern politicians made clear, their region desperately needed and wanted the cornucopia of assistance provided by the AAA, the CCC, the NRA, and the TVA. The South, in fact, shared more bountifully in New Deal largesse than any other section and paid the least per capita in taxes. Running for reelection in 1936, Pat Harrison frequently boasted that Mississippi received more per capita federal funds than any other state. Accordingly, Southern congressmen overwhelmingly supported the President in 1933 and 1934. Only Harry Byrd of Virginia and Josiah Bailey of North Carolina joined Glass in the Senate in expressing vehement Southern opposition to the New Deal. For his part, Roosevelt did nothing to upset local elites or encourage the proponents of Negro rights. Neither executive nor congressional spokesmen had much to say about race. The "gentleman's agreement" that held the party together—the understanding that support for the administration would be rewarded with a willingness to let the South handle its own racial relations—appeared unshakable. The White House and the Dixie courthouse seemed solidly allied.[1]

A small minority of Southerners dissented, foreshadowing the opposition to come. William Ball of the Charleston *Mercury* broke with the New Deal because he feared any emphasis upon change would inevitably destroy the racial status quo. Others chided the NRA for being a "Negro Relief Association." How, they demanded of Roosevelt, were they going to get blacks to pick and chop cotton when Negroes were receiving $12 a week from federal work programs, more than twice as much as they had ever been paid. "The blue eagle was fast becoming a bird of prey," claimed Glass. Southerners, he wrote, were "privately cursing the symbol as a black buzzard." Still others complained of the New Deal's radicalism. Senator Richard Russell of Georgia explained his vote against the confirmation of Rexford Guy Tugwell as under secretary of agriculture in 1934 because "we have all but been completely Russianized." Governor Eugene Talmadge of Georgia denounced the President's program as being run by socialists and communists. He taunted Northerners for not solving their own unemployment problems: "What you need in New York is not La Guardia but Mussolini." Most commonly, however, opposition to the New Deal started to come from the banker-merchant-planter-industrialist governing class. Such organizations as the Southern States Industrial Council and the Southern Tariff Association began to lash out at the New Deal for its excessive spending and alleged pro-labor orientation.[2]

The sudden swelling of the Democratic ranks with Northern liberals after the elections of 1934 and Roosevelt's reform proposals in 1935 lengthened the list of Southern conservatives in opposition to the New Deal. The President received congressional approval for the social security, labor relations, relief, tax, and public utilities holding-company bills. But he paid a price. "Cotton Ed" Smith and Walter F. George of Georgia joined the ranks of the "irreconcilables." And on the "death sentence" provision of the utility bill, which Roosevelt considered a "must," eight of the twenty-two Southern senators and fifty-five of the ninety-nine Dixie representatives deserted the administration—a far greater display of opposition than that from Democrats of any other section.[3]

Most important, a growing number of Southern politicians in 1935 (although still decidedly a minority of those in power below the Mason-Dixon line) openly voiced their discontent with the new directions of Roosevelt's policies. It gradually dawned on an increasing number of them that they had remained ideologically much the same since the Wilson days while their Northern counterparts had changed markedly. They still wanted a carefully circumscribed national government, one strong enough to umpire the economy and respond temporarily to calamities like the depression, but one too weak to interfere with the local oligarchies that controlled the business of the South. Yet they saw their more socially democratic brethren from the urban North advocating sweeping powers for the federal government and pushing relief and reform schemes that would reduce the competitive advantages of the South's major economic interests while stimulating the have-nots in labor and agriculture to demand their due. Their fears were heightened by the formation of farm labor unions and the threats by labor organizers to unionize Southern factory workers. Slowly the race issue came out of the bag. The growth of federal power was pictured as a dagger pointed at the heart of the state's right to regulate its own racial affairs. To counter the appeal of New Deal proposals that would increase the pay of those on work relief, build housing for the poor, and assist tenants and croppers, Southern conservatives raised the spectre of equal wages for blacks, of integrated housing, of social equality, and of intermarriage between the races. They also combined sectional and racial rhetoric in denouncing the organizing efforts of the Southern Tenant Farmers' Union and United Mine Workers.[4]

Amidst a resurgence of Southern sectionalism, highlighted by renewed interest in the Confederate cap and flag, some conservatives sought to organize opposition to Roosevelt. They pointedly referred to themselves as "Jeffersonian Democrats" or "Wilsonians." Those hostile to the New Deal in the Lone Star State coalesced in the "Constitutional Democrats of Texas." Border

state anti-New Dealers organized the "National Jeffersonian
Democrats." Governor Talmadge formed a "Grass Roots" anti-
Roosevelt movement and hosted a convention in Macon, Georgia,
early in 1936 to fuse together the disparate elements opposed to
an extension of the New Deal. Financed by the American Liberty
League and the Southern Committee to Uphold the Constitution,
and particularly by Will Clayton's Texas cotton brokerage firm,
Joe Pew of the Sun Oil Company, Millionaire Texas lumberman
John K. Kirby, and the Du Ponts, Talmadge's followers mixed
Negrophobia and anti-Semitism in concocting the charge that
alien radicals had taken over the New Deal to undermine the
states' right to handle the race problem as they saw fit. The convention delegates resolved to be "united to oppose Negroes, the
New Deal and . . . Karl Marx."[5]

Rather than arguing substantively against the New Deal's social and economic reforms, the conservatives appealed to the
white South's racial pride and fear. Eleanor Roosevelt was made
the symbol of everything wrong with the "damnyankee," race-
meddling New Deal. The followers of Talmadge attacked her
for hosting a garden party for inmates of the National Industrial
Training School for Girls, labeling it just entertainment for "a
bunch of 'nigger whores.'" They distributed thousands of pictures throughout the South of "Nigger Lover Eleanor" dancing
with a black youth. Another widely-reproduced picture showed
Mrs. Roosevelt with some ROTC cadets at Howard University.
Its caption read: "A picture of Mrs. Roosevelt going to some nigger meeting, with two escorts, niggers, on each arm." They also
circulated rumors that blacks "come to the White House banquets
and sleep in the White House beds," and popularized the ditty:

> You kiss the negroes,
> I'll kiss the Jews,
> We'll stay in the White House
> As long as we choose.

Virtually all their speeches against the New Deal included at
least one accusation against Eleanor Roosevelt of having Negro

blood or a black lover. Other targets of their wrath included the Black Cabinet, Ickes, Foreman, and other "nigger loving" New Dealers, especially the Jewish ones. Touring the South with Gerald L. K. Smith, Thomas Dixon, and the leaders of the Sentinels of the Republic, Talmadge made much of those misleading the President as "Mordecai Ezekiel, Morgenthau, and other names I cannot spell and cannot pronounce."[6]

Few Southern conservatives in either Congress or the Democratic hierarchy joined Talmadge in openly attacking President Roosevelt in 1936. Party loyalty ran deep, especially in an election year. Southern voters, far more than their elected representatives, looked forward to additional succor from the New Deal trough. Many Southern politicians believed they still had more to gain than to lose from a second term for FDR. The President, after all, had done little overtly to threaten the white power structure in Dixie. Accordingly, most Southern leaders who shared the apprehension of Senator Carter Glass for the passing of the Old South and the future of states' rights seethed privately but remained officially silent. Political opportunism dictated that they sublimate their fears and doubts. Damning Roosevelt for helping blacks more than any president since Lincoln, Glass wrote to a friend during the campaign: "This has incensed me beyond expression and but for the very peculiar political situation at this time I would bitterly denounce it in a public statement."[7]

That silence ended after 1936. Almost without exception conservative Southern politicians considered the abrogation of the 104-year-old rule requiring a two-thirds vote to nominate a candidate at the Democratic convention as a mortal blow to their power within the party. This trump card had always given the South veto power over the Democrats national candidates and platforms. Now they would have to play without it, becoming just one of a growing number of interest groups at the political table. Senator James F. Byrnes of South Carolina, writing about the convention's action, recalled bitterly that "the chairman put the question and so quickly announced adoption that delegates had no opportunity to voice opposition."[8]

Many Southern conservatives also abhorred the new players at the Democratic table. Blacks, Jews, liberal intellectuals, representatives of the new industrial-urban disadvantaged poor, and, above all, labor unionists began to jostle Southerners for their share of Washington's seats of influence. The United Mine Workers emerged as the party's single largest contributor; the Committee for Industrial Organization, Labor's Non-Partisan League, and the American Labor Party in New York (often elbowing the regular Democratic organization aside) entered the fray on behalf of Roosevelt and pronounced liberal candidates; and labor leaders conspicuously undeferential to the South, especially John L. Lewis and Sidney Hillman, sought to influence Democratic policy and strategy. This rise of a politically aggressive labor movement intensified the gloom of Southern conservatives determined to block the unionization of labor below the Mason-Dixon line. So did Roosevelt's break with party regularity. The President had snubbed some of his own party's nominees to assist a Republican, George Norris of Nebraska, the Farmer-Laborites in Minnesota, and the La Follette Progressives in Wisconsin. Many in the South wanted a regular Democratic loyalist, not a social democratic liberal, in the White House. They feared they had helped elect the opposite.[9]

Contemporaries regarded the Grand Coalition forged by FDR in 1936 as a definite break with the traditional Democratic party. Many articles written in the late 1930s pictured the radical representatives of Negroes, small farmers, relief recipients, intellectuals, and labor unions usurping the power of the old professional party wheelhorses. Others described the Jeffersonian–states' rights–limited government–white supremacist Democratic credo as being superseded by a political philosophy that esteemed human rights above property rights, that favored an extension of federal power at the expense of the states, that prized executive supremacy over the other branches of government, and that codified the sympathies of Robert Wagner of New York rather than Carter Glass of Virginia. Still others viewed the changes as a prelude to political realignment. Conservatives, they hoped, would leave the party, and the Democrats would then forcefully champion all manners of reform. In the South, however, few conservatives desired to quit the Democratic party; they wished to reclaim it, cleanse it of its new elements, and make it again the pristine embodiment of race, God, and Southern womanhood. A disgruntled High Johnson, in close concert with Bernard Baruch and the congressional conservative leadership, appealed for Democrats to support the party of "the Pat Harrisons, the Joe Robinsons, the Jimmy Byrnes, the Georges of Georgia, the Cordell Hulls," and not that of "the Hopkinses, the Ickes, Corcorans, or Wallaces." He accused the President of disloyalty to the South and denounced his 1936 coalition as "a new party, not a recognizable Democratic Party, but a one-man Roosevelt Party, conceived with superficial cleverness, but stuck together with spit and tied into a unit with haywire—a composite of inconsistencies. You get," Johnson continued, "at the very heart and center, the Solid South, tied in with Northern Pro-Negro policy."[10]

Indeed, the zeal of the administration for Negro votes in 1936 provided the most emotional pretext for an open assault on the New Deal by Southern conservatives. "I am not opposed to any Negro praying for me," Senator Smith of South Carolina explained after his walk-out at the 1936 convention, "but I don't want any blue-gummed, slew-footed Senegambian praying for me politically." Addressing himself to the dangers to the white South of the Democratic appeal to the black electorate, Smith added: "The doors of the white man's party have been thrown open to snare the Negro vote in the North. Political equality means social equality, and social equality means intermarriage, and that means mongrelizing of the American race." Glass complained: "To any discerning person it is perfectly obvious that the so-called Democratic party of the North is now the negro party, advocating actual social equality for the races." On another occasion he wondered if the white South "will have spirit and courage enough to face the new Reconstruction era that northern so-called Demo-

crats are menacing us with." Glass further feared "the Southern
people may wake up too late to find that the negrophiles who are
running the Democratic Party now will soon precipitate another
Reconstruction period for us." Bailey seconded this concern:
[The President] "is determined to get the Negro vote and I do
not have to tell you what *this* means." Catering to the black electorate in the North, Bailey fumed, has brought the Democrats to
the "lowest depth of degradation." It has led to the capturing
of the party "from us by John Lewis, Harold Ickes, Robert Vann,
White of the Society for the Advancement of Negroes [*sic*],
Madame Perkins, Harry Hopkins, Cothran [*sic*], and Cohen."
This new party of blacks, city bosses, and labor barons, Bailey
worried, would soon impose upon the South "a new Reconstruction Era."[11]

Many Southern congressmen reiterated that fear. Like Martin
Dies of Texas, they began to identify Roosevelt and the New
Deal with "the men from the big cities" of the North, which "are
politically controlled by foreigners and transplanted Negroes."
During the filibuster against the anti-lynching bill in 1938, almost
every Southern senator emphasized this change in the Democratic party. Byrnes claimed that "90 percent of the Negroes in
the North . . . are voting for Democratic candidates. The Negro
has not only come into the Democratic Party," he thundered, "the
Negro has come into *control* of the Democratic Party." That "epochal new fact" of political life, wrote John Temple Graves, one
of the South's most prestigious editors, "and that alone, was the
rock on which the party in the South could at last be split."[12]

Certainly, the relative decline in importance of Southerners
within the Democratic party fed the Negrophobia of the late
thirties. The South had been largely responsible for nominating
FDR in 1932. But not in 1936. In 1932 James Farley leaned heavily for support on such Southerners as Cordell Hull, Josephus
Daniels, John Rankin, and Pat Harrison. Four years later he
handily managed the convention for Roosevelt without their assistance. The President, moreover, had not needed a single South-

ern electoral vote to win in either election. Long the backbone of Democratic strength, the votes of the South in the electoral college dropped from 90 percent of the party total in 1920 and 1924 to 74 percent in 1928; to 26 percent in 1932; and finally to 23 percent in 1936. They were dispensable.[13]

Equally foreboding, Roosevelt's coattails carried a majority of non-Southern Democrats into Congress. Between 1896 and 1930 the Southern and Border states had accounted for two-thirds of the Democrats elected to Congress. Under Roosevelt, their total dropped to under half. The thirty Democratic senators from the South and the Border regions were part of a majority of 60 in 1933–34, 69 in 1935–36, and 76 in 1937–38. Likewise, those states contributed 130 representatives to the Democratic majorities of 311, 320, and 331 in the Seventy-third, Seventy-fourth, and Seventy-fifth congresses. Roosevelt's Southern opponents also had to face the prospect in 1937 of 13 Progressive and Farmer-Laborites in the House, and Norris, La Follette, and Minnesota's Ernest Lundeen and Henrik Shipstead in the Senate, which further swelled the bloated New Deal majority.[14]

The arithmetic of the Seventy-fifth Congress boggled the minds of liberals, much as it dismayed conservatives. A national liberal majority appeared in the offing. Not a single Southern or Republican vote would be needed to pass New Deal legislation. Civil rights leaders even believed that a successful cloture vote to cut off a filibuster on anti-lynching bills was now feasible. "The water of liberalism has been dammed up for forty years by the two major parties," rejoiced William Allen White. "The dam is out."[15]

White had not counted on Roosevelt's proposing a court reform plan that would enable him to pack the judiciary. All the congressional discontent that had been simmering now boiled over. Roosevelt could not contain the rebellion. The dam was up again. After 1937 Roosevelt faced a shifting, informal, but highly effective, conservative coalition resolved to block, or at least limit severely, all efforts to aid Negroes, labor unions, urban areas, and disadvantaged workers and farmers. The prominence of Southerners in that coalition proved to be yet another development weakening the defenders of white supremacy and strengthening the cause of civil rights.[16]

Democrats from the South voted against Roosevelt's domestic program more often than did representatives from any other section. Their opposition, however, except on issues directly pertaining to race, was never "solid." Many Dixie congressmen remained emphatic in their support for the New Deal. For every Bailey there was a Hugo Black of Alabama. For every Byrd there was a Theodore Bilbo of Mississippi. Both FDR's extreme antagonists and champions in the South spanned the spectrum in their racial beliefs and practices. Neither the sympathy for Negro rights expressed by Luther Patrick of Alabama and Maury Maverick of Texas nor the racial demagoguery of Martin Dies of Texas and John Rankin of Mississippi barred them from voting on most occasions with their Northern liberal colleagues. Yet, by the end of the decade racism and economic reaction had become interwoven. Quite perceptibly, a majority of congressmen from below the Mason-Dixon line turned against the New Deal. Roll call votes indicate a steadily increasing percentage of Southern Democrats joining with the Republicans to oppose measures favored by the administration. Even more of them, as journalists and New Dealers recognized, backed Roosevelt on a final vote but fought against his program in their respective committees, in conference committees, in supporting crippling amendments, in maneuvers to block consideration of certain measures, and in their private attempts to put pressure on the White House. And when they did make their aversion to the New Deal public, they resorted to racial and sectional rhetoric.[17]

In 1937, for example, not a single Southern congressional leader endorsed the President's requests for $700 million for slum clearance and public housing, a fair labor standards act, or $1.5 billion to continue the WPA. In both the House and Senate, Southerners provided most of the Democratic opposition to the relief bill. Congressmen Clifton A. Woodrum of Virginia and Sam McReynolds of Tennessee, and Senators Joseph Robinson of Arkansas, James Byrnes of South Carolina, and Pat Harrison of Mississippi led the effort for drastic cuts in the WPA appropriation. Of the 49 Democratic votes in the House for an amendment to curtail relief spending by one-third, 35 came from the South. Half the Dixie senators voted for a similar amendment. The same number also favored Byrd's amendment to slash the expenditures in the Wagner housing bill, contrary to the pleas of non-Southern Democrats. Only 40 Democrats in the House opposed the 1937 housing act; 31 of them were Southern. Half the Dixie delegation in the Senate defied Roosevelt's wishes on the fair labor standards bill that year, compared to the less than one-quarter of the non-Southern Democrats. When the House recommitted Wagner's proposal, 81 of the 99 Dixie representatives voted with the Republican majority; only 51 of the remaining 230 Democrats joined them. A majority of Southerners in both houses also favored investigating the National Labor Relations Board and the sit-down strikes. The administration wanted neither inquiry. Forty-three of the 78 Democrats who broke with Roosevelt on the House motion to pry into the new labor tactic hailed from the South. By the end of the year, moreover, the House Rules Committee had become the chief stumbling block to New Deal legislation. Five Southern conservatives, led by Edward E. Cox of Georgia and Howard W. Smith of Virginia, dominated the 14-man committee. Prior to the 1938 elections, Labor's Non-Partisan League singled out 26 Democrats it wanted defeated; 17 of them represented Dixie.[18]

Although such opposition to the New Deal in 1937 exemplified the antipathy of rural representatives to the needs of an industrial-urban constituency, Southerners usually spoke in racial terms when explaining their break with Roosevelt. Many editorials in the Southern press and the resolutions of all the bar associations below the Mason-Dixon line joined senators Byrd, George, Smith, and Connally of Texas in denouncing court-packing as the first step toward the destruction of white supremacy. The rights of the states to handle their own racial problems, asserted Bailey in his attack on the President's proposal, "would be violated again and again; and our people would be reduced to the very conditions under which our forefathers suffered." Glass, in a nationwide radio address in opposition to the court plan, announced that the "frightful proposition" aims at "another tragic era of reconstruction for the South." He blamed civil rights minded "political janizaries" like Ickes for pushing the plan. The secretary of the interior, Glass continued, "recently reproached the South for providing separate public schools for the races . . . he urged repeal of every statute and ordinance of segregation . . . he practically committed the administration at Washington to a new force bill for the South." Glass closed by depicting the court bill as an act of rape by "visionary incendiaries" who "would like to see the reversal of those decisions of the Court that saved the civilization of the South."[19]

Talk of a "nigger-loving New Deal" and condemnations of the vile liberal appeal for the votes of blacks punctuated congressional debates on relief, housing, and labor legislation in the next three years. Civil War and Reconstruction analogies reverberated. Analyzing this rhetoric, a young Southern journalist, W. J. Cash, underscored its appeal "to all the old bloody shirt themes to rouse up sentiment against" Roosevelt and the New Deal. He depicted all the liberal economic proposals then current as "Sherman's Second March." Senator Wagner complained in a speech in 1938 that "the ancient shibboleths are heard once again," particularly "the rights of States." Southern conservatives preached states' rights as the ark of their covenant, the Tenth Amendment as their First Commandment.[20]

Stymied by the conservative Democrats' refusal to pass the bills he proposed, Roosevelt announced on June 24, 1938, that he would intervene in certain primaries to insure the election of congressmen who would legislate "the definitely liberal declaration of principles set forth in the 1936 Democratic platform." This decision—in no way related to civil rights—nevertheless turned out to be yet another development linking support for the New Deal to the civil rights cause. Except for the effort to oust New York Congressman John O'Connor, the administration centered its fire on senators Millard Tydings of Maryland, Walter George, and "Cotton Ed" Smith—particularly the latter two. Many of the shapers of public opinion in the South reacted as if Roosevelt had advocated burning Atlanta. Their war was on.[21]

Roosevelt set the tone of the conflict when he compared the selfish, "feudal" elites of the South with fascists in Europe. "When you come right down to it," the President addressed his audience in Gainesville, Georgia, "there is little difference between the feudal system and the fascist system. If you believe in the one, you lean to the other." Roosevelt then called on Georgians to elect liberal legislators, with minds "cast in the 1938 mold and not in the 1898 mold." Walter George responded with a torrent of condemnation for Northerners who catered to the Negro vote. Playing up his role in the recently-concluded successful Southern filibuster against an anti-lynching bill, he contrasted his racial views with those of FDR's "left-wing brain-trusters," as well as those of carpetbaggers like Harold Ickes and scalawags like Clark Foreman, the latter, being pictured by George as a sinister traitor to the Southern tradition. George termed Roosevelt's attempted purge as a "second march through Georgia." "It made one of the neatest niggah-baiting tricks you ever saw," confided an aide. Raising the spectre of a Negro-dominated national Democratic party, George easily won renomination by appealing to his constituency to vote for states' rights and white supremacy.[22]

In South Carolina, Smith went all out in depicting the New Deal as a conspiracy to force civil rights down the throat of the South. At every opportunity he recounted, with increasing embellishment, his walkout in "Philly-delphy." "The Negro minister was not put there to invoke divine blessing," he informed his listeners. "He was there to invoke Negro votes. He was not asking divine blessing, but *primary* blessing." When pressed to discuss the issue of his opposition to the New Deal, Smith replied that he was just about to do that during his first primary speech "when I felt somebody was watching me. Of a sudden I looked down. There, hunkered up near the platform was an old farmer, with a torn black hat on his head and tobacco juice running down both sides of his mouth. I looked at him. I heard him croak, 'Aw, hell, Ed! Tell us about Philadeffy.' And, by God, I did!"

He did indeed, over and over again. Reporting on the primary, Harry Ashmore remembered Smith telling his constituents:

> . . . when I came out on the floor of that great hall, bless God, it looked like a checkerboard—a spot of white here, and a spot of black there. But I kept going, down that long aisle, and finally I found the great standard of South Carolina—and, praise God, it was in a spot of white!
>
> I had no sooner than taken my seat when a newspaperman came down the aisle and squatted by me and said, 'Senator, do you know a nigger is going to come out up yonder in a minute and offer the invocation?' I told him, I said, 'Now don't be joking me, I'm upset enough the way it is.' But then, bless God, out on that platform walked a slew-footed-blue-gummed, kinky-head Senegambian!
>
> And he started praying and I started walking. And as I pushed through those great doors, and walked across that vast rotunda, it seemed to me that old John Calhoun leaned down from his mansion in the sky and whispered in my ear, 'You did right, Ed.'

Then, his voice raising to a roar, Smith inevitably would conclude: "This is the time when, whether you like Ed Smith or not, every red-blooded white man should vote for Smith. Outside forces are seeking to defeat me because of my stand for White Supremacy." He won handily. The night after the election, standing beside the Wade Hampton statue on the State House grounds, Smith vowed to battle forever the New Deal Reconstruction.[23]

The word "demagogue" used as a verb, wrote a political scientist in 1938, came into vogue in Washington that year. Roosevelt's failure to purge Southern conservatives proved the potency of racism as a campaign issue once again in Dixie. The attempt of

Northern legislators to enact anti-poll tax and anti-lynching measures ended all Southern restraint. Even relatively pro-New Deal
senators now damned the administration for its "race-meddling."
They distrusted Roosevelt's racial proclivities and said so publicly. "The Man Bilbo," as he advertised himself, began an ora-
torical rampage that would last until his reelection in 1940.
Having done nothing to distinguish his record in three years
as a senator, "The Man" pulled out all the stops in arousing the
racial prejudices of his discontented, poor, rural, "redneck" constituency in the hills and bayous of the Magnolia Commonwealth.
"It has become necessary for us now to consider and to openly
discuss the forces which are today attempting to destroy the color
line," he would announce when defending the poll tax. "We will
tell our negro-loving, Yankee friends to 'Go Straight to Hell.' "[24]

"Why is it now, after three-quarters of a century . . . that an
attempt is made to cram down the throat of the South this insulting, undemocratic, un-American piece of legislation," Bilbo asked
during his stint in the 1938 Southern filibuster against the Wagner-
Costigan anti-lynching bill. Because of "Negro lovers, Negro
leaders, and Negro voters," he answered. "To defeat this measure,
so help me God, I would be willing to speak every day of the
year 1938." The folks back home loved it. Two months later he
introduced an amendment to the relief bill that would provide
for the deportation of all Afro-Americans to Liberia. A four hour
tirade followed. Bilbo reiterated his views on the inferiority of
blacks and the impossibility of racial equality in the United
States. "Race consciousness is developing in all parts of the
world," he perorated: "Consider Italy, consider Germany. It is
beginning to be recognized by the thoughtful minds of our age
that the conservation of racial values is the only hope for future
civilization. It will be recalled that Hitler . . . gave as the basis
of his program to unite Germany and Austria 'German blood ties.'
The Germans appreciate the importance of race values."[25]

Less than a year later he brought his proposal up again, requesting Congress to appropriate a billion dollars to finance a

Negro hegira to Africa. Only through physical separation, insisted "The Man" can miscegenation be prevented and civilization be preserved. The alternative would be the "unspeakable horrors of amalgamation, blood pollution, and hybridization." Those civil rights leaders who opposed his scheme Bilbo branded "amalgamationists" who "want white wives," who "want to see white women nursing black babies—their babies!" In 1940 he summed up his views in a *Living Age* article, "An African Home For Our Negroes," emphasizing the poll tax and the white primary as the bulwarks protecting Southern white womanhood from forced racial intermarriage.[26]

Many liberals laughed off such ranting as the "Bilbonic Plague," but few found funny the epidemic of Bilboism contaminating North-South congressional relations after 1937. The differences between the Southern filibusters against anti-lynching bills in 1935 and 1938 highlighted what had happened. The 1935 talkathon had been a gentlemanly tea party. Neither Northern nor Southern Democrats considered civil rights important enough to risk splitting the party or jeopardizing Roosevelt's program. Proponents of the measure made no effort to keep the Senate in round-the-clock sessions or to attempt cloture. It ended calmly after six days. But not in 1938. For nearly seven weeks the Northerners refused to give in; they insisted on night sessions and twice sought to invoke cloture. Almost every Southern senator took the floor to blame Roosevelt personally for alienating the South from the Democratic party and to link the demands for civil rights legislation with the pro-leftist, pro-CIO, and pro-Negro forces that had supplanted them in the party hierarchy. Not since the filibusters of the 1890s had the Senate witnessed such a barrage of explicit, overt Negrophobia.[27]

To liberals, no individual in the House of Representatives better personified Bilboism than Martin Dies, Jr., of Texas. As chairman of the Special House Committee on un-American Activities and organizer and self-proclaimed president of the House Demagogues Club, Dies, more than any other congressman in the late thirties, added anti-labor, anti-Communist, and anti-Semitic, as well as anti-New Deal and anti-Negro, connotations to the Southern byword "states' rights." Once a loyal New Dealer, he declared in 1937: "Now that the emergency is over, it is time to retrench and economize." Dies now demanded "an end to fruitless experimentation." He scoffed at the New Deal playing Santa Claus and "wet nurse for every local community." To get the government to return to the principles of a constitutional democracy his committee focused on the "un-American" forces at work in the New Deal rather than on the fifth-column activities of fascists the House had intended when it authorized the Special Committee in 1938. From its inception the Dies Committee attacked the New Deal and the labor and civil rights movements for their Communistic ties. It made much of the interracialism in the WPA's Theatre Project. Ickes, Perkins, and Frank Murphy were also singled out for censure.[28]

Between 1939 and 1941 Dies lost no opportunity to hamper the liberal thrust of the New Deal by "red-baiting" those in the administration identified with the labor and civil rights movements. He came to be considered the *beau ideal* of reactionaries throughout the country, particularly in the South. His 1940 account of what the committee had uncovered devoted six pages to the left for every one about the right. A whole chapter was devoted to "A Trojan Horse for Negroes." Virtually every civil rights leader, Dies intimated, had either been duped by the Communists or worked as a paid agent of Joseph Stalin. According to the Texan, Negroes were treated far better in the United States than anywhere in the world; propaganda to the contrary came from foreign sources intent on stimulating racial unrest. He also blamed Negro demands for civil rights on the same "alien" influence. His treatment of labor unions and the New Deal's concern for the forgotten men similarly blurred any distinction between liberalism and foreign radicalism. With good reason, therefore, the NAACP, the National Negro Congress, the Civil Rights Federation, the Public Affairs Committee, the National Board of the

Young Women's Christian Association, the American Civil Liberties Union, and other organizations supporting Negro rights joined to oppose continuation of the Dies Committee. In Congress, those most outspoken in their disavowal of Dies's efforts included Emanuel Celler, Samuel Dickstein and Vito Marcantonio of New York, Frank E. Hook of Michigan, Lee Geyer and Jerry Voorhis of California, and Maury Maverick of Texas—the very leaders of the House bloc for anti-lynching and anti-poll tax legislation.[29]

Conversely, the roster of Dies's supporters featured almost every major opponent of the New Deal and civil rights. Edward Cox of Georgia, J. Bayard Clark of North Carolina, John Rankin of Mississippi, and Joseph Starnes of Alabama led the House debate to continue the work of the Dies Committee. They also took the lead in denouncing the Roosevelt Administration for meddling in the racial affairs of the South and in opposing the liberal housing, labor, and relief legislation proposed by the President during his second term. Outside the White House, Dies garnered the applause of nearly every pro-fascist group he was supposed to be investigating. The Ku Klux Klan showered him with praise. George Deatherage of North Carolina, leader of the Knights of the White Camellia, lauded his work. When informed that Dies would investigate "the Jewish plot," Deatherage wired him "a great big kiss" from "all the boys." William Dudley Pelley and his Silver Shirts endorsed his efforts to uncover the Jewish-Negro-Bolshevist alliance destroying the American way of life. So did George Christian and his White Shirts of Chattanooga. William Blanchard of the White Front in Miami, wondering "Must the American white man accept the nigger as his equal by a brace of Jewish commissars?" placed his hope on Dies. So did Vance Muse, head of the Christian-American Front, who had organized the Grass Roots anti-Roosevelt convention for Talmadge in 1936. All these organizations and their hapless fuehrers took their cues from Father Charles E. Coughlin, who had chosen Dies as *Social Justice* "Man of the Year" in 1938. Weekly, these men tuned in to

the broadcasts from the Shrine of the Little Flower for information on the Jewish and black New Deal liberals they viewed as
the enemy at the gate. In addition to Dies and Bilbo after 1938,
they began to hear of Senator Robert Rice Reynolds of North
Carolina.[30]

Following his reelection that year, Reynolds broke with the
President on domestic policy and became his most strident opponent in foreign affairs. He mixed his condemnations of the New
Deal with Negrophobia, red-baiting, and isolationism. He had
nothing but contempt for Joseph Stalin, yet endorsed Benito
Mussolini's invasion of Ethiopia, justified Adolph Hitler's seizure
of Czechoslovakia, and defended Francisco Franco against the
"so-called Loyalists, the liberals." Borrowing the idea from Dies,
he announced in January 1939 the formation of the Vindicators,
"an association of Patriotic Americans." The association was supported by Coughlin, the KKK, and a score of minor pro-fascist organizations in the South, and, like their supporters, it barred
blacks and Jews from membership. "We are faced with a foreign
invasion," Reynolds announced. "The country is running riot
with isms." The extremity of his attacks on the President, and
Reynolds's warm embrace of the most rabid white supremacist
groups provided Democratic liberals with yet another prominent
Southerner in their demonology.[31]

Although many who supported the anti-labor views of Dies or
the isolationism of Reynolds were neither fascists nor white supremacists, liberal publicists often pictured the exception as the
rule. A rash of articles and books intended to discredit the opposition to Roosevelt ballyhooed the resurgence of the Ku Klux Klan
in the late thirties. The Klan came to typify the extremes of
Southern hostility toward Negroes, Jews, unionists, and liberals.
Opponents blamed it for the success of strike-breaking in the
South and for the failure of the movement to repeal the poll tax.
For its part, the Klan welcomed such publicity. It propagated
this notoriety with repeated tirades against the Roosevelts, the
CIO, and Negro rights organizations. Although the Klan never

became the mass organization it had been after the First World War, it served the causes of liberalism and civil rights by besmirching the standards of Southern sectionalism and states' rights.[32]

By the end of the 1930s the KKK had given the face of Southern conservatism an unmistakable fascist tinge. Since the Klan and Fritz Kuhn's German-American Bund both raged against Franklin Roosevelt, blacks, and Jews it probably did not shock Northern liberals in 1940 to read in their newspapers that the two organizations had jointly staged several mass meetings, replete with fiery crosses and fiery swastikas. Several of the Southern leaders working closely with the Bund, including Deatherage, Blanchard, and Pelley, were later indicted for sedition. "Fascist" became an epithet liberally applied to all manner of Southern conservatives. Journalists labeled Bilbo the "Mussolini of Mississippi," Talmadge, the "Fuehrer of Sugar Creek." Articles in the *New Republic* and the *Nation* often stressed the synonymity of fascism and racism. The South was pictured as Nazi-like for its white supremacist beliefs, and its representatives were censured for their "Hitler-like praise of racial homogenity." The Institute of Propaganda Analysis warned of scores of fascist groups in the South, each brewing a poison composed of equal measures of anti-New Deal, anti-union, anti-leftist, anti-Semitic, and anti-Negro bigotry. Southern liberals themselves took the lead in condemning the area's conservative extremists as fascists. W. J. Cash referred often to Nazi ideas on race as "Ku Kluckery." "We can't do much pointing of the accusing finger at Adolf Hitler or ell Doochey for trying to give their people an exaggerated idea of the supremacy of their blood," Ralph McGill wrote in the Atlanta *Constitution.* "We have the Klan." Clarence Cason, who taught journalism at the University of Alabama, titled Dixie politics "Fascism: Southern Style." Allan Michie and Frank Ryhlick agreed. "As a means of distracting the whites of the South from fundamental economic and social issues, the Negro has been to the Bourbons what the Jews have been to Hitler." White supremacy became so identified with Hitler-ite racism that W. T. Couch, director of the University of North Carolina Press, had to complain in sorrow: "Is there any sanity in the view now often stated that no one but a Fascist or Nazi can believe one people or race superior to another."[33]

Not everyone in the South, however, wanted to fire again on Fort Sumter. The same New Deal currents that had stirred Southern conservativism had also stimulated a new emergence of liberalism in the South. Its proponents resented the fact that the South had closed the door to Darwin and Freud, as well as Marx; they viewed with shame the stereotype of their South as a land of poverty, pellagra, and poll taxes; and they considered it imperative that a biracial alliance of disadvantaged farmers and laborers be enfranchised to overturn the rule of the Rankins, Bilbos, Byrds, and Coxes. Recognizing that local elites had paid off their poorer brothers with the status that came from being white instead of coin of the realm, some quite willingly and others with hesitancy and trepidation came to the realization that they would have to join the battle for Negro rights to make real their dreams of a New South.[34]

Southern liberals, although few in number, occupied positions that enabled them to make their opposition to the old sectionalism resound. They shattered the image of a white South solidly united on racial matters, much as Southern blacks by their political activities destroyed the myth that Negroes were content with the status quo. From such journalists as Jack Cash of the Charlotte *News*, Virginius Dabney of the Richmond *Times-Herald*, Jonathan Daniels of the Raleigh *News and Observer*, and John Temple Graves of the Birmingham *Age-Herald*, the South heard its obsession with white supremacy linked to the paucity of its economic progress. From such university presidents and social scientists as Frank Graham, Homer Rainey, Howard Odum, and Rupert Vance, it learned that the economic ills of Dixie could not be cured unless real democracy replaced the South's poll tax plutocracy. Such labor unionists as Lucy Randolph Mason and H. L.

Mitchell propounded the necessity of interracialism to counter the divide-and-conquer tactics of industrialists determined to keep the South an open shop. Representatives of the Roosevelt Administration, particularly Will Alexander, Clark Foreman, and Aubrey Williams, emphasized the indispensability of treating Negroes equitably to diminish the poverty of the South. And such politicians as Brooks Hays of Arkansas, Senator Claude Pepper of Florida, Birmingham Congressman Luther Patrick, and San Antonio Mayor Maury Maverick broke the unanimity of the South's political spokesmen on civil rights issues. "There was a mighty surge of discussion, debate, self-examination, confession, and release," the editor of the Atlanta *Constitution* recalled. "We saw and we talked. There was a stimulation in those days. Gone, finally, were the myths of white-pillared mansions, and a magnolia-scented civilization."[35]

The forces loosed by the depression and the New Deal, Ralph McGill went on, "rubbed out 'Nigger is Nigger and cotton is cotton' and all that this crude inanity implied." King Cotton had died. In its place the liberals saw a New South dawning, a South of large cities, robust industrialism, and agricultural diversification. Despite the persistence of many old habits and traditions, liberals had good reason to believe that the Twentieth Century had finally overtaken the South in the 1930s. The increasing number of radio sets and blacktop roads pulled both blacks and whites out of isolation. Tractors replaced mules, and the need for hundreds of thousands of unskilled farm laborers gave way to mechanical pickers. Cotton acreage dropped drastically, from 43,227 acres in 1929 to 22,811 in 1939. At the same time, the phosphates, nitrates, and potash produced by the TVA and distributed by the AAA speeded up the conversion of subsistence farming to commercial agriculture, while the availability of cheap electrical power, made possible by the Rural Electrification Administration, attracted new manufacturing establishments. Municipalities and states began to advertise, to offer tax concessions and bond issues, and to pass new zoning laws to entice industry. The Old

South was changing. But the representatives of the Old South would not accept the change. They expressed a mood of *ressentiment,* a nostalgia for the old verities. In their speeches and votes they favored the homogeneously ethnic small town over the racially polyglot big city, the religion of fundamentalism over modernity, the rights of capital over those of labor, a strong legislature rather than a powerful executive, and the rights of states instead of national planning and coordination. They resented the shift of power to Washington, as did they resent deficit spending, controls on business, taxation to pay for relief and public housing, and the government's encouragement of labor unionization. Their absolute refusal to accept any modification in race relations symbolized their more encompassing determination to thwart change. The battle lines were drawn, further connecting liberalism to the cause of Negro rights.[36]

None better exemplified the spirit of Southern liberalism than Lucy Randolph Mason, the rebel daughter of the Confederacy; Senator Pepper, the renegade thorn in the side of his racist, reactionary Dixie colleagues; and Jack Cash, the poet laureate of those in revolt against the bigotry, social irresponsibility, and violence of the Old South. Mason, the embodiment of white womanhood Southern politicians claimed to be protecting, turned from her work with the YWCA to become a propagandist for interracial unionism. A daughter from a pure first family of Virginia, she perturbed sheriffs, mayors, mill owners, and bank owners up and down the South by her lectures on the Fourteenth Amendment and the rights of blacks and unions. McGill fondly remembered:

> Many a tough sheriff in a small town that had a CIO organizer in jail looked up to see a small lady in a dark suit, wearing a little white-trimmed black hat on gray hair, come smiling into his office. Being, of course, sure of his image of himself as a Southern gentleman, and a protector of Southern womanhood, he would offer a chair before he heard even her name. Some legend has it, swallowed their cuds of chewing tobacco on

hearing that she was with the CIO and had come to talk about civil rights.

Not everyone took kindly to the stern lectures, even when given in a girl-like fashion. A local politician clamored: "What's back of you? Who sent you here anyhow? And by what right do you come into the state of Virginia to make trouble about civil rights?" "And," McGill continued, "so Miss Lucy told him."

> She ticked off her ancestors. George Mason, who wrote the Virginia Declaration of human rights, was her great-great-great-grandfather. Three of her ancestors signed the Declaration of Independence. Chief Justice Marshall was her mother's great-great uncle. The Randolphs, the Carters, the Beverleys, the Bollings, and the Chichesters of the colonial days were of her family. And if he wanted to come down to the Confederacy, her great-grandfather, James Murray Mason, had gone with John Slidell as Confederate envoy to Britain; General Robert E. Lee was her father's cousin and her father himself had served in the Confederate army. And, she concluded, her brothers had served in the First World War and one had been killed in action in France. Drawing a deep breath, Miss Lucy said, "Young man, I believe I have a right to come into Virginia to talk civil rights to her people." "Madame," said the visitor as he walked to the door, "whatever the CIO pays you, you are worth it."

"And she was," concluded McGill, "many times over."[37]

Pepper assumed the role of the Southern conscience in the Senate. Loudly and continuously, he raised his voice to condemn the racist isolationism of Senator Reynolds and his backers. He voted with Northern New Dealers more than any other Southern senator. Unlike a majority of Dixie's spokesmen in Congress, he backed the administration on large relief appropriations, expansion of the NYA and the FSA, public housing and wages and hours legislation, and the court and executive reorganization issues. On May 2, 1938, Pepper beat several conservative, Negrophobic opponents in the Democratic senatorial primary to gain reelection. He considered his victory a mandate to follow Roosevelt rather than his Southern colleagues, but he could not influence them. Minutes before the 1939 session adjourned, Pepper took the floor to "decry the unrighteous partnership" of Dixie Democrats and Republicans that had sabotaged New Deal legislation "because they hate Roosevelt and what Roosevelt stands for." He accused them of forming an "unholy alliance."

> I accuse that alliance of putting personal grudge and party feeling above the welfare and safety of the American people. I accuse that designing alliance of a deliberate attempt to sabotage the first real effort ever made in this nation to secure for the workers of America industrial democracy and economic emancipation. I accuse them of having prostituted their power to serve the U.S. Chamber of Commerce, the Manufacturer's Association, and the beneficiaries of special privilege, who hate in their hearts the man who has tried to lighten the burden of toil on the back of labor.

Southern senators fumed. Bailey called him "a coward and a liar." They demanded he sit down and permit a motion to adjourn. Pepper would not relinquish the floor. He again denounced the "Machiavellian alliance," and concluded to a rather un-senatorial accompaniment of hisses and hoorays by vowing to fight his conservative colleagues as long as he could, however he could.[38]

Meanwhile, W. J. Cash labored on his manuscript entitled *The Mind of the South*. Throughout the thirties he composed articles and editorials for the Baltimore *Evening Sun* and the Charlotte *News* denouncing lynching, supporting unionization, and lambasting Southern opposition to the New Deal, all the while stealing time to hone the prose of his critique of the Old South. He finished in 1940. Published early in 1941, *The Mind of the South* instantly gained recognition as a classic work of Southern history and contemporary analysis. Liberal reviewers, North and South, welcomed its moving restatement of all the concerns then current in the New South. Cash championed the organization of Southern labor. He applauded the academics blueprinting plans for cooperative regionalism. He stressed the need to replace the fallen

King Cotton with a progressive economy fully integrated with the rest of the nation. Indignantly, Cash described all the forms of racial brutality, discrimination, injustice, and oppression suffered by blacks. He laid bare the economic motivations behind Dixie demagoguery. Most of all, Cash dissected what he called the "Proto-Dorian consensus," the blind obsession of the Southern lower classes with the trappings of white supremacy and sectional loyalty, with the chimeras of the "Lost Cause" and "White Purity," which kept them enthralled to the oligarchs.[39]

Numerous other Southern liberals similarly ended their acquiescence. What George Washington Cable once called the "Silent South" became vocal. Opposition to the Southern credo became public. Following the lead of Howard Odum the most prominent Southern sociologist, social scientists emphasized the toll on the South exacted by racism. They detailed the ways in which the race issue kept the South in bondage. To present a publicly liberal view on political matters, one contrary to the ideas of the demagogues, Brooks Hays, Francis Pickens Miller, and H. C. Nixon organized the Southern Policy Committee. The committee helped persuade members like Virginius Dabney, who had become editor of the Richmond *Times-Dispatch* in 1936, to publish articles denouncing the poll tax and calling for passage of a federal anti-lynching law. Jonathan Daniels, editor of the Raleigh *News and Observer,* took the same positions in his newspaper and in his column, "Native at Large," in *The Nation.* A score of newspapers in the urban South followed suit. So did Lillian Smith and Paula Snelling, who began publishing *Pseudopodia* in 1936, changed its name to the *North Georgia Review* the next year, and soon thereafter won a reputation for their journal as the most militant white-run advocate of Negro rights in the South. Smith and Snelling called for the total abolition of all segregation.[40]

With the President's approval and Mrs. Roosevelt's active involvement, the academic, labor, political, and journalistic apostates joined together in Birmingham in November 1938 to organize the Southern Conference for Human Welfare (SCHW). The SCHW had its origin in four separate but related concerns. First, CIO officials and members of the Communist-controlled National Committee for the Defense of Political Prisoners in the South, headquartered in Birmingham, wanted to call a conference to focus on anti-union violence and the denial of constitutional rights to labor organizers. Led by Joseph Gelders, they won support for the calling of a meeting on civil liberties and civil rights in the South from Eleanor Roosevelt, the Southern Policy Committee, and Frank Graham, the president of the University of North Carolina. They were significantly aided in this endeavor by Lucy Randolph Mason, who had been revolted by the brutal beating of Gelders in 1936 by the agents of the Tennessee Coal and Iron Company. Second, President Roosevelt in 1938 warmed to the idea of a Southern-based campaign to abolish the poll tax. He viewed this as a part of his larger effort to liberalize the Democratic party. Roosevelt believed that the hundreds of thousands of disfranchised in the South, if able to vote, would support his programs to aid the needy, and might help him defeat the conservatives blocking his bills in Congress. The genius of a Southern organization working against the poll tax, from Roosevelt's point of view, was that it would leave him unimplicated. If it succeeded, he would have a liberal, united party supporting him; if it failed, he would be free of the campaign's taint and would still be able to work with Dixie politicos.[41]

Third, Roosevelt and the Southern regionalists, for their own reasons, wanted to publicize the South's economic problems. As a part of his effort to purge conservatives from the party, Roosevelt wanted a pamphlet that would detail the plight of the South and point clearly to the solution: the need to elect liberal candidates who would vote for the President's program. Roosevelt asked the National Emergency Council to prepare the document. During the summer of 1938, the President officially released the *Report on Economic Conditions of the South,* terming that region "the Nation's No. 1 economic problem—the Nation's problem, not merely the South's." The response was the opposite of what he had hoped for. Opponents of the New Deal denounced it as a libel on the South and its way of life. It became a storehouse of ammunition put to use against Northern liberals. Instead of being taken as a plea for economic reconstruction, it was cited to prove the shibboleth of the South as an economic colony, literally in bondage to the North. Because it had been written by Southerners prominent in civil rights activities, especially Clark Foreman, Lucy Mason, and H. L. Mitchell of the Southern Tenant Farmer's Union, conservatives caricatured it as another FDR scheme to upset the racial system of the South and win the Negro votes of the North. The Kiplinger "Washington Letter" depicted the Report as part of FDR's "plan to undercut conservative leaders in the South," to "wean the masses" away from "their present conservative representatives in Congress." A flood of mail to the White House from Southern chambers of commerce, state legislatures, and governors branded the report as insult and demanded a congressional resolution of censure for all those having anything to do with it.[42]

The regionalists, however, wanted to play up the NEC's report in order to focus public attention on their proposed prescriptions for the South's ills. Led by Howard Odum and Rupert Vance, they abhorred the Old South prattle of sectional conflict. They propounded a doctrine of cooperation, development, and planning, whose end was the integration of all sections into one harmonious and bountiful nation. Therefore, they joined the denunciation of "Neo-Confederate" leaders bent on keeping the South separate and unequal. The regionalists did not want to hide Southern shortcomings. They wanted the veil removed so that the South could face itself honestly and begin the work that had to be done. Many regionalists wanted the SCHW to trumpet these concerns, as well as to add Southern backing for New Deal research and planning. They also hoped the SCHW would follow the regionalists in emphasizing the problems of labor relations, farm tenancy, and black economic inequality, the three main stumbling blocks to Southern prosperity.[43]

Fourth, some Southern liberals, particularly those close to the administration, wanted a robust organization in Dixie to supplant the infirm Commission on Interracial Cooperation. They believed that the issues of the color line could no longer be left to the white supremacists or silently swept under the rug. They saw racism as the barrier to their hopes for an economic and political reconstruction of the South. Like Cash, these liberals wanted the "Proto-Dorian consensus" destroyed so that the mass of Southern whites could understand and vote their real class interests. To counter what they called the threat of facism at home, such men and women as Clark Foreman, George S. Mitchell, Aubrey Williams, Lucy Randolph Mason, and Louise O. Charlton yearned for an interracial populist organization that would be the basis for a liberal-labor-Negro coalition. They were joined by Southern blacks active in the CIC but now disenchanted with its cautiousness.[44]

The impressive list of sponsors and participants in the first session of the Southern Conference for Human Welfare augured well for the four related goals. The notable educators included Frank Graham, Arthur Raper, Charles S. Johnson, and Howard K. Beale. The whole galaxy of progressive journalists appeared; most prominent were Virginius Dabney, Mark Ethridge, John Temple Graves, Ralph McGill, and George Fort Milton. The AFL, the CIO, the STFU, the Railroad Brotherhoods, and the National Farmers' Union all sent delegations, as did many of the Communist and Socialist youth and labor groups. Senator Pepper, and Senator Lister Hill of Alabama, Democratic National Committeeman Brooks Hays of Arkansas, San Antonio Mayor Maury Maverick, Alabama Governor Bibb Graves, and Birmingham Congressman Luther Patrick were the spokesmen for the politics of the New South. Eleanor Roosevelt and Mary McLeod Bethune joined Foreman, Mitchell, Williams, and R. W. Hudgens of the FSA in signifying the New Deal's interest. The President also sent the SCHW a warm letter of greeting. Perhaps most important, black constituted one-third of the conference membership. The race issue would be faced. The initial convention, indeed, approved resolutions advocating an end to the poll tax, freedom for the Scottsboro Boys, and both state and federal anti-lynching laws.[45]

Most shocking of all to the Old South was that the SCHW conducted its first two sessions without segregating the races. After Birmingham police commissioner Eugene "Bull" Connor compelled the convention to obey the local Jim Crow ordinance, the SCHW voted to condemn the city officials for enforcing such a statute and resolved to meet in the future only where "the practice of the past few days would not be applied." Eleanor Roosevelt deliberately placed her chair in the middle of the area separating whites from blacks to protest Connor's order. The identification of the New Deal could hardly have been more graphic. Such actions caused the Negro press to cheer. The *Defender* called it a "rare and precious moment in the social history of America." Lillian Smith described it as "not simply an unusual happening but the symbol of a changing South, a good South." Conversely, a speaker addressing the South Carolina Sheriff's Association declared that the behavior of the Roosevelt Administration was "an insult to every white man and woman in the South."[46]

The following year the SCHW established a Committee on Civil Rights. Headed by Maury Maverick, the Committee met in Chapel Hill, North Carolina, to determine its priorities. "We chose the issue which we considered the key to other problems—the abolition of the poll tax," said Joseph Gelders, secretary of the committee. In 1939 eight Southern states still retained the poll tax as a requirement of voting. The SCHW began its campaign by getting a grant from the William C. Whitney Foundation for research on suffrage in the South. Then it began instituting test cases in the federal courts, publishing literature on the tax's inequities, distributing buttons and stamps proclaiming "Free American First–Abolish the Poll Tax," and drafting the legislation to be introduced in Congress by Senator Pepper and Congressman Geyer. In concert with a host of other groups promoting New Deal issues, including the AFL and the CIO, the ACLU, the National Lawyers' Guild, the National Farmers' Union, the National Women's Trade Union League, the Townsend Plan, the Church League for Industrial Democracy, the National Federation of Constitutional Liberties, the National Conference on Social Work, and every major Negro and civil rights organization, the SCHW's Committee on Civil Rights merged its campaign with that of the National Committee to Abolish the Poll Tax, formed in 1940 by Congressman Geyer.[47]

Initially, most Southern liberals tried to keep the race issue out of the movement against the poll tax. They understood fully that the fear of Negro suffrage would complicate their efforts. Some Southern opponents of the tax went so far as to publish studies showing that while repeal permitted formerly disfranchised whites to vote, other devices continued to keep blacks disqualified. Most of what they wrote pertained to poor white farmers and union members, not to Afro-Americans. Much of it emphasized the support for the New Deal by proponents of repeal and the anti-Roosevelt record of those fighting to retain the poll tax. But Southern conservatives would not permit this argument to define the conflict. They turned it into a racial issue. They insisted that the purpose of those who advocated the abolition of the poll tax was Negro suffrage and that the movement had little to do with white poverty. The "Big Mule" industrialists of Alabama declared that those favoring repeal wanted "nothing short of complete social equality [on the statute books], abolition of all race segregation, and a strong pressure to bring about interracial marriage." The Tuscaloosa *News* added that "it believes that the poll tax is one of the essentials for the preservation of white supremacy." The Byrd machine in Virginia used the same reasoning against New Dealers campaigning for abolition of the poll tax there. So did the conservative political organizations of Tennessee, Georgia, Mississippi, and Texas. An Alabama judge told the Montgomery *Advertiser* that he opposed political equality for Negroes because it would lead to social equality. "We've been apprehensive since the Negroes have been participating in the AAA elections," the judge confided. "It gives them notions." "All niggers—uneducated and educated—have one idea back in their mind," said the chairman of the county board of registrars in Montgomery, "that they want equality. . . . It is necessary to keep the Negro from voting, for voting would lead to social equality."[48]

This metamorphosis of the poll tax issue established yet another link between the New Deal and the cause of Negro rights, because the President and many of his closest supporters publicly endorsed repeal. "The right to vote," Roosevelt declared, "must be open to all our citizens irrespective of race, color, or creed—without tax or artificial restriction of any kind. The sooner we get to that basis of political equality, the better it will be for the country as a whole." Roosevelt had supported Pepper's efforts in Florida to win repeal there in 1937, and the following year he made public a letter to Brooks Hays giving his backing to the anti-poll tax movement in Arkansas. Poll taxes, claimed Roosevelt, "are inevitably contrary to fundamental democracy and its representative form of government in which we believe." At a press conference later in 1938, the President again announced that he favored ending all poll tax requirements for voting. These were highly significant words and actions by a President on an issue clearly identified as a racial matter. When Representative Geyer submitted the anti-poll tax bill drafted by the SCHW to the House in 1939, scores of Northern New Dealers came out for its passage. Angrily, Mississippi's Pat Harrison took pains to note that, "of course, John L. Lewis and the Southern Conference, and Mrs. Roosevelt and the President are all against the tax."[49]

A third major liberal organization pushing repeal of the poll tax, the Southern Electoral Reform League (SERL), entered the fray in 1941. Headed by Moss A. Plunkett, an antagonist of the Byrd machine, the SERL had the active support of Clark Foreman and Frank Graham. It featured among its many Northern sponsors such proponents of civil rights as Van Wyck Brooks, John Dewey, Arthur Garfield Hays, Gardner Jackson, A. Philip Randolph, Norman Thomas, and Oswald Garrison Villiard. At its first meeting in February, Eleanor Roosevelt delivered the major address supporting the Geyer bill. Like the SCHW and the National Committee to Abolish the Poll Tax, its funds came mainly from the AFL and the CIO. All three, moreover, regularly received publicity for their pronouncements and activities in the *New Republic, The Nation,* and *Common Sense,* as well as in numerous labor and religious journals. In addition, they all had the blessings of the White House. Together, the SERL, the SCHW, the NCAPT, and the major Negro rights groups focused their attack on the "poll tax congressmen" as the most anti-labor, anti-Semitic, anti-Negro, and anti-New Deal representatives in Washington. Their statistical demonstrations that many of the most extreme racists were also the last progressive on economic issues further intertwined the causes of liberalism with those of the civil rights movement. They battled a common enemy. Time and again they emphasized the opposition both to Roosevelt and to Negro rights by Cox of Georgia, Smith of Virginia, Dies and Sumners of Texas, Rankin of Mississippi, and Starnes and Hobbs of Alabama. Scores of articles, books, and editorials written in the late thirties condemned the poll tax as the handmaiden of economic conservatism and racism. Pamphlets on the poll tax published by the American Association of University Women, the American Council on Public Affairs, and the United Auto Workers underscored the indivisibility of liberalism in race and class, pointing out the close connections between prejudice and poverty. The Research Committee on the Suffrage in the South, which included Ralph Bunche of Howard University, Max Lerner of Williams College, and C. Vann Woodward of the University of Virginia, and which was sponsored by the New School for Social

Research, similarly stressed the poll tax as an obstacle to both racial and economic reform. It is a weapon of the South's ruling elite used to oppose Roosevelt, wrote Maury Maverick, and "anybody else who won't do his bit to keep the colored people, the white sharecropper, the whole lowest third down in the dirt."[50]

On matters of race, the poll tax issue closed the linked circle that isolated the dominant politicians of the South from much of the rest of the Democratic party. For over a hundred years, Dixie's representatives had relied on the votes of Democrats from the North to thwart every challenge to white supremacy. They could do so no longer. The rift in the party ended Northern deference to the South on civil rights. The vote on the 1942 anti-poll tax bill in the House demonstrated the magnitude of that change. After being able to sit for nearly four years on the Geyer bill in the Judiciary and Rules committees, the South now stood alone. The House overwhelmingly adopted the measure by a vote of 254 to 84. Only 4 Southerners favored the bill; 70 voted nay. Only 6 Northern and Western Democrats opposed the measure; 102 voted aye. Even the Border Democrats split 20 to 4 in favor of Geyer's proposal. It required a filibuster to kill the bill in the Senate. Every Southern senator, except Pepper, vehemently denounced the move to abolish the poll tax by federal legislation. Not a single Northern Democrat joined them.[51]

A decade after Roosevelt's election to the presidency and despite these dramatic developments, the Negro leadership still waited in vain for a major civil rights bill to be enacted into law. Northern Democrats would vote for such legislation, but not yet battle all-out for it. New Dealers would identify themselves with the black struggle for equality, but not to the detriment of their greater concerns. President Roosevelt, for the most part, remained above the battle, continuing to offer symbolic assistance at different times both to the foes and to the proponents of the Negro vote, hoping to alienate neither group too decisively. He spoke out against the poll tax but never led the fight against it. He well understood how disfranchisement, malapportionment and the one-party system, and the seniority of Southerners left him dependent upon the very congressmen and senators he had wished to purge from the party. The resurgence of Republican strength in the 1938 elections and the priority of foreign and military policy issues after 1939 placed the South back in the saddle again. No other section proved more internationalist and interventionist than Dixie. Roosevelt needed its votes. To gain the full support of the white South he once again compromised the black struggle.[52]

The continued weaknesses of Southern liberalism gave Roosevelt little choice. Organizations like the SCHW made more headlines than progress. Except for the existence of a vocal liberal intellectual establishment, the basic elements needed for a New Deal South stayed inert. Below the Mason-Dixon line the labor movement remained weak, blacks and lower-class whites did not vote, and neither urban machines anxious for the workers' vote nor ethnic-religious minorities sensitive to issues of civil liberties and rights flourished. Not surprisingly, many liberals backed away from the SCHW and the poll tax issue upon being labeled pro-Red and pro-Black. The leaders of the Old South still prevailed.[53]

"Yet if the New Deal did not dislodge those who dominated the power structure in the South, it threatened them as they had never been threatened before," concluded Dewey Grantham, an historian of the South. Although it generated intransigence, the New Deal also stimulated movement toward the substitution of the Southern credo by the American creed. "By nationalizing most issues, by liberating the Democratic party from the dictation of southern leaders, and by bringing to political consciousness elements in the region which had long been unable to exert any influence in politics, the New Deal threatened the old power structure and nourished forces that eventually began to reconstruct the region's political affairs." These developments aided immeasurably the cause of civil rights. Whatever Roosevelt's needs of 1940 might have dictated, the momentum of the preceding five years could not easily be stopped. For a variety of reasons, other groups influential in the Democratic party now opposed any total capitulation by the President to Southern conservatives. The rift in the party caused by the New Deal had helped place civil rights on the agenda of the new national majority coalition and had forced the spokesmen for white supremacy to take the defensive.[54]

6

The Red and The Black

"The Depression affected people in two different ways. The great majority reacted by thinking money is the most important thing in the world. Get yours. And get it for your children. Nothing else matters," recalled Virginia Durr, one of the architects of the SCHW campaign against the poll tax. "And there was a small number of people who felt the whole system was lousy. You have to change it." That small number of people—the Stalinists, Trotskyists, Socialists, followers of A. J. Muste, and assorted fellow-travellers—failed to destroy capitalism in the thirties but succeeded in revolutionizing the status of civil rights issues. In tandem with New Dealers, black politicians, and Southern liberals, the American Left made the struggle for black equality a part of the progressive agenda. This assistance to blacks came at a price. Communism, especially, repulsed many Americans, who transferred their antipathy to causes associated with the Communists. Untold numbers of potential adherents to the cause of civil rights were alienated by its affiliation with "un-American" radicalism. Particularly in the South, the fear of being labeled a Red scared away potential supporters of Negro rights. Conservatives found it easy to rationalize opposition to anti-lynching and anti-poll tax legislation by pointing to the prominence of radicals in many of the groups lobbying for these measures. Guilt by association implicated many black rights leaders and assemblages. At the same time, the disruption, deceit, and duplicity often practiced by the Communist party, and the use of the race issue for its own sectarian ends complicated the work of established civil rights organizations. Well-founded distrust of Communist leaders prevented the NAACP, the Urban League, and the CIC from total cooperation with the Left in their battles against the common foe of white supremacy.[1]

Yet, on balance, the positive effects of the Left's involvement in racial matters outweighed the negative, at least in the 1930s. Like the abolitionists, the Left functioned as an irritant to the American conscience. It too had an impact on American thought disproportionate to its numbers. The Left publicized the evils of racism and the benefits of integration to a far greater extent than any other white organization. Its battles for the freedom of the Scottsboro Boys and Angelo Herndon, as well as its endeavors in behalf of the black unemployed and sharecroppers, aided in the politicizing of Afro-Americans. It sparked and financed new civil rights groups whose radicalism made the established Negro organizations more militant in their tactics and yet more respectable to the American mainstream. The many journals of the Left highlighted cultural and intellectual trends undermining the racist foundations of white superiority and influenced a small but vital coterie of Negro authors to abandon black nationalism and separatism in favor of interracialism. In addition, it spurred leftist labor unions to recruit blacks, to mobilize white workers to combat racial discrimination, and to commit their financial and political resources to the quest for legislation that would assist blacks. Many liberals, moreover, joined with the Left in the Popular Front of the mid-thirties in asserting that the fight for Negro rights was an integral part of the struggle against fascism at home and abroad.[2]

Prior to the Great Depression, the Left had emphasized the ideology of the class struggle at the expense of immediate issues of concern to Afro-Americans. Throughout the 1920s the Socialists continued to follow Eugene Debs's policy of making no special appeals to the Negro. The Socialist party platform of 1926 even warned blacks "that the social, civil, and industrial injustices of which they so rightly complain cannot be materially remedied until the present industrial system has given place to a cooperative commonwealth." "What the Negro wants and needs, Norman Thomas announced, "is what the white worker wants and needs; neither more nor less. This is what we Socialists stand for." While formally a restatement of the Socialist party's philosophy of color-blind working class unity, Thomas's disregard for the excessive disabilities of black labor reinforced the traditional antagonism of most Negro spokesmen toward Socialists. The *Courier* ridiculed as pie in the sky the leftist belief that the end of capitalism would bring the demise of race prejudice.[3]

The Communists, on the other hand, bent over backwards in the twenties to try to capitalize on the nationalistic sentiment of blacks. In 1921 the African Blood Brotherhood (ABB) became the first Negro contingent to join the American Communist movement. Such separatist and African-oriented ABB leaders as Cyril V. Briggs, W. A. Domingo, Otto Huiswood, Lovett Fort-Whiteman, and Richard B. Moore dominated the formulation of Communist party policy on race. They had the Communist party flirting with Garveyism. ABB officials arranged for Communist speakers at Garveyite conventions, edited Garvey's *Negro World*, and echoed Garvey's sentiments in their own *Crusader*. In 1925 Moscow ordered the ABB replaced by the less nationalistic American Negro Labor Congress (ANLC). It never got off the ground. According to the *Defender*, only thirty-seven delegates attended its first convention in Chicago that year. Over half were from Chicago. The NAACP, the Urban League, and the Negro press castigated the ANLC for still being too separatist. Prominent Afro-American unionists, led by A. Philip Randolph, boycotted the ANLC. An ANLC organizer in the twenties sadly admitted that the American Negro Labor Congress had failed to recruit many blacks.[4]

In the summer of 1928 the Sixth World Congress of the Communist International announced the doctrine of "the right of self-determination of the Negroes in the Black Belt." Afro-Americans, according to the party line, were not simply a racial minority but an oppressed separate nation seeking self-determination. This theory, in part, reflected Stalin's own understanding of the minority problem in the Soviet Union. It also underscored the degree to which American Communists in the twenties had been impressed by Garvey's ability to attract mass support. It further demonstrated the crucial role in Communist affairs still being played by such ABB members as Cyril V. Briggs, Otto Hall, and Harry Haywood. But the doctrine hardly spoke to the needs of most blacks. Recalling the impossible dream of a separate "Negro Republic," Benjamin Gitlow, once a Communist functionary, stated that regardless "of our efforts and the large sums of money spent on that sort of propaganda, we made very little headway among the Negro masses." Gitlow soon stopped advocating separatism or even referring to the scheme for a separate nation.[5]

In fact, a close reading of the International's resolution indicates that it stressed only the *right* of self-determination, not its fruition. It "does not necessarily imply that the Negro population should make use of this right in all circumstances, that is, that it must actually separate or attempt to separate the Black Belt from the existing governmental federation with the United States." The International, moreover, resolved that if the Black Belt "prefers to remain federated with the United States it must be free to do that." It hedged its advocacy of separatism by distinguishing between the needs of Northern and Southern blacks and by maintaining that after the "proletarian revolution" Negro Communists should oppose the disjunction of the Black Belt from the rest of the nation. Given the desire of blacks in the North for assimilation, the International required American Communists to make "equal rights" its main slogan and to fight all segregation within the party. "It must be born in mind that the Negro masses will not be won for the revolutionary struggles until such time as the most conscious sections of white workers show by action that they are fighting with the Negroes against all racial discrimination and persecution." White workers had "to march at the head of this struggle . . . to everywhere make a breach in the wall of segregation and Jim Crowism which have been set up by the bourgeoise slave market mentality." The resolution ordered the party to carry on "a relentless struggle against all manifestations of Negrophobia."[6]

The ambiguity of the Comintern resolution left the American Communists free to emphasize interracialism and to downplay separatism. Self-determination became little more than a ritualistic slogan in the party's theoretical journals. The party opted to stress "Black and white, unite and fight." Party Secretary Earl Browder demanded that the mobilization of unemployed blacks be made a top priority. Any unemployment movement, he warned, that did not feature blacks "in the foreground would be doomed to failure."

During the 1929 textile strike in Gastonia, North Carolina, the party's central committee ordered its labor organizers to discuss "equal rights for Negroes" in their speeches at workers' rallies. When a surprised Communist reported back to his superiors that the company he was organizing employed only two blacks, they admonished him: "We must prepare the workers for the coming revolution. We must look ahead and smash all feelings of inequality." A black Communist party official commenting on Gastonia in *The Communist* went further: "It is not only necessary to fight the chauvinism of the white workers but the segregation tendencies of the Negro workers themselves." The party's first two district meetings in the South, held in Charlotte and Birmingham, emphasized the struggle for civil rights. By 1930 *The Communist* had interred all articles in favor of separatism and racial nationalism, which had been one of its most popular themes in the twenties. It now specifically denied the separate nationality of blacks, maintaining that they were only a racially persecuted minority and quite unlike the Africans and Caribbeans who constituted an oppressed colonial people. Even Harry Haywood recanted, attacking black nationalism as contrary to the "revolutionary solution of the question by a fighting alliance of the Negro masses and white workers." In 1930 *The Negro Worker,* the separatist party journal for blacks, switched its editorial line. Black nationalism was now defined as reactionary and utopian, a tool of Negro "misleaders" to prevent blacks from supporting revolutionary trade union movements.[7]

Still, the Communists floundered in their efforts to gain black support. The League of Struggle for Negro Rights (LSNR) had little more success than its predecessor, the American Negro Labor Congress. It could generate neither black membership nor favorable editorial comment in the Negro press. At the beginning of the thirties, perhaps 150 to 200 Afro-Americans belonged to the Communist party out of a total party membership of about 7500. James Ford later wrote that prior to 1932 the party was "completely isolated from the basic masses of the Negro people." Its policy of dual and revolutionary organization, permitting no cooperation with "social fascists" and "betrayers of the Negro people," had flopped. The LSNR's campaign to "win the masses away from their bourgeois and petty-bourgeois leaders" by labeling established Negro spokesmen as "lickspittle" of white capitalism only shut even tighter the doors of the black community to Communists. Moreover, to the extent that the party gloried in its isolation, shunning all other leftist and Negro groups and being shunned by them in return, it had little attraction to blacks. Only true believers could find the powerless and persecuted Communist organization appealing in the twenties. This was doubly so for blacks who knew well the disadvantages of being a target of oppression. "It's bad enough being black," went a street saying, "why be red?" "The American Negro is not going to embrace

Communism or Socialism" the *Courier* editorialized late in 1928, because his "position is precarious enough without making it more so by joining a crew that espouses the overthrow of the government and the dictatorship of the proletariat."[8]

Few blacks cared a whit about Socialism. As Claude McKay had bitterly observed, "Karl Marx's economic theories are hard to digest, and the Negroes, like many other lazy-minded workers, may find it easier to put their faith . . . in that other Jew, Jesus." At the start of the depression most blacks did just that. The Communists had as yet done nothing to demonstrate their usefulness to the black struggle, and they knew it. Admitting its failure early in March 1931, the party pledged that it would have to "prove to the Negro workers, NOT in WORDS, but in DEEDS, that the white workers will fight for the rights of Negroes."[9]

Then came March 25, 1931. Like depression youth all over the country, some two dozen teenagers in search of employment or excitement hopped a freight train southbound from Chattanooga. Midway in the trip a group of black youths clashed with several whites, forcing them off the train. The white boys reported the incident to the police, who telephoned ahead to stop the train. Near Paint Rock, Alabama, the local sheriff removed nine black youths and two young white women from the freight. Fearful of arrest, the women of questionable repute accused the blacks of raping them at knifepoint. This ugly charge caused crowds to gather at the Paint Rock jailhouse. Talk of lynching filled the air. The sheriff moved the blacks to the jail at Scottsboro, the county seat. The governor dispatched twenty-five armed National Guardsmen to keep the uneasy peace. Within two weeks and amid a continuing atmosphere of hostility over the "nigger rape case," an all-white grand jury in Scottsboro had indicted the nine blacks for forcible rape, the trial judge had assembled a jury panel of one hundred whites and casually appointed all six white lawyers in Scottsboro as defense counsel, and the court had tried and found guilty all of the accused. Despite the haste of the proceedings, the contradictory testimony given by the women, and the protestations of innocence by the nine blacks, all but the youngest were sentenced to death in the electric chair.[10]

On the day of the sentencing the Communist party's Central Committee issued a long statement condemning this "legal lynching" by the "parasite landlords and capitalist classes of the South." Within twenty-four hours, the LSNR, the Young Communist League, the Trade Union Unity League, and the Anti-Imperialist League of the United States had trumpeted their outrage against "capitalist justice." A day later the Communist-dominated Marine Workers Industrial Union in New Orleans called a meeting "to take the offensive and to expose the rottenness and corruption of Southern justice before all the American people." Every Communist organization leaped into the fray, demanding freedom for "the Scottsboro Boys," as they would be called throughout the decade. The Communist party sponsored demonstrations in behalf of the defendants in every major city in the country during the summer of 1931. Its International Labor Defense took charge of the legal appeals. The party was beginning to prove its mettle to blacks. Scottsboro, wrote Harry Haywood, was "a godsend."[11]

The Communists made the most of it. In Chicago they conducted fourteen protest rallies over a three-month period. Thousands of Harlem's residents marched alongside Communists in 1931 to condemn the "framing of nine Negro boys at Scottsville [sic]." A "March on Washington" brought four thousand to a demonstration in front of the White House. The Communists even staged interracial demonstrations in Atlanta and Birmingham. The mothers of the imprisoned youth, or at least Negro women posing as these mothers, appeared under Communist auspices in hundreds of towns and cities. These women always linked the fate of their sons to the larger cause of racial injustice. They regularly praised the courageous role of the Communist party. "I haven't got no schooling, but I have five senses and I know that Negroes can't win by themselves," one mother told a rally in New Haven. Only the Communists had managed to prevent the electrocution of her son so far, Mrs. Patterson exclaimed, "and I have faith that they will free him if we all is united behind them. . . . I don't care whether they are Reds, Greens, or Blues. They are the only ones who put up a fight to save these boys and I am with them to the end."[12]

The Communists also triggered a series of fiery, and often violent, confrontations at United States consulates in Latin America and Europe to demonstrate their advocacy of "the brotherhood of black and white young proletarians . . . and an end to the bloody lynching of our Negro co-workers." Scottsboro superceded Sacco and Vanzetti as the preeminent symbol of American injustice. No news coming out of the United States in 1931 and 1932 received more coverage in the European press than did stories on Scottsboro. Maxim Gorky, the Russian novelist, interpreted the affair for Russian readers of *Pravda*. Albert Einstein, H. G. Wells, and Thomas Mann arraigned American white supremacy for their fellow countrymen. Hundreds of internationally prominent authors, labor leaders, politicians, and scientists signed Communist petitions demanding freedom for the Scottsboro Boys. In Atlanta a young black Communist, Angelo Herndon, could not contain his joy as he witnessed the party making "the Scottsboro case a battering-ram against Jim-Crowism and oppression. I watched the protests in the Scottsboro case swelling to a roar that echoed from one end of the world to the other."[13]

Simultaneously, Communist propaganda transformed Scottsboro into the most searching indictment of Jim Crow yet to appear in the United States. The number of articles, books, plays, and poems written by Communists about the nine blacks numbered in the hundreds. The *Daily Worker, New Masses, Negro Worker, Harlem Liberator,* and *Southern Worker* ("the Communist paper for the south") devoted greater attention to Scottsboro in the first half of the thirties than to any other subject. Much of what they wrote also found its way into such liberal journals as *The Nation, New Republic,* and *Christian Century,* and ulti-

mately their writings reached a mass audience in the pages of the
New York *Times* and other Northern newspapers. The Negro
press, unable to pay travel expenses for its reporters, borrowed
heavily from the Communists for news and analyses of Scottsboro. Dozens of well-known authors in the Communist party orbit, including Sherwood Anderson, John Dos Passos, Lincoln
Steffens, Langston Hughes, and Theodore Dreiser, wrote and
lectured on the racial oppression epitomized by Scottsboro. Virtually every demonstration, rally, march, protest parade, and
mock trial got publicized. Thousands upon thousands of letters,
often following the format outlined by the party poured into the
White House, the Supreme Court, and the office of the Alabama
governor demanding the freedom of the Scottsboro Boys.[14]

During the period that the party orchestrated what it termed
the "development of revolutionary mass action outside of courts
and legislative bodies," its International Labor Defense (ILD)
pressed the legal campaign for a reversal of the Scottsboro decision. In March 1932 the Alabama Supreme Court upheld the convictions and death sentences for all but the youngest defendant.
The ILD appealed to the United States Supreme Court. A week
after Roosevelt's election, the High Court reversed the verdict.
With only the arch-conservatives Pierce Butler and James C. Mc-
Reynolds dissenting, the tribunal ruled that Alabama's failure to
provide truly adequate counsel denied the Scottsboro Boys due
process of law. The justices remanded the case to the state.[15]

The ILD returned to the courtroom and the CP went back to
the streets, staging demonstrations and interracial rallies. After
1933, however, the Communists did not battle alone. Two years
before the adoption of an official "united front" strategy, the
party tacitly began accepting the assistance of other leftist and
Negro movements. In return, the party muted its calls for a violent revolution against racist capitalism. Rather than a broadside
assault on the whole of white supremacist-capitalist-repressive
American society, the Communists, like the NAACP and other
civil rights organizations, discussed particular manifestations of

racial discrimination and segregation. This shift both reflected and accelerated the willingness of non-Communists to join with the party in demonstrations about Scottsboro. Now the doors of Negro churches and civil associations opened to Communist speakers. In 1934 the party called for a "solid front in the fight for the unconditional freedom of the Scottsboro Boys."[16]

The tactical switch of the Communist International the following year in asking for a united front to meet the "towering menace of fascism" facilitated the entrance of Communists into the mainstream of the civil rights movement. All sectarian tendencies in Communist propaganda were checked. The lawyers of the NAACP were welcomed by the ILD to join in the second appeal for the Scottsboro Boys before the Supreme Court in 1935. Wary of any alliance with the Stalinists, the NAACP hesitated and then gingerly agreed, circumscribing the area of cooperation. Once again the High Court overturned the Alabama convictions. Speaking for the narrow five-to-four majority (in which all four outstanding anti-New Dealers dissented), Chief Justice Charles Evans Hughes announced that the systematic exclusion of Negroes from Alabama juries constituted a clear denial of due process of law. Few blacks still cared about the intricacies of Marxian Socialism, but many now considered Communists useful to the black struggle. The decisions in the Norris and Patterson cases were the most progressive civil rights victories yet won before the Supreme Court. Black spokesmen credited their leftist allies with these achievements. A host of non-Communist organizations, including the ACLU, the Methodist Federation for Social Action, and the Socialist League for Industrial Democracy, labored with the Communists and the NAACP throughout the remainder of the decade in the Scottsboro Defense Committee to secure the release of all the defendants. Tension and disharmony pervaded the inner workings of the joint committee, but publicly a solid front was presented.[17]

In a similar manner, the Communist defense of Angelo Herndon aided both the cause of civil rights and that of new party membership. Through Herndon many whites were newly awakened to the problems of race. Likewise, among these new supporters as well as among those whites already concerned with civil rights issues, were a number of persons to whom the party turned in its never-ending search for new members. Herndon, arrested in Atlanta in 1932 for leading a biracial demonstration of the unemployed on the steps of the Fulton County Courthouse, served as the party's second most publicized case of black martyrdom when he was found guilty of incitement to insurrection under a statute originally enacted to prevent slave uprisings. The Communists took advantage of the episode. The overt racism of the trial judge, the use of an old slave law against a black radical in the depression, and the harsh sentence of eighteen to twenty years on a chain gang combined to provide the CP with another platform to propagandize against white supremacy in the South. During the following five years the Communists reached out to bring additional black, liberal, and labor organizations into the struggle for Herndon's freedom. Once again, the publicity generated by the party played down sectarianism as it emphasized the role of Communists in the civil rights movement. No other whites, wrote Benjamin Davis, Jr., Herndon's black attorney, more forcefully arrayed "the world of white supremacy and racial hatred against the forces of freedom and dignity." Davis, a graduate of Amherst College and Harvard Law School, and the son of Atlanta's most prominent black Republican, joined the party in January 1933 in the midst of the Herndon case. During the course of his association with the Communists in their involvement with Herndon, Davis "found the only rational and realistic path to the freedom which burns in the breast of every Negro. It required only a moment to join, but my whole lifetime as a Negro American prepared me for the moment."[18]

As with the Scottsboro trials, the Communists organized conferences, marches, rallies, and committees throughout the country to fight for the freedom of Herndon. Thousands of prominent white jurists, academicians, artists, and authors helped make the

case a matter of international concern. In a similar vein, Socialists, fellow-travellers, progressives, unionists, and liberals joined
together to issue proclamations, sign petitions, raise defense
funds, and speak at open meetings in Herndon's behalf. The
party certainly benefitted, as did the cause of civil rights. Americans unaccustomed to hearing discussions of Negro affairs were
encountering an increasing number of whites who addressed
themselves to that matter. Across the nation, observed Ben Davis,
"churches passed resolutions, ministers preached sermons; fraternal societies took a stand; young people and college students became active campaigners for the issues."[19]

The party published in 1934 Herndon's own appeal for justice,
You Cannot Kill the Working Class. A clever blend of autobiography and exhortation, it credited the Communists with being the
most effective opponents of white supremacy. Herndon, as did
the party that year, straddled both calls for "self-determination"
and violent revolution and proposals for a reformist coalition of
civil rights activists. Three years later his book *Let Me Live* emphasized just the latter. By 1937, the party line was solidly for a
united front against racial discrimination. Not a hint of separatism
or nationalism or even a suggestion of disdain for the "reactionary" NAACP intruded upon Herndon's demand for unity in the
quest for total integration. The exigencies of the Popular Front
against fascism subordinated all racial matters to the progressive
ideal of black-white unity.[20]

That notion gained additional force in 1937 when the Supreme
Court reversed Herndon's conviction. In May 1935 the Supreme
Court dismissed Herndon's appeal. Only the liberal jurists Benjamin Cardozo, Louis Brandeis, and Harlan Fiske Stone dissented. Following Roosevelt's proposal to pack the Court, however, Chief Justice Charles Evans Hughes and Owen Roberts
switched sides and agreed to hear the appeal, leaving the four
conservatives in the minority. On April 26, 1937, by a five-to-four
vote, the Supreme Court ruled that Herndon had been deprived
of the liberties guaranteed by the Fourteenth Amendment. Once

again the four arch-conservative opponents of the New Deal on
the High Court stood out as the opponents of the rights of struggling blacks. The liberal and Negro press once again heralded
the decision as a vindication of the strategy of the Popular Front.
The NUL, the NAACP, the Brotherhood of Sleeping Car Porters,
the ACLU, the League for Industrial Democracy, the Federal
Council of Churches, the Central Conference of American Rabbis, and numerous labor, social welfare, and religious organizations had joined with the Communist and Socialist parties to free
Herndon. Never before had civil rights groups been so much a
part of such a broad coalition. Fighting for the "immediate demands" of blacks was becoming the progressive thing to do.[21]

The Left also doggedly insisted that blacks be given a better
economic break during the depression. Every major leftist group
made special efforts to feature blacks in the various "Hunger
Marches" on Washington, state capitals, and city halls. The
Communist-led Unemployed Councils initiated mass demonstrations and rent strikes to protest the inadequacy of relief payments to blacks in Baltimore, Chicago, Cleveland, Detroit, Pittsburgh, and New York. The Unemployed Council in St. Louis
worked closely with the LSNR, persistently raising issues of
black oppression and racial discrimination and portraying themselves as anti-fascistic. In 1934 the two groups campaigned for a
"Bill of Rights for Negroes," a city ordinance that would ban segregation in public facilities, prohibit discrimination in hiring by
both public and private employers, and declare illegal any attempt to thwart blacks from renting apartments or homes. In
Ohio and New York the militant National Unemployed leagues
demanded special financial assistance for impoverished Afro-
Americans. Established by A. J. Muste's Progressive Labor Action, they too proclaimed the necessity for black and white workers to struggle jointly to build the new society.[22]

The Workers' Committees on Unemployment set up by the Socialist party in Chicago and New York proclaimed similar objectives. They organized demonstrations and picket lines to end

discrimination in relief and work-relief programs. In 1935 the
Socialist party transformed the Committees into the Workers' Alliance of America, claiming a membership of six hundred thousand. The following year, the Unemployed Councils and National Unemployed Leagues both merged with the Workers'
Alliance of America (WAA). For the rest of the decade, the
WAA assigned a high priority to wiping out racial discrimination
in the WPA by sponsoring interracial sit-down strikes in numerous relief bureaus and WPA offices.[23]

Leftists also joined blacks to prevent the eviction of Negro
families for failure to pay rent. "When eviction notices arrived,"
Drake and Cayton reported, "it was not unusual for a mother to
shout to the children, 'Run quick and find the Reds!' " Leaders of
the Unemployed Councils would rush to the houses to replace
the furniture put out on the sidewalk. Clashes with the police ensued. Inevitably, these led to protest rallies. The old Negro spiritual "I shall not, I shall not be moved" became the theme song of
the fight against evictions, and many a black community grew accustomed to white men and women orating on streetcorners, denouncing the "fire-traps" and "rent hogs" and urging blacks and
whites to unite and fight.[24]

One Communist attempt to prevent the eviction of a black
family in Chicago in 1931 precipitated a minor riot in which the
police shot three Afro-Americans. The party's Central Committee did not hesitate to take action. By nightfall, fifty thousand
leaflets had been readied for distribution throughout the Southside. The leaflets bore the slogan: "DEMAND DEATH PEN-
ALTY FOR THE MURDERERS OF THE WORKERS!" A series of demonstrations to protest the "Chicago Massacre" was
hastily arranged. "The barbarous murder of our three class comrades by the Chicago Bosses," the CP proclaimed, "must be
answered by the sternest pledge of revolutionary solidarity and
fighting strength; by the mobilization of large masses of Negro
and white workers who must take the streets in tremendous solidarity demonstrations." Nearly twenty thousand blacks filed past

the slain Negroes lying in state at the Odd Fellows' Hall. Above the coffins hung a huge picture of Lenin, flanked by paintings of blacks and whites laboring together. Overhead, a banner spelled out the message that had been reiterated through the summer: "NEGRO AND WHITE WORKERS, UNITE TOGETHER!" More than fifteen thousand Chicagoans crowded State Street for the funeral procession. Scores of Communists lined the march route with placards reading "They Died For Us! We Must Keep Fighting!" and "Fight Against Lynching—Equal Rights for Negroes!"[25]

"Here was something new: Negroes and whites *together* rioting against the forces of law and order," observed Drake and Cayton. "The Renters' Court immediately suspended all eviction proceedings for an indefinite period." Mayor Anton Cermak, hoping to avert further violence, ordered that increased attention be paid to the needs of black relief. During the following month Chicago Communists enrolled some five hundred new black members in the party. Ten times that number signed up in the Unemployed Councils. The party claimed several thousand new converts in Harlem and many more blacks rallied to the New York Unemployed Councils. However inflated or transitory such membership figures might have been, "the Reds," as Drake and Cayton and numerous non-Communist blacks observed, emerged as leaders in the civil rights movement. The fight against evictions, the demonstrations for adequate relief payments, and the campaign to free the Scottsboro Boys had convinced many that the Reds would fight, as Herndon put it, "for political, economic, and social equality for Negroes." Indeed, interracialism itself became associated with Communism in the early thirties.[26]

"The Communists appear to be the only party going our way," exclaimed Carl Murphy, publisher of the Baltimore *Afro-American,* "for which Allah be praised." P. B. Young of the Norfolk *Journal and Guide* wrote: "The Communists in America have commendably contended for and have practiced equality of all races, and in their many activities have accepted Negroes into their ranks in both high and lowly positions; more, they have dramatized the disadvantages of the Negro by walking in a body out of a jim-crow Pittsburgh hospital by aiding ejected tenement dwellers, and in industrial strikes directed by them fighting against the practice of excluding Negroes from labor unions." The NAACP in mid-1932 had solicited the Negro press for its views on Communism. This was the period of greatest conflict between the CP and the NAACP, and the latter must have been taken aback by the response of black editors. From the Philadelphia *Tribune* came a depiction of the Communist party as the "symbol of absolute equality." It credited them with courageously condemning the persecution of blacks and battling for the Scottsboro Boys. Franklin M. Davis of the Atlanta *World* commended the Communists for their insistence on social equality, open friendliness to blacks, and unprecedented use of "Mr." and "Mrs." when addressing Southern blacks. The editor of the Oklahoma *Black Dispatch,* a member of the NAACP Board of Directors like Murphy, applauded the party for denouncing "Jim Crow, segregation and anti-marriage laws, yes, everything which has hitherto separated the white and black here in America." "Since the abolitionists passed off the scene," said Murphy in summing up the consensus of the Negro press, no other white group "has openly advocated the economic, political, and social equality of black folks."[27]

Not all blacks agreed. Many had serious reservations. Some felt that Communists "used Negroes," and that "if they ever gain power they'll be just like the other crackers." Others regarded the Communist party's flaunted interracialism as "bait." "But Negroes are realists," wrote Drake and Cayton. "They take 'friends' and allies where they can find them."

> Most of them were attracted to the Communists primarily because the 'Reds' fought for Negroes *as* Negroes. Thousands of Negro preachers and doctors and lawyers, as well as quiet housewives, gave their money and verbal support to the struggle for freeing the Scottsboro Boys and for releasing Angelo Hern-

don. Hundreds, too, voted for Foster *and* Ford, Browder *and* Ford, for what other party since Reconstruction days had ever run a Negro for vice-president of the United States? And who had ever put Negroes in a position where they led white men as well as black? Every time a black Communist appeared on the platform, or his picture appeared in a newspaper, Negroes were proud; and no stories of 'atheistic Reds' or 'alien Communists' could nullify the fact that here were people who accepted Negroes as complete equals and asked other white men to do so.

The head of Baltimore's largest Negro church made the same point in an article in the Urban League's journal in 1933. That year, moreover, Mordecai W. Johnson, president of Howard University, told a meeting of church leaders: "I don't mind being called a Communist. The day will come when being called a Communist will be the highest honor that can be paid to any individual; that day is soon coming." Even the NAACP admitted in 1935 that due to some Communist actions "the whole Negro race is far ahead of where it would have been" without the party in the struggle for civil rights.[28]

Among the accolades bestowed on the Communists by Afro-Americans, none appeared more frequently than praise for the party's overt interracialism. The CP mandated that a higher proportion of blacks than their numbers in the party might warrant be placed in all executive committees and offices. Three times the Communists nominated James Ford for the vice-presidency. Ford, whose grandfather had been lynched by the KKK, had been a steel worker in Birmingham before the CP made him nationally known as a vice-presidential candidate and prominent as a black expert on history and political affairs. William L. Patterson, whose mother had been born into slavery, worked the dining cars of the Southern Pacific Railroad to save enough money to attend the law school of the University of California before joining the party and becoming the head of the ILD. Another Afro-American, Henry Winston, presided over the Young Communist League. The CP designated still other blacks as congressional candidates and district heads. Howard University was chosen as the campus to host the first national convention of the National Student League in December 1933. Melech Epstein, a party functionary in the thirties, later bitterly described the extremes to which "Negroes were coddled in the party . . . It became an unwritten rule that every committee must include a certain proportion of Negroes . . . More Negroes were sent to Party schools in Moscow and here. Harlem and the Southside in Chicago were 'concentration' points, with special headquarters. The South, where the party was practically nonexistent, was dotted with Negro organizers." The Communists particularly encouraged blacks to write for its publications and speak before its gatherings. They campaigned openly for the nullification of all state bans on racial intermarriages, as well as an end to segregation in major league baseball.[29]

To prove their sincerity on the racial issue, the Communists ostentatiously practiced "social equality." In 1931 party leaders in New York published a manifesto, "On the Struggle Against Chauvinism." The Stalinists insisted that the CP insure "the proper attraction of Negroes to all social affairs, dances, concerts, etc." All party functions were to be interracial. White female Communists were to fraternize with black males. "The greatest degree of fraternization," they concluded, "the closest association of the white with the Negro comrades in social life inside and outside of the Party is imperative." Most Communists obeyed the directive. In Chicago, for example, police often harassed interracial couples, assuming that the woman was either a prostitute or a Red. "Heaven spare the Party 'comrade' who at the mixed black and white Communist dances fails to dance with partners of the other race!" reported the ultra-conservative Elizabeth Dilling in her lurid account of how the Communist party roped Negroes into the class struggle.

> I have never attended a Communist Party mass meeting without observing the public petting of Negroes and whites. This is a deliberate and staged policy. At one meeting three burly

Negroes were pawing their white girl companion, a college-type blond wearing a squirrel coat. At the huge American League Against War and Fascism Congress in Chicago, a Negro in front of me sat with one arm around his girl companion; with his other hand he stroked her leg.

Such charges, in fact, became a staple of anti-Communist propaganda. The Special Committee on Un-American Activities chaired by Martin Dies viewed with alarm the numerous instances of "social equality" it uncovered, especially the fact that black men danced with white Communist women and that "communist girls have been sent among Negroes to practice 'social equality.' "[30]

Many black leaders could not help but be impressed. "The Communists are showing that it is possible for Negroes to sit side by side with white people without defiling them," proclaimed the Philadelphia *Tribune*, ". . . that Negro men and white women can socialize without scandal." But not all blacks agreed. Black women in the CP banded together to protest the excessive display of interracial intimacy. They considered the startling number of marriages between black men and white women within the party an insult to Negro womanhood. Party officials, black and white, denounced such expressions as "bourgeois nationalist deviations." They warned blacks in the party against "anti-white tendencies." The party removed Cyril Briggs and George Padmore, former members of the African Blood Brotherhood, from their editorship of the *Harlem Liberator* and *Negro Worker*, respectively, replacing both with blacks who unreservedly endorsed the integrationist thrust of Communism in the thirties.[31]

Some of the civil rights publicity garnered by the Communist party came from its staged trials against "white chauvinism." Party leaders ordered that it be a policy that no Communist display even the faintest trace of anti-Negro behavior or attitudes. According to Len De Caux, a party publicist and labor organizer, what followed "was as intense, at times as extreme, as any party campaign. White members went around in a tizzy. They had to check every figure of speech they used. . . . They had to reexamine all the conventional attitudes of white life." In the spring of 1931 in Harlem, over fifteen hundred attended the public trial of August Yokinen, an immigrant party member working as a janitor in the Finnish Workers Club. He was charged by the CP with treating blacks disrespectfully. The prosecuting attorney dutifully denounced all manifestations of white supremacy in American life. Richard B. Moore, who defended Yokinen, echoed the denunciations. He blamed racism on anti-union employers. "We must unite all workers, white and Negro, native and foreign born, to fight against the white chauvinist, fascist lynchers and terrorists," he declared. "Together," Moore added, "we must also combat the opportunistic Negro bourgois-nationalist misleaders . . . who are doing the dirty work of the bosses by attempting to stir up the Negro masses against the white workers." Yokinen pleaded guilty, admitting the errors of his ways. The "worker's jury" voted unanimously to expel him from the party and to give him an opportunity to win readmission by playing a special role in the black freedom struggle. The audience ratified the verdict. Yokinen accepted it gratefully.[32]

In Chicago a Communist who inadvertently slapped an Afro-American during an argument over the distribution of leaflets found himself tried before a jury of one hundred workers. He was suspended from the party for two months and required to prove himself by performing additional tasks in the battle for civil rights. Another white Communist was drummed out of the party for threatening two black members who had socialized with his daughter. Commenting on a similar case in Milwaukee, the Chicago *Defender* exclaimed: "How under such circumstances, can we go to war with the Communist party? Is there any other political, religious, or civic organization in the country that would go to such lengths to prove itself not unfriendly to us? . . . We may not agree with the entire program of the Communist party, but there is one item with which we do agree wholeheartedly and that is the zealousness with which it guards the rights of the Race." That opinion also stemmed from the interracial demonstrations staged by the party at restaurants, hotels, and beaches that excluded blacks, and from the ordinances against discrimination that sometimes resulted from these episodes of direct action.[33]

The association of Communism with zeal for civil rights seemed even greater after the promulgation of the new Soviet Constitution in 1936. Its widely heralded provisions for ethnic equality underscored the failures of the United States in this matter. Few Americans knew much about the actual internal affairs of the Soviet Union, but numerous books and articles, by both Communists and non-Communists contrasted the two nations' successes in solving their minority problems. The Soviet Union, wrote Drake and Cayton, "to thousands of Negroes, was the one 'white' nation that treated 'darker folks right.'" Long after he broke with the party, Richard Wright still remembered the powerful attraction of the Soviet Union's concern for ethnic diversity and justice.

> I had read with awe how the Communists had sent phonetic experts into the vast regions of Russia to listen to the stammering dialects of peoples oppressed for centuries by the Czars. I had made the first total emotional commitment of my life when I read how the phonetic experts had given these tongueless peoples a language, newspapers, institutions. I had read how these forgotten folks had been encouraged to keep their old cultures, to see in their ancient customs meanings and satisfactions as deep as those contained in supposedly superior ways of living. And I had exclaimed to myself how different this was from the way in which Negroes were sneered at in America.

Douglass Southall Freeman of the Richmond *News-Leader* stated:

> The Russian nation has for a generation shown what could be done to outlaw race prejudice in a country with many kinds of people. They did not wait for a people's mind to change. They made racial discrimination and persecution illegal. . . . The Russians have welcomed cultural *differences* and they have refused to treat them as *inferiorities*. No part of the Russian program has had greater success than their racial program. How about applying that to America?

After a trip to the colored Soviet republics of central Asia, Langston Hughes recalled "what the natives themselves told me: 'Before, there were no schools for Uzbek children—now there are. Before, women were bought and sold—now no more. Before, the land and water belonged to the beys—today they are ours, and we share the cotton." One did not have to be a sharecropper, or a Communist, to appreciate the difference.[34]

However much such impressions distorted the truth, they gained currency in the United States. It became an article of faith in the Popular Front that cultural pluralism could be attained, that racial prejudice could be ended. These did not remain just Communist or Negro ideas. Other leftist, labor, and student groups adopted them and made them a part of urban liberalism. A. J. Muste and his American Workers' party (AWP) reiterated all the Communist party shibboleths on race. They battled discrimination in industrial unions and the New Deal relief programs; they joined the defense campaigns for Herndon and the Scottsboro Boys; and they insisted on racial equality within their own operations and gave blacks a chance for leadership and self-expression found in few movements other than those of the Communists. The establishment of the Congress of Racial Equality (CORE) in 1942 would bring to fruition many of the precepts and practices of Muste and the AWP. In a similar manner, the DeLeonist Socialist Union Party, and its journal *The New Industrial Unionist,* served as a conduit of ideas initially associated with civil rights and Stalinist organizations. The DeLeonists popularized the view that the race problem was more than just a class problem. Reversing the dogma of the 1920s, their party declared that socialism in the United States would never be achieved until the victimization of blacks was ended.[35]

Also reversing the position it had maintained throughout the first third of the century, the Socialist party in the New Deal era attacked racism directly. Indications of a shift in policy came in 1929, when the party established the United Colored Socialists of America (UCSA). "This is the first real and substantial effort made by the American Socialist party to reach the members of my race," announced Frank Crosswaith, the head of the UCSA. Later that year Norman Thomas chose an NAACP officer as one of the national executive secretaries of the Socialist party, appointed a special black organizer for the South and convinced the Young Peoples Socialist League to adopt a resolution condemning racial discrimination in trade unions.[36]

Not until 1933, however, did the *American Socialist Quarterly,* the party's official journal, announce the new emphasis on black rights. Ernest Doerfler's "Socialism and the Negro Problem" directly criticized Debs for the view that the Socialists could make no special appeals to blacks. He insisted they could and urged a broad program of support for civil rights as the way to do it. So did Margaret I. Lamont, who went even further in denouncing the Socialist party's prior colorblindness and in calling upon all Socialists to act against racial oppression. She outlined an ambitious agenda for educating white workers to overcome their racism and for fighting to secure Afro-American political and social rights. "Socialists must take an active and militant place in the campaign against lynching," Lamont proclaimed, "against Jim-Crowing in its innumerable forms, against the flagrant discrimination in education, in the giving of relief, and in the courts, and against depriving Negroes of the vote."[37]

They did. During a meeting of the Socialist-sponsored Continental Congress of Workers and Farmers in Washington in 1933, the SP began to gain press coverage for their new policy. Hundreds of Socialist delegates, led by Norman Thomas, marched in a body to the Cairo Hotel to demand cancellation of their reservations because the management would not permit a black to register. As Thomas had expected, the incident aroused a storm of publicity in the Southern-minded capital. No other hotel would accommodate the interracial assemblage. Thomas and his followers then moved to a tourist camp operated by the War Department. It too discriminated against Afro-Americans. "How can we either protest Hitlerism with good grace or hope to escape similar

ills in America," Thomas exploded with rage at a press conference, "when we chronically carry out a more thoroughgoing discrimination against our colored fellow citizens than he has yet
imposed upon the Jews." In a letter to the *New Republic,* Thomas
justified the Socialist party's response to Washington mores:
"Speaking for myself and for the Socialist party, we believe that
all this discrimination—economic, political and social—is not only
unjust in itself, but fraught with menace to the country." Thomas
called on all white workers to put immediate pressure on the
government to abolish discrimination against Negroes.[38]

In the years that followed, the Socialists tried to do just that.
Norman Thomas appeared regularly at Negro conferences, lambasted FDR for not doing enough to aid Afro-Americans, demanded the enactment of federal anti-lynching and anti-poll tax
legislation, took up the cudgel for black sharecroppers and tenants, elevated Frank Crosswaith and A. Philip Randolph to major
positions within the SP, and lent his name to a host of *ad hoc*
committees for racial justice. The most prominent white Socialists, including Franz Boas, John Dewey, Reinhold Niebuhr, and
Goodwin Watson, identified their advocacy of civil rights with
their socialistic beliefs. The annual conventions of the Socialist
party methodically adopted resolutions against all forms of discrimination and segregation. The party called often and loudly
for federal civil rights laws. Such Socialist satellites as the League
for Industrial Democracy and the Student League for Industrial
Democracy added their voices to the command by the Popular
Front for racial equality in the labor and youth movements. The
heavily Socialist Fellowship of Reconciliation, which would also
play a major role in the establishment of CORE, took the lead in
injecting concern for racial justice into the social gospel. Moreover, Socialists active in the Brookwood Labor College and Highlander Folk School, training centers for labor leaders in the
South, integrated those institutions and included civil rights materials in the curriculum taught young union organizers. And like
the CP and AWP, the Socialists attracted extensive publicity by

their vocal insistence on ending Jim Crow in all areas of American life and by their practice of interracialism in all party activities.[39]

No individual better illustrated the connection between civil rights and the Popular Front than Paul Robeson. A tall, handsome black actor and singer, Robeson advocated Negro rights as militantly as anyone in the thirties. Strongly influenced by the Communist views of his wife, the former all-American football star, Phi Beta Kappa, and valedictorian of his class at Rutgers University, left for the Soviet Union in mid-decade. He returned in 1939, lavishing praise on the Soviet Union for its absence of white racism. "In Russia, I felt for the first time like a full human being —no color prejudice like in Mississippi, no color prejudice like in Washington." Shocking many, he announced that he would send his son there for his education. Robeson had nothing but good things to say about the Communists, and millions detested him for it. The Left, on the other hand, idolized him. In Spain he sang for the Loyalist troops; in the United States he worked on behalf of Jewish refugees from Nazism. Robeson depicted his ballads as songs for both Negro freedom and for "those seeking freedom from the dungeons of fascism in Europe today." He insisted that "the struggle for Negro rights was an inseparable part of the anti-fascist struggle." Hardly a leftist or racial cause went unendorsed by the black entertainer, a fact much ballyhooed by the Negro press. Most significant, however, was that white leftist publications made even more of it, just as they—perhaps more than blacks—popularized Robeson's version of "Ballad of Americans," an avowedly integrationist song that contemporaries connected with the civil rights movement.[40]

The Left further underscored its interracialism by changing the image of civil rights as an issue of interest primarily to Afro-Americans. Such white Communists as James S. Allen, Herbert Aptheker, and Philip S. Foner came to be the main representatives of the party in its quest for black rights, as well as the major interpreters of Negro history and culture, in the late thirties. The

CP even chose a white to head its Harlem branch. White Trotsky-
ites played leading roles in the development of the interracial
sharecropper movement and in some labor campaigns for civil
rights legislation. Where they had political power, as in the CIO
Council of Minneapolis and the Michigan Democratic Federation, they associated themselves with all issues concerning the
rights of blacks. Socialists followed Norman Thomas in asserting
that the "war against fascism" must begin "in our country" against
the evils of Jim Crow. Jewish Socialists, in particular, in the International Ladies Garment Workers Union (ILGWU), the American Labor party, and in American intellectual affairs became
commonplace in civil rights organizations and as financial and
political supporters of the movement. A galaxy of first- and second-generation immigrants assumed leadership positions in the
struggle for racial equality. At meetings such as the conference
in 1937 of the American League Against War and Fascism in
Pittsburgh, they quite typically took time from their proceedings
to picket places of public accommodation that refused service to
blacks.[41]

By the end of the decade no civil rights leader or group con-
sidered it anything but normal that a Socialist organization, the
Workers Defense League, would want to sponsor a journalistic
series on racism in the South; or that a young white Communist,
Richard Rovere, and a liberal white reporter with the Scripps-
Howard chain, Thomas Stokes, would want the assignment; or
that those who planned and financed the project would include
representatives of the *Catholic Worker,* the American Jewish
Committee, the Federal Council of Churches, the Workmen's
Circle, the ILGWU, the Textile Workers Union of America, and
the ACLU, as well as leaders of the NAACP and the National
Negro Congress; or that the articles would first be published in
The Nation and the *Jewish Daily Forward;* or even that the strategy meetings for the project would be held in Norman Thomas's
apartment.[42]

The Workers Defense League, established by Socialists in 1936 as a counterpart to the ILD, fought for anti-poll tax and anti-lynching legislation, pushed an "End Peonage" campaign, and handled legal matters for the Southern Tenant Farmers Union (STFU). Beginning that year, it also sponsored an annual National Sharecroppers Week to raise funds for the STFU and to direct attention to the plight of black agricultural workers. Prominent Broadway and Hollywood figures, including Tallullah Bankhead, John Barrymore, John Garfield, Barry Fitzgerald, Olsen and Johnson, and Paul Muni, cooperated in publicizing the week. A Writers Committee headed by John Chamberlain and Margaret Marshall sponsored manuscript sales of the contributed works of such authors as Van Wyck Brooks, Theodore Dreiser, and John Steinbeck. A Labor Committee, chaired by David Dubinsky and A. Philip Randolph, conducted parallel drives among trade unionists. In 1940 Mayor Fiorello LaGuardia directed the program of the New York Committee for National Sharecroppers Week, which featured Eleanor Roosevelt as its keynote speaker.[43]

Similarly, Communist and Socialist student groups made civil rights one of their top priorities on college campuses. The American Student Union, an offspring of the Socialist Student League for Industrial Democracy and the Communist National Student League, regularly proselytized for black rights in its publications. Its conventions approved resolutions on all racial issues then current. Such Southern chapters as Bennet College, Duke University, and the North Carolina Women's College boycotted theaters Jim-Crowing blacks. Its main journal, the *Student Advocate,* demanded an end to all segregationist and Jim Crow practices in college athletics, ROTC units, military academies, and Southern state universities. In 1937 it chose as the best college editorial of the year a call for federal anti-lynching legislation by the student paper of Millsaps College in Mississippi. The *Student Advocate* also championed courses in Negro history and culture, insisted on the hiring of black college instructors, and often reprinted editorials on civil rights, such as the one from the *Daily Northwestern* summoning its students "to take up the defense of Negro rights. The status of the Negro at Northwestern makes ridiculous our claim to glory as a *liberal* institution. The fight for Negro rights is the fight for every person who believes in democracy and freedom."[44]

In the eight years following its founding in 1934, the American Youth Congress (AYC) also made civil rights a part of the antifascist struggle. At its first national conference, the AYC adopted a Declaration of Rights of American Youth which fully placed it on the side of minority rights. The Congress passed scores of resolutions supporting freedom for the Scottsboro Boys, an end to Jim Crow in education, the enfranchisement of Southern blacks, and the study of Negro history. Many of its leaders, such as Harriet Pickens, the daughter of an NAACP official, and Dorothy Haight of the Christian Youth Council, were particularly vocal in equating racism with Hitlerism. The Congress, moreover, associated its work with that of the Southern Negro Youth Congress (SNYC). It provided the SNYC with publicity and financial support; officials of the two organizations addressed the conventions of the other. And in virtually all its forays on the racial front, the AYC received the public backing of Aubrey Williams and Eleanor Roosevelt.[45]

The Popular Front, which terminated with the signing of the Hitler-Stalin pact in the summer of 1939, hardly brought an end to racial discrimination. Nor did it produce a firm alliance between established race betterment groups and Communist-led organizations. Cooperation between the two remained episodic and fraught with suspicions. But the Popular Front did reiterate the Left's commitment to political and social equality for blacks, to interracial unity, and to opposition to Jim Crow in all its manifestations. It spoke also to scores of peace, church, labor, and student associations and to hundreds of thousands of whites attracted to the Popular Front because of its aversion to fascism and its advocacy of economic justice. Because of that, many whites began to espouse ideals of racial equality and justice and to endorse the campaigns for anti-lynching and anti-poll tax legislation. Some would cease supporting civil rights when the Communists considered it convenient to deemphasize their commitment during the Second World War. Others developed a lifetime adherence to the cause. In the 1930s these new converts would have their greatest impact on the labor movement.[46]

7

Organized Labor and Civil Rights

The egalitarian policies of some of the labor organizations forged another link between urban liberals and the black struggle. Racial discrimination persisted in many unions. Some excluded blacks completely; most maintained segregated locals in the South. Almost all kept blacks out of top policy-making positions. Yet by the end of the thirties a former major antagonist had become an ally of the civil rights movement. In part this occurred because of the activity of determined leftist cadres in many of the organizing drives. It was also due to the conflict between craft and industrial unions and the novelty of labor leaders having to vie for black support. Primarily, however, it happened because the Congress of Industrial Organizations required the backing of Afro-Americans to succeed. Consequently, by 1941 numerous CIO unions, as well as some American Federation of Labor unions, had joined the ranks of those battling Jim Crow. By their advocacy of legislative reform, their rhetoric for racial justice, their financial support of black protest groups, and their practical demonstrations that interracialism could work, their quest for racial equality attained new vigor.

None of this seemed likely at the beginning of the depression.

With few exceptions, labor unions adhered to their anti-black traditions. The craft unions justified their discrimination by insisting that they had to follow the prevailing racial attitudes of the day, by arguing the need to restrict membership to safeguard their job monopolies, and by emphasizing the role of black workers as strikebreakers. Although blacks never constituted a majority of the scabs in any industry, their crossing of picket lines helped defeat organizing drives by auto, coal, railroad, slaughterhouse, steel, and textile workers. In 1929 angry unionists blamed blacks for breaking the Boston longshoreman strike. The hostility engendered fanned the racial antipathy of Afro-American spokesmen and white workers alike. The hierarchy of the AFL adamantly refused even to meet with the NAACP or the Urban League to discuss discrimination in the union movement.[1]

Most black leaders responded in kind, bristling with anti-union denunciations. Few blacks had a stake in the labor movement. Although about 8 percent of all non-agricultural workers, Negroes comprised only 1 percent of union membership. Nearly half the fifty thousand black unionists, moreover, belonged to one segregated union, the Brotherhood of Sleeping Car Porters. The BSCP remained unrecognized by the Pullman Company and by the federal government's Mediation Board. It could gain entry into the AFL only as a federated affiliate under the jurisdiction of its Executive Council. Not surprisingly, Afro-American spokesmen defended strike-breaking on the bases of black necessity and lily-white unionism. Kelly Miller's "logic aligns the Negro with labor but good sense arrays him with capital" was widely quoted, as was the unanimous resolution adopted by fifty-two black editors at a meeting of the National Negro Press Association in 1924 "condemning all forms of Unionism and economic Radicalism." They chose "to stand 'squarely' behind capital." Booker T. Washington's distrust of unions and reliance upon the goodwill of the white upper class still reigned.[2]

The first breach in this wall of mutual antagonism came with the efforts of leftists to organize biracial unions in the South. Directly challenging the AFL's United Textile Workers, which refused to enroll black mill workers, the Communist National Textile Workers preached and practiced racial equality. So did the Sharecropper Union established by the Communist party in Alabama and the United Citrus Workers organized by the party in Florida. None of these unions succeeded in enlisting the support of many workers or in acting as an effective bargaining agent for their members. But they did receive publicity in the Negro and radical presses for their interracialism.[3]

More prominently, the Southern Tenant Farmers Union (STFU), founded in 1934, focused national attention on the question of racial unity within the labor movement. With the encouragement of Norman Thomas, a small interracial group of Socialists and tenant farmers met by the dim light of kerosene lamps in a rickety old schoolhouse near Tyronza, Arkansas, to form their union. Immediately, a white farmer raised the question on everyone's mind: "Are we going to have two unions, one for whites and one for colored?" The men debated the relative advantage of both possibilities. Then an elderly black man rose to speak. "It won't do no good for us to divide because there's where the trouble had been all the time," he said slowly. Reminding them of the failures of segregated farmers' unions in the region, the old man concluded: "The same chain that holds you holds my people too. If we're chained together on the outside we ought to stay chained together in the union." The others agreed. They resolved that the STFU would welcome black and white croppers, tenants, and day laborers.[4]

From the outset, the STFU crusaded for racial as well as economic justice. Funded by the Socialists and a number of civil rights organizations, it functioned primarily as an organ of protest. Collective bargaining came second. This reflected the views of the STFU leadership. H. L. Mitchell, an associate of Norman Thomas, presided over the union. From the time he had witnessed his first lynching as a boy in Tennessee, Mitchell thirsted for answers to the racial question. Howard Kester and Claude

Williams, two white preachers who had learned their racial gospel from Dr. Alva Wilmot Taylor at Vanderbilt University, assisted Mitchell. Before joining the STFU, Kester had served as a member of the Socialist party's executive council, as an investigator of lynchings for the NAACP, as a founder of the Fellowship of Reconciliation's student interracial program, and as a close ally of Reinhold Niebuhr in the Committee on Economic and Racial Justice. Williams also had journeyed far toward racial egalitarianism before entering the STFU. His reputation as a Communist battler for Negro rights within the Federal Council of Churches and the Methodist Federation for Social Service made him a hero to many Christian Socialists from the Commonwealth College in Arkansas to the Union Theological Seminary in New York.[5]

Mitchell, Kester, and Williams gave the STFU immediate access to liberal journalists and to a score of leftist, labor, and religious groups concerned with Negro rights. After 1936 Gardner "Pat" Jackson lent his aid. A wealthy liberal and skilled propagandist, Gardner first gained fame as a key organizer of the Sacco and Vanzetti defense committee. He brought to the STFU additional sources of publicity, financing, and alliances. Consequently, throughout the second half of the thirties, such magazines as the *New Republic, The Nation, New Masses, Opportunity, The Crisis, Common Sense, Commonweal, Survey Graphic, Social Forces*, as well as *Time*, the Scripps-Howard newspaper chain, and the New York *Times*, focused on the interracialism of the STFU. Some articles dwelled on the election of blacks to union offices. Others editorialized on the necessity of surmounting race prejudice in order to build a united labor front or predicted that black and white laborers would join together to quell the racial bourbons. Many emphasized the theme: "Hitler stalks the cotton fields of the South." The violence of plantation owners against croppers became a staple in the literature of the Popular Front. The STFU played it to the hilt. "As a means of bringing home to the country the situation," Mitchell suggested, "we ought to station the men who have been shot, beaten, and driven from their homes in front of Henry Wallace's office with signs or banners telling who was responsible for these acts of violence." His own articles stressed the slogan: "Hitler over the plantations." Such publicity and tactics did little to unionize the sharecroppers or to stop the bickering between Stalinists and Socialists, which kept the STFU divided and weak. More a paper organization than a real union, with greater support in New York than in the South, the STFU did nonetheless succeed in making some influential Americans conscious of Karl Marx's dictum: "Labor in the white skin cannot be free as long as labor in the black is branded."[6]

However much these radical ventures in the rural South accustomed liberal and Negro readers to the idea of interracial unionism, not until A. Philip Randolph won his battle against the Pullman Company would the AFL even begin to consider the problem of racial discrimination in its ranks. A magnificent orator, Randolph radiated idealism. He alternately pleaded, thundered, cajoled, and threatened to get the AFL moving down the road of racial egalitarianism. Jacob Potofsky of the Amalgamated Clothing Workers remembered him as "a voice in the wilderness." To John Brophy of the United Mine Workers, he was "a thorn in the side of prejudice and discrimination. . . . He emphasized the ethical as well as what was practical for the trade union." Almost singlehandedly, Randolph led the way.[7]

Born in 1889 in Crescent City, Florida, Asa Philip Randolph grew up in the warm yet moralistic household of an African Methodist Episcopal clergyman. Asa "followed the drinking gourd" north to New York City to become an actor. He enrolled in City College and became a Socialist. In 1917 Randolph and Chandler Owen began editing *The Messenger*, "The only radical Negro magazine in America," according to its subtitle. After the war he taught at the Rand School of Social Science, perennially ran as a Socialist candidate for state and local offices, and changed *The Messenger*'s subtitle to "A Journal of Scientific

Radicalism." It hardly mattered. Few blacks read *The Messenger* or stopped to listen to Randolph orating on a soapbox about the need for a socialist alliance of Negro and white workers. He was a leader without followers. Much of his energy went into opposing Marcus Garvey. Randolph disdained all forms of black nationalism and separatism. He insisted on "as much contact and intercourse—social, economic, and political—as is possible between the races." Until 1925 few took note.[8]

That year, a small group of Pullman porters searching for a spokesman not dependent on the Pullman Company for his wages asked Randolph to organize a union for them. He switched the masthead of *The Messenger* to read "The official organ of the Brotherhood of Sleeping Car Porters," and launched a decade-long effort to unionize the black porters against the opposition of their employer and most of the Negro press and leadership. He made the battles for unionization and for civil rights one and the same. "The principle of social equality," Randolph told his audiences, "is the only sure guarantee of social progress." To stir porters to join the Brotherhood of Sleeping Car Porters (BSCP), he appealed to their desire for full citizenship rights. The right to unionize merged with the rights of blacks to enjoy equality of opportunity. "When I heard Randolph speak, it was a light," remembered E. D. Nixon. A Pullman porter who would later head the NAACP branch in Montgomery, Nixon played the key role in initiating the bus boycott in that city in 1955. "Most eloquent man I ever heard," he went on about Randolph. "He done more to bring me in the fight for civil rights than anybody."[9]

By the end of the 1920s blacks considered the Brotherhood another organization promoting the cause of racial equality, but Randolph could not gain union recognition for the BSCP, and the Pullman Company ignored it. The Mediation Board established by the 1926 Railway Labor Act would not compel the employer to negotiate. The Great Depression took its toll. By 1932 hard times had decimated the powerless union. Branches closed. *The Messenger* folded. Sterling Spero and Abram Harris concluded their 1930 study, *The Black Worker*, with a respectful obituary for the BSCP: "The great pity of the virtual collapse of the porter's union lies . . . in its effect upon Negro labor generally. The hope that this movement would become the center and rallying point of Negro labor as a whole is now dead."[10]

"And then Roosevelt came along," recalled an associate of Randolph's, "started the New Deal, and they started passing laws." Section 7a of the National Industrial Recovery Act guaranteed the right of employees "to organize and bargain collectively through representatives of their own choosing." Described by John L. Lewis as the emancipation proclamation of the union movement and by William Green as labor's Magna Carta, this same clause appeared verbatim in the 1933 Emergency Railroad Transportation Act. It stimulated an upsurge in union organizing. The following year, Congress amended the transportation act to define the term "carrier" specifically to include sleeping car companies. The Brotherhood was jubilant. Porters rushed to join the BSCP. In mid-1935 a reconstituted Board of Mediation supervised a secret ballot to certify the BSCP as "the duly authorized representative" of the sleeping car porters. Acknowledging the critical role of the New Deal in his victory, Randolph wrote to Walter White: "This is the first time that Negro workers have had the opportunity to vote as a national group in an election, under federal supervision. . . . It is an extraordinary occasion." The election, he summed up, "will mark an historic point in the efforts of the Negro workers in the trade union movement."[11]

Future triumphs, however, came slowly and painfully. The AFL procrastinated. At its 1934 convention, the resolutions committee disallowed the motion proposed by Randolph to expel "any union maintaining the color bar." "The A. F. of L. cannot interfere with the autonomy of National and International Unions," it replied summarily. As a sop, the AFL resolved to establish a Committee on Problems of Negro Labor "to investigate the conditions of the colored workers of this country and report to the next convention." The committee met in Washington in

July 1935. Randolph and representatives of the NAACP, the NUL, and the Joint Committee on National Recovery testified for two days on the discriminatory practices of the AFL. They urged the committee to hold regional meetings to gather additional evidence. Green vetoed the idea. In fact, the AFL head wanted the committee to cease operating altogether. He had his hands full with those who clamored for the Federation to organize industrial unions; he wanted no part of another potentially divisive issue.[12]

Against Green's wishes, the committee issued a courageous report along with its recommendations. John Brophy, espousing the egalitarian policies of the United Mine Workers and the deep-seated concern for racial justice inculcated by his father, convinced the rest of the committee to propose "a full and free opportunity to discuss frankly the cause of differences and discriminatory practices within the unions against colored workers, with the object in view of finding solutions that lessen friction and produce more goodwill among the races." Accordingly, the committee called for: 1) all unions now discriminating against Negroes to change their rules and practices in conformity with the "oft-repeated declaration of the A. F. of L. conventions on equality of all races within the trade union movement"; 2) no future charters to be issued to unions excluding blacks; 3) a Federation campaign "to get the white worker to see more completely the weakness of division and the necessity of unity between white and black workers to the end that all workers may be organized." The NAACP could hardly believe it. The report, it announced, amounted to "an evolutionary policy of ending all racial discrimination" in the AFL.[13]

But William Green and his allies would not give up easily. At the historic 1935 convention, which saw the issue of industrial unionism erupt into a bitter debate climaxed by the fight between John L. Lewis of the United Mine Workers and "Big Bill" Hutcheson of the Carpenters Union, few delegates paid much attention to the racial problem. President Green refused to submit

Brophy's report. Contrary to the rules of the AFL, Green turned the report over to the Federation's executive council. The council dumped Brophy's report unceremoniously and substituted a proposal drawn up by the head of the racially exclusionist Railway Clerks that advocated that the AFL take no action. Green waited until late in the evening of the final session of the hectic convention to introduce the executive council's resolution.

Randolph leaped to his feet to object. He demanded that the AFL act on the Brophy report. Green demurred: "I believe we ought to make provisions for the admission of [blacks]," he announced, but "that is neither here nor there." The only issue, Green continued, is whether or not unions are autonomous. "Can we suspend the charter of the international union because it does not provide for the admission of colored members? Can we do that? Would you be willing to order that to be done? Are you ready to do that? There is the issue." In vain, Randolph regained the floor. He insisted that the "American Federation will not be able to hold its head up and face the world so long as it permits any section of workers in America to be discriminated against because they happen to be black." Few listened. The harried, tired delegates, anxious to adjourn, hastily approved the Green substitute.[14]

The racial issue had at least come out in the open within the AFL. It would remain there for the next six years. Green began to act less and less high-handedly with the proponents of racial change. He had little choice. Civil rights groups picketed AFL conventions. Negro spokesmen denounced the Federation. He had to meet the challenge of John L. Lewis' Committee for Industrial Organization, busily competing for black support and membership. And Randolph would not quit. The AFL's full acceptance of the BSCP as an internationally chartered union in 1936 augmented Randolph's power and prestige.[15]

Randolph made the most of it. He joined with civil rights groups in their picketing of subsequent conventions. He aided the NAACP and the National Negro Congress in their attacks on the AFL. He organized the Negro Labor Committee to publicize the need for racial equality within the labor movement. Randolph annually introduced resolutions at AFL conventions calling upon the Federation to pursue a vigorous program of bringing blacks into the trade union movement, demanding that the AFL expel unions guilty of excluding black members.

"Autonomy is not something absolute," Randolph answered back to the usual Federation response. "The white and black workers in the South cannot be organized separately as the fingers on my hand," he told the Tampa convention in 1936. "They must be organized altogether, as the fingers on my hand when they are doubled up in the form of a fist. . . . If they are organized separately they will not understand each other, and if they do not understand each other they will fight each other, and if they fight each other they will hate each other, and the employing class will profit from that condition." To back up his rhetoric, the BSCP staged jurisdictional raids on other railway craft unions, announcing that they would cease if the other brotherhoods reformed their racial practices. Randolph also brandished the threat that black workers would go Communist or join the CIO in order to force Federation officials to act against racism.[16]

Randolph's activities got some results. Green gradually began urging AFL affiliates to end their color bans. About half of those with exclusionist clauses deleted them from their constitutions. But widespread informal prohibitions remained in many craft unions. They ignored black applicants, restricted membership to relatives, rigged examinations so that blacks would fail them, and refused to admit Afro-Americans into their apprenticeship programs. Covert discrimination replaced formal exclusion. Randolph succeeded, however, in getting Green to support the main items of the civil rights agenda.[17]

The AFL president took to the stump to speak out for the freedom of Angelo Herndon and the Scottsboro Boys and to campaign for anti-lynching and anti-poll tax legislation. Nor was Green alone in "getting religion," as Randolph chortled. Individual unions such as the Hotel and Restaurant Employees' International Alliance and the Bartenders' International League of America echoed the BSCP's condemnation of Jim Crow in the AFL. The Federation itself, at its annual convention in 1938, 1939, 1940, and 1941, endorsed policy statements authored by Randolph calling "upon the fair state of Alabama, in the name of justice and humanity and fair-play" to free the Scottsboro Boys, opposing the white primary and poll tax, supporting federal anti-lynching legislation, and demanding that the government safeguard the equal rights of blacks in the military services and in any federal act to aid education.[18]

This shift by the AFL, however, proved to be only a ripple compared with the wave in race relations created by the Committee for Industrial Organization. Renamed the Congress of Industrial Organizations in 1938, the CIO's racial liberalism stemmed in part from the prior experience of many of its early leaders with organizing blacks. Negro strikebreakers in 1927 had doomed the UMW's attempt to unionize Southern coal mines. To prevent a reoccurrence, the United Mine Workers' campaign in 1933–34 had made an unprecedented effort to gain the backing of Negro leaders, to employ black organizers, to elect Afro-Americans to union offices, and to demand equal pay for equal work for everyone regardless of race. The success of this program in winning black miners over to the UMW led John L. Lewis and his associates to insist on following "the U.M.W. Formula" in their attempts to organize the meat packing, tobacco, and iron and steel workers. David Dubinsky, who aided Lewis in founding the CIO, had also successfully promoted an egalitarian racial policy in organizing black workers in the International Ladies Garment Workers Union in 1933–34. In addition, the leadership of the Amalgamated Clothing Workers and the International Mine, Mill, and Smelter Workers, which also withdrew from the AFL with Lewis, had followed the same pattern in unionizing blacks previously considered "unorganizable."[19]

These unionists brought to the CIO an existing reputation for fairness to blacks. At the ILGWU convention in Chicago in 1934, Dubinsky ordered the whole assemblage to move to another hotel when he learned that black delegates had been discriminated against. A motorcade of trucks and taxis dramatically transported all the delegates to a new meeting place. The major traffic jam in downtown Chicago that ensued caused Dubinsky's gesture to be reported in newspapers across the country. The ILGWU "practices what it preaches concerning civic equality of all people," Dubinsky told a cheering convention, "and will continue to help in that fight against race discrimination outside and inside the labor movement, until it is won."[20]

John L. Lewis had gained an even more positive reputation among black leaders. His insistence on organizing Afro-American miners on an equal basis with whites, his early endorsement of civil rights legislation, and his open support for "Phil" Randolph and the BSCP won him the plaudits of most black spokesmen. The Negro press wrote of him as the most progressive white labor official on racial issues. Four days after Lewis resigned as AFL vice-president in 1935, Walter White congratulated him on his stand for industrial unionism and affirmed that "Negro workers feel confident that the new movement will be guided by the same policy of freedom from racial discrimination which has characterized the United Mine Workers under your leadership."[21]

The racial progressivism of the CIO stemmed also from the humanitarianism and radicalism of many of its organizers. Thousands of young labor intellectuals, Communists, Socialists, idealists, and social gospel ministers flocked to the CIO after 1935. To further her commitment to racial justice in the South, Lucy Randolph Mason signed aboard as a publicist. Myles Horton, the founder and director of the Highlander Folk School, who believed that the CIO "would be a democratic, radical, social movement," headed the first Textile Workers Organizing Committee. "I didn't talk about integration," said Horton, "we just did it." The Reuther brothers, who had organized their first picket lines to protest racial discrimination at Detroit's City College and to fight a ban on blacks at a local swimming pool, rushed to join the movement to unionize auto workers. Grover Hathaway, repulsed by the Jim-Crowing of Negroes in the South, distinguished himself for his racial fairness as an organizer for the Steel Workers Organizing Committee and the Packinghouse Workers Organizing Committee. Wyndham Mortimer and John Santo, who joined the Communist party because of the compassion they felt for the disadvantaged and their belief that the Soviet Union had solved the problem of racial persecution, helped organize auto and transportation workers for the CIO. Philip Murray, the number two man behind Lewis, brought to the union movement a concern for civil rights rooted in the religious teachings of his faith. Such unionists brought to the CIO a dedication to racial equality rarely present in the AFL.[22]

No group within the CIO initially crusaded for racial justice more than the Communists. Organizers such as John Santo, in the New York subways; Julius Emspak, in the electrical industry; Ralph Shaw, in the St. Louis steel industry; and Wyndham Mortimer, in the auto industry went further than most labor leaders in articulating their racial beliefs. So did such editors as Len De-Caux of the *CIO News* and Henry Kraus of the *United Auto Worker*. The Communist-dominated unions joining the CIO—Harry Bridges' Marine Workers Industrial Union (MWIU); the United Office and Professional Workers Union, led by Lewis Merrill; Mervyn Rathborne's radio telegraphists; the fur workers, led by Ben Gold; and "Red" Mike Quill's Transport Workers Union—consistently pushed progressive resolutions on civil rights matters at CIO conventions. They also did the most to publicize the black struggle in their union newspapers and workers' education programs.[23]

Communist party policy sometimes of necessity became union policy. Negro scabbing had broken a west coast maritime strike in 1925. After Harry Bridges instituted an aggressive non-discriminatory policy in all union affairs, however, no blacks passed through the MWIU pickets in 1936. Bridges understood that be-

cause of the sizable number of Negro maritime workers an egali-
tarian policy was necessary if his union was to succeed. On the
other hand, the minimal number of black transportation laborers
in New York City left the almost all-Irish Catholic Transport
Workers Union (TWU) free to disregard the race issue if it
chose. It did not. Under the leadership of Quill and Santo the
TWU drove home the analogy of "the struggle of the oppressed
Negro workingmen" with the "Irish workers under the yoke of
British imperialism." "Scratch a Racist and You Will Find a
Labor-Hater Under the Skin," proclaimed the *Transportation
Bulletin.* Besides vigorously siding with Adam Clayton Powell's
People's Committee demonstrations that blacks be hired as bus
drivers for the first time, the TWU also resolved in favor of every
current civil rights proposal in the Popular Front. So did Ben
Gold's virtually all-Jewish fur workers union.[24]

The Communists also did the most in the thirties to get blacks
into union leadership positions. Such black Communists as Ferdinand Smith of the National Maritime Union, Jesse Reese of the
Steel Workers Organizing Committee, Revel Cayton of the long-
shoremen's union, and Henry Johnson of the packinghouse workers union devoted much of their efforts to increasing the number
of black officers, delegates to conventions, and members of bargaining or grievance committees in all CIO unions. They largely
succeeded. In addition, their prodding helped to convince whites
in the CIO to contribute financially to the NNC, the NAACP, the
Southern Negro Youth Congress, and the SCHW. This forged an
important link in the organized labor-civil rights movement alliance.[25]

However much the idealism and radicalism of certain leaders
helped, the CIO adopted progressive policies and practices primarily because industrial unionism could not otherwise succeed.
The congress trod the path of necessity. The large numbers of
black workers in the mass production industries made unionization imperative. Outside the unions they constituted a dangerous
strikebreaking—perhaps fatal—union-busting force. Thus, wher-

ever blacks appeared essential to the successful unionization of an industry, the CIO's liberalism on civil rights stood out.

No clearer case of this existed than in the steel industry. Here blacks constituted roughly 20 percent of all laborers. According to widespread belief, black scabs had been responsible for crushing the Homestead strike of 1892 and the steel strike of 1919. Immediately after establishing the Steel Workers Organizing Committee (SWOC) in 1936, Murray urged a special campaign to gain the loyalty of Negroes. He declared SWOC's "policy to be one of absolute racial equality in Union membership." Money and emissaries were sent to the NAACP, the NNC, and the Workers Councils of the Urban League to entice their cooperation. Afro-Americans were placed on the national staff. Black steelworkers became union organizers. In Atlanta, the SWOC ended the practice of segregated union meetings. An Urban League official reported from St. Louis in 1937:

> The S.W.O.C. organizers are making it a point to have a Negro officer in each lodge, composed from a plant in which there are Negro workers. They have not stopped there. But in a dance sponsored by the Women's Auxiliary, *all* workers and their friends participated. I attended this affair, and rejoiced at this new beginnning in the social history of St. Louis.

Indeed, in every local with a sizable number of black workers the SWOC appointed Afro-Americans to prestigious offices, placed them on all grievance and bargaining committees, refused to hold meetings in hotels or halls which discriminated against blacks, and publicly allied itself with the cause of civil rights. The SWOC made generous contributions to the major Negro rights groups. Murray spoke before them. By its resolutions, articles, and editorials in the union press, the SWOC wooed the Afro-American community. This strategy worked. Most black spokesmen and associations supported SWOC. The *Courier* and the *Defender* offered critical assistance in the Pittsburgh and Chicago areas, the two largest areas of concentration of black

steel workers. All the civil rights groups gave SWOC their backing. The NNC alone distributed over a quarter of a million leaflets to blacks in the steel industry. It held regional and national
conferences to stir enthusiasm for unionization. And it furnished
SWOC with volunteer speakers, pickets, and organizers. Negroes
flocked to the CIO's steel union as they never had to the AFL's
Amalgamated Association.[26]

The CIO Packinghouse Workers Organizing Committee
(PWOC) employed "the U.M.W. Formula" with the same results
as SWOC. Afro-American scabs had often broken strikes of the
meatpackers. Constituting over a quarter of the packinghouse
workers, blacks had to be convinced by the PWOC not to scab
and not to join either the company unions or the AFL Amalgamated Meat Cutters. So it outdistanced the other unions in its
egalitarianism. In addition to what SWOC had done, the packinghouse workers' union leaders demanded an end to the practice
of "tagging" the time cards of Afro-Americans; they extracted
from Swift & Company a pledge to hire blacks in proportion to
their numbers in the Chicago population; and they loudly protested instances of discrimination by the meat companies and
competing unions. In one NLRB election after another, the great
majority of black meatpackers voted to go with the CIO.[27]

The auto industry, particularly the Ford Motor Company, presented the CIO with the same problem. Although blacks comprised only about 4 percent of the auto workers in the 1930s, they
were concentrated in a very few strategic plants. The percentage
of Negroes at Ford was over 12 percent, with 99 percent of them
in the massive River Rouge plant. In order to organize Ford, the
United Auto Workers had to organize blacks.[28]

The UAW had their work cut out for them. No Negro communities and civic leaders in the thirties appeared more steadfastly
anti-union than did those in and around Detroit. Not even the
announcement in 1937 that the UAW would permit no Jim Crow
and would follow "the U.M.W. Formula" helped at first. Blacks
refused to sign up with the UAW. Most blacks played a passive

role in the 1937 and 1938 auto sit-down strikes. They neither actively opposed nor sided with the UAW. But in 1939 Afro-Americans made up a majority of the workers who crossed picket lines in Chrysler strikes in St. Louis and Detroit. Looking ahead to its next major campaign, CIO strategists knew they had to do something to alter the situation or the UAW would surely fail at Ford.[29]

Henry Ford had won the respect and support of the Detroit Negro community by leading the way in the industry in offering blacks jobs and equal pay with whites. His black workers constituted a higher percentage of all his workers than that of Afro-Americans in the Detroit region. Moreover, Ford employed them in all departments and positions, including foreman. He also contributed liberally to many of Detroit's Negro churches and civic associations, financed the all-black model suburb of Inkster, personally provided relief for unemployed blacks, subsidized the research of George Washington Carver, and featured such black stars as Marian Anderson and Dorothy Maynor on the Ford Sunday Hour. His tight grip on the Negro Wayne County Voters District Association kept the black political leadership solidly anti-union, especially anti-UAW. In 1937 Detroit black leaders threatened to boycott the NAACP annual conference scheduled to be held in that city unless the association dumped a UAW organizer from the program. After Dr. Mordecai Johnson of Howard University urged blacks to join the auto union, Detroit Negro ministers banded together to bar him from speaking at a local church. When Walter White met with the NAACP branch in the Motor City, he sensed "an atmosphere as definitely anti-union as would have been that of a meeting of the board of directors of the Ford Motor Company." Local officials of the Urban League disregarded the policy of their national office; they sided 100 percent with Ford against the UAW.[30]

Accordingly, the UAW drive to organize Ford in 1940 emphasized racial egalitarianism and support for civil rights more than any previous unionizing campaign. With much fanfare, the UAW dismissed prejudiced white organizers and replaced them with blacks. Henry Kraus filled the columns of the *United Auto Worker* with news of the civil rights movement and promises of racial justice. R. J. Thomas and other union officials spoke before black rallies and conventions. Civil rights leaders addressed union meetings. An ambitious program of worker education was established to minimize racial friction and foster interracial contacts. The UAW markedly enforced a non-discrimination edict for all its athletic, cultural, and social facilities. After black delegates to the 1940 convention in St. Louis complained of discrimination by the host hotel, the UAW voted unanimously to hold future meetings only where blacks would receive completely equal accommodations.

Guided by Walter Hardin, the UAW's General Negro Organizer, the union leapt into the forefront of labor groups allied with the civil rights movement. It became the most vocal advocate in the labor movement of anti-lynching and anti-poll tax legislation, the most lavish contributor to Negro rights associations, and the most constant lobbyist for legislation favorable to blacks in Congress. For their part, Walter White and other civil rights spokesmen marched in the UAW picket line around the River Rouge plant. Their speeches and writings urged blacks to join the UAW. Most black auto workers did, helping to convince Ford to capitulate in 1941, recognize the UAW, and agree to wage increases.[31]

The millennium had not arrived. Plenty of discrimination, covert and overt, persisted in the unions of both the CIO and the AFL, at both the national and local levels. Even those unions most vocal in their support for civil rights, like the UAW and TWA, countenanced anti-black actions by employers and their own members. Union officials proved as capable of opportunism as the leaders of other American organizations. The Communists, particularly, shelved their egalitarian zeal after 1941, when the defense of Mother Russia became paramount. Frequent backsliding, in fact, marked the advance of all unions toward a color-blind labor movement. Few white workers "get religion," in the sense A. Philip Randolph meant. Given the pervasiveness of racism in American society, not many laborers suddenly converted to the cause of racial justice because of the speeches of their leadership or the presence of blacks in their unions.[32]

Still, a decisive change in the fortunes of the movement for racial equality occurred in the thirties. Because of its new alliance with labor chieftains, it now communicated its needs to millions of whites, not thousands. The sense of isolation from the rest of American society which had so plagued the movement at the start of the decade faded. The conventions of the CIO annually recapitulated the message of the civil rights movement in their many resolutions condemning Jim Crow and supporting legislation favored by blacks. The comic books, pamphlets, and posters issued by the CIO did the same. So did the *CIO News*, delivered monthly to five million American families. Never before had the proponents of the black struggle reached so broad an audience.[33]

Nor had they ever had such powerful political allies. All the major CIO leaders personally identified their positions with the Negro rights movement. Brophy, Lewis, and Murray appeared often at the conventions of civil rights associations; at meetings of white unionists they regularly made a pitch for racial justice. Brophy usually tied the oppression of blacks to the rights of workers to organize, strike, and gain a better living. "Behind every lynching is the figure of the labor exploiter," he orated, "the man or the corporation who would deny labor its fundamental rights." John L. Lewis sounded the anti-fascist theme, equating racism with Hitlerism. Murray, too, made union rights and civil rights synonymous. Once, the black and white workers attending a CIO gathering in the deep South, where local ordinances forbade desegregation, cut the rope dividing the races and freely intermingled after listening to Murray speak.[34]

Many a local CIO leader followed the example of the national officers. In New York, the CIO's Industrial Council worked

closely with the NAACP and the NNC to support Adam Clayton
Powell's civil rights campaigns and to increase black leverage in
Democratic politics. The American Labor party organized several
ward clubs in Harlem. Labor's Non-Partisan League did the same
in Chicago, adeptly intermingling labor issues and civil rights.
In Detroit, UAW blacks wrested power from the Ford-controlled
Negro political machine and with the assistance of the NAACP
and CIO Council became a major force in municipal affairs. The
Pennsylvania CIO Council pushed a bill in the state legislature to
make it illegal for anyone to distribute literature intended to in-
cite racial prejudice or hatred. Other state councils worked for
legislation to increase housing, employment, and educational opportunities for blacks. Nationally, the CIO won its battle for the
establishment of a special Negro division in the administration
of the wages and hours law to prevent the discimination which
flourished in the early years of the New Deal.[35]

The labor movement also helped politicize blacks and increase
the militancy of civil rights groups in the 1930s. The CIO's educational programs made blacks more conscious of the struggle
for racial equality and less willing to tolerate gradualism and
supplication. Thousands of blacks experienced interracialism for
the first time and grew accustomed to being treated like men and
to being addressed as "Brother" or "Mister." Black unionists could
feel that they were needed. They sensed being an integral part
of a union's bargaining power, working together with whites for
a common goal, not being a ward of charity. Participation in
NLRB and local union elections, representation on bargaining
and grievance committees, holding office, and speaking out at
union meetings all schooled blacks in political skills and tactics,
augmenting the teachings of the black churches, lodges, and betterment organizations. From the labor movement they also
learned the importance of mass action, the power of boycotts and
disruptions, and the organization and discipline necessary for
strength. Few lessons were repeated more than the need for enfranchisement and wise use of the ballot. In addition, the devel-

opment within unions of a young black leadership cadre acted as leaven on the civil rights movement.[36]

At the time, no change seemed more paramount than the labor movement's overt interracialism. It had never been attempted on a mass scale before. Many racists and conservatives had doubted its feasibility. Even Charles S. Johnson considered the pursuit "itself an intellectual revolution." Yet more remarkable, Johnson continued, interracialism had been made concrete in "actual organizations, institutions, and social experiments." Here the CIO stood out. Even before the 1930s ended, social scientists cited the CIO as prime proof that increased racial contacts reduced prejudice and improved relations between the races. That would long remain a key article of faith for the believers in racial justice.[37]

8

Changing Ideas:
Race and Racism

A variety of cultural and intellectual developments in the thirties further incremented the aid given to the black struggle by liberals, leftists, and labor leaders. The research of biologists, psychologists, and social scientists undermined the shibboleths long used to rationalize second-class citizenship for blacks. A new intellectual consensus emerged. It rejected the notion of innate black inferiority; it emphasized the damage done by racism; and it depicted prejudice as a sickness, afflicting both individuals and the very well-being of the nation. These findings, in turn, emanated from the stages, movie screens, radio broadcasts, and popular fiction of the day. The prominence accorded Negro scholars and authors, moreover, belied the stereotype of the Afro-American as a Sambo unable to contribute to American civilization. Together these developments played a vital role in the reversal of racist attitudes.

From every side scholars whittled away at the scientific affirmation of the inherent inferiority of blacks to whites. Franz Boas and a handful of followers had been struggling to counter that notion since the turn of the century, but not until the 1930s did they succeed. By the end of the depression decade it had become

axiomatic among many educated Americans that race did not determine intelligence or personality, and that environment, not
genes, most influenced human behavior. These changes came
about because of the gradual accumulation of new data discrediting old explanations and because of the impact of Hitlerism and
the Great Depression on the climate of opinion.[1]

One aspect of the scientific attack on racism centered on the
concept of the uniqueness of the races and its corollary that
whites had made greater progress on the road of evolution than
blacks. Again and again Boas and his students demonstrated that
no "pure" races existed. They asserted that all mankind evolved
from the single species *homo sapiens* and that racial intermixture
had been continuous throughout history. Melville Herskovits estimated that at least 80 percent of the Negroes in the United States
in 1930 possessed combinations of black, white, and Indian
blood. J.B.S. Haldane claimed that all notions of race were fic-
tions. Ashley Montagu entitled his summation of the decade's
research *Man's Most Dangerous Myth: The Fallacy of Race*. "The
indictment against the anthropological conception of race," Montagu asserted, "is (1) that it is artificial; (2) that it does not agree
with the facts; (3) that it leads to confusion and perpetuation
of error, and finally, that for all these reasons it is meaningless,
or rather more accurately such meaning as it possesses is false.
Being so weighted down with false meaning it were better that
the term be dropped altogether than that any attempt should be
made to give it a new meaning." Few scientists disagreed. Julian
Huxley demanded that "the question-begging term 'race'" be
banished "from the vocabulary of science," as well as "from all
discussion of human affairs." The Nobel Prize winning biologist
Herbert J. Muller associated usage of the concept "race" with
"defenders of vested interests. . . . Fascists, Hitlerites, and reactionaries generally."[2]

Boas and others also exploded the notions that brain size, prog-
nathism—the degree of protrusion of the jaw—and mortality and
morbidity rates demonstrated that blacks constituted a lower or-

der of species than whites. Along with Aldous Huxley, Lancelot Hogben, and Theodore Dobzhansky, Boas proved that cephalic and prognathic indices vary within races as much as between them. They also pointed out that somatic features such as body hair and hair texture could as easily be deduced to prove that Negroes are at a more advanced stage of evolution than whites. S. J. Holmes and Julian Lewis demonstrated the higher susceptibility of whites to certain diseases than blacks, further casting doubt on the concept of white biological superiority. They related differentials in mortality and morbidity not to genetic differences in race but to variations in housing, nutrition, sanitation, and medical care. All these findings emphasized the importance of environment in determining physical characteristics.[3]

Even more discomforting to theorists of white supremacy was research conducted in England and the United States that challenged the dictum that racial interbreeding produced morphological "disharmonies." This view had often been advanced as scientific proof for the necessity of rigid segregation. In 1936 Harry L. Shapiro's widely publicized study of the descendants of the mutineers of the *Bounty* on Pitcairn Island concluded that the hybrids of white-Tahitian unions were more vigorous, robust, and healthy than either the average Tahitian or Englishman. It substantiated earlier studies in the 1930s by W. E. Castle and Herskovits, who asserted that "the undesirability of crossing cannot be substantiated by objective proof."[4]

Other followers of Boas destroyed the notion that race determined culture, another cornerstone of the white supremacy doctrine. Developing Boas's theory that "culture makes man, not race," they pinpointed the social determinants of what had once been considered hereditary racial characteristics. Ruth Benedict depicted the extreme temperamental variations in the Kwakiutl and the Zuni tribe of the Pueblo Indians. Both were of the same Mongoloid race, but their similarities ended there. Margaret Mead made the same point in her writings on southern Pacific cultures. She disclosed how the vastly dissimilar socializing proc-

ess of three Papuan tribes resulted in three quite distinct personality types, each peculiar to its culture. Mead also emphasized
the differences in the crises of adolescence in Samoan and Western civilization, again relating them to culture and not race. Social forces and not genes, Benedict and Mead stressed, mold human behavior.[5]

Paralleling this idea, Boas, Benedict, and their associates contributed to the relativistic view of culture. The many variants of
the doctrine of cultural relativity all diminished the idea of the
superiority of the white race and of western civilization. Scores
of anthropological studies underscored the contributions of African and Asian cultures. Others demonstrated the manner in
which whites lagged behind other races in certain social developments. In 1938 Boas added to his new edition of *The Mind of
Primitive Man* the bold declaration that no group of humans was
more or less advanced than any other. Admirers hailed it "a
Magna Carta of self-respect for the 'lower races.' "[6]

The single most crucial blow to scientific racism came from
Otto Klineberg, a social psychologist inspired by Boas. Ever
since Alfred Binet had first devised a quantitative test to measure
intelligence in 1905, racists had trumpeted the results of I.Q. (intelligence quotient) examinations to bolster their belief in white
superiority. Few defenders of Jim Crow in the 1920s failed to
echo the conclusions of the chairman of the committee of psychologists that administered the intelligence tests for the U.S.
Army in World War I that the numerical scores "brought into
clear relief . . . the intellectual inferiority of the negro." Most,
but not all, scientists in the twenties were content to accept the
Binet scale as a true test of inborn intelligence. It appeared that
"science" had proved the inferiority of blacks. However, the emphasis on environmentalism propounded by Boas led Klineberg
in 1923 to begin to reexamine the World War I tests, particularly
the effect of migration to Northern cities on the scores of blacks.[7]

In 1935 Klineberg overturned many of the academic community's attitudes toward innate intelligence and I.Q. tests by pub-

lishing *Negro Intelligence and Selective Migration* and *Race Differences.* Synthesizing some of his earlier studies, as well as those of other scholars, Klineberg found that the I.Q.'s of individuals of different races changed according to education and socioeconomic background. He showed that second-generation black migrants from Ohio, Illinois, New York, and Pennsylvania had higher I.Q.'s than both Southern blacks and Southern whites. This struck at the heart of the evidence for inherent black inferiority. Klineberg then proved that the I.Q.'s of Negroes in New York City increased in proportion to their length of residence in the city. "It is safe to say," Klineberg concluded, "that as the environment of the Negro approximates more and more closely that of the White, his inferiority tends to disappear." The leading psychologists concurred. Thomas R. Garth, who had initially believed in "clear-cut racial differences in mental traits," now concluded that they could not be proved. He admitted that it was "useless to speak of the worthlessness of so-called 'inferior peoples' when their worth has never been established by a fair test." C. C. Brigham also recanted publicly. Referring to the studies of the 1920s that had asserted the superior intelligence of certain races, Brigham confessed: "In particular one of the most pretentious of these comparative racial studies—the writer's own—was without foundation."[8]

Other investigators stressed the cultural biases inherent in the Binet tests. Some pointed out that language handicapped certain groups. Many emphasized the importance of motivation in influencing results. Still others dismissed the I.Q. results as not having any bearing on racial inferiority because of the absence of "pure" races. By the start of World War II, few academics would any longer state that genetic racial differences determined intelligence. A new consensus had emerged: that there are no inborn or innate racial differences in aptitude but only differences caused by educational, cultural, economic, and other environmental determinants. When the twenty-two thousand members of the

American Psychological Association were called upon to affirm the validity of that view, only three publicly dissented.[9]

The APA action came within a month of the news of Munich and of violent anti-Jewish pogroms in Germany. Outraged by Hitlerism, other professional groups quickly approved resolutions deriding any scientific claim for racism. At Boas's urging, the American Anthropological Association declared late in 1938: "Anthropology provides no scientific basis for discrimination against any people on the ground of racial inferiority." Its convention that year adopted resolutions denouncing Nazi race theory, as did a national meeting of biologists. In December the American Association of University Professors condemned totalitarian regimes for "persecuting teachers on account of their race or religion." Nazism had given racism a bad name, and that undoubtedly accelerated the speed with which scientists discredited genetic concepts of race in the thirties. Many were shocked by the racist mouthings of Goering and Goebbels, and by Lothrop Stoddard's effort to vindicate his own views by praising the Nazi concept of race. When Hitler talked of racial equality as "this Jewish nonsense," it filtered into the laboratory. When he incorporated his own prejudices into the Nuremberg Laws and the officially established Nazi sciences of *Rassenkude* (study of race) and *Rassenforschung* (racial research), other scholars eagerly accepted the new findings of their colleagues demolishing racial superiority. A rash of books in the late thirties followed Jacques Barzun in labeling race "a modern superstition" and in denouncing eugenics with Edward H. Hooton as little more than "a lay form of ancestor worship" clothed in "Ku Klux Klan regalia." At the World's Fair in 1939, Henry Wallace led a panel on "How Scientists Can Help Combat Racism."[10]

Franz Boas did not need such instruction. He had been battling what he called the Nazi race mania since the early 1930s. In concert with other Jewish Americans and the refugees from Germany, he believed science could be an opponent of racism.

His influence on the National Research Council's Committee on the American Negro led that committee to support financially the research of Herskovits, Klineberg, Mead, and his other students who shared his abhorrence of Nazism and racism. In 1933 he established the Institute of Race Relations at Columbia University to provide a "more detailed study of Negro-white race relations in the United States" and "to study and appraise various techniques employed in correcting typical problem situations." In the mid-thirties the Society of Friends and Swarthmore College took over the institute. Boas, with the assistance of Ruth Benedict, also turned the Department of Anthropology at Columbia University and Popular Front organizations like the American Committee for Democracy and Intellectual Freedom toward a preoccupation with racial issues. Fittingly, when he suffered a fatal heart attack at the Columbia Men's Faculty Club in 1942, Boas's last words concerned the need for eternal vigilance against racism.[11]

Kurt Lewin, a Jewish refugee from Nazism, influenced social psychologists much as Boas did anthropologists. He focused their work on a host of problems of racial prejudice. His work on the behavioral effects of frustration laid the basis for the explanation of racism as a personality malady of the racist, rather than something caused by the character or behavior of the group against whom the prejudice is directed. The Society for the Psychological Study of Social Issues, established by Lewin in 1936, and the Commission on Community Interrelations of the American Jewish Committee, which he chaired, spawned numerous social psychological investigations into the roots and nature of prejudice. Virtually all concluded that race hatred was generated by the frustration of individuals blocked from realizing their biological needs or social desires. They viewed prejudice as a symptom of maladjustment or neurosis. As Ben Hecht popularized this thesis for the American reading public: "Prejudice is our method of transferring our own sickness to others. It is our ruse for disliking others rather than ourselves."[12]

Other scholars broadened Lewin's explanation of the roots of prejudice. Many sociologists set out to discover why prejudice was directed toward some groups and not others and why even relatively secure and stable personalities acted with prejudice. Two major concepts dominated their work: the "social distance scale" and the "tradition of prejudice." Developed by Emory S. Bogardus late in the 1920s, the scale enabled researchers to measure the extent and persistence of prejudice. They uncovered wide variations in attitudes toward Negroes based on the degree of social intimacy involved in the question. Thus, whites responded quite differently when asked about racial intermarriage rather than about equal employment or citizenship rights for blacks. The measuring of degrees of friendliness with or social distance from Afro-Americans then led to attempts to correlate scores on these scales with such matters as age, sex, education, social class, courses in race relations, and contact with blacks. Many such studies lent credence to the arguments of civil rights leaders that interracialism decreased prejudice. The more contact between the races, they agreed, the less chance of racial conflict. The "tradition of prejudice" theory concentrated scholarly attention on the dysfunctional patterns of racism imbedded in American folkways and on their malleability. "Attitudes toward Negroes," Eugene Horowitz explained, "are now chiefly determined not by contacts with Negroes, but by contact with the prevalent attitude toward Negroes." Following the work of Lewin and his associates, sociologists in the 1930s removed the onus for discrimination from blacks. They also bolstered the conviction that racism could be cured.[13]

That persuasion acquired additional momentum from the research of social scientists on racial stereotypes, on the transmission of bigotry, and on the personality damage done by racism. Beginning with Sterling Brown's epochal article in 1933, "Negro Character as Seen by White Authors," studies of the falsehoods, exaggerations and omissions in the stereotypic picture of Afro-Americans multiplied. Each indicated the dangers of generalizing

from a few particulars and illustrated how stereotypes rationalized racial proscriptions. All agreed that the irrational picture of
Negroes held by most whites created a "contrast conception," in
which the Afro-American became the "antithesis of character and
properties of the white man." These scholars also affirmed the
tenuous nature of such beliefs. One school of sociologists taught
that stereotypes would wither away as interracialism and education increased. Another pressed the hypothesis that distorted
thinking served a function, that it elucidated the defense mecha-
nism of whites who feared competition from blacks. They saw
the problem as getting whites to understand that their interests
did not actually conflict with those of Negroes. Once that was
apparent, stereotypes would become dysfunctional and ultimately disappear.[14]

Both schools also researched the socialization process which
inculcated whites with their distorted image of blacks. Following
Bruno Lasker's pioneering study published in 1929, *Race Attitudes in Children,* they investigated the sources of racial prejudice; how parents, teachers, and clergymen fostered bigotry; and
what could be done by society to curb or dispel misguided racial
attitudes. They all rejected the notion of innate prejudice, of natural aversions, of an "instinct of race feeling." Those concepts had
been central to the sociological study of race in the twenties.
Even as critical and anti-white supremacist a scholar as Robert
E. Park in the 1920s described racial prejudice as "an instinctive
factor," largely immune to correction by interracial contact or
education. But by the end of the thirties, Park shared with most
sociologists a view of prejudice that no longer held it innate.
Rather, it was caused by cultural and social tensions and could
thus be modified.[15]

The movement away from biological explanations of behavior
and personality reached its apex in the socio-psychological analyses of John Dollard and his colleagues. With painstaking clarity
they depicted the social processes and patterns which caused
prejudice. They made the concepts of class and caste central to

the cultural milieu in which discrimination flourished. And, without minimizing their indignation, they exposed the psychic toll of racism on the personality development of both whites and blacks. They labeled the disease caused by mutual suspicion and hostility between the races "paranoia." Dollard described white racism as a "psychotic spot, an irrational, heavily protected sore through which all manner of venomous hatreds and irrational lusts may pour." Kenneth and Mamie Clark documented the self-devaluation by blacks growing up in an atmosphere of racial discrimination. Others detailed the effects of caste and class on such matters as Negro ambition, criminality, family disorganization, aspiration, and achievement. As a clear warning, some emphasized the repressed violence lurking just below the surface of America's seemingly placid accommodation between the races.[16]

Intellectual revolutions can rarely be dated with precision. Much as scholars often appear to have a penchant for avoiding deadlines, so too their ideas usually resist categorization by the calender. Yet, clearly the attitudes of social scientists in the United States changed markedly in the thirties. Studies of undergraduate courses in race relations, of sociological textbooks, and of theories of race indicate pronounced differences between the 1920s and the depression decade. Studies of race relations and of blacks ranked at the bottom of research interests of American sociologists in the twenties, and most of those published supported white supremacy.[17]

E. Franklin Frazier expounded on the distinction in his presidential address to the American Sociological Association. In the earlier period, claimed Frazier:

> When the sociologist began to direct his attention to the Negro, it was to study him as a "social problem" in American life. The general point of view of the books and articles published by this group of sociologists was that the Negro was an inferior race, because of either biological or social heredity or both; that the Negro because of his physical characteristics could not be assimilated; and that physical amalgamation was bad

and therefore undesirable. These conclusions were generally supported by the marshalling of a vast amount of statistical data on the pathological aspects of Negro life.

He explained the change as a consequence both of the maturation of the concepts and techniques of sociology and of the altered social outlook of sociologists. In an article published in 1947 Frazier amplified the extent to which sociological theory reflected public attitudes "during the first two decades of the present century." These writings, he noted, "on the Negro problem were merely rationalizations of the existing racial situation," which he defined as the Northern acceptance of the Southern solution to the racial problem, especially regarding disfranchisement and segregation. In the third decade, however, "as the relation of the Negro to American life changed and the problems of race relations throughout the world became more insistent," different viewpoints on race relations dominated the profession.[18]

Concurrently, the other social sciences changed. They, too, reflected the altered temper of the times, the reactions to Nazism, and the plight of the forgotten men. Much was written about black poverty, about discrimination in the New Deal recovery program and in the labor movement, and about a liberal coalition that knew no color line. Political scientists emphasized the racism extant in politics and in the administration of justice. Their writings became weapons in the battles against the poll tax, the white primary, peonage, police brutality, and lynching. Others focused on the inequities in education and housing for Afro-Americans. Particular attention was paid to the many problems of the South, and the manner in which an obsession with race retarded economic growth and social development. Historians began to delve into the nexus between white supremacy and class exploitation in their research on Africa, the slave trade, Reconstruction, and Populism. A positive portrait of Negroes helping to build and defend American civilization began to replace the picture of slovenly, ignorant blacks as mere recipients of white uplift. The Sambo image of contented darkies loyal to their owners was challenged by one dwelling on the extent of slave insurrections. A few historians depicted the role of Negroes in the abolitionist movement and their continual quest for greater freedom and dignity.[19]

Not content merely to write about race problems, a growing number of social scientists actively participated in the Negro rights campaigns. Followers of Boas joined him in attacking various manifestations of white supremacy. Scholars associated with the SCHW cooperated with the civil rights leadership in the fight against lynching and the poll tax, as did many who sympathized with the Popular Front. Some younger historians like C. Vann Woodward and Howard K. Beale, in revolt against the conservative majority of their profession, battled for the freedom of Angelo Herndon and for desegregated education in the South. At the National Conference on Fundamental Problems in the Education of Negroes held in 1934 under the auspices of the United States Office of Education, academicians from across the country gathered for the first time officially to condemn segregation in schools as inimical to the black student's incentive, self-pride, and esteem. In words close to those the Supreme Court would use twenty years later in ruling segregation in public education unconstitutional, Beale told the conference that "separate schools stigmatize the Negro and give his children a sense of inferiority and the white man's children a feeling of superiority which can never be outgrown in later life." No one dissented. The scholars formally resolved that: "Enforced segregation, whether by law or local pressure, in education as in the general life of the people is undemocratic."[20]

The cultural changes that had made such a declaration possible also stimulated government and philanthropic officials to champion the new intellectual consensus on race. The Office of Education funded many of the psychological and sociological studies. The WPA assisted in the preparation of *Deep South* by Allison Davis, Burleigh Gardner, and Mary Gardner. The Rosenwald Foundation, the Rockefeller Foundation, and the Yale Institute of Human Relations sponsored scores of research projects on race relations. In 1937 the Carnegie Corporation invited the Swedish social scientist Gunnar Myrdal to come to the United States to direct "a comprehensive study of the Negro." The result was *An American Dilemma,* a classic exposition of the racial egalitarianism of social scientists in the thirties. Ultimately, Myrdal would be aided by some seventy American scholars, as well as the NAACP, the Urban League, the Commission on Interracial Cooperation, the Social Science Research Council, the General Education Board, and numerous agencies of the federal government. The American Council on Education and the American Youth Commission collaborated in 1937 on a massive investigation of "the effects upon the personality development of Negro youth of their membership in a minority racial group." Homer P. Rainey, Will Alexander, Robert C. Weaver of the USHA, and Ambrose Caliver of the Office of Education played key roles in organizing the project, which brought together Dollard, Davis, Frazier, Charles S. Johnson, Ira DeA. Reid, and other Negro and white sociologists to produce the landmark series of publications detailing the effects of a racist environment on young blacks.[21]

Black scholars constituted nearly half the social scientists employed in the massive Carnegie Corporation and American Council on Education research projects. This, too, marked a significant break with the past. It helped in whittling away at the stereotype of the Afro-American as a non-achiever and an inferior thinker. Only forty-five blacks had received doctorates in the first three decades of the century, compared to nearly two hundred in the 1930s. More important, in the thirties blacks began to receive public acclaim for their scholarship. Ira DeA. Reid, Bertram W. Doyle, Allison Davis, St. Clair Drake, Horace Cayton, Charles S. Johnson, and E. Franklin Frazier in sociology; Ralph Bunche in political science; Abram Harris and Robert Weaver in economics; and Rayford Logan, Benjamin Quarles, and Carter Woodson in history all gained recognition within their disciplines and from the educated reading public.[22]

A number of Negro scientists also won the esteem of the aca-

demic community. Percy L. Julian successfully isolated and syn-
thesized male and female hormones and the drug physostigmine,
essential in the treatment of glaucoma. Herman Y. Chase conducted important studies on the effect of radiant energy upon
animal cells, as did Samuel M. Nabrit with biological regenera-
tion. Charles Stewart Parkes published some sixty scholarly articles in the 1930s on plant species. Thomas Wyatt Turner detailed
the physiological effects of various minerals on plants. Most high
school students began to learn of George Washington Carver's
work on crop diversification and soil conservation. A physicist,
Elmer Samuel Imes, pioneered investigations in infrared absorption bands. And Ernest E. Just, who had graduated Phi Beta
Kappa and *magna cum laude* from Dartmouth, was honored with
the vice-presidency of the American Society of Zoologists for his
discoveries in egg fertilization, cell division, and artificial parthe-
nogenesis.

In addition, blacks became more visible in the musical and
artistic worlds of the thirties. Black sculptor Richard Barthe and
artists Aaron Douglas, Jacob Lawrence, and Hale Woodruff
gained increasing attention. Concert singers Marian Anderson,
Dorothy Maynor, Roland Hayes, and Paul Robeson appeared frequently on the stage and on national radio broadcasts. The
Roosevelts invited the black opera stars Florence Cole Talbert
and Lillian Evanti to sing at the White House. Katerina Yarboro
performed with many of the leading opera companies in the
country. In 1935 William Dawson's *Negro Folk Symphony* had
its premiere with Leopold Stokowski and the Philadelphia Orchestra. Soon after, the New York Philharmonic introduced William Grant Still's *Afro-American Symphony,* and the Chicago
Symphony Orchestra presented the Negro composer Florence
Price's *Symphony in E Minor.* Still's African ballet *Sahdji* and
Asadata Dafora Horton's dance opera *Kykunker* in the early
1930s awakened choreographers to the distinctive cadence of African and Negro dances, as did the work of Katherine Dunham.
Within a few years, their tempos would be part of the new ballet

popularized by Martha Graham and Doris Humphrey. So would many of their themes and stock characters. By the end of the decade Graham and Humphrey were devising their own Negro dances of social significance, often with titles like *Lynch Town*.[23]

Even the radio networks, ever fearful of offending a part of their mass audience, changed somewhat. For the first time, such entertainers as Ethel Waters, Louis Armstrong, and the Mills Brothers had their own radio revue shows. Civil rights organizations had some success in diminishing the stereotypic roles for blacks. Eddie "Rochester" Anderson was a small advance over Amos 'n' Andy. Although "Rochester" displayed many of the same tendencies toward dice, drink, and dames, he also proved to be a lot smarter and hardier than his stingy, often foolish, somewhat effete boss, Jack Benny. Significantly, Anderson's jokes came at Benny's expense, reversing the traditional pattern for blacks and whites; "Rochester" addressed Benny as "Boss" rather than "Sir," as in the servant-master dialogue of the 1920s; and most episodes ended with "Rochester" having to use his wit and resourcefulness to extricate Benny from some entanglement. In the thirties such tiny movements counted as steps forward. So did the many broadcasts of Paul Robeson's rendition of "Ballad for Americans," with its explicit plea for racial equality, and the editorials by major stations in favor of federal anti-lynching legislation.[24]

In a like manner, the spirit of racial protest affected Hollywood, but just barely. The percentage of servile parts for Negroes, which had exceeded 80 percent of the movie roles for blacks in the 1920s, dropped to 40 percent in the thirties. Yet, W. C. Fields still joked "Get along, you Senegambian" to his Negro coachman. "Beulah," Mae West commanded her black maid, "peel me a grape!" *The Green Pastures* caricatured black religion as one everlasting weekend fish fry. Little Miss Curlytop captivated her audience with the demeaning "Uncle Billy can do anything. He can sing. He can dance. He can climb trees." The stereotypes remained: dancing Bill "Bojangles" Robinson; that

shufflin' and stammerin' handyman Stepin Fetchit; big, black
bossy Hattie McDaniel; dim-witted Willie "Sleep 'n' Eat" Best;
Charlie Chan's "terr'fied of de ghosts" chauffeur; Mantan More-
land, whispering "Feets! Do your stuff"; and the panicky house-
girl Butterfly McQueen—"Gee, Miss Scarlet, 'Ise don't knows
nothin' 'bout birthin' babies." But now, at least, they were joined
by Clarence Brooks as the dignified Negro doctor in *Arrow-
smith;* by Rex Ingram as the heroic, un-servile Nigger Jim in *The
Adventures of Huckleberry Finn,* and as the towering black genie
in *A Thousand and One Nights* bellowing "Free! I'm free at
last!"; by Daniel Haynes's manly performance in *The Last Mile;*
by Clarence Muse's rebellious and valiant characters in *So Red
the Rose* and *O'Shaughnessy's Boy;* and, most of all, by the proud,
defiant Paul Robeson.[25]

Robeson's *The Emperor Jones* presented Americans with a
colossal, determined black man who refused to kowtow to anyone. He personified the Afro-American asserting himself, cutting
"whitey" down to size. Robeson radiated confidence. His gestures
suggested nothing but strength. Reviewing the film in 1933, *Time*
commented: "To have a black man playing the star part in a film
in which the white actors were of lesser importance was indeed
something of a filmic revolution."[26]

The rarity of such roles for blacks itself became a civil rights
issue, as did productions considered demeaning to Afro-Americans. The NAACP and the National Negro Congress boycotted
and picketed theatres playing films like *Gone With the Wind.*
Progressive and leftist journals featured articles on the racial
slanders produced by Hollywood. Some film critics subjected
movies to more racial analysis than artistic commentary. A few
filmmakers responded in ways other than Joseph Schenck who
complained that the industry "doesn't mold the public, the public
molds us." Mervyn Le Roy produced the hard-hitting *I Am a Fu-
gitive from a Chain Gang* and *They Won't Forget.* First National
gave black actors and actresses dignified roles in productions

such as *Cabin in the Cotton.* Universal's *Imitation of Life,* based
on Fannie Hurst's best-selling novel, sympathetically dealt with
the problem of Negroes trying to "pass" as whites in order to live
a decent life. *Black Legion,* starring Humphrey Bogart, and Fritz
Lang's powerful *Fury* spoke out against the subjects Hollywood
had never before dared to indict: the KKK, lynching, and racial
injustice. Limited but significant changes had occurred. "Aestheti-
cally what had been achieved by the summer of 1942," wrote
Thomas Cripps in his comprehensive history of blacks in film,
"was the final step of a dissolution of the monopoly that Southern
literary attitudes had held over the depiction of racial life in
America."[27]

Unlike the film industry in that it was not dependent upon a
mass audience, the American theatre went still further in spot-
lighting the oppression of blacks and in eroding the old meta-
phors. In place of the crap-shooters of Marc Connelly's *The Green
Pastures,* dutifully included in Burne Mantle's *The Best Plays of
1929–1930* with a note about the "kindly sympathy" of the Southern Negro and "his trusting and childlike religious faith," there
appeared dramas focusing on the inhumanity of racism and the
new fighting spirit of blacks. To delineate the sadism inherent in
white supremacy, Paul Green dramatized Erskine Caldwell's
Kneel to the Rising Sun. James Millen's *Never No More* illustrated the lynch mania in the South in the early thirties. *Blood
Stream* by Frederick Schlick scrutinized the brutal treatment of
black convict labor. In 1934 John Wexley's *They Shall Not Die*
presented the case against Alabama's "rape frame-up" of the
Scottsboro Boys. That same year, *Stevedore,* starring Rex Ingram,
told the story of an Afro-American's awakening to the consciousness of the class struggle. The necessity of revolution in order to
overcome racial exploitation even gained the praise of *Variety.
The Magazine* made the same point later in the decade in lauding Orson Welles' production of Richard Wright's *Native Son.* In
addition, such Broadway plays as *Mulatto* by Langston Hughes,

Samson Raphaelson's *White Man,* and *Brass Ankle* by DuBose Heyward, although not specifically propagandistic, broke new ground in their sympathetic and fully developed presentation of black characters and problems.[28]

Scores of little theatres in Northern cities featured "agitprop" plays about racial oppression. Most preached the virtues of union organizing and interracial class unity. These ever-present panaceas became the mainstay of the new black theatre groups—the Rose McClendon Players, the Harlem Players, the Negro People's Theatre, and Langston Hughes's Harlem Suitcase Theatre. Probably no single "proletarian" play was performed more frequently than Hughes's *Don't You Want to Be Free.* With the quality of a ritual, the actors repeatedly joined hands with the audience at the end of Huhges's drama to sing:

> Oh, who wants to come and join hands with me?
> Who wants to make one great unity?
> Who wants to say, no more black or white?
> Then lets get together, folks,
> And fight, fight, fight.[29]

In all likelihood, those already committed partook in that scene; however, tens of thousands watched the appeal for racial justice for the first time in the productions of the WPA Theatre Project. Fourteen of the eighty-one new plays put on by the project dealt directly with problems of race prejudice and discrimination. The WPA, in addition, presented historical pageants about John Brown, Nat Turner, Toussaint L'Ouverture, and Harriet Tubman, which highlighted the Negro's quest for freedom. Its "Living Newspaper" shows editorialized against the chain gang, lynching, disfranchisement, and the Italian invasion of Ethiopia. Only strong pressure from Southern congressmen forced the Theatre Project to cancel *Liberty Deferred,* an unrelenting expose of segregation, sharecropping ills, and the injustice at Scottsboro. The willingness of the project to involve itself in the controversial race issue became a major topic of criticism for Southern politicians. When it got the chance, Congress killed the Theatre Project at the end of the decade.[30]

Indeed, virtually every cultural medium in the thirties did something to lift the veil that hid the oppression of blacks and the damage done by racism. The American Artists' Congress and the American Writers' Congress expressed the need to counter fascism by fighting "against white chauvinism (against all forms of Negro discrimination or persecution)." Margaret Bourke-White, Erskine Caldwell, Lewis Mumford, Stuart Davis, William Gropper, and Ben Shahn called for art and literature to serve the cause of racial justice. Scores of novels, plays, radio and art shows, and motion pictures reflected an abhorrence to Nazism and a depression-born concern with the problems of the poor and powerless. In one art form after another, sympathy for the persecuted and the down-and-out led from the unemployed white worker to the displaced Okie and then to the forgotten Negro. In each medium, moreover, black cultural achievements helped diminish the persuasiveness of the Sambo stereotype.[31]

The combined effects of Nazism and the Great Depression gave black and white authors an audience receptive to narratives of racial subjugation. Much of the fiction about the South, with the notable exceptions of works by Margaret Mitchell and Stark Young, condemned that region's obsession with race and the exploitation of blacks. Even William Faulkner, for all his denigration of novels of social protest and his love of tradition in Mississippi, did much to reorient Southern literature by turning the happy-go-lucky Sambo into a victim of the hate-ridden, brutal, hypocritical, senselessly prejudiced South. Erskine Caldwell went much further. In one memorable story after another he revealed the utter depravity of the Southern caste system. As no one before, he depicted the crushing effect of racism on both white and black. "If the treatment of the colored man is ever more humane," an intellectual historian would write in 1941, "we are going to owe a very great debt to Erskine Caldwell." Hamilton Basso,

James Saxon Childers, and Lyle Saxon followed Caldwell's lead, as did William March and Carson McCullers. They scorned Southern paternalism, dwelled on the economic basis of racism, illustrated its barbaric components, and gave prominence in their stories to complex, exemplary black characters.[32]

The Communist party took the line that all progressive authors had to focus on the tribulations of blacks and to depict the conflicts between integration and segregation, civil rights and black nationalism as ones of progress versus reaction. "To select other themes was tantamount to betrayal of the race," Wilson Record later wrote. Party historians ignored or criticized Marcus Garvey and Booker T. Washington; they depicted Negro history as an uninterrupted chronicle of Afro-American protest. Whatever happened in the thirties was given a racial meaning. In the midst of the furor over the kidnapping of the Lindbergh baby, *New Masses* editor Mike Gold penned a column about another crime— the murder of a three-year-old black boy in Jacksonville, Florida, who died of appendicitis because the white-only hospital would not admit a dying Negro. The proletarian novels of Olive Durgan, Josephine Johnson, Grace Lumpkin, Myra Page, T. S. Stribling, and Leane Zugsmith dramatized the whole litany of black protest. Readers of this literature became accustomed to black protagonists being cheated in company stores, abused and beaten for no reason, lynched without cause, sexually abused by lecherous white exploiters, and discarded in old age or sickness by the supposedly paternalistic white boss. Most of the novels, expectedly, ended with poor whites joining the blacks, renouncing the old ways of race hatred, and striking in solidarity to defeat capitalist prejudice. Scott Nearing's *Free-Born*, one of the best of the proletarian novels, traced the life of a poor Afro-American from hopeless sharecropper to dedicated revolutionary. Nearing documented the misery of blacks, the lynch spirit in the South, and the Communist hope for white and black workers "fighting shoulder to shoulder" to win a world without racism "under working class control."[33]

Numerous authors outside the party orbit addressed themselves to the same problems and themes, often with less dogma
and more skill. Newspaper headlines were expropriated for stories about the inequities of caste, peonage, police brutality, and,
especially, lynching. Although the number of lynchings in the
South decreased markedly in the mid-1930s, the incidence of in-
nocent blacks being tortured, mutilated, and burned by sadistic
mobs in fiction steadily increased in the thirties, culminating in
Erskine Caldwell's best-selling *Trouble in July*. John Spivak and
Robert Burns barely fictionalized stories in the press of the
convict-lease system and the murdering of overworked black
convicts by weighting their bodies and dropping them in a
swamp. Other novels repeated the indictment of sharecropping
then current in the social science and liberal political journals.
Various writers borrowed from the journalistic exposes of the day
to dramatize the horrors of the third-degree and other tortures
employed by Southern police to extract confessions from blacks.[34]

Black authors, Richard Wright counseled, should transcend
nationalism for "the highest possible pitch of social consciousness." Langston Hughes called upon his fellow black writers to
end their absorption in the "soul-world" and to join the struggle
against oppression. Most did. The interests of the writers of the
Harlem Renaissance stood in sharp contrast to the social realism
of the thirties. Strike meetings replaced sultry jungle nights for
background and atmosphere; the leading characters became em-
battled croppers and proletarian workers rather than quaint and
religious black folk peasants; the problems of economic necessity
and survival in a racist culture took precedence over those of
"passing" and black identity. All separatist themes were subordinated to those of interracial unity and the struggle for civil
rights.[35]

Hughes put aside his nationalist credo of 1926 in favor of one
"to explain and illuminate the Negro condition in America." For
Hughes this meant Marxism. Throughout the thirties he illustrated his notion of the Afro-American as a twin victim of eco-

nomic racial exploitation. The "Jazzonia" of cabaret Harlem in *The Weary Blues* gave way to the depressed ghetto of *Shakespeare in Harlem*.

> Down on the Harlem River
> Two A.M.
> Midnight
> By yourself!
> Lawd, I wish I could die—
> But who would miss me if I left?

His first novel, *Not Without Laughter*, told a bitter tale of racial prejudice in a small Kansas town. He travelled to the Soviet Union, associated with Arthur Koestler and Boris Pasternak, contributed to *Izvestia, International Literature, New Masses*, and the Communist party publications for blacks, founded left-wing Negro theatre and literary groups in Chicago, Harlem, and Los Angeles, covered the exploits of blacks fighting in the International Brigade in the Spanish Civil War, and campaigned for civil rights in innumerable poems, essays, stories, plays, and speeches. Typical of his work in the depression decade, his "Let America be America Again," protested against the oppression of all subordinated groups and envisioned a future egalitarian, color-blind society. Such writings profoundly influenced the generation of young black artists coming of age in the thirties.[36]

Two of them, William Attaway and Waters Turpin, acknowledged Hughes's impact and exemplified the committed artistry he called for. In a series of novels, Turpin traced the effects of bigotry, poverty and lynching on three generations of blacks in the South and in Chicago. Attaway, whose *Blood on the Forge* was hailed by critics as the black man's *Grapes of Wrath*, savagely described the oppression in Kentucky that forced Negroes into the steel mills of Pennsylvania. Attaway saw no promised land in the North. He described the tedium, drudgery, racism, and economic exploitation in the North as every bit as dehumanizing as the plight of the black farmer in the South: enslaved to debt, on the verge of starvation, inevitably forced to flee a lynch mob. The three black brothers, whose tales Attaway related, helplessly watched their hopes crushed and obliterated.[37]

The black protest novel of the thirties culminated in Richard Wright's *Native Son*. The day it appeared, wrote Irving Howe a quarter of a century later, "American culture was changed forever. No matter how much qualifying the book might later need, it made impossible a repetition of the old lies." Born in Mississippi in 1908, abandoned by his father, brought up by indifferent relatives and orphanages, Wright drifted to Chicago in 1927. He worked at assorted odd jobs. As the depression worsened he gravitated toward the Communists. Early in the thirties he joined the John Reed Club. In 1933 Wright got his membership card for the party. After that he went to work on the *Daily Worker*, wrote for the Federal Writers Project in Chicago and New York, and started publishing his short stories in *Left Front, International, Midland, New Masses,* and *New Challenge.*[38]

Wright gained prominence in 1937, bringing to light the stultifying effects of discrimination and segregation in his "Big Boy Leaves Home" and "The Ethics of Living Jim Crow: An Autobiographical Sketch." The following year he won a WPA writing prize. *Uncle Tom's Children* expressed the suffering of alienated, frustrated, oppressed blacks who daily faced violence, Jim Crow, and the inability to prevent the sexual exploitation of their women by whites. Reviewers lauded Wright's four novellas for communicating the agony of racism more graphically than anything previously written and for pointing to the necessity of interracial solutions. " 'Black and white, unite and fight.' It is the old communist slogan that Wright is pressing in terms of action," wrote Malcom Cowley, "and it is a good slogan too, even for those like myself who are more attached than the Communists to things as they are." Wright remained unsatisfied. He brooded that he "had written a book which even bankers' daughters could read and weep over and feel good about." His next work, Wright promised, "would be so hard and deep that they would have to face it without the consolation of tears."[39]

In early 1940 the Book-of-the-Month Club selected *Native Son* for its members. From the ring of an alarm clock awakening Bigger in a squalid Chicago tenement to his encountering a rat feeding off the garbage to his helplessness in the death cell, Wright probed the effect of repressive prejudice upon the human personality. American racism had created a monster, and Bigger incarnated it. Wright's fictional character epitomized most of what sociologists had written in the thirties of the negative consequences of growing up in a racist environment, and his actions confirmed the direst prophecies of social psychologists on the pathology spawned by white supremacy. Wright made his readers both feel shame for the existing racial situation and recoil in horror at its results. He captured all the yearning and restlessness of blacks stirring in the 1930s, appealing a bit to white consciences but primarily warning of an impending doom; for, buffeted by forces he could neither understand nor control, Bigger found meaning only in violence. Blacks would not be denied their humanity, even if they had to "go Communist" or to murder to get it. Bigger's killing a white woman—the symbol of white sickness—chopping up her body, and burning it in a furnace was Wright's metaphor for all the "bad niggers" of Georgia and Harlem who would destroy the nation if the race problem remained unsolved.[40]

"A blow at the white man," wrote Irving Howe describing *Native Son*, "the novel forced him to recognize himself as an oppressor."

> Speaking from the black wrath of retribution, Wright insisted that history can be a punishment. He told us the one thing even the most liberal whites preferred not to hear: that Negroes were far from patient or forgiving, that they were scarred by fear, that they hated every minute of their suppression even when seeming most acquiescent, and that often enough they

hated *us*, the decent and cultivated white men who from complicity or neglect shared in the responsibility for their plight.[41]

Fittingly, Dorothy Canfield Fisher, who wrote the introduction to the first edition, related the meaning of *Native Son* to the reams of social science research on the race issue published in the 1930s. She quoted at length from the studies sponsored by the American Youth Commission and American Council on Education. Their investigations, Fisher wrote:

> present conclusive evidence that large percentages of Negro youth by virtue of their combined handicap of racial barriers and low social position subtly reflect in their own personality-traits minor or major distortions or deficiencies which compound their problem of personality adjustment in American society. More specifically, the research studies have revealed: That being a Negro in most cases means living in the presence of severe physical limitations, but, more important for personality development, also means living in an intimate culture whose incentives, rewards, and punishments prevent the development of that type of personal standards, attitudes, and habits which the general community deems desirable.

According to Fisher, moreover, not only was the characterization of Bigger Thomas firmly grounded in the scholarship of the thirties, but the audience's awareness of its findings made it possible for Wright to delineate with much subtlety the cause-and-effect relationship between Bigger's brutal crime and his victimization by white society. "He knows he does not have to prove this," Fisher concluded. "He assumes that every one of his readers will know all that without being told. And he is right. We do."[42]

The nation had been warned, coaxed, beseeched, and inundated with evidence. But how many read and learned? We cannot know. Extensive public opinion polling and surveying of attitudes toward race relations would not develop until the following decade. Nor can we know the extent of the gaps between belief and behavior. Fisher assumed that the shocks of the depression and the rise of Nazism had opened the minds of her audience to the new research and writings discrediting old prejudices. She supposed that the outpouring of scholarship on the "unfinished business of democracy," and the empathetic treatment given it in the arts and literature, had badly eroded the old scientific and stereotypic bases of racism, and that new concepts of race, of environment, of the costs of prejudice and discrimination, and of the place of blacks in American society had come to the fore. So did Richard Wright. A year after *Native Son* he expressed the black hopefulness wrought by the changes in the 1930s:

> The differences between black folk and white folk are not blood or color, and the ties that bind us are deeper than those that separate us. The common road of hope which we all have traveled has brought us into a stronger kinship than any words, laws, or legal claims.
>
> Look at us and you will know yourselves, for *we* are *you*, looking back at you from the dark mirror of our lives!
>
> What do we black folk want?
>
> We want what others have, the right to share in the upward march of American life, the only life we remember or have ever known. The lords of the land say: "We will not grant this!"
>
> We answer: "We ask you to grant us nothing. We are winning our heritage, though our toll in suffering is great!" The bosses of the building say: "Your problem is beyond solution!" We answer: "Our problem is being solved. We are crossing the line you dared us to cross, though we pay in the coin of death!"
>
> The seasons of the plantation no longer dictate the lives of many of us: hundreds of thousands of us are moving into the sphere of conscious history.
>
> We are with the new tide. We stand at the crossroads. We watch each new procession. The hot wires carrying urgent appeals. Print compels us. Voices are speaking. Men are moving! And we shall be with them. . .[43]

9

The Law of the Land

Addressing a Southern white audience in 1900, Judge Emory Speer of Georgia warned that some day blacks would gain funds, hire first-class lawyers and go before the courts to attack successfully the statutes and practices branding them second-class citizens. In the thirties, the NAACP and other organizations substantiated Speer's credentials for prophesy, even though it had never occurred to that white judge that the task would be accomplished mainly by black attorneys. Yet William Hastie, Charles Houston, Thurgood Marshall, and their colleagues did just that. They won the reversal of previous decisions that had legitimized the exclusion of blacks from jury service, the subjugation of Afro-Americans in peonage and mob violence, the inability of Negroes to obtain a fair trial, and the unequal status of blacks before the law in education, employment, housing, and public accommodations.[1]

This reversal rested in the main on the constitutional revolution begat by the New Deal, which, according to historian William Leuchtenburg, "altered fundamentally the character of the Court's business, the nature of its decisions, and the alignment of its friends and foes." No group would benefit more from these changes than Afro-Americans. The Court discarded its preference for a tightly confined, non-interventionist national government. It transferred the special solicitude once reserved for property rights to a vigorous concern for human rights. Although evidence of this development appeared early in the 1930s, it did not became fully manifest until after the Roosevelt appointees constituted a new majority on the High Court at the end of the depression decade. Though some historians have dated the Court's switch from a restrictive interpretation of Negro rights to an egalitarian view of the Fourteenth Amendment from the first Scottsboro decision in 1932, both the number of cases involving blacks that the Supreme Court agreed to hear and the percentage of outcomes favorable to Negro litigants leaped significantly after 1937.[2]

In part the reversal also flowed from the transformation of the NAACP's legal personnel, procedures, and practices. During the association's first decade, Du Bois often complained of civil rights cases being lost because of faulty arguments and briefs.

> It has happened time after time, in case after case. The Negro has taken his cause before the Courts half prepared. He has been warned of this: He ought to have learned by bitter experience but he has not yet learned. Law is not simply a matter of right and wrong—it is a matter of learning, experience, and precedents.

Justice Louis Brandeis made the same point in the 1920s, indicating that civil rights cases had been lost because of flawed preparation and presentation. The NAACP's legal effort was more of a disjointed attempt to respond to crises as they arose rather than a carefully planned and organized, well-financed campaign. The association was short on money, assistance from legal groups and theoreticians, and on black talent. At the start of the Great Depression, the law school at Howard University lacked accreditation, and not a single course in civil rights law existed in the country. Only about a thousand black lawyers, less than one percent of the nation's total, were in practice, and fewer than a hundred had graduated from ranking law schools. "There were not ten Negro lawyers, competent and willing to handle substantial civil rights litigation," throughout the South, wrote William Hastie.[3]

That situation changed in the thirties. Charles Hamilton Houston, a Phi Beta Kappa at Amherst and graduate of Harvard Law School, succeeded a lethargic retired white judge as dean of the law school at Howard in 1929. He enlisted assistance from his close friend William Hastie, who had followed Houston to Amherst and the Harvard Law School; Leon A. Ransom, who graduated first in his class from Ohio State University's law school; and James M. Nabrit, Jr., an attorney trained at Northwestern Law School who would teach the first civil rights law course in the country. In 1931 Howard won full accreditation from the American Bar Association. Two years later its graduates included Thurgood Marshall and Oliver W. Hill, who would lead the NAACP in Virginia and become the first black ever to serve on the Richmond City Council. Numerous others followed. "The most hopeful sign about our legal defense," Houston told the 1935 NAACP convention, "is the ever increasing number of young Negro lawyers, competent, conscientious, and courageous, who are anxious to pit themselves against the forces of reaction and injustice."[4]

Moreover, the NAACP's courtroom offensive against Jim Crow benefited from the financial and technical assistance of other organizations. In 1929 the American Fund for Public Service (AFPS) agreed to allocate one hundred thousand dollars to the association to finance "a large-scale, widespread, dramatic campaign to give the Southern Negro his constitutional rights." The decision had been based on the desire of Charles Garland, an eccentric, leftwing millionaire who established the AFPS to give his money away "as quickly as possible, and to 'unpopular causes,' without regard to race, creed, or color." Money had already been given to the Urban League and to A. Philip Randolph to organize the sleeping car porters. The determination to spur the NAACP's courtroom activities was aided by a brilliant report to the fund by James Weldon Johnson, Lewis Gannett, and Morris Ernst outlining the feasibility of a successful series of legal suits for racial justice. However, the onslaught of the Great Depression forced board members of the AFPS and the NAACP to question the wisdom of fighting Jim Crow in the courts. The money could be better spent, some argued, on the immediate economic needs of the black masses. Others wanted it used to forge a "union of white and black workers against their common exploiters." After a succession of bitter meetings, they decided that legal equality was "the necessary basis of any real economic independence." Planning for the court battles would proceed.[5]

In 1930 a joint AFPS–NAACP Committee on Negro Work retained the white New York attorney Nathan Margold to direct the legal campaign. Famed for his defense of the American Indians' interest, Margold began by preparing a comprehensive 218 page report on the legal status of the Afro-American. He depicted the worsening position of blacks by summarizing the implications of every court decision relating to Negroes since *Plessy* v. *Ferguson*. He envisioned a concerted offensive against Jim Crow, but the stock market crash eroded AFPS funds and forced the Committee on Negro Work to resolve to concentrate only on educational inequalities.[6]

Margold proposed a direct challenge to the constitutionality of segregated education. He based his strategy on the unanimous opinion of the Supreme Court in *Yick Wo* v. *Hopkins* (1886). In invalidating a San Francisco ordinance whose covert purpose was to exclude Chinese from the laundry business, the Court had declared:

> Though the law itself be fair on its face and impartial in appearance, yet, if it is applied and administered by public authority with an evil eye and an unequal hand, so as to practically make unjust and illegal discriminations between persons in similar circumstances, material to their rights, the denial of equal justice is still within the prohibition of the Constitution.

Margold believed a case could be made that the unequal appropriation of school funds for blacks and whites throughout the South constituted a similar "denial of equal justice" and thus violated the equal protection clause of the Fourteenth Amendment. He admitted the audacity of his contention but countered his critics that it "would be a great mistake to fritter away our limited funds on sporadic attempts to force the making of equal divisions of school funds in the few instances where such attempts might be expected to succeed." Such a policy, Margold claimed, would eliminate only minor pockets of discrimination and establish no new precedents against "white supremacy" and the "separate but equal" rule.[7]

The NAACP Board of Directors overruled Margold. It opted for a low-key series of piecemeal taxpayers' suits "to force equal if separate accommodations." This strategy, the board stated, would:

> (a) make the cost of a dual school system so prohibitive as to speed the abolishment of segregated schools; (b) serve as examples and give courage to Negroes to bring similar suits; (c) cases will likely be appealed by city authorities, thus causing higher court decisions to cover wider territory; (d) focus as nothing else will public attention north and south upon the vicious discrimination in the apportionment of public school funds so far as Negroes are concerned.

In the main, finances dictated the NAACP's strategy. The continued dwindling of AFPS funds, from the promised hundred thousand dollars to but a few thousand between 1931 and 1934, made it difficult for the NAACP Board to feel "bullish" about Margold's plan. At this time the association was scaling down all its programs. It dreaded risking all on one gamble before the Supreme Court. In addition, the NAACP feared appearing too provocative and exacerbating an already tense situation in the South. After dropping to ten in 1928 and seven in 1929, the number of lynchings jumped to twenty-one in 1930. The same number

were committed in each of the next two years, and the figure rose
to twenty-eight in 1933. The board did not want to stir the wrath
of white supremacists. The stakes were too high and the NAACP
had little confidence in the cards it held.[8]

The campaign against educational inequality remained dor-
mant until 1935 due to the combination of declining resources,
disagreement over legal strategy, and conflict over leadership.
Ickes's offer of the post of solicitor in the Interior Department led
Margold to resign in 1933. Walter White was preoccupied with
the anti-lynching fight and his controversy with Du Bois. Other
staff members devoted themselves to securing an equal share of
the New Deal's economic benefits for Afro-Americans. Starved for
funds and personnel, the program drafted by Margold gathered
dust. Karl Llewellyn would not leave Columbia for the salary the
NAACP offered. No other top attorney seemed interested in filling
Margold's position. Finally, in 1934 Charles Houston, Dean of
Howard University Law School, agreed to help the association.
Roger Baldwin of the American Fund for Public Service, however, held up his appointment, insisting that the NAACP campaign be headed by a white lawyer. Only White's persistence
finally forced Baldwin to yield. But because of his commitment
to Howard, the first black editor of the *Harvard Law Review*
could not begin working full-time for the NAACP until mid-1935,
further stalling the suits planned.[9]

Once Houston settled into his new position, the drive to win
legal equality for the Negro picked up speed. With his two chief
lieutenants—William H. Hastie, a fellow Felix Frankfurter pro-
tégé, and Thurgood Marshall, his star pupil at Howard—the
former dean began attracting financial contributions and offers
of legal assistance. The three Negro lawyers disregarded the pattern followed by previous NAACP attorneys of waiting for cases
to come to them. They established the precedent of carefully
selecting, readying, and arguing each case in conjunction with an
intensive effort to educate the public as to the nature and extent

of racial inequality. The three wanted to be an integral part of the struggle for civil rights, not a legal aid society. Their briefs would be weapons for that fight, as useful to an editor, politician, or speechmaker as to a jurist. Houston vastly expanded the NAACP Legal Committee. Previously an honorific group, the committee was given a role in formulating strategy and tactics. He recruited a score of young black lawyers throughout the country to join the attack on Jim Crow. Houston also established liaisons with many of the nation's leading law school professors to help research constitutional problems and to publish in legal journals the evidence in favor of reversing past decisions detrimental to blacks.[10]

Houston complied with the NAACP Board's decision "to force equal if separate accommodations" rather than pursue Margold's proposed direct assault on Jim Crow. Recognizing the conservatism of the federal judiciary and the inclination of most courts to avoid abrupt reversals of precedent, the NAACP sought to force racial equality incrementally. It planned to begin at the graduate level. There could be no pretense of even "separate but equal" since no facilities existed for black professional education in any of the Southern states, except for Howard and Meharry Medical College in Nashville, and only two border states provided out-of-state tuition grants. The NAACP hoped that the combination of the tiny number of black applicants for graduate work and the prohibitive expense of a state's establishing separate facilities for Negroes would convince state officials to admit the few blacks. That would establish a precedent to be pushed eventually at lower levels. The NAACP believed that in addition to the huge costs involved the South might give in and desegregate its graduate schools because whites regarded integration in professional education as less dangerous than in secondary or primary schools. As Marshall later recalled jocularly:

> Those racial supremacy boys somehow think that little kids of six or seven are going to get funny ideas about sex and marriage just from going to school together, but for some equally funny reason youngsters in law school aren't supposed to feel that

> way. We didn't get it but we decided that if that was what the
> South believed, then the best thing for the moment was to go
> along.

Houston, however, left no doubt as to the ultimate purpose of
this strategy. The "objective of the association," he wrote in his
first article in *The Crisis*, "is the abolition of all forms of segregation in public education."[11]

Actually, the disputation began before Houston's carefully
orchestrated campaign even started. In 1933 Thomas Hocutt applied for admission to the University of North Carolina College of
Pharmacy. The university rejected him because of his race and
Hocutt asked the NAACP for assistance. The association agreed
to file for a writ of mandamus in Hocutt's behalf. William Hastie
argued the case for the NAACP. Fearing the implications of an
adverse decision to its entire segregated educational system,
North Carolina assembled the state attorney general, leading
members of the state bar, and the dean of the university law
school to oppose the twenty-three-year-old Hastie. Hocutt lost on
a technicality—not fully complying with the admission requirements—because Dr. James E. Shepard, president of the North
Carolina College for Negroes and the leading exponent of black
conservatism in the state, would not supply Hocutt with a recommendation or transcript. Still, the NAACP seemed pleased with
the publicity the case had attracted, with the judge's contention
that the state must supply "substantially equal" facilities to its
black citizens, and with the expressed determination of young
blacks in other states to mount similar challenges.[12]

In 1934 Donald Murray, an Amherst graduate, asked the
NAACP to file a suit to compel his admission to the University
of Maryland Law School. Arguing for the NAACP, Marshall
claimed that Maryland's provision for out-of-state tuition grants
did not constitute equality of treatment. The trial court and the
Maryland Court of Appeals agreed. They ordered the regents of
the university either to establish a separate law school for Negroes
equal to that for whites or to admit Murray. Maryland chose the

far less expensive course of quietly accepting Murray into its previously all-white law school.[13]

The United States Supreme Court's involvement in civil rights, however, accelerated because of cases involving the procedural fairness of trials, not educational inequality. Following the Scottsboro trial in 1931, attorneys for the International Labor Defense (ILD) argued in an appeal to the Alabama Supreme Court that the defendants had been denied due process of law as required by the Fourteenth Amendment. Walter H. Pollak, who had gained fame for his work in the *Gitlow* and *Whitney* civil liberties cases, contended that the due process clause had been violated by the courtroom atmosphere in Scottsboro, which made a fair and impartial trial impossible, by the failure to provide the defendants with adequate counsel and the opportunity to prepare a defense, and by the systematic exclusion of blacks from both the grand and trial juries that indicted and convicted the black youths. The high court of Alabama rejected the ILD's plea, ignoring the first contention, denying the second, and finding no sufficient evidence for the third. The United States Supreme Court agreed to review the proceedings.[14]

On the first decision-Monday after Franklin Roosevelt's election, Justice George Sutherland, speaking for a seven-to-two majority, ordered Alabama to hold new trials for the Scottsboro Boys. For only the second time in its history, the High Court decided that the Fourteenth Amendment guarantee of due process applied to the Sixth Amendment right to a fair trial. Justices Pierce Butler and James McReynolds dissented. Decrying the demise of states' rights, Butler denounced the decision as "an extension of federal authority in a field hitherto occupied exclusively by the several states." To offset the bitterness of the dissenters, Chief Justice Charles Evans Hughes tactfully assigned the majority opinion to Sutherland. The Utah railroad lawyer and his equally conservative colleague Willis Van Devanter generally voted with Butler and McReynolds, and to hold them with the majority Hughes agreed to the narrowest possible opinion on the case. Sutherland said nothing about the ILD's claims of the systematic exclusion of blacks from Alabama juries and the impossibility of a fair trial for Negroes in Scottsboro. Instead, he restricted the Court's ruling to the question of the right to counsel, and even hedged that with numerous qualifications. "The failure of the trial court to make an effective appointment of counsel," intoned Sutherland, in a "capital case, where the defendant is unable to employ counsel, and is incapable adequately of making his own defense because of ignorance, feeblemindedness, illiteracy, or the like," constituted a "denial of due process within the meaning of the Fourteenth Amendment."[15]

The limited nature of the decision touched off the kind of debate that followed every civil rights case before the Supreme Court in the thirties. Because the Court generally expanded its scope incrementally, upsetting the least possible number of precedents and existing relationships, its rulings failed to win favor with those demanding fundamental changes. They condemned the Court for justifying delay and evasion, for dealing with the appearance and not the substance of racism, for attacking symptoms and not the disease, for often speaking in grand terms but allowing the existing pattern of white superiority and black subordination to remain unchanged. Such critics howled that the Supreme Court would allow Alabama to re-try the convicted defendants. The *Daily Worker* called the decision a sham: "The Supreme Court has taken great care to instruct the Alabama authorities how 'properly' to carry through such lynch schemes." American Civil Liberties Union officials Morris Ernst and Arthur Garfield Hays denounced the Court for its deception. In their view it had ignored the most basic points raised by the defense and left the outcome of the second trial just as certain as the first one had been. The Urban League, on the other hand, lauded the decision for its symbolic value. Great changes must begin with small steps; new majorities must be educated and won over to new doctrines. Moreover, the Court had in fact ruled for these poor, uneducated blacks against the state of Alabama. In the past, wrote Felix Frankfurter in the New York *Times,* the Supreme Court had been "insistently cautious in subjecting State criminal trials to the limitations of the Fourteenth Amendment." Now the high court appeared ready to assert its responsibility in insuring equal justice to blacks, after six decades of leaving the supervision of civil rights to the states and utilizing the due process clause primarily to protect property and business interests.[16]

As the debate continued, the Supreme Court extended the reach of the Fourteenth Amendment in its incremental fashion. In 1933 Alabama again tried, found guilty, and sentenced to death Haywood Patterson and Clarence Norris. The other trials facing the Alabama Court were postponed pending a ruling on the ILD's claim that the exclusion of blacks from the grand and trial juries constituted a denial of due process of law. The defense established that no one in either Jackson County, the site of the indictment, or Morgan County, where the trials had been held, could recall a Negro serving on a jury. Alabama officials countered that no blacks met the requirements for jury duty, these being "male citizens who are generally reputed to be honest and intelligent men, and are esteemed in the community for their integrity, good character, and sound judgment." The Alabama Supreme Court accepted the jury commissioner's argument that there had been no deliberate exclusion of blacks. The Supreme Court decided to review the cases again. It may have been emboldened by the patent weaknesses in the prosecutor's allegations revealed in the second trials. Ruby Bates had changed her testimony. Appearing for the defense she claimed that she had not been raped and did not see Victoria Price raped.

Lower court rulings had probably also influenced the justices of the Supreme Court. The Maryland Court of Appeals in 1932 had taken it upon itself to determine whether blacks had been denied the right to serve on juries. It ordered a new trial for a black man convicted of murder because it found evidence of a "long, unbroken absence of Negroes from juries." The following year, George Crawford, a Negro indicted for murder in Virginia, escaped to Massachusetts and filed a writ of habeas corpus in the United States District Court at Boston that the all-white jury system in Loudoun County violated his rights under the Fourteenth Amendment. Federal Judge James A. Lowell granted the writ. He reasoned that the unconstitutional exclusion of blacks from the Loudoun County grand jury voided its indictment of Crawford. The United States Court of Appeals for the First Circuit, however, reversed Lowell. Crawford was extradited, tried, and found guilty in Virginia. The NAACP, stung by criticism in the Negro press that it lacked the militancy of the ILD shown in the Scottsboro case, made much of the fact that no blacks had ever served on a Loudoun County grand jury. That argument may have helped save Crawford's life, although the court rejected it as a reason to quash the indictment. The NAACP then tried again in a case involving a black Oklahoman sentenced to death for raping a white girl in 1931. The NAACP appealed on the ground that no blacks had ever served on juries in Okmulgee County. On May 13, 1935, the Supreme Court declared the Negro's conviction unconstitutional in a *per curiam* decision. The matter of the absence of blacks from the Southern jury system, moreover, had started to receive scrutiny in the legal journals by the time the *Norris* and *Patterson* cases reached the Supreme Court in 1935.[17]

Speaking for the Court, Hughes spurned the contention of the Alabama courts that they alone had the right to determine whether discrimination against Afro-Americans existed in jury service. When a federal right was involved, the Chief Justice declared, the Supreme Court itself would decide "whether it was denied in substance and effect." Reversing earlier precedents that placed the burden of proof on blacks to demonstrate intentional discrimination in the selection of jurors, Hughes stated that the Court would infer such discrimination from the facts. Emphasizing the "long-continued, unvarying, and wholesale exclusion of Negroes from jury service," the high court set aside the Scottsboro convictions. The trials would have to begin all over again.

For the first time in the twentieth century, the Supreme Court asserted its power to supervise the administration of justice to blacks in the states by examining for itself the evidence of discrimination. The Court's caveat that it would not be bound by state court determinations regarding discrimination but would independently see whether "in truth a federal right had been denied" reversed the course set in the *Slaughter-House Cases* in 1879 of relegating the protection of civil rights to the states.[18]

Yet on the same day of the Scottsboro decisions the Supreme Court also indicated the limits of its desire to intervene in a state's racial affairs. It unanimously upheld the right of a political party to exclude blacks from its primaries. In 1927 the Court had declared unconstitutional the white primary law of Texas because of the state's overt and direct discrimination. Shortly after, the Texas legislature gave the "power to prescribe the qualifications of its own members" and to "determine who shall be qualified to vote or otherwise participate in such political party" to the State Executive Committee of every political party in Texas. Dr. A. L. Nixon of El Paso sued a second time for the right to vote. In 1932 the Supreme Court divided in a five-to-four vote in his favor. Speaking for the majority, Benjamin Cardozo invalidated the action of the Texas legislature on the ground that the State Executive Committee's power to exclude Afro-Americans from a primary was "statutory. If the State had not conferred it, there would hardly be any color of right to give a basis for its exercise." Justices Butler, McReynolds, Sutherland, and Van Devanter dissented, claiming that the Democratic party was a private association and could exclude anyone it wished.[19]

The Texas Democratic convention understood the cue. It formally resolved to limit its membership to whites. The state had to do nothing. Despite the transparency of the maneuver, and despite the Democratic primary in Texas being tantamount to the official election, a unanimous Supreme Court on April 1, 1935, accepted the fiction of a political party as a private organization and validated its right to exclude blacks from voting in a primary.

The Court was not yet about to undertake a campaign to end the disfranchisement of blacks, although that had been the very purpose of the Fifteenth Amendment. Nor would it yet champion civil rights through a broad and expansive interpretation of the Fourteenth Amendment. As one lawyer wrote in 1935, "It is perhaps remarkable that more than sixty-six years after the adoption of the Fourteenth Amendment, with its operations in many directions well defined, its effectiveness in accomplishing the chief purpose of its adoption—the protection of the Negro—is still largely undecided." Andrew McLaughlin, in his massive *Constitutional History of the United States* published that year, agreed: "For fifty years or more, the relationship of the freedman to the fourteenth amendment has been practically lost to view."[20]

After 1937, however, the Supreme Court's responsiveness to black litigants wanting the full protection promised by the Fourteenth and Fifteenth amendments quickened perceptibly. In one sense, the Court followed the trend in the nation toward a greater awareness of and solicitude for the plight of Afro-Americans. It is unlikely that the justices did not know of the egalitarian teachings propagated by academics, clergymen, popular authors, and some members of the media, or that some of their own stereotypic views of blacks went unaltered by the cultural shifts in the thirties. They probably were not unmindful of the growth of a rather well-financed, unified, broadly-based interracial civil rights movement, and the support for civil rights coming from New Dealers and labor leaders. The swelling agitation regarding the injustices associated with Scottsboro, lynching, and the poll tax undoubtedly penetrated the judicial chambers. Such Roosevelt appointees as Hugo Black (1937), Stanley Reed (1938), Frank Murphy (1940), and Robert Jackson (1941), moreover, well understood the political importance of the Negro vote to the Democrats. They had been practical New Deal politicians before their elevation to the Court and realized the pragmatic necessity of the alliance between blacks and the national Democratic party.

Generational considerations also differentiated the Roosevelt Court from "the nine old men" who preceded it. The Hughes Court had been dominated by conservative business lawyers whose outlook on racial matters had been shaped in the heyday of the Court's retreat from Reconstruction. They had received their education, come of age politically, and ascended to the Supreme Court at a time when the ideology of white supremacy went virtually unchallenged. The reverse was true of the younger jurists selected by Roosevelt. Educated in the twentieth century and schooled in liberal New Deal politics, oriented toward reform and championing the underdog, and associated with the egalitarianism being taught at the elite law schools, the justices of the Roosevelt Court could well have been expected to be more concerned with civil rights than their predecessors, although that certainly is not why FDR appointed them.[21]

In the most fundamental sense, however, the Supreme Court's increasing willingness to protect the civil rights of blacks stemmed from the crisis of the Court in 1937 and the subsequent revolution in constitutional law. The High Court responded to the political pressures that grew out of Roosevelt's attempt to pack the judiciary and also out of the needs of citizens in the throes of a depression. Their response was to broaden the regulatory powers of the national government. States' rights was one casualty of this development; "dual federalism" was another. Once begun, the propensity of the Court to take a national approach to the questions before it continued. The path led from economic matters to those concerning civil liberties and rights. As the Supreme Court came to allow the executive and legislative branches greater discretion in regulating property and business relations, it assumed more concern for the problems of procedural fairness to persons on trial for crimes and for the equal rights of minorities—religious and political, as well as racial. In a footnote to an opinion in 1938, Justice Harlan Stone indicated the Court's directions when he wrote that laws involving the Bill of Rights required "more exacting judicial scrutiny" than other laws. By the end of the decade, the Roosevelt Court had assigned the protection of civil rights and liberties to the preferred position once reserved for guarding the welfare of business interests.[22]

In 1938 the Supreme Court restated the constitutional guarantee to the right of counsel in a capital case and overturned the conviction of a Kentucky Negro for murder because no blacks served on the county grand jury panel. The next year, Justice Hugo Black, speaking for a unanimous court, ruled that all attempts to exclude Afro-Americans from grand juries denied them equal protection under the law. In announcing another unanimous decision in 1940, Black reiterated the Court's demand that Negroes not be excluded from the jury system. That exclusion, wrote Black, "not only violates our Constitution and the laws enacted under it but is at war with our basic concepts of a democratic society and a representative government." The Supreme Court again asserted that it would determine for itself the issue of exclusion rather than rely on what state courts said and that it would infer that a long-continued absence of blacks from juries was proof of systematic exclusion. It repeated its view at least a dozen times in the subsequent two decades, yet the United States Commission on Civil Rights in the 1960s continued to find Southern counties in which no blacks had ever served on a jury. The Roosevelt Court wounded the white jury system, but left it functioning.[23]

Much the same pattern occurred in the High Court's extension of procedural safeguards for a fair trial, particularly in its effort to put an end to the use of the "third degree" to obtain confessions. In 1936 the Court first ruled that the use of a coerced confession in a state trial denied a defendant due process of law. Following Hughes's decisions in the 1935 Scottsboro cases, the Court asserted its power to determine itself whether *in substance* due process had been followed. In a long series of opinions emphasizing this claim, the Supreme Court emphatically added the right to be free from self-incrimination through forced confessions to the growing list of rights that states were forbidden to deny.

In rural Mississippi in the spring of 1934, three impoverished, illiterate blacks, accused of killing a white man, had been taken to a county jail, beaten, whipped, and tortured until they confessed. At their trial, the sheriff admitted mistreatment of the prisoners but insisted that the confessions were voluntary. One of the deputy sheriffs, who acknowledged having whipped the defendants, explained that he had not beaten them excessively for Negroes, "not as much as I would have done if it were left to me." The three blacks swore that they had confessed only to escape further torture. They repudiated their confessions. Nevertheless, the trial judge admitted their earlier confessions as proper evidence, and the jury found them guilty as charged. On appeal, the Mississippi Supreme Court upheld the verdict.

Speaking for a unanimous Court, Chief Justice Hughes reversed the convictions of the three black Mississippians in 1936. He solemnly affirmed the right of the Supreme Court to ascertain whether due process had been denied. Pointing to the "undisputed evidence of the way in which the confessions had been procured," Hughes's opinion stated that the "duty of maintaining constitutional rights of a person on trial for his life rises above the rules of procedure, and whenever the court is clearly satisfied that such violations exist, it will refuse to sanction such violations and will apply the corrective." Reminding the Mississippi Supreme Court of its duty, the Chief Justice proclaimed: "The rack and the torture chamber may not be substituted for the witness stand."[24]

In 1940 the Court extended its 1936 ruling to prohibit "the drag net methods of arrest on suspicion without warrant, and the protracted questioning and cross questioning" of prisoners denied "friends, advisers, or counselors." The case began with the murder of a white man in a small Florida town. A day after the killing, some twenty-five to forty blacks in Pompano were rounded up, arrested without warrants, and confined to the county jail for six days, all the while being held incommunicado and enduring persistent grilling by the police. On the confession extracted from one Negro, four blacks were convicted of murder and sentenced to death. Two Florida courts upheld the penalty. The NAACP petitioned the United States Supreme Court for a grant of *certiorari* on behalf of the black defendants, asserting that "sunrise confessions" extracted under conditions of duress and fatigue were no more voluntary than those taken at gunpoint. The Court granted the writ.

On Lincoln's Birthday, 1940, Black announced for the Court that mental torture, no less than physical torture, constituted compulsion and a denial of due process. Utilizing the brief prepared by Thurgood Marshall, as well as the reports of the 1931 National Commission on Law Observance and Enforcement and the American Bar Association Committee on Lawless Enforcement of the Law, Black made a special point of the prevalent use of the third degree against Southern Negroes. His opinion concluded eloquently:

> Under our constitutional system, courts stand against any winds that blow as havens of refuge for those who might otherwise suffer because they are helpless, weak, outnumbered, or because they are non-conforming victims of prejudice and public excitement. Due process of law, preserved for all by our Constitution, commands that no such practice as that disclosed by this record shall send any accused to his death. No higher duty, no more solemn responsibility, rests upon this Court, than that of translating into living law and maintaining this constitutional shield deliberately planned and inscribed for the benefit of every human being subject to our Constitution—of whatever race, creed, or persuasion.

Later that year, Black again wrote the opinion for a unanimous court, which this time set aside the conviction of a Negro defendant who had been mentally tortured. In 1941 the Supreme Court twice overturned the convictions of blacks who had been tried on the basis of involuntary confessions. In each case, the NAACP appealed to the precedent of the Chambers ruling and the High Court agreed.[25]

The shift of the Roosevelt Court further showed in its decisions on picketing against discrimination in employment and on racial restrictive covenants. Boycotts of merchants who refused to hire blacks became a common form of racial protest in the 1930s. A number of Northern cities witnessed major "Buy Where You Can Work" campaigns. The one established in Washington, D.C., by the New Negro Alliance, included Mary Bethune, William Hastie, Charles Houston, and a score of other black government officials, lawyers, and educators. In the mid-thirties, a federal court issued an injunction restraining the New Negro Alliance from parading in front of stores to protest their refusal to hire Afro-Americans. The District of Columbia Court of Appeals upheld the injunction, but the Supreme Court thought differently. Over the denunciatory dissents of Butler and McReynolds, the Court ruled that members of a particular race could organize and picket against job discrimination under the protection of the Norris-La Guardia Act forbidding federal court injunctions in labor disputes. "Race discrimination by an employer," wrote Roberts, "may reasonably be deemed more unfair and less excusable than discrimination against workers on the ground of union affiliation."[26]

Two years later, in 1940, the Supreme Court reversed an Illinois Supreme Court decision upholding the validity of a racial restrictive covenant. In a highly technical ruling written by Harlan Fiske Stone, which avoided the issue of the constitutionality of the covenants that the NAACP counsels had raised, the Court decided that the black purchasers could occupy the land in question. The decision only partially pleased civil rights leaders, yet it was a far cry from the Supreme Court opinion in 1926 that gave local courts permission to enforce racial restrictive covenants and that dismissed the Negro's appeal as "so insubstantial as to be plainly without color of merit and frivolous." The 1940 decision at least opened up twenty-seven city blocks surrounding the University of Chicago previously closed to black occupancy. But by 1945 practically every white family had left the area.[27]

Many of the Supreme Court's initial decisions on racial matters had minimal effect. Progress came at a painfully slow pace, even in cases involving interstate transportation. The protracted effort to end enforced segregation in interstate travel developed out of Congressman Arthur Mitchell's decision to purchase a first-class Pullman ticket for his trip from Chicago to Hot Springs, Arkansas, in April 1937. The Congressman travelled comfortably in his Pullman accommodations until Memphis. As the train crossed the Mississippi River into Arkansas, the conductor on the Rock Island Railroad instructed Mitchell, a Negro, to comply with the Jim Crow laws of Arkansas by leaving the air-conditioned Pullman car for the crowded, dirty, and inferior car reserved for baggage and blacks. The Afro-American protested in vain; the conductor would not back down. After the completion of the journey, Mitchell filed a complaint with the Interstate Commerce Commission. The ICC upheld the railroad's contention that it had to comply with Arkansas's law requiring separate facilities for the races and that the extremely small number of blacks desiring Pullman accommodations justified there being so little Pullman space available for Negroes. When Mitchell turned to the courts, the United States District Court of Northern Illinois dismissed his suit on the ground that it had no jurisdiction. Upon Mitchell's appeal, the Supreme Court agreed to hear the case.[28]

At this point, Mitchell broadened his plea to assault the constitutionality of the *Plessy* decision, and Francis J. Biddle, the Solicitor General of the United States, filed a brief in behalf of the black Congressman. For the first time, the Justice Department submitted an *amicus curiae* brief on the side of a black defendant, even though the government itself was being sued by Mitchell. In response, Governor Frank Dixon of Alabama called a conference of Southern governors to coordinate strategy, and ten Dixie attorneys general prepared briefs to justify the continuation of the separate-but-equal rule. On April 28, 1941, the Supreme Court unanimously announced in favor of Mitchell. However, it did so in a manner that completely sidestepped Mitchell's challenge to the *Plessy* v. *Ferguson* decision. The Court left the 1896 ruling in effect, demanding only that blacks be afforded equality of Pullman accommodations: "The comparative volume of traffic cannot justify the denial of a fundamental right of equality." The legal debate on the consequences of the Supreme Court's actions went on. Some were dismayed that the *Plessy* rule had been left in full force and effect. They blamed the Court for informing the South that it would merely have to exercise greater care in how it discriminated against Afro-Americans. Contrarily, a law professor at Washington University viewed the decision as a step toward the ultimate "federal prohibition of segregation as well as inequality." A Southern lawyer observed: "All of this is disruptive of Southern traditions and portends a terrific wrench in readjustment that must occur in the near future."[29]

Another Southern institution, peonage, came under sustained attack in the 1930s, and, resulted in the Supreme Court again aligning with the proponents of civil rights. Under pressure from the NAACP and the Communist-backed Abolish Peonage Committee of America, the Justice Department began to move in 1940 to indict peonage bosses. Concomitantly, the state of Georgia indicted and convicted a black man for not paying a debt, sentencing him to forced labor. James Taylor asked the Supreme Court to intervene. The U.S. Solicitor once more filed a brief *amicus curiae* in behalf of the Negro's cause. Biddle reviewed the evidence of widespread peonage in the South and quoted a resolution of the Georgia Baptist Convention in 1939 declaring that "there are more negroes held by these debt slavers than were actually owned as slaves before the War between the States." In 1941 the Supreme Court unanimously overruled the Georgia high court and struck down the state law permitting such coerced labor.[30]

Inadvertently, the Justice Department again came to the aid

of the civil rights movement in 1941, when in a case not involving black rights it persuaded the Court to rule that party nominating conventions constituted an integral part of an election. The Court agreed with the government's argument that for falsely counting ballots the Louisiana Democratic party's primary election officials had acted under color of state law. The crucial *Classic* decision set the stage for the Supreme Court to outlaw the "white primary" three years later. In fact, as soon as the Court had announced its opinion in 1941 the NAACP began its work to challenge Texas's white primary on the very grounds taken by the Supreme Court in *United States* v. *Classic.* The association persuaded Dr. Lonnie Smith to attempt to vote in the Democratic primary and, when he was denied the ballot, to bring suit against the registrar. Hastie and Marshall hurried to Texas to prepare the case. They contended that, because of *Classic,* the denial of the ballot to blacks in a primary solely because of race violated the Fifteenth Amendment.[31]

The association had been given further cause for optimism in this endeavor by the tone of the High Court's 1939 ruling in *Lane* v. *Wilson.* In this case the Court, over the dissents of Butler and McReynolds, invalidated an Oklahoma law which contrived to keep the outlawed grandfather clause in effect through subterfuge. In no uncertain terms Frankfurter proclaimed that the Fifteenth Amendment "nullified sophisticated as well as simpleminded modes of discrimination. It hits onerous procedural requirements which effectively handicap exercise of the franchise by the colored race although the abstract right to vote may remain unrestricted as to race. . . . We believe that the opportunity thus given Negro voters to free themselves from the effects of discrimination to which they should never have been subjected was too cabined and confined." Frankfurter's assertion that the Court would look beyond the letter of the law to ferret out discrimination augured well for the NAACP's efforts to end disfranchisement.[32]

Most of all, the legal campaign against educational inequality and Jim Crow stimulated hopefulness among black leaders and their liberal allies. In 1936, Hastie, Houston, and Marshall formulated a strategy for the attack on the gross inequities in the expenditure of public monies for Afro-American and white education, particularly the practice of offering Negro teachers lower salaries than white teachers. The United States Office of Education had estimated early in the 1930s that it would take twenty-six million dollars annually to bring black education in the South up to a material par with that of whites. The NAACP hoped that the South would give up segregation before approving such expenditures. Although slowed down by the opposition of black teachers fearful of antagonizing their local school boards, the NAACP attorneys agreed to institute a series of suits to eliminate the salary differential.[33]

In December 1936 the NAACP filed its first petition for equal salaries in the Circuit Court of Montgomery County, Maryland. By 1938 five such suits had been started. In each, the NAACP made the claim that pay given to black teachers in the South averaged about one-third that of whites, and that the salary gap had more than doubled in the thirty years between the turn of the century and the start of the depression. The association's first major victory came in 1939 when the United States District Court in Baltimore granted an injunction to a black teacher restraining the Anne Arundel County Board of Education from discriminating in the payment of teachers. "The plaintiff, as a colored teacher," declared the court, "is unconstitutionally discriminated against in the practice of his profession by the discrimination made between white and colored teachers." Rejecting the argument that salary equalization would impose a heavy financial burden on the county, the court declared that "these considerations cannot control the supreme law of the land as expressed in the Fourteenth Amendment."[34]

A sweeping decision the following year by Judge John J. Parker for the Circuit Court of Appeals wiped out an annual differential of $129,000 created by the underpayment to black teach-

ers by the School Board of Norfolk. "This is as clear a discrimination on the ground of color as could well be imagined," stated
Parker, "and falls squarely within both the due process and equal
protection clauses of the Fourteenth Amendment." On November
4, 1940, the Supreme Court declined to hear an appeal by the
Norfolk School Board. Parker's decision stood as the law of the
land. Within two years, fifty-three school districts in Virginia
had begun to equalize salaries.[35]

More than a victory against racial wage differentials, these
decisions illustrated the expanding application of the Fourteenth
Amendment to protect Negro rights. They established the rule
that a state as an employer may not discriminate in any way
against its employees on the basis of race. Further, the opinions
indicated again the Court's readiness to accept the facts of inequality as *prima facie* evidence of discrimination. The number of
blacks directly aided was small, but once established, the doctrine
of "substantial equality" would have ramifications in every aspect
of Afro-American life.[36]

For that reason, no decision of the Supreme Court in the thirties held greater promise than *Missouri ex rel Gaines* v. *Canada*.
In 1936 the University of Missouri had rejected Lloyd Gaines's
application to its law school. Although Missouri provided no facilities for legal education for blacks, its high court ruled that
"separate but equal" could be met by the state if it would send
Gaines at its expense to a law school in an adjacent state. The
NAACP asked the Supreme Court for a writ of mandamus forcing
the university to admit Gaines.[37]

Speaking for a six-to-two majority of the Court on December
12, 1938, Chief Justice Hughes announced that the equal protection of the laws entitled blacks to be admitted to the state university in the absence of other provisions for legal training within
the state. Hughes carefully emphasized that Gaines's right "was
a personal one. It was as an individual that he was entitled to
equal protection of the laws." The chief justice even cited *Plessy*
with favor. However, the "admissibility of laws separating the

races in the enjoyment of privileges afforded by the State rests
wholly upon the equality of the privileges which the laws give to
the separated groups within the State." Justices Butler and Mc-
Reynolds once more dissented. "For a long time Missouri has
acted upon the view that the best interest of her people demands
separation of whites and negroes in schools," stated McReynolds.
"Under the opinion just announced, I presume she may abandon
her law school and thereby disadvantage her white citizens . . .
or she may break down the settled practice concerning separate
schools and thereby, as indicated by experience, damnify both
races." The justice from Tennessee apparently spoke for others.
Mysteriously, Gaines shortly disappeared and never attempted
to enter the University of Missouri law school. Rumors persisted
that he had been drowned or run out of the state. Just in case another Negro would press for the right that Gaines had claimed,
the state soon erected a separate law school for blacks.[38]

The denouement aside, civil rights spokesmen without exception hailed the *Gaines* decision as the beginning of the end of
segregated education. Raymond Pace Alexander, a distinguished
black attorney in Philadelphia and former president of the National Bar Association, wrote of it as "one of the most brilliant,
courageous, and forceful statements supporting the fundamental
purpose of the 14th Amendment that has ever been declared by
our Supreme Court." The NAACP went out of its way to stress
that, although it had not asked the Court to overrule *Plessy* (believing the time not quite ready for that yet), a majority of justices agreed to reevaluate the basic meaning of "separate but
equal." For the first time, the Supreme Court weighed the "intan-
gible" factors of equality. "Petitioner insists," wrote Hughes, "that
for one intending to practice in Missouri there are special advantages in attending a law school there, both in relation to the opportunities for the particular study of Missouri law and for the
observation of the local courts, and also in view of the prestige
of the Missouri law school among the citizens of the State, his
prospective clients." The Court concurred. It ruled that the offer

of tuition in an out-of-state school could not match these advantages. This presaged the intensive examination of what constituted equality that led the Supreme Court in the following decade to strike down one instance of Jim Crow in education after another. As legal historian Robert J. Harris observed: "What makes the Gaines case unusual is that the Court looked beyond the formula to question the fiction, and, in law, to question a fiction is to kill it."[39]

In 1896 Justice Henry Billings Brown, delivering the opinion for the Court in *Plessy* v. *Ferguson,* had maintained that the framers of the Fourteenth Amendment "could not have intended to abolish the distinctions based upon color." Yet, in the 1930s, that is exactly what the Supreme Court began to assume. Brown wrote that "legislation is powerless to eradicate racial instincts, or to abolish distinctions based upon physical differences, and the attempt to do so can only result in accentuating the difficulties of the present situation." The Roosevelt Court, however, abrogated racial wage differentials, progressed toward eliminating the white primary, peonage, restrictive covenants, and discrimination in employment, and insisted upon putting teeth into the due process clause to guarantee black defendants a fair trial and to include Negroes in the jury system. Reversing a half a century of legal discrimination against Afro-Americans, the Court in the thirties expanded the concept of "state action" and commenced the nationalization of the Bill of Rights. Both innovations would leave blacks less at the mercy of states' rights and decrease the area for state-enforced private discrimination.[40]

Moreover, the Roosevelt Court's chipping away at separate-but-equal diminished the possibility of maintaining segregation. Speaking for the Court in 1927, Chief Justice William Howard Taft affirmed that the question of segregated schooling had "many times been decided to be within the power of the state legislatures to settle without the intervention of the federal courts." Eleven years later in *Gaines,* the Court made clear its intention to intervene. It did so again in *Mitchell.* Those decisions sounded a muffled death knell for *Plessy* in education and public accommodations.[41]

The actions taken by the Roosevelt Court, moreover, altered the psychological climate in which the civil rights movement battled racial discrimination and inequality. They gave Afro-Americans cause for hope, and hope stimulated scores of additional legal challenges to Jim Crow. To coordinate the many lawsuits initiated independently by their branches, the NAACP appointed Thurgood Marshall to the new post of special counsel for the association in 1938. The next year it established a Legal Defense and Education Fund to raise money for its mushrooming legal campaign. Incorporated in New York, the fund enabled the NAACP to solicit tax-deductible contributions for its litigation, greatly augmenting the resources it could pour into future courtroom fights against Jim Crow.[42]

The gains made in the courtroom also strengthened the position of the NAACP as the nation's leading civil rights organization. Each minor victory against Jim Crow weakened the defenders of the status quo in the black community. Increasingly, the goals of the association became those of black America. No longer content with separate-but-equal, black spokesmen at the end of the thirties demanded integration. By 1939 hardly a major Afro-American leader would dare assert, as had Robert R. Moton in 1929, that blacks would accept segregation as long as it was "equitable and voluntary." In 1937 the Urban League roundly condemned segregation in all phases of life, especially in education because of the sense of inferiority it instilled in black children. There could be no equality, proclaimed *Opportunity,* until the demise of separatism. "No matter how attractive segregation may be at first," the *Courier* editorialized, "all informed minorities know full well that it spells death in the long run." To a cheering NAACP convention in 1939, Charles Houston vowed the association's determination never to compromise with segregation: "It is not a question of wanting to sit in the classroom with white students. It is a question of vindicating one's citizenship."[43]

Neither the decisions of the Court nor such rhetoric fundamentally changed the patterns of race relations in the thirties. They did little to end the daily humiliations and oppression encountered by most Afro-Americans. As the reports of the United States Commission on Civil Rights in the 1960s made abundantly clear, the caste order still stood in the administration of justice, education, employment, housing, public accommodations, and the right to vote. Nine justices in Washington could not quickly reconstruct the stateways and folkways, ingrained over centuries, of a vast nation without the assistance of the other branches of government and, at least, a significant minority of aroused citizens.

Still, its actions had important effects. The cases the Supreme Court agreed to hear provided the civil rights movement with reams of publicity and helped focus national attention on the plight of the Afro-American. The ringing tone of some of the decisions played a role in shifting the attitudes of whites toward issues of race. The new climate of opinion included the egalitarian ideas articulated by Black, Hughes, Murphy, and their brethren on the Court. And, if the Supreme Court in the 1930s did not cripple the underpinnings of the Jim Crow system, it did make them wobble.[44]

These early victories heightened the expectations of the civil rights movement, spurring it to request that the Supreme Court do yet more and more. It also legitimized the Negro's quest for equality outside the judicial arena. Increasingly, blacks had the law on their side in their struggle against discrimination and segregation. They became less the supplicant having to beg for whatever concessions white America would grant. Entitled to equality under the law, blacks demanded their due rights. The movement could now cloak itself with the Constitution and proclaim to the rest of the nation in the most persuasive and unqualified terms: "We are asking you to do what you have written into your fundamental creed."[45]

10

The Struggle

A host of race advancement, interracial, and protest organizations battled for racial equality and justice in the thirties, spurring and exploiting the civil rights developments fashioned by jurists, intellectuals, and public spokesmen. The fight was fought on a scale, and with an intensity, unseen in any previous decade. Forsaking accommodation, more blacks than ever before marched, struck, boycotted, lobbied, and rallied against racial discrimination. Established groups adapted, found new allies and sources of support, augmented their rapport with Afro-Americans outside the "Talented Tenth," and acted and spoke in an increasingly radical manner. New militant organizations prodded those more conservative to greater aggressiveness and amplified the volume and visibility of the whole movement for human rights. Nonetheless all the sound and fury brought about few concrete changes in the lives of most Afro-Americans; it was not an era of fruition for the black struggle. Neither the NAACP nor any of the Negro rights groups could mobilize enough blacks or whites to work toward effecting the reforms the civil rights movement desired. Still, the movement acquired in the thirties a strength and hopefulness it never had before. This turn of events held out the promise of substantial change.

Initially, the depression cast a gloom on the quest for civil rights. Afro-Americans found themselves in a desperate battle to hold onto what little they had. The struggle for survival dwarfed every other concern. All but a tiny number of well-to-do blacks considered the luxury of membership in a traditional civil rights movement beyond their means, financially and emotionally. Out of work or on reduced income, many blacks in the NAACP ceased paying their dues—at a time when the association depended on membership dues for 80 percent of its income. Others no longer took an active part in branch affairs. Subscriptions to *The Crisis* fell so sharply that the board of directors contemplated suspending publication. Middle-class supporters of other race betterment and interracial organizations also could no longer afford their contributions. The National Urban League scuttled several of its programs, and a few NUL branches closed their doors. The Chicago Urban League could not meet its payroll in 1931 and stopped operating. The Commission on Interracial Cooperation had to fire experienced race relations experts from its field staff and national office.[1]

Until the mid-1930s, most civil rights organizations considered themselves fortunate just to continue to exist. All fought a serious morale problem as they constantly were forced to postpone needed tasks, scale down their efforts, and beg for resources. The NAACP curtailed drastically its regular research, publicity, and lobbying operations when its major backers reduced their contributions. The loss of monies from the Carnegie Corporation and other patrons had the same effect on the Urban League, and diminishing dividends from the Phelps-Stokes, Julius Rosenwald, and Laura Spellman funds kept the Commission on Interracial Cooperation struggling to survive. At the end of 1932, Walter White pleaded with NAACP sponsors for funds merely to keep the national office functioning. He had already reduced the staff, cut salaries twice, and contemplated a further salary reduction at the start of 1933. That year, the total income of the association dropped to thirty-four thousand dollars, its lowest point in over a decade.[2]

Unable to succeed alone, the NAACP, Urban League, and other interracial groups increased their cooperation in joint ventures. Many such groups had worked together before, but the need to cooperate even more was never greater. They pooled their meager resources to establish a Joint Committee on National Recovery (JCNR), since no single civil rights organization could afford to finance a watchdog and lobbying office in Washington. Officially backed by some twenty groups, the JCNR had an annual budget of less than five thousand dollars and only one paid full-time worker. Lacking the resources to compete with well-heeled lobbies in Washington, the JCNR failed to dent the discrimination of early New Deal programs. Its only success came as a publicity agency. It provided the Negro press and civil rights movement with numerous examples of Jim Crow and inequality in the relief and recovery effort.[3]

The depression also forced the Negro rights movement to devote more attention to the economic plight of blacks. In contrast to their earlier emphasis on education and social work in the twenties, the CIC and the NUL increasingly directed their efforts toward influencing government economic policies. Along with the NAACP, they attempted to secure representation within New Deal agencies and to exert pressure on administrators and legislators. Given the extremity of the economic crises, no organization ostensibly committed to the Negro's welfare could follow any other course. Correspondence to the national office from NAACP branches throughout the 1930s demanded an increasing preoccupation with bread-and-butter issues. The combination of the decrease in white philanthropy and the growth of the federal government made it imperative to utilize the state as an instrument of reform, and the civil rights movement responded accordingly. In part it modified its traditional programs because the depression magnified its ineffectuality in aiding the black masses and, in part, the expansion of New Deal social services preempted much of the work previously done by Negro betterment groups. In addition, these organizations altered their priorities to ward off the challenge of the Communists. Although some civil rights spokesmen decried the new involvement with labor and welfare issues, this new emphasis strengthened the movement. To the extent that the NAACP and the Urban League supported New Deal economic legislation and unionization, they gained rapport with the black community and the assistance of concerned liberals and labor leaders.[4]

Rather than rely almost exclusively on employers for charity and jobs, as it had done since its founding, the Urban League in the thirties became a proponent of interracial unionism and the expansion of the welfare state. It lobbied for more Negroes in government policymaking and administrative posts, for an end to discrimination in federal projects, and for increased funding for the WPA and other relief programs. Urban League officials T. A. Hill, Lester B. Granger, Ira Reid, and Eugene K. Jones travelled back and forth between Washington and New York, lobbying and testifying before Congress so often they got tagged "the brief-case boys." In 1935 the Urban League opened its own government liaison office in Washington. At its annual convention that year, Hill claimed the Urban League's major accomplishment to be its new popularity with blacks.[5]

One of the reasons for that development, according to Hill, was the NUL's establishment at the beginning of the New Deal of its Emergency Advisory Councils (EAC). The Councils were designed to "organize public opinion" against discrimination by government agencies and to inform the Negro masses of the benefits they could derive from the New Deal legislation. By December 1933 some 196 Councils in thirty-two states were in operation. Much of their effort went toward requesting more funds from Congress for PWA and WPA work projects.[6]

In 1934, moreover, the Urban League founded the Negro Workers' Councils (NWC). For both employed and unemployed blacks, the NWC hoped to "develop their bargaining power in the labor market," to get Negroes into established labor unions, and to promote interracial unionism. The league chose Granger to set out on a campaign of "mass education." "This is no time for soft words and seeking after interracial amity at the expense of the race's future," he wrote in *Opportunity*. Local councils were schooled in protest techniques. Unless the AFL stopped discriminating against blacks, Granger warned, the NUL would support company unions. *Opportunity* kept preaching the "line" of strength through unity and numbers. "You must organize to compel the breakdown of discriminatory barriers that keep you out of unions, and, consequently, out of employment. You must organize to prevent the passing of legislation that will be a further aid to discrimination-practicing unions and employers. You must organize to demand, with other workers, a new deal for labor." The league's pamphlets—*Any New Deal can be the same Old Deal, Where the Trouble Really Lies, Employer vs. Labor, A Football Game, White Workers vs. Black Workers, A Tragedy, The Friends of Negro Workers,* and *Can We Afford to Strikebreak?*—emphasized class and labor, but not race, consciousness. Granger proclaimed unionism as the most important solution to the Negro's problems.[7]

In sum, the National Urban League began to change in the thirties. It heralded its support for civil rights and New Deal liberalism. Like other race betterment organizations, it placed great reliance on the expanding powers of the federal government to bring about the ultimate integration of the Negro into all phases of American life. It was outspoken in its support of the CIO, urging black workers to sign up with the United Auto Workers, Steel Workers Organizing Committee, and Packinghouse Workers Organizing Committee, and it associated itself with numerous united front ventures for the Scottsboro Boys and for anti-lynching and anti-poll tax legislation.

As many of its critics averred, however, the decentralized nature of the league and the dependence of its locals on contributions from the Community Chest and industrial philanthropy kept many of its branches from following the policies of the national office. Some remained little more than middle-class employment agencies and often sided with management against labor. And the national office itself often differed tactically from some of the other interracial groups. However much it shared their goals, the NUL sometimes eschewed the militancy of other organizations campaigning for Negro rights.

Nevertheless, the Urban League augmented the cause of civil rights. It became more a protest and pressure group and less an accommodationist one. Some of its branches went considerably beyond the national office in supporting "Don't Buy Where You Can't Work" campaigns and demonstrations against Jim Crow. How far the NUL had shifted from its conservatism of 1929 can be gauged by its early association with the National Negro Congress in the mid-thirties, its espousal of an end to Jim Crow in the military and in all federal programs at its 1940 annual convention, and its endorsement of A. Philip Randolph's proposed March on Washington the next year.[8]

The NAACP went even further in redirecting its program and tactics. Although its insistence on anti-lynching legislation and a legal offensive against educational inequality did not slacken, association officials prominently involved themselves in Congressional battles over many New Deal measures. They demanded an end to discrimination by the AFL and urged black workers to sign up with the CIO. In united front ventures, the association campaigned for the freedom of the Scottsboro Boys and Angelo Herndon, and for federal assistance to Southern black sharecroppers. William Hastie summarized the course of the NAACP at its annual convention in 1939: the more the federal government expanded the more the association had to change to keep track of and influence all government policies affecting blacks. This meant a reordering of priorities.[9]

These changes did not come easily or quickly. Many of the more economically conservative board directors and branch leaders fought tooth-and-nail against any modification of the NAACP's basic civil libertarian approach. In addition, the association constantly worried that an abrupt shift in the direction by the NAACP, as its more militant critics urged, would be ineffectual and would lead to a Communist takeover of its Northern branches. Charles Houston, Walter White, and Roy Wilkins expressed reservations about a "mass-oriented" program that would destroy their efforts to build a movement in the South at the same time driving away the support of their more moderate followers without resulting in any real gains or new membership. Uttering radical threats, they cautioned, was a far cry from truly being able to organize mass pressure on the government. Given the tremendous difficulty of welding together the largely poor, uneducated, and socially disorganized black masses into a unified protest movement, the NAACP continued to rely on litigation, lobbying, muckraking, and agitation as the best means of influencing public opinion and mobilizing liberal assistance. Nevertheless, the NAACP gradually altered its program.[10]

The NAACP, ever since its founding, had been accused by its critics of benefiting only the black bourgeoisie while ignoring the plight of the Negro masses. As the depression intensified, so did this criticism. In 1932 allegations that the NAACP callously disregarded the misery of millions of blacks reached a crescendo. Board Chairman Joel E. Spingarn asked a group of some forty Afro-American intellectuals and leaders to meet with him the following spring at his Amenia estate. The letters of invitation posed the following questions: "How adequate is the present program of the N.A.A.C.P. in this changing state? In 1916, the association's program was regarded as radical, as being a generation ahead of its time. How is the program regarded today? How should the program be changed or enlarged or shifted or concentrated toward certain ends?"[11]

The answers Spingarn received could hardly have pleased him. Such conferees as Ralph Bunche, E. Franklin Frazier, William Hastie, and Abram Harris denounced the shortsightedness and inadequacy of the NAACP, particularly its cautious legalism and disregard of the critical need to forge an alliance of black and white workers. Much influenced by the various Marxist analyses then popular with white intellectuals, the young blacks at Amenia talked boldly of interracial class unity. They accented the insufficiency of white paternalism and the need for the Negro elite to devote itself to the black masses. Their recommendations to the NAACP at the end of the conference stressed immediate attention to economic issues and to the urgency of an interracial labor movement.[12]

Du Bois transmuted these criticisms into an attack on the association's quest for integration. Throughout the first half of 1934, the editor of *The Crisis* derided the NAACP's concentration on civil rights and lack of concern for pocketbook issues. Although Du Bois never really abandoned the fight against discrimination, or the goal of integration, his desire to prod the association to do more about the immediate economic needs of blacks led him to propose an interim plan of "voluntary segregation." Instead of declaiming against a hostile world, Du Bois advocated that "We segregate ourselves. We herd together." He envisioned blacks joining in a "voluntary determined cooperative effort" as consumers and producers. "I do not consider this compromise," Du Bois asserted. "I consider it common sense." When White and the board of directors retorted that Du Bois had compromised with white supremacy, Du Bois went out on a limb in charging that the NAACP's program led to "loss of self-respect, the lack of faith in ourselves, the lack of knowledge about ourselves, the lack of ability to make a decent living by our own efforts and not by philanthropy." For good measure, Du Bois accused White of having "more white companions and friends than colored" and of being too light-skinned to understand what segregation and discrimination really means to a black, the very same charges that Garvey levelled at Du Bois a decade earlier. Du Bois vilified the

NAACP for awaiting "the salvation of a white God." Blacks, he concluded, must "develop in the United States an economic nation within a nation."[13]

The NAACP counterattacked fiercely. White and Spingarn proclaimed that blacks must never accept segregation as desirable, even temporarily. They made the conflict with Du Bois one of being "*for* integration and *against* segregation." James Weldon Johnson, the retired executive secretary of the NAACP, quickly wrote a slim volume outlining the possible courses that Afro-Americans might take in their present predicament. Much of it lambasted Du Bois's ideas of self-sufficiency as an acceptance of permanent second-class citizenship. "The most logical, the most feasible and most worthwhile choice for us," Johnson concluded, "is to follow the course that leads to our becoming an integral part of the nation, with the same rights and guarantees that are accorded to other citizens, and on the same terms." Francis J. Grimke, one of the first to sign the call for the NAACP in 1909, angrily added his voice to the chorus of condemnation. Du Bois's acceptance of Jim Crow, wrote the respected black minister, means an end to his leadership in the Negro community.[14]

Virtually every major Negro leader and newspaper sided with the NAACP and against Du Bois. "I can see no hope nor place for a Negro nation within the United States," wrote Claude McKay. "The idea seems just a waste of intellectual energy to me." Frazier claimed that "Du Bois's racial program needs not to be taken seriously." Church leaders and Negro college presidents took the same position. The NUL urged its supporters to read Johnson's book. A popular black columnist lamented that Du Bois had "left the ship of race equality for a safer and quieter retreat in the harbor of proscription and race segregation." *The Defender* captioned a picture of Du Bois: "Is He a Quitter?" Its editor asserted that the former battler for civil rights "has now hung up his armor and capitulated to the enemies of his cause." The Great Depression had destroyed the attraction of black nationalist visions of a separate economy by its destruction of Negro businesses. More than half the black retail merchants and savings and loan associations failed in the 1930s. The payrolls of Negro-owned stores dropped to two-thirds of what they had been in 1929. Of the more than one hundred Negro banks established between 1890 and the start of the depression in the early thirties, only twelve remained in 1936. Accordingly, the full integration of blacks into the economy and into American society, replaced self-sufficiency as the dominant motif in black thought. With few exceptions black spokesmen were united in their support of the NAACP's opposition to separatism and segregation.[15]

"By its very existence," the NAACP's Board of Directors resolved, segregation, "carries with it the implication of a superior and inferior group and invariably results in the imposition of a lower status on the group deemed inferior." A month later, in May 1934, the board went further in stating the association's official view of segregation which deemed it an evil that must "be combated to the greatest extent possible." Du Bois resigned.[16]

The controversy over the economic policies of the NAACP, however, did not end with Du Bois's departure. Younger critics took up his cause. They denounced the association's hesitancy in promoting unionism and programs to aid the unemployed. As the criticism mounted, officials like Charles Houston echoed the demands of those who complained of White's obsession with antilynching and the national office's imperviousness to "problems affecting the masses." Two Howard University professors, Ralph Bunche and Abram Harris, circulated studies explaining the necessity of a reformulation of objectives by the association and called upon the NAACP to take the lead in establishing an alliance of black and white workers.[17]

To mollify the critics, the NAACP in July 1934 established a Committee on Future Plan and Program under the direction of the militant Abram Harris. Mary White Ovington, James Weldon Johnson, and the famous Negro surgeon, Louis T. Wright—representing the traditional civil rights emphasis of the association—served on the committee, along with the Socialist-oriented Harris, social worker Rachel Davis Du Bois, and the radical literary critic Sterling Brown. They set up a series of advisory committees run by other young radicals, including Bunche, Frazier, Hastie, and Benjamin Stolberg. Their final Report on Future Plans and Programs called upon the NAACP to foster "the building of a labor movement, industrial in character, which will unite all labor, white and black, skilled and unskilled, agricultural and industrial."

Little in the Harris report should have caused a stir in 1935. The NAACP had already started to respond to the recommendations of the Amenia conference. No other group contributed more to the Joint Committee on National Recovery. *The Crisis* regularly featured articles critical of the New Deal's economic treatment of blacks. It had begun to lobby against discrimination by Washington agencies, to attempt to get more Negroes into government advisory and administrative positions, and to cooperate with white liberals pushing for economic reforms. These activities all spoke to points urged by Harris. In addition, the NAACP hierarchy became more pro-labor following the progressive stands on race taken by the UMW and ILGWU. That policy would increase as the CIO became more liberal on civil rights and the AFL took steps to appear less discriminatory. Controversy erupted only because Harris demanded that the association totally shift its resources from civil rights to economic activity, and because he proposed to diminish the powers of Walter White and the board of directors.[18]

The challenge posed by Harris went to the heart of the NAACP's purpose. Harris argued, no doubt correctly, that if a new economic program was to amount to something really different from what the NAACP had done in the past then control of it must reside in an autonomous Advisory Committee on Economic Affairs. "You can't rely upon the James Weldon Johnsons and the Walter Whites for any new program, for they represent just those values that I think stand in the way of clear thinking on the present relation of the Negro to world forces," he wrote to Du Bois. "Thus as important as a practical economic program is, we must have people behind us who are sick of the old intellectual rubbish. . . . This is going to take a lot of internal purging which we ourselves have got to do." Harris frankly admitted his aim "to liquidate the influence of certain Negroes and whites who are now assuming leadership." Du Bois, nursing his wounds in Atlanta, agreed: "There's simply nothing to be done so long as Walter White and Roy Wilkins are running the Association." Harris's plan would have reduced White's position to that of a figurehead. It would have transformed the national office into a weak coordinating agency. The board of directors would have been left with supervisory powers over little but a drastically reduced legal program.

Though some members of the Board supported Harris, almost all recoiled from the notion of dropping the litigation, legislation, and lobbying for civil rights. Such a step, they reasoned, would leave the nation bereft of a single organization concerned primarily with the rights and liberties of Afro-Americans. It would drive almost all the middle-class blacks and whites out of the association, leaving it penniless and powerless, and it would mean abandoning the fight against lynching, disfranchisement, and inequality in education just as the association was on the verge of success.[19]

The outcome resembled that of the Du Bois squabble. The association reaffirmed its commitment to civil rights, as well as to a concern with the economic needs of the black masses. It insisted upon fighting for blacks on both fronts. Some critics of the NAACP, like Ralph Bunche, kept damning the NAACP for clinging "to its traditional faith, hope and politics." They derided the association's economic program as mere lip service. However, the great majority of Negro spokesmen commenting on the Harris challenge approved the NAACP's rejection of the attempts to cease emphasizing civil rights and to curtail the powers of the national office made at its annual convention in 1935. The association, moreover, did place greater emphasis on influencing the growing activities of the federal government and on working with organized labor and the Popular Front alliance.[20]

In the second half of the thirties, the NAACP's economic program took full shape. It pressed for an expansion of the personnel and authority of the Black Cabinet and lobbied in Congress for legislation to ameliorate the plight of blacks. Using its influence with Eleanor Roosevelt and other New Dealers, the NAACP sought to protect the interest of Negroes in federal programs such as the Civilian Conservation Corps, the Tennessee Valley Authority, the Works Progress Administration, the Federal Housing Authority, and social security. It raised funds for organizations like the STFU and joined with labor groups in fighting for federal assistance to the downtrodden—particularly domestic and agricultural workers. White twice headed the "Equal Protection under the Law" Committee for the Conference on the Problems of the Negro and Negro Youth. He strongly recommended additional federal action to aid Afro-American workers and the unemployed. In addition, the NAACP established its own Committee on Economic Problems Affecting the Negro and appointed Hastie head of a special committee to counteract discrimination by labor unions. Both the resolutions of its annual conferences and the programs of activities for the Association approved by the board of directors reflected the increased concern of the NAACP for improving Negro employment opportunities. Even its legal division participated. The NAACP furnished legal aid to the STFU, to organizations battling against peonage, and to the New Negro Alliance, the group in Washington, D.C. that boycotted white employers who refused to hire blacks.[21]

The NAACP's cooperation with the CIO most strikingly illustrated its departure from previous policies. Like the Urban League, the association responded to the racial egalitarianism preached and practiced by the CIO by assuming a position of leadership in the Negro community in lauding interracial unionism. The NAACP invited such union officials as Walter Reuther and Philip Murray to join its board of directors, and association and labor leaders increasingly addressed one another's conventions. Association spokesmen worked with the CIO in lobbying for housing and wages-and-hours legislation, as well as for amendments to the social security act. It supported labor in its efforts to establish the committee on civil liberties headed by Senator La Follette and to oppose Congressman Dies's Un-American Activities Committee. The surest sign of its maturing alliance with labor came in 1940 when Virginia Congressman Howard Smith proposed amending the National Labor Relations Act to prohibit unions which discriminated from being designated as the exclusive bargaining agent for workers in any given industry. Negro leaders had long called for such an amendment, but because of the tremendous progress made by blacks in entering the labor movement and because of Smith's obvious intention to emasculate the act the NAACP joined with labor in opposing the proposal. Similarly, the association went all-out in supporting the UAW during the River Rouge strike and in preventing its more conservative branch in Detroit from encouraging black strikebreaking. Correspondingly, the UAW backed the NAACP's antilynching campaign, sponsored rallies to secure passage of a federal bill, called for its adoption in radio addresses, and bombarded Washington with telegrams demanding the immediate enactment of the legislation desired by the NAACP.[22]

This expansion of the NAACP program also reflected the competition it received from leftists. The association feared its being supplanted by the Communists as the leading protest group for blacks. From the opening of the campaign to free the Scottsboro Boys to the drive for equality of opportunity in the defense program, the NAACP rarely made a move without first evaluating its potential in stealing the thunder of the Left. The more the CP and its fronts involved themselves in civil rights, the more the NAACP tried to match their militancy in asserting the demand for sweeping changes in America's race relations. The Communist challenge accelerated the association's commitment to interracial unionism and its struggle for equality of economic opportunity. NAACP lawyers adopted bolder tactics because of the courtroom battles of the International Labor Defense in behalf of the Scottsboro Boys and Angelo Herndon. The involvement of such CP fronts as the National Committee for the Defense of Political Prisoners and the Woman's International League for Peace and Freedom in the campaign for anti-lynching legislation influenced the NAACP to picket the Justice Department's 1934 National Crime Conference in Washington and to stage militant youth demonstrations on college campuses in 1937. And the sponsoring of "Don't Buy Where You Can't Work" drives by the League of Struggle for Negro Rights and the National Negro Congress led the NAACP to champion similar movements in Toledo, Richmond, and Washington.[23]

In the mid-thirties, the CP poured its resources into the National Negro Congress to forge a United Front of the Negro People and to wrest the leadership of the civil rights movement. Black spokesmen had been speculating about the need for a Negro Sanhedrin or broad coalition of Afro-Americans to exert maximum power in the quest for Negro rights since the end of Booker T. Washington's hegemony. Ralph Bunche decided to do something about it in 1935. He used the occasion of a conference in Washington on the economic status of the Negro, co-sponsored by Howard University and the Joint Committee on National Recovery, to convene a meeting of Afro-American leaders sympathetic to his proposal for a unified Negro pressure group which would lead the black masses and force the government to respond to their needs. Out of these deliberations came the call for a National Negro Congress (NNC). The CP secured the appointments of James W. Ford to the founding committee and of John P. Davis, closely identified with the Communists, to the chief post of organizer-secretary. From its inception, when the party took the lead in publicizing the new Congress and planning its program, and until its eventual demise, the CP retained control, even though the NNC's catholic support for all the civil rights and liberal economic demands present in the thirties won it the endorsement of many non-Communist black leaders and enabled it to retain A. Philip Randolph as president of the Congress until 1940.[24]

Although Bunche and Davis promised that the NNC would not "usurp the commendable work and programs of any one of the numerous interracial and Negro organizations already existing," the congress constantly tried to steal the NAACP's thunder. The resolutions and activities of the Congress's national office and more than seventy local councils closely paralleled those of the NAACP. From 1936 to 1940 they sought many of the same goals in many of the same ways. Both derided the nationalist approach. Both favored developing interracial alliances with the liberal and labor communities. Both emphasized to blacks the advantages of adopting pro-CIO and pro-New Deal policies. Moreover, both stressed civil rights issues and relied on mobilizing white public opinion as the primary means of inducing racial change in the society. When the NNC followed the NAACP in making federal anti-lynching legislation its top priority for 1937 and 1938, it too lobbied on Capitol Hill, sponsored demonstrations, urged its locals to write their representatives, and sought endorsements for its goals from prominent whites. Similarly, the NNC followed the NAACP in stressing the importance of Negro voting power, organizing registration drives, and backing liberal Democrats. Like the NAACP it testified before Congress in favor of new housing and education bills, and for amendments to the Social Security and Fair Labor Standards acts to include domestic and agricultural workers.[25]

The NNC and NAACP shared a commitment to most of the issues and causes considered "progressive" in the thirties. Their conventions not only attacked lynching and the poll tax, but also condemned the Italian invasion of Ethiopia, supported Randolph's efforts to reduce discrimination in the AFL, backed the sharecroppers, the Scottsboro Boys, and Angelo Herndon, tied the struggle against fascism abroad to fighting the evils of Jim-Crowism and the KKK at home, vigorously supported the racial egalitarianism of the CIO, and maintained their ultimate objective to be the total political, economic, and social integration of blacks in the United States. On the local level, NNC councils fought against police brutality and discrimination in higher education. They campaigned for racial equality in employment opportunities and recreational facilities. In conjunction with NAACP branches, NNC councils undertook to register blacks in Baltimore, to secure jobs for Negroes on the busses and trains of Chicago and New York, and to open up positions for Afro-Americans in the Detroit city government. Both organizations aided the CIO drive to unionize Negro workers in the auto, packaging-house, steel, and textile industries. Both challenged the anti-labor sentiment and conservative leadership in the Negro community and helped shift black public opinion toward a friendly attitude toward the CIO.[26]

In much the same manner, the Communist-controlled Southern Negro Youth Congress (SNYC) aided the civil rights movement both by its espousal of the same aims as the NAACP and by its encouragement of greater aggressiveness. In 1937 the Communists in the NNC established the SNYC as an additional front to compete with the NAACP for civil rights leadership. The SNYC filled the gap left by the NAACP's indolence in developing a youth program and in organizing in the South. The New Southern group sponsored annual conferences for black youth and established local councils in several urban areas. Though it had little success in reaching the mass of Negro lower-class youth, the SNYC added its voice to the Popular Front's demands for anti-lynching and anti-poll tax legislation, full enfranchisement, and total racial equality before the law. The SNYC also cooperated in efforts to ameliorate the sharecropping system and to organize an interracial textile union. Such activities stirred the NAACP to greater militancy, prodding the association to pay greater attention to the bitter impatience of some blacks in Southern colleges. The very existence of the SNYC helped belie the myth of Southern Negro contentment with the status quo. It became a bit harder for Southern demagogues to blame the quest for civil rights on just Northern agitators when the youth of their own section called for the right to vote, to serve on juries and to participate in all primary elections, as they did at the first SNYC convention in Richmond in 1937, or when the SNYC in 1939 declared its opposition to segregation and its hope for an integrated educational system.[27]

The Southern Conference for Human Welfare (SCHW) also emerged from the ferment of the New Deal and the Popular Front. It supplanted the more cautious CIC as the voice of racial liberalism in the South. The SCHW conducted some non-segregated conclaves, approved many of the same resolutions being passed by Northern civil rights groups, and spearheaded the drive to abolish the poll tax. The SCHW's Council of Young Southerners, endorsed by such notables as Justice Hugo Black, Will Alexander, and Eleanor Roosevelt, condemned segregation and eventually affiliated with the SNYC. Some of the individuals associated with the SCHW boldly called for racial equality in the political life of the South. Such expressions were unique for Southern liberalism. Gunnar Myrdal, who attended the first convention in Birmingham in 1938, recalled having

> a feeling that the real importance of this meeting was that here for the first time in the history of the region, since the era of the American Revolution, the lonely Southern liberals met in great numbers—actually more than twelve hundred—coming from all states and joined by their colleagues in Washington; and that they, in this new and unique adventure, experienced a foretaste of the freedom and power which large-scale political organization and concerted action give.

This may well have been doubly true for the blacks, who comprised over a third of the conference. To Sterling Brown it meant that "the South is on the move. The hind wheel may be off and the axle dragging, but the old cart is moving."[28]

Brown's comment may well stand as a metaphor for the effect of the depression decade on the civil rights movement. The tide had shifted. The movement started to recruit personnel and to found councils in sufficient numbers to stimulate hope. An aggressiveness superceded the virtues of gradualism and paternalism. More than ever before, black leaders spoke out against segregation and discrimination. "These are times of a great awakening and new opportunities for all," wrote Mary Bethune in 1938. "The spirit of democracy is being galvanized into realistic action." Despite hard times, the NAACP grew from about 21,000 in 1929 to nearly 54,000 ten years later. Its budget jumped from $34,000 in 1933 to $65,000 in 1940. New civil rights organizations sprouted in most urban areas. The Committee on Civil Rights and the Civil Rights League fought against racial discrimination in Detroit, as did the Council of Negro Organizations in Chicago. Representing over a hundred thousand people, and some fifty-seven civic, religious, fraternal, and labor organizations, the council, according to Drake and Cayton, made it "respectable to support a demonstration or a boycott in the struggle for Negro rights." The Future Outlook League and the Vanguard League did the same in Ohio. Scores of court suits were brought and won to stop racial discrimination in public accommodations in Cleveland's hotels, parks, and swimming pools. Organized protest demonstrations also led the Ohio State Employment Service to establish a Race Relations Unit that would promote the hiring of blacks. The "old cart" even creaked a bit in the South. Various Associated Negro Democratic clubs and Independent Colored Voters Leagues began to register blacks and to oppose the poll tax. Black students held sit-ins at the municipal library of Alexandria, Virginia. In Greensboro, N.C., students boycotted a local theater which barred all films portraying blacks in other than menial roles.[29]

In many Northern ghettos, blacks took to the streets to protest police brutality, racial stereotyping in Hollywood movies, and Jim Crow public accommodations. They joined with the Communists in hunger marches, sit-down demonstrations for jobs and relief, rent strikes, and efforts to stop evictions. Nearly a dozen cities had their schools boycotted by black parents objecting to separate schools. At least thirty-five cities witnessed pickets and boycotts by "Don't Buy Where You Can't Work" campaigns struggling to get jobs for blacks in white-owned businesses. Those in Cleveland and New York lasted for years, engaged large segments of the Negro community and leadership, and secured thousands of new jobs for blacks. "Indeed," wrote August Meier and Elliot Rudwick in a recent essay on Afro-American protests, "direct action during the Depression contrasted sharply both quantitatively and qualitatively with the history of such tactics during the entire preceding century, and achieved a salience in black protest that would not be equalled or surpassed until the late 1950's and 1960's." "Never before," opined Ralph Bunche at the end of the thirties, "have Negroes had so much experience with picket lines, and it may be a lesson that will sink in."[30]

This upsurge in black protest, in fact, led numerous contemporary commentators to exaggerate its meaning. Dollard described blacks who could no longer "ignorantly accept their 'place' as once they could." Virginius Dabney of the Richmond *Times-Dispatch* wrote of "a growing awareness on the part of the dominant race that the Negro is not a serf or a helot, but a human being with legitimate aspirations for the improvement of his education, political, and financial status, aspirations which are slowly being realized." Myrdal believed the age of segregation "was just on the verge of being broken."[31]

The upsurge of white support for Negro rights in the thirties also stimulated such optimistic forecasts and the hopefulness of the civil rights movement. Progressive leaders increasingly set the tone of discourse on racial issues in union halls and universities. They gave the civil rights movement the necessary corroboration that Du Bois considered imperative in 1903. Writing in *The Souls of Black Folk*, Du Bois contended that "while it is a great truth to say that the Negro must strive mightily to help himself, it is equally true that unless his striving be not simply seconded, but rather aroused and encouraged by the initiative of the richer and wiser environing group, he cannot hope for a great success." A third of a century later, Du Bois's hopes began to be realized.[32]

In many parts of the country, white individuals and organizations joined the fight for Negro rights. Whites resigned from the Kansas Authors Club to protest its racially restrictive policy. They called for an end to segregation in professional baseball. They refused to attend a celebration in a New Jersey park that did not admit blacks. Still other whites joined hundreds of blacks to picket the opening of the World's Fair in New York, and the protests gained four hundred new jobs for Negroes at the fair. Whites in such organizations as the American Civil Liberties Union, the National Federation for Constitutional Liberties and the Council Against Intolerance in America regularly proposed legislation to end discrimination in the civil service and to stop lynching. Unions, women's clubs, and civil associations refused to hold conventions in segregated accommodations. Increasing numbers of politicians followed Mayor Fiorello La Guardia of New York and Governor Elmor Benson of Minnesota in condemning all forms of racial discrimination. Whites contributed to and became active members of organizations such as the Urban League, the NAACP, and the National Negro Congress. New York's governor and two senators, as well as the heads of the AFL and the CIO, Aubrey Williams, Frances Perkins, and Eleanor Roosevelt, addressed the 1940 convention of the Brotherhood of Sleeping Car Porters. Various state legislatures established commissions to investigate the extent of racial inequality in education, employment, housing, and the administration of justice. Connecticut, Indiana, New Jersey, New York, Ohio, and Pennsylvania passed new civil rights laws prohibiting discrimination in public accommodations. Numerous professional associations took stands on virtually every civil rights cause of the thirties: freedom for the Scottsboro Boys; ending segregation in interstate travel; abolishing the poll tax and the white primary; and enacting legislation against lynching and discrimination in the expenditure of public funds.[33]

Students and educators added their voices to the white call for civil rights. Teachers' associations passed resolutions in favor of equalizing the salaries of blacks and whites in their profession and promoted Negro History Week and courses stressing the need for interracial cooperation. Professor Broadus Mitchell resigned from Johns Hopkins to protest the administration's refusal to admit blacks to graduate or professional schools. White students at Northwestern, Butler, and Washington universities, and at the state universities of Illinois, Missouri, Michigan, and Minnesota, fought discrimination against blacks in dormitories, cafeterias, and campus athletics. Other student groups demanded the admission of blacks on an equal basis with whites. Racial quotas and discrimination in fraternities especially came under fire. The Connecticut Conference of Youth boycotted beaches that excluded blacks. The Young Communist League sponsored the first interracial dance to be held in Washington since President Grant's inauguration in 1873. The Student League for Industrial Democracy, the National Student League, and the American Student Union regularly supported the work of the youth divisions of the SCHW, the NAACP, and the NNC, emphasizing civil rights as part of the larger fight against fascism at home.[34]

Perhaps no white group shifted more on racial questions in the thirties than the clergy. Beginning with the declaration of Northern Baptists in 1930 terming "race prejudice the greatest hindrance to the establishment of the Kingdom of God on earth," a growing number of Protestant churches ceased to be silent on civil rights issues. The Northern Baptist, Methodist, and Presbyterian churches endorsed federal anti-lynching legislation. So did the Disciples of Christ, the Episcopalians, and the National Council of Congregational Churches. Proclamations by these churches also deprecated Jim Crow in education, employment, and the administration of justice. Most resolved not to "meet except in cities where there is no segregation."[35]

A number of specialized Protestant groups persistently demanded reforms in race relations. The Congregational Council for Social Action and Commission on Inter-Racial Relations, the

Presbyterian Fellowship for Social Action, the Methodist Federation for Social Science, and the Council of Methodist Youth espoused the policies of the leading civil rights organizations. So did the followers of Reinhold Niebuhr and A. J. Muste in the Fellowship for Reconciliation, Fellowship of Southern Churchmen, and Fellowship of Socialist Christians, who sought to make "the principles of brotherhood concrete in the relationship between the races." Headed by Dr. George Haynes, the Department of Race Relations of the Federal Council of Churches instituted Race Relations Sunday in 1932 and Interracial Brotherhood Week in 1938. The department also promoted the exchange of pulpits by black and white ministers, annually awarded the Harmon medal to persons making outstanding contributions to racial justice, and worked with the NAACP and the NNC in lobbying for civil rights legislation.[36]

A small number of progressive Catholics correspondingly began to move their church officers toward a commitment to civil rights. In 1933 George K. Hunton and Father John LaFarge of the Clergy Conference on Negro Welfare met with a group of lay Catholics and clergymen at Manhattanville College in New York to draw up the "Manhattanville Resolutions." This was the first major statement in behalf of civil rights ever made by Catholic officials. A year later, they established the first Catholic Interracial Council and began to publish the *Interracial Review*. Supported by Monsignor John A. Ryan of the Social Action Department of the National Catholic Welfare Conference, the Interracial Council prodded *American* and *Catholic World* to proselytize for racial equality. It convinced the Catholic Youth Organization to desegregate its summer camps and persuaded "The Catholic Hour" to broadcast talks for Negro rights. In the mid-thirties, New York parochial schools began to integrate. Catholic University in Washington admitted its first Negro students in 1936. The following year, the National Federation of Catholic College Students formed a committee on interracial justice. In 1938 concerned clergymen organized the Catholic Committee of the

South to campaign for civil rights. And at the end of the decade, Pope Pius XII and the National Catholic Alumni Association called for dropping the color bar at all Catholic institutions of higher learning.[37]

Religious liberalism on civil rights, however, remained exceedingly limited. Church actions rarely matched their rhetoric. The gap between leaders and followers kept most churches from responding effectively to local racial issues. Sunday church hour was still the most segregated hour of the week. Still, the change had started. In preceding decades, many clergymen had been the chief spokesmen for white supremacy and most denominations refused to take a stand on any matter affecting Negroes. In the thirties, they established the precedents that would place the churches in the forefront of the campaign for Negro rights in the following two decades. The leaders of the black struggle could now appeal to the Bible as well as the Constitution.[38]

A viable coalition had been formed. Writing in the mid-1930s, Malcolm Cowley emphasized that "the most critical aspect of the Negro question" now was that "the Negroes no longer stand alone." The alliance could not yet legislate its will. But it did further the expectations and optimism about the decade ahead. So did the growth of black militancy, which revealed both a greater Negro impatience with racial inequality and the changes in white attitudes which gave blacks hope for success. And so did the increasing strength of established interracial groups. So much so that Mary Bethune could conclude: "We are on our way."[39]

11

"Strange Fruit"

The anti-lynching crusade of the thirties especially buoyed the hopefulness of the black struggle. Although the civil rights movement failed to obtain the enactment of federal legislation, its battle against this most criminal and atrocious manifestation of racism aroused blacks more than any other issue, altered the attitudes of many whites, and forged a sturdy interracial coalition, which attracted scores of major organizations and thousands of prominent Americans for the campaigns to follow.

Throughout the nation, and particularly in the South, the Great Depression intensified racial animosity by heightening competition for a share of the dwindling economic pie. Black Shirts and kindred organizations intimidated Negroes into giving up their jobs to whites. A reign of terror swept through the lower Mississippi Valley as white railroad workers fought to oust Afro-American trainmen. Battles between black scabs and white trade unionists in several cities grew more numerous and bloody. "Look out, brown man!" a horrified Sherwood Anderson wrote in the *Nation*. "These aren't good times for a Negro man to be proud, step too high. There are a lot of white men hard up. There are a lot of white men out of work. They won't be wanting to see

a big, proud black man getting along. There'll be lynchings now."
There were. After a drop from twenty-three in 1926 to sixteen
the following year, and then ten and seven in 1928 and 1929 respectively, at least 21 lynchings occurred in 1930. J. Thomas
Heflin of Alabama defended the practice in a speech to the Senate: "Whenever a negro crosses this dead line between the white
and negro races and lays his black hand on a white woman he
deserves to die." The Tuskegee Institute recorded another
twenty-one lynchings in each of the following two years and
twenty-eight in 1933. This marked increase gave new life to
organizations like the Commission on Interracial Cooperation.
Although the commission had languished in the late twenties, the
upsurge of lynchings provided it with the single most vivid issue
to demonstrate the discrepancy between America's ideals and its
practices.[1]

The Commission on Interracial Cooperation remained a cautious venture. It considered agitation detrimental to progress in
race relations and assaults against Jim Crow as irresponsible.
Few of its state committees, ranging from about two thousand
members in North Carolina to eighty-eight in Mississippi, often
ventured beyond helping blacks to gain a housing project or a
new school. The national office focused on improving Southern
racial attitudes. It promoted Race Relations Sunday and directed
its publications, conferences, and speakers to the churches, press,
and religious journals. It introduced sociology courses in race
relations in seventy Southern colleges. Hundreds of university instructors distributed some two hundred thousand copies of CIC
bulletins on the racial situation to their classes in education, history, and literature. More than a thousand public schools adopted
commission materials highlighting Negro history and achievements in American life as well as problems of race relations.
Seven Southern states wrote the CIC program into their official
curriculum. The study of matters long taboo in Southern schools
gained respectability. The "sympathetic study of the Negro in
colleges and universities, and the appearance of influential Negro

leaders before selected audiences of white people, to discuss the race question from the Negro's angle," added Mary Bethune at the end of the thirties, "are some of the unusual and salutary concrete results of the activities of the Interracial Commission." Most importantly, Bethune credited the CIC with helping to decrease lynchings.[2]

At the start of 1930, Will Alexander predicted that lynching would soon be a "lost crime," a most unusual happening. As Alexander addressed the Quadrennial Conference of the Methodist Church in May, a white mob in nearby Sherman, Texas, dragged a Negro on trial for rape from the courtroom, hung him from a tree, slowly burned his body, and then looted and destroyed many of the black homes and stores in town. Alexander felt humiliated. He also knew he had to act to undermine the Communist appeal to blacks, particularly as the worsening of the depression caused an upsurge of racial violence. Alexander quickly awakened the moribund state councils to launch educational programs on how to prevent lynchings. Under the direction of Robert Eleazer, the various state groups worked through the political structure from the governors down to the most backwoods police officers. They concentrated on showing communities the harm done to them by lynching. "We built a network of persons all over the South who reported immediately to our office in Atlanta any threatening situation," recalled Alexander. "These facts were passed on immediately to the office of the governor in whatever state was involved. The governors usually cooperated in whatever way they found possible—some governors used the state guard. In some cases they intervened personally." The councils also made a special effort to present awards to sheriffs who had thwarted vigilantism. "When an officer was alert and intelligent in handling a threatened lynching," Alexander continued, "all possible recognition was given him in the press, and the techniques he used were broadcast to peace officers throughout the South."[3]

That summer, Alexander convinced George Fort Milton, the

young liberal editor of the Chattanooga *News,* to chair a committee "to study the causation of these examples of group sadism." Alexander wanted its findings published, hoping this would hasten the day when "mob murder" would no longer besmirch the South. He believed that "a better understanding of the causes underlying the resort to mob violence" was essential "to plan effective preventive steps." Officially called the Southern Commission on the Study of Lynching (SCSL), it included such established Negro leaders as R. R. Moton, John Hope, and Charles S. Johnson, and such whites as Howard Odum of the University of North Carolina, Julian Harris of the Atlanta *Constitution,* and W. J. McGlothin, the president of Furman University and of the Southern Baptist Convention. Its distinguished roster of supporters was deliberately designed to gain a respectful hearing for the various reports and pamphlets it issued. Meeting for the first time on September 5, 1930, the SCSL decided to prepare exhaustive analyses of the causes, circumstances, and consequences of all the lynchings that year, hoping "that a people better informed as to the facts of lynching, and the economic, social, and mental factors involved, will cooperate to the utmost in the complete elimination of these assaults upon civilized society." Under the imprimatur of these well-known journalists and educators, such case studies as *Lynchings and What They Mean, The Mob Murder of S. S. Mincey, The Flight of Tuscaloosa,* and *The Mob Still Rides* entered into the Southern dialogue on race relations. Each of the publications highlighted the tenuous connection between crimes of rape and lynchings. They underscored the indifference of peace officials to the fate of blacks, the sadism and barbarism of lynchers, and the high incidence of mob violence in counties of extreme poverty, divesting lynching of the cloak of chivalry that Southern leaders had garbed it in.[4]

The commission sent two landmarks of research, *The Tragedy of Lynching* by Arthur Raper, and James Harmon Chadbourn's *Lynching and the Law,* to every Southern editor, library, and college in 1933. "Never again," Alexander stated, "could any honest, intelligent man say that lynchings were ever justified or unpreventable. The lynchings were inexcusable, they could have been prevented, and any honest, vigorous effort on the part of the law enforcement officers could have found those who did the lynching." Both works exemplified the objectivity and thoroughness the CIC insisted on to undermine the mythology supporting lynching. Only a dispassionate onslaught of facts and figures, the commission believed, would open eyes to the barbarism previously justified as essential to the Southern way of life. By concentrating on greed, rather than woman's honor, as the cause of lynching, "we had stripped lynching of its last shred of respectability," Alexander claimed.[5]

The commission further pierced the unity of the South by calling for federal legislation to stop lynching. Previously, most Southern liberals had decried mob murder but insisted that the states could end vigilantism by themselves. In the mid-thirties, however, the logic of the commission's involvement in the fight against lynching propelled it closer toward the mainstream of the civil rights movement in the North. Like the Urban League and the NAACP, its greater militancy reflected both the vigorous role in the black struggle then being played by the Communists and the mark of the New Deal on liberal thought. The growing acceptance of the idea that the federal government had the right and duty to intervene on behalf of the economic well-being of its citizens led to the corollary that the federal government had the obligation to protect the lives and constitutional rights of Afro-Americans. Responding to this changing relationship between the states and Capitol Hill and to the din from the Communist ranks, the Commission on Interracial Cooperation broke with tradition. It endorsed the Costigan-Wagner anti-lynching bill being pushed by the NAACP in 1935.[6]

Adherence to the CIC's male supremacy tradition, moreover, led to the third front in the commission's campaign against lynching. The exclusion of females from the Southern Commission on the Study of Lynching caused a howl of protest, recalled Mrs. Jessie Daniel Ames, who had become Director of Woman's Work for the CIC in 1929. It insulted the women who donated their efforts to the commission and they "read the riot act about it to Dr. Alexander." Ames suggested to Alexander, "If you'll underwrite the expenses, I'll call a meeting from all of the Southern states. We'll have a meeting here *as women* and see what we can do in this field." Twenty-six women met on November 1, 1930. Using statistics gathered by the SCSL, Ames repudiated the myth that Southern ladies needed lynchings for their safety. "Public opinion," she informed them, "has accepted too easily the claims of lynchers and mobsters that they were acting solely in the defense of womanhood." Of the two hundred-odd lynchings in the 1920s, Ames went on, less than 30 percent of the victims had even been accused of crimes against white females. Of all the lynchings since 1890, less than one in eight victims had been charged with rape. "In the light of the facts, this claim can no longer be used as a protection to those who lynch." Ames also emphasized that lynching discredits Christianity, and impedes the work of American missionaries among non-white peoples.[7]

Twenty-five of the women signed the first resolution declaring that lynching "is an indefensible crime, destructive of all principles of government, hateful and hostile to every ideal of religion and humanity, debasing and degrading to every person involved." They repudiated and condemned the rationale for lynching as necessary for the protection of white women:

> We are profoundly convinced that lynching is not a defense of womanhood or of anything else, but rather a menace to private and public safety, and a deadly blow at our most sacred institutions. . . . It brutalizes the community where it occurs, including the women and children who frequently witness its orgies. . . . The mob sometimes takes the lives of innocent persons, and often inflicts death for minor offenses. It brings contempt upon America as the only country where such crimes occur, discredits our civilization, and discounts the Christian religion around the globe.

> We, therefore call upon all our public officials to use every
> power at their disposal to protect from mob anarchy the laws
> they are sworn to defend; upon our religious leaders to cry aloud
> against the crime till it ceases to exist; upon parents and teach-
> ers to train up a generation incapable of such relapses into bar-
> barism; and upon all right-thinking men and women to do their
> utmost in every way for the complete eradication of this crime.[8]

Twelve agreed "to promote a movement of Southern white
women through the existing organizations, the chief purpose of
which was to inform the public on the real nature of lynching."
On November 1, 1930, the Association of Southern Women for
the Prevention of Lynching (ASWPL) was born. It debated the
idea of pursuing legislation, but decided to leave political action
to other groups. "It was a question of educating," Ames emphasized. So the twelve women "went home and began to work and
to talk and to retell the facts as they had learned them." They
faced opposition and ridicule, recalled Ames, "Nor did they forget
to pray," often being refused permission to speak. By the end of
1931, thirty-three hundred women had signed a declaration of
opposition to lynching and had pledged "to create a new public
opinion in the South which will not condone for any reason the
acts of mobs or lynchers."[9]

By 1935, twenty-three thousand women had signed. In 1940
the number of signatures topped forty thousand. More than
fifteen hundred Southern sheriffs took a similar ASWPL pledge.
State councils existed in thirteen Southern states. Over a hundred
regional and national women's organizations, with a membership
of more than two million, endorsed the ASWPL campaign. The
association published scores of pamphlets on racial violence,
including *This Business of Lynching, Death by Parties Unknown,
Lynching is Wholesale Murder,* and *Southern Women Look at
Lynching.* It also had speakers at most of the church conferences
in the South, emphasizing the adverse effects of lynching on missionaries abroad. "Well, you know that moved all the women
because they were so dedicated and they were putting so much

money in their foreign missions," Ames later stated. "That was one of the strongest appeals we could make." Another was retaliation at the polls against sheriffs who did not cooperate. A mailing to all ASWPL members asked:

> Do you know your sheriff? Have you talked with your sheriff? If it is an election year, have you talked with the candidates for sheriff? Have you asked each candidate what he will do to prevent lynchings if elected? The voters will decide for or against lynchings this year.

In addition, the association held numerous anti-lynching institutes, visited scores of Southern colleges, and addressed hundreds of civil groups. In 1936 alone it distributed more than seventy-six thousand pieces of anti-lynching material. Many commentators, moreover, credited ASWPL members with preventing the lynching of scores of blacks, because of their timely phone calls to a sheriff or visits to a local jail.[10]

But unlike the CIC, the association never endorsed the NAACP's drive for federal anti-lynching legislation. The YWCA and the Methodist Woman's Missionary Council immediately backed the bill announced by the NAACP late in 1933, much to Mrs. Ames's displeasure. She maintained, throughout the decade, that such a bill could never surmount a filibuster in the Senate and that "we were trying to reach the women in those little rural towns, the wives and mothers of the men who lynched. . . . I don't believe they would have gone along with us if we had endorsed a federal anti-lynching bill. They'd say we were following the Yankees and doors would have been closed to us." Suspicious of "the Northern Negro" and "starry-eyed blueprint designers in Washington," Ames kept in check those ASWPL members more militant than she. But Ames met them halfway. Early in 1934 the association resolved: "We regard with favor any legal measure that promises a sure and permanent eradication of lynching." Because local authorities still often failed to punish lynchers, the resolution continued, "it is our conviction that some plan should be derived by which State and Federal authorities may cooperate in eradicating this evil."[11]

In her report to the association in early 1935, Ames emphasized that although the ASWPL must continue to try and change public opinion in the South "we have no word of condemnation or destructive criticism for others who feel that they must attempt other methods. We are all working toward the same point. . . . Even if we pursue different roads . . . we will meet at the end." On several occasions in the next few years she urged ASWPL members to write their senators to "keep us out of the debate on the Senate floor." Still insisting publicly that the ASWPL should take no stand on a federal bill, Ames confided to the executive council on January 26, 1939, "Of course the agitation for a Federal anti-lynching measure has been of inestimable value . . . because it has made lynching news when we were not lynching and it has been national news." But that was as far as she would go. Jealous of her own power and the distinctiveness of *her* organization, fearful of too much racial change too fast and of the influence of the NAACP, Ames never permitted the ASWPL to deviate from its original mission.[12]

Yet many of its members did. They travelled the path from the ASWPL to broad support of the civil rights movement. Ames herself joined the campaign to aid in the equalization of black teachers' salaries. Others followed Mrs. Dorothy Tilly of Atlanta, described in a *Harper's* article as "the Dowager Duchess" of Southern women crusading for an integrated society, in fighting against the poll tax and peonage. Many joined the SCHW and the Southern Regional Conference, which would supplant the CIC during the Second World War. The very novelty of the South's leading churchwomen, "the little old ladies," usually married to men of prominence and power, tracing "lynching directly to its roots in white supremacy" insured them coverage in the nation's newspapers. Too respectable to be denounced as radicals, too locally rooted to be accused of being outside agitators, the ASWPL remained a thorn in the side of Dixie demagogues throughout the 1930s, its mimeograph machines and printing presses headlining the crack in the once solid white Southern opposition to the black struggle.[13]

In the North, assorted civil libertarian, youth, labor, leftist, and religious organizations also mobilized public opinion against lynching. The American Jewish Committee, the Congregational Church, the Federal Council of Churches of Christ in America, the Interdenominational Ministers Alliance, and the Society of Friends' Race Relations Committee each labored in its own vineyard. While the Urban League condemned the crime as a blot on America's conscience, the American Federation of Teachers emphasized the relationship between the anti-lynching cause and the labor movement. The National Student Council of the YWCA and the Public Affairs Committee of the YWCA called for an end to lynching, as part of a new deal in race relations. The CP's International Labor Defense and League of Struggle for Negro Rights boisterously associated the issue with the battle against fascism. So too did a variety of leftwing groups, including the National Committee for the Defense of Politcial Prisoners, the Women's Peace Society, the League for Industrial Democracy, and the Women's International League for Peace and Freedom.[14]

In September 1930 the American Civil Liberties Union (ACLU) also entered the fray. Initially, through correspondence, it hoped to persuade lawmakers of the need for anti-lynching legislation. Its annual report and a special publication in 1931, *Black Justice,* focused on the ACLU's plans to arouse the public to the broad problems involved in the denial of civil rights to Negroes. After 1933, when the NAACP launched its anti-lynching campaign, the ACLU merged its membership files, added the Costigan-Wagner bill to its "must" legislative list, and sponsored a Conference on Civil Liberties Under the New Deal which featured anti-lynching speeches by Senators Edward Costigan of Colorado and Robert Wagner of New York. In 1937 the ACLU made passage of a federal anti-lynching bill its top priority. Other straws in the wind indicating an awakening interest included the awarding of the Pulitzer Prize to Louis Jaffe of the Norfolk *Virginian-Pilot* for his journalistic efforts against lynching, and the beginning of publication by *The Nation* in 1933 of a special honor roll for public officials who opposed lynching.[15]

That year, moreover, the NAACP announced its decision to concentrate on anti-lynching legislation as its main activity. The association desperately needed funds and believed the emotional issue of mob violence against blacks to be the most potent appeal for contributions. A majority of its board of directors thought that only a highly charged cause could pry loose the money tightly withheld by former white and black benefactors. In addition, the board wanted to meet the noisy challenge from the Left, as well as the competition from other liberal and race betterment groups. Ever since its founding the NAACP had taken the lead in fighting lynching. It could not do less now, with the number of lynchings spiraling upward and agitation for federal legislation crescendoing louder than it had ever been. The association had already taken a back seat to the Communists on the Scottsboro affair. To do so on lynching, the board reasoned, would confirm the charges made by critics of the NAACP that it was too weak, timid, and bourgeois to battle for blacks against the political leaders of the South. The NAACP had to prove its mettle by succeeding at what it had always claimed it could do best.[16]

The accession of Walter White to the position of executive secretary further impelled the NAACP to emphasize a drive for federal anti-lynching legislation. Ever since James Weldon Johnson's retirement in 1930, White had confronted challenges to his leadership. W. E. B. Du Bois, Abram Harris, Ralph Bunche, and numerous other black intellectuals all contested his views, ability, and right to head the NAACP. Their allies on the board, particularly president Joel E. Spingarn and Mary White Ovington, made White's tenure hazardous. To silence his critics, White had to demonstrate his skill in leading the association on a major campaign, or else suffer the fate of being replaced. In 1933 no other course seemed more likely to accomplish his purpose than a battle against the upsurge in lynchings.[17]

White's own talents and temperament provided additional cause for taking this step. Campaigning against racial violence had been White's primary function for the NAACP since 1918, when he first went to work for the association as an investigator of lynchings. Just out of Atlanta University, the blond, blue-eyed, and fair-skinned son of a Georgia Negro postman fitted perfectly the NAACP's requirement for someone light enough to infiltrate lynch mobs. He succeeded so well that Johnson made him his assistant. White won a loyal following in the association during the twenties by risking his life while investigating lynchings, performing yeoman work in the attempt to gain congressional approval for an anti-lynching bill in 1922, and writing *Rope and Faggot,* a scathing analysis and history of mob violence against Afro-Americans. White's gregarious, sociable manner, while grating to some of his more aloof colleagues in the NAACP, suited the association's need for a leader who could lobby effectively and secure support from prominent white individuals. Unlike his predecessor who craved the contemplative, scholarly life, the dapper White loved nothing more than hobnobbing with artists, writers, and politicians, buttonholing editors and congressmen, appearing on radio shows, and mobilizing the talents of his many white friends in the professions. Thus, many of the same qualities that most offended Du Bois and Spingarn ideally equipped White to orchestrate a massive interracial protest against lynching.[18]

White and the board of directors, moreover, believed with Will Alexander that the New Deal had paved the way for a major effort to enact federal anti-lynching legislation. Roosevelt had generated reform impulses and stirred sympathy for the forgotten men. The New Deal's shift of power to the federal government made the argument for states' rights appear increasingly obsolete. Every civil rights leader, moreover, considered anti-lynching his most persuasive moral issue, the one best calculated to impress on the American conscience the utter shame of racial injustice. It was also the single cause that could most likely gain white allies and generate united action by the Afro-American community. This combination of institutional and personal needs, plus the horror of the twenty-five lynchings that had already occurred in 1933, set the NAACP on a course it would follow for the rest of the decade.[19]

In November 1933 the lynching of two white men in San Jose, California, set off a nation-wide protest that the NAACP used to launch its campaign. A score of leading politicians and journals condemned the vigilante action, and President Roosevelt denounced lynching as "a vile form of collective murder." White immediately telegraphed the President that "twelve million Negroes" applauded his "every word." Oswald Garrison Villard, editor of the *Nation*, similarly commended Roosevelt and called for federal action. Two days later, a mob in St. Joseph, Missouri, tortured, burned, and hanged a nineteen-year-old black. The lynching toll for the year stood at twenty-eight.[20]

The NAACP announced its intention to press for a federal anti-lynching statute. White quickly organized a Writers League Against Lynching, which blasted the columnist Westbrook Pegler's defense of vigilantism. He then requested Senator Costigan to introduce a bill that the NAACP would soon draft. The Senator from Colorado accepted the task, exclaiming to the press on November 29: "If mob violence is to run riot in America in place of orderly justice the end of free government on this continent will have to come. The sober sense of this country does not, and will not, sanction such menacing lawlessness." That same day, a joint letter from the NAACP and the ACLU requested some two dozen liberal and Afro-American organizations to meet with them at the New School for Social Research in December to plan collective action as a Federal Anti-Lynching Legislation Committee.[21]

News of the involvement of Costigan and the actions of the NAACP stimulated additional support. Senator Wagner, who had addressed the annual convention of the NAACP in 1931 and collaborated with White to fight discrimination in public works projects in 1932, endorsed the proposed measure and then agreed to be its co-sponsor after a stroke partially disabled Costigan. Congressman Emanuel Celler of Brooklyn urged White to let him introduce the bill in the House. His position on the Judiciary Committee, Celler claimed, could "be of considerable help to you in this matter." But White refused. For strategic purposes he wanted a Southerner to sponsor it in the House. None would. Reluctantly White accepted the offer of Representative Thomas Ford of California. The recent lynchings in Ford's home state made him at least a reasonable alternative to a congressman from the South.[22]

Outside the halls of Congress, the Methodist Episcopal Church, the National Council of Jewish Women, the World Alliance for International Friendship through the Churches, the YWCA, the Women's Missionary Council, and numerous other organizations endorsed the NAACP's proposal. In June the association announced that forty million people belonged to groups officially supporting anti-lynching legislation.[23]

Karl Llewllyn of Columbia University Law School, Charles Tuttle, a former U.S. District Attorney in New York, and famed civil libertarian Arthur Garfield Hays meanwhile joined White to draft the anti-lynching bill. Two assumptions guided their deliberations: lynchings occurred because of the cooperation or indifference of local officials; and lynchings could be prevented if community leaders really so desired. Their bill accordingly provided penalties for law enforcement officers delinquent in averting lynchings. It empowered the federal government to prosecute lynchers if after thirty days the state proved unwilling, and it levied a fine of up to ten thousand dollars on the county in which the lynching took place, to be paid to the dependents of the victim. Like so many other bills submitted to Congress during the depression, Costigan-Wagner emphasized the economic stake in the issue.[24]

In February 1934 the Senate Judiciary Subcommittee headed by Frederick Van Nuys of Indiana opened hearings on the anti-lynching bill. NBC broadcast nationwide the testimony given to Congress. Walter White and attorneys Arthur Spingarn and Herbert K. Stockton testified for the association. Their arguments summed up the case the NAACP would make until the outbreak of World War II. All stressed the recent condemnation of lynching by the President. White emphasized the broad interracial backing for the bill, pointed out the states' inability or unwillingness to protect black prisoners, and hinted of the likelihood of black radicalism, even Communism, unless the nation showed a readiness to respect the most basic rights of Afro-Americans. Spingarn and Stockton argued the constitutionality of the bill and the legal precedents for a vigorous federal role. Costigan and Wagner repeated the NAACP claims in their testimony supporting passage of the measure. On March 28, the full Judiciary Committee recommended that the Senate approve S. 1798. Now the NAACP had to get the bill to a vote.[25]

The energetic White crisscrossed the country to increase the pressure on Roosevelt to endorse the Costigan-Wagner bill. The NAACP wanted the President at least to get Majority Leader Robinson to let the Senate consider the bill. White carefully modulated a series of announcements in behalf of the bill to achieve maximum coverage in the press. First came Rabbi Stephen S. Wise's comparison of Hitler's persecution of the Jews with the violence against Afro-Americans; then H. L. Mencken's statement on the absolute need for federal authority to prevent lynchings; then the YWCA's plea to Roosevelt to aid passage of S. 1798; and finally a deluge of endorsements for the measure. The *New Republic* and *The Nation* gave extensive publicity to the bill. The Reverend John T. Gilard of Baltimore mailed out hundreds of letters to parish priests urging their support for the anti-lynching campaign. The Federal Council of Churches passed a powerful resolution backing Costigan-Wagner, and at least ten major church conventions followed suit. Keeping her husband informed of these developments, Eleanor Roosevelt finally convinced the President to meet with Walter White.[26]

For nearly an hour and a half the NAACP head importuned the President at their White House conference. White presented Roosevelt with detailed charts on the strategic value of the Negro vote in the next presidential election. He reassured the Chief Executive of the bill's necessity and constitutionality. Finally, he informed Roosevelt of the numbers and prominence of those requesting that the President place Costigan-Wagner on his "must" list: nine governors, fifty-four college presidents and distinguished academics, twenty-seven mayors, fifty-eight church leaders, and nearly two hundred authors and jurists. The President listened attentively, expressed his desire to see lynching banished from the land, and then explained why his need for recovery and relief legislation precluded his being able to challenge the Southern leadership of the party. White pleaded with the President that the bill would easily pass if it could only be brought to a vote. Roosevelt refused to commit himself. He closed the interview by telling White that he would confer with Costigan and Wagner to seek a means of reaching a vote before adjournment.[27]

Roosevelt met with the bill's sponsors on May 24. The dialogue followed the line that had ensued between the President and White two weeks earlier. Roosevelt repeated his desire for an end to lynching and his fear of what a filibuster might do to party unity. Stopping just short of doing absolutely nothing for the bill, Roosevelt let Costigan and Wagner inform Senator Robinson "that the President will be glad to see the bill pass and wishes it passed." Roosevelt confirmed that at a press conference the next day, telling reporters that while he had some doubts about this particular bill "I am absolutely for the objective." He concluded by affirming his desire for the bill's sponsors "to go ahead and try to get a vote on it in the Senate."[28]

Understanding the President's half-hearted support, Majority Leader Robinson refused to cooperate with Costigan and Wagner. Mississippi Senator Hubert Stephens vowed that the bill would come to a vote only over his dead body, and Robinson wanted no part in forcing a filibuster that would shatter the harmony of the session. Costigan, reminding his colleagues of Roosevelt's sentiments on lynching, called for the Senate to act on May 28, but Robinson ignored his plea. Desperately, White proposed staging a mass silent parade in Washington to demonstrate support for anti-lynching legislation. The bill's sponsors dissuaded him, arguing in favor of giving the Senate another chance. In June, Costigan tried to bypass the Senate leadership, which kept the legislation buried in committee. He requested unanimous consent to bring the bill up for consideration. "Cotton Ed" Smith of South Carolina and Kenneth McKellar of Tennessee said no. The Congress adjourned without voting on the anti-lynching measure. Louis Howe buried the bill in his files with the note: "Not favored at this time—may create hostility to other crime bills."[29]

Outwardly, the NAACP looked forward to the 1935 congressional sessions. Congress had not been so close to acting on a bill to deter lynching in over a decade. Costigan vowed he would reintroduce it. Indicative of the growing force of the anti-lynching movement, the Congress would have before it thirty-three separate bills opposed to lynching. Not one single bill had been submitted from 1925 to 1932, only two in 1933, and ten in 1934. The NAACP claimed to have organizations with a combined membership of over forty-two million people behind the Costigan-Wagner proposal. New groups endorsing the measure included the American Federation of Labor, the Methodist Federation of Social Services, the Social Justice Commission of the Central Conference of American Rabbis, and the National Baptist Conven-

tion, as well as the state legislatures of Indiana, New Jersey, and
New York, and the city councils of Duluth and Cleveland. A
symposium in *The Crisis* entitled "Public Enemy Number One!"
featured statements in favor of the NAACP bill by Villard, W. E.
Woodward, Du Bose Heyward, Fannie Hurst, Sherwood Anderson, George F. Milton, Pearl Buck, and other well-known writers.
Dozens of letters from senators and congressmen backing the
legislation were reprinted in *The Crisis*.[30]

At the beginning of the year, the NAACP, the Federal Council
of Churches and thirteen affiliated organizations sponsored a
series of mass rallies for the bill around the country. NBC and
CBS offered free radio time for programs opposed to lynching.
On one such program, an all-star cast including George Gersh-
win, José Iturbi, John McCormack, Lily Pons, and Lawrence
Tibbet appealed for federal anti-lynching legislation. Senators
Wagner and Costigan appeared on a special CBS Lincoln Day
program to ask for support of their bill. "I tremble for the future
of my country when I remember that God is just," Costigan
quoted Jefferson on slavery. "At this hour," the senator from
Colorado went on, "13,000,000 people in this country practically
dwell from sun to sun under the unlifting shadows of potential
mob violence, despite all lessons taught the world by our fatal
experience with human slavery."[31]

Thousands viewed the NAACP's "An Art Exhibit Against
Lynching" in one of Manhattan's poshest galleries. Timed to open
the same day that the 1935 congressional hearings on Costigan-
Wagner began, the show included works by George Bellows,
Thomas Benton, John Steuart Curry, Julius Bloch, E. Simms
Campbell, Jose Clement Orozco, and some forty others. A paint-
ing by Harry Sternberg graphically depicted the castration of a
manacled black by an angry mob. One by Alan Frelan illustrated
a crowd of white women and children passively watching a mutilated Negro being burned at the stake. Reginald Marsh's award-
winning *New Yorker* cartoon pictured a mother holding her
little daughter on her shoulders to get a better view of the violent

mistreatment of a Negro. The caption read: "This is her first lynching." The prose in the exhibition catalogue written by Sherwood Anderson and Erskine Caldwell expressed a revulsion toward lynching equally vivid. So did the address at the opening by Pearl Buck. "This exhibition may do much to crystallize public opinion," wrote the art critic of the New York *World-Telegram*. "It is an exhibition which tears the heart and chills the blood. Remember, this is not an exhibition for softies. It may upset your stomach. If it upsets your complacency on the subject it will have been successful." The Communists sponsored their own art show, "The Struggle for Negro Rights." The pieces by Noguchi, Jacob Burck, and William Gropper further aroused indignation against lynching and attacked the forces responsible for it.[32]

No art show, however, could match the impact of the lynching of Claude Neal. Although the crime occurred on October 23, 1934, it did not become a *cause célèbre* until the beginning of 1935, when the NAACP widely distributed an eight-page pamphlet recounting in grisly detail the abduction of the young black by an Alabama mob that crossed state lines to lynch Neal in Florida. The whites had cut off his fingers and toes, castrated Neal and forced him to eat his genitals, mutilated his body with red-hot irons, and then hung him from a courthouse tree. The pamphlet and the many periodical and journalistic accounts based on it also emphasized the indifference of local officials to the crime and the fact that some fifteen newspapers published notices of the planned lynching during the week before it happened. Despite the federal government's usual quickness in intervening in cases of kidnappings across state lines, the Justice Department denied that it had jurisdiction in the Florida lynching because no ransom had been demanded. That line of reasoning proved a bit too legalistic for many who had been shocked by the details of the affair. Thousands of letters poured into the White House and Capitol Hill demanding action on the Costigan-Wagner bill.[33]

Following swift hearings by the Van Nuys Subcommittee

again, the Judiciary Committee reported the bill favorably. Roosevelt asked Robinson to get the bill placed on the calendar, which the majority leader did. On April 9, Senators McKeller and Richard Russell of Georgia blocked Costigan's attempt to have his proposal considered. A week later, Senator George requested postponement because of an illness in his family. After another week, Robinson urged Costigan to lay the bill aside so Congress could act on social security, agricultural, and other urgent legislation. But Costigan had had enough. He demanded a record vote without debate on April 24. Senator Connally objected, forecasting the filibuster to come.[34]

First Costigan, and then Wagner, traced the long history of lynchings in America, emphasizing the racially discriminatory nature of the crime, the necessity of federal intervention, and the constitutional grounds for federal sanctions. "Certain living American principles which in the long run affect our conduct and determine history should be called into action," Costigan concluded:

> One is that ours is a government of laws and not of men; another, that justice to human beings and the equal protection of our laws are foremost concerns of the State. The manner in which we practice these principles fixes our choice between Hitler and Mussolini on the one side, and Washington, Jefferson, Lincoln, Henry Grady, Woodrow Wilson, and Franklin Delano Roosevelt on the other. . . . No man can be permitted to usurp the combined functions of judge, jury, and executioner of his fellow men; and whenever any State fails to protect such equal rights, I submit that the Federal Government must do its utmost to repair the damage which is then chargeable to all of us.[35]

Led by Tom Connally, the representatives of the South then gained the floor and kept it for six days. Bailey denounced the measure as a force bill; Byrnes, George and Glass decried federal intervention in local affairs; and "Cotton Ed" Smith insisted that the virtue of Southern white women must be defended—at any cost. Supporters of the anti-lynching bill made no effort to keep the Senate in round-the-clock sessions or to attempt cloture. Although many Northern Democrats had announced their intention to vote for the proposal, neither they nor the President considered it important enough to divide the party and risk the loss of the New Deal's 1935 program. On May 1, the Senate laid the anti-lynching measure aside by voting 48 to 32 in favor of Robinson's motion to adjourn. The Republicans split eighteen to five against adjournment. Only fourteen Democrats answered aye and nine did not bother to vote.[36]

"All along I've been telling you that your President had no real courage and that he would chisel in a pinch," Charles Houston exploded to White. The feeble effort of most Democratic senators to press for a vote on the anti-lynching measure accurately reflected Roosevelt's lack of commitment. White resigned from his honorific position in the Virgin Islands and blasted the President in several articles. Roy Wilkins, the new editor of *The Crisis,* also focused his wrath on Roosevelt. Mary White Ovington wanted the NAACP to work with the Republicans to embarrass the Chief Executive. Several articles in the *New Republic* and *The Nation* roundly condemned Roosevelt's handling of the issue.[37]

Stung by these criticisms, the President agreed in the fall to confer with White on future strategy. They met shortly after noon, January 2, 1936, and talked for nearly an hour. White alternately cajoled, pleaded, and exhorted; but to no avail. Although the NAACP now claimed to have fifty-nine senators pledged to the bill and the endorsements of organizations with over fifty million members, the Chief Executive insisted that there was no desire in the Senate to press the matter at this time. He acknowledged his support for the bill but excused himself from being able to force it through. Roosevelt closed the interview by suggesting that a less controversial Senate investigation of lynchings might have the same salutary effects as legislation in reducing the number of such crimes. But the Southern senators cut the appropriations for the investigatory committee to be headed by Van Nuys and then Byrnes killed the proposal by never reporting it out of his Committee on Audit and Control.[38]

White refused to give up. Following the 1936 election he sounded a call to arms to renew the battle for anti-lynching legislation. Believing that the Democrats had been amply impressed with the power of the Negro vote and that the Republicans understood that they needed to recapture it, White appeared more encouraged than ever before. Dozens of new groups added their names to the list of supporters for the Costigan-Wagner bill. Particularly important were many of the recently established CIO unions because they had large memberships, ample money, and political muscle. In addition, the newly organized National Negro Congress threw its influence with labor and leftist groups behind the association's proposal. As always, the NAACP played up the endorsements of Southern whites. Newspapers around the country reprinted a Richmond *Times-Dispatch* editorial in which Virginius Dabney dramatically reversed his previous stand which favored leaving the matter to the states. Some of the leading dailies in Southern cities followed suit. A Gallup poll reported 53 percent of Southerners in favor of federal action. Congressmen deposited more than sixty anti-lynching bills in the hopper for the 1937 session. Each one signified the Negro's advances toward full citizenship, the NAACP proudly exclaimed. Each was a part of the larger battle against all forms of discrimination and racial injustice.[39]

In April the House took up the anti-lynching matter. Congressman Joseph A. Gavagan, who represented Harlem, beat back an attempt by Hatton Sumners in the Judiciary Committee to substitute a toothless measure for the Costigan-Wagner bill, and then won a 282 to 108 vote to discharge that bill from committee and bring it to the floor for consideration. Maury Maverick of Texas and Franklin W. Hancock of North Carolina were the only Southerners to support Gavagan. The Border state congressmen split about evenly on the discharge petition, but the other non-

Southern Democratic representatives voted 68 to 10 to consider the NAACP proposal.[40]

Just as the House debate began, news of a lynching in Duck Hill, Mississippi, as ghastly as that of Claude Neal came over the news ticker. Congressman Michener of Michigan read the press account to his shocked colleagues. On the very day that Mississippi Governor Hugh Lawson White boasted that his state had not had a lynching in fifteen months—thus negating the need for federal legislation—a mob abducted two handcuffed blacks from the Winona County sheriff and threw them into a waiting school bus. Followed by forty cars, the bus sped toward a predetermined clearing in the woods where over five hundred whites gathered for a carnival of violence. With no interference from local officials, the white townsfolk chained the two blacks to trees, horsewhipped them, mutilated their bodies with a blow torch, disfigured them, fired round after round of buckshot into the dead Afro-Americans, and then piled their remains onto a gasoline-drenched brush fire. The sheriff claimed he and his deputies could not identify any of the whites who took the prisoners or joined the crowd. The stunned House sat in silence until Michener finished. Three days later, 277 congressmen voted for the Gavagan bill; 120 voted no. Every Southerner but Maverick of Texas opposed the measure. The Border Democrats again divided evenly. Northern Democrats went 173 to 14 for the bill.[41]

The Senate, however, proved an impassable barrier for the NAACP. The new majority leader, Alben Barkley, kept the bill mired at the bottom of the Senate's calendar. The fight over "court-packing" had damaged party unity enough; most moderates wanted to adjourn as quickly and quietly as possible to bring the bitter 1937 session to an end. But the experienced Wagner, who had replaced Costigan as floor leader for the NAACP, outmaneuvered Barkley. On August 11, the New York Senator suddenly moved to bring up the anti-lynching bill immediately. Wagner had caught everyone off guard. All hell broke loose in the Senate cloakroom. Tempers, rubbed dangerously raw by the

Court fight, flared. Southerners, damning Roosevelt and the North, threatened to filibuster until Christmas if necessary. Having tasted victory in their first mass desertion of the President, they would brook no compromise on anti-lynching. Writing to an ASWPL official, Senator Bailey fumed:

> I know that this proposed lynching bill is the forerunner of a policy studiously cultivated by agitators, not for the purpose of preventing lynching, but for the purpose of introducing the policy of Federal interference in local affairs. The lynching bill would promptly be followed by a civil rights bill, drawn upon the lines of the bill which Thad Stevens tried to put upon the South.

Wagner relented. He agreed to Barkley's compromise that the bill be withdrawn, on the understanding that it would be considered right after the farm bill in the next session.[42]

At the beginning of January 1938, Roosevelt met with Wagner and Van Nuys to set the strategy for dealing with the forthcoming filibuster. The Negro press interpreted the move as a definite indication of Roosevelt's support for the NAACP bill. Several days later, on January 6, the Southern senators and William E. Borah of Idaho began a filibuster that would last for nearly seven weeks. Nothing like it had been seen in Washington since the post-Reconstruction talkathons of the 1890s. A far cry from the restrained filibuster which shelved Costigan-Wagner in 1935, the 1938 battle smacked of fratricide. Virtually every Southern Senator denounced the President's meddling in the matter. They particularly blamed him for Garner's announcement that he would enforce the rules "in a technical manner" and Barkley's vow that he would hold night sessions if necessary. Such moves heightened Walter White's optimism that the time for anti-lynching legislation had come.[43]

The decisive swing of public opinion behind the measure also quickened White's hopes. George Gallup reported the South 57 percent, and the nation 72 percent, favorable to Senate passage of anti-lynching legislation. Many of the most respected newspapers, North and South, blasted the obstructionism of the filibustering senators. Resolutions supporting the NAACP's position poured in from all over the country. Over two-thirds of the all-white student body at the University of Texas voted to back the bill and condemn the talkathon. Scores of youth groups protested the filibuster in nationwide rallies on National Youth Demonstration Against Lynching Day. Conventions of various CIO unions lashed out against both lynching and the right of Southerners to filibuster civil rights legislation to death. So did the *Daily Worker* and popular front groups like the Southern Negro Youth Congress. The National Negro Congress held numerous rallies to drum up support for the bill. An overwhelming number of Protestant churches and religious journals, and sixty senators, pledged their support for the bill.[44]

The Southerners turned the debate into a paean to the fair name of Southern womanhood and an attack on the President and the New Deal's aid to blacks. Their speeches reverberated with threats to the White House to end its backing for civil rights or lose the votes of the South. "I give you warning," Bailey proclaimed, "that no administration can survive without us." The South, he emphasized, would not tolerate a Democratic party catering to the Negro vote. Byrnes, directing his comments to the people of the South, claimed that they had "been deserted by the Democrats of the North." Bilbo unveiled his scheme for the African colonization of all American blacks, and Allen J. Ellender of Louisiana talked for six days on white supremacy. "I believe in white supremacy, and as long as I am in the Senate I expect to fight for white supremacy," he began. After recounting in great detail the battle to subjugate Afro-Americans, Ellender exclaimed: "It was costly: it was bitter, but oh, how sweet the victory."[45]

In a long address, Pat Harrison depicted the many ways in which civil rights had alienated the South from the Democratic party. Was the faith and love of the South for the party to be squandered away for Negro rights, the Mississippian asked of the President.

> We see the people of the South confronted with the terrible situation of a Democratic majority betraying the trust of the Southern people, destroying the things that they have idolized and in which they believe. I read the other day that the Negro representative from Illinois has introduced a bill to abolish Jim Crow laws in the States, to abolish those laws which provide for the segregation of the races. The next thing, in all probability, will be a bill to provide that miscegenation of the races cannot be prohibited, and when that has been accomplished, they will come back here and seek the help of the majority party in power to take away from the States the right to say who shall vote in their elections, to say that every colored man in every Southern State should take part in the primaries in the State!

For good measure, Senators Connally and Russell closed by linking the demands for anti-lynching legislation with the Communist influences in the New Deal, a tactic that would be repeated with ever increasing frequency in later attacks on the racial views of the Federal Theatre Project, the FSA, the WPA, and the National Labor Relations Board.[46]

Undaunted, most Northern Democrats insisted that the Senate majority favoring the bill be allowed to legislate its will. In a completely unprecedented move, they sought to invoke cloture and end the filibuster. The breach between North and South grew wider, and communication between them more acrimonious. This was no longer the charade of 1935 in which each side went through the motions. When Roosevelt's son James called Byrnes to ask: "Father would like to know what likelihood there is of the filibuster's ending?" Byrnes shot back: "Tell him not until the year 2038, unless the bill is withdrawn before then!"[47]

On February 16 the Senate voted forty-six to forty-two against a motion "to bring to a close the debate upon the bill (H.R. 1507) to assure to persons within the jurisdiction of every State the equal protection of the laws and to punish the crime of lynching," sponsored by eighteen Democrats. Every Southerner voted nay. The Border senators divided down the middle. The other Democrats supported cloture by an almost four-to-one margin. The Republicans, however, voted ten-to-three against stopping the filibuster. The tide then shifted southward. The President and the nation wanted the Senate to act quickly on his request for an emergency appropriation of $250 million for relief far more than they cared about an end to lynching. On February 21 the Northern Democrats gave in.[48]

The NAACP could not admit defeat. Having come tantalizingly close, the board of directors voted to re-introduce the bill in 1939. Walter White, who had invested so much in the massive effort, announced to the press:

> Nothing has happened to change our opinion that a federal anti-lynching law is needed if lynchings are to be checked and lynchers punished. The five authenticated lynchings of 1938 may be fewer than in previous years, but they have been just as savage, and have shown greater contempt for law and order. . . . Furthermore, in not a single case has anyone been arrested for these lynchings. In other words, the states have continued as they have in the past, to do nothing about lynching. The federal government must act.

Van Nuys and Gavagan pledged to sponsor the measure again. Once more the endorsements rolled in. Eleanor Roosevelt, Philip Murray, John L. Lewis, the Southern Conference for Human Welfare, the Wisconsin legislature, the Connecticut American Legion, and scores of previously unheard from organizations lined up behind the legislation. NAACP youth groups led a series of mass marches. In Chicago they paraded through the South Side with flaming torches. In Harlem over a thousand youths wore black armbands to mourn the filibuster. A late 1938 protest rally for the bill sponsored by the National Negro Congress drew representatives from over one hundred groups.[49]

Little had changed in Congress or the White House however.

On January 10, 1940, the House overwhelmingly passed the Gavagan bill by 252 to 131. The lineup remained essentially the same.
Not a single Southerner voted aye; Border Democrats went 19 to
15 against the bill; and the Democrats from the North, Midwest,
and West supported the measure by an almost five-to-one ratio.
Southern senators vowed to filibuster if the bill was brought up
again. The impossibility of obtaining cloture, given the united
Republican stand in favor of what the GOP leader Charles L.
McNary called "the last barrier to tyranny," made another cloture attempt an exercise in futility. Moreover, new issues relating
to defense and foreign policy, which topped Roosevelt's priority
list, put a high premium on Democratic unity.[50]

The result in Congress notwithstanding, the cause of civil
rights gained much from the decade-long struggle against lynching. At the very least, lynchings diminished. From a high for the
decade of twenty-eight in 1933, the number of those murdered
by mobs dropped to eighteen in 1935, to eight in the following
two years, then to six in 1938, and finally dropping to two in
1939. The states themselves started to take greater care to prevent lynchings. To ward off federal legislation a number of Southern states enacted their own anti-lynching measures. Mississippi
provided the death penalty for the crime. Roosevelt ordered the
Justice Department at the end of the decade to investigate carefully all cases of mob violence that possibly involved a denial of
some federal right. The anti-lynching campaign also served as the
civil rights movement's baptism of fire. From it, more than any
other issue, the movement learned the intricacies of modern public relations, fund raising, and legislative lobbying. In the 1930s
the black struggle became professionalized. Moreover, the battle
for an anti-lynching bill proved crucial in the development of
new allies. Many initially attracted to the cause because of the
patent injustice of lynching stayed on to join the NAACP and
other Negro groups in fighting against the poll tax, discrimination in the defense program, and segregation in education and
housing.[51]

The campaign also augmented the power of White and the NAACP. Time and again during the filibusters of 1935 and 1938, one Southern senator after another laid the blame for the furor at their doorstep. Bailey caustically told White: "You ought to go out and make an honest living instead of trying to attend to other people's business and taking up collections from people who are deluded by the folly which you put forward." Pointing his finger directly at the NAACP secretary sitting in the Senate gallery, Byrnes exclaimed: "One Negro, whose name has heretofore been mentioned in the debate—Walter White of the Association for the Advancement of Colored People—has ordered this bill to pass. If a majority can bring about a vote, the bill will pass. . . . If Walter White . . . should consent to have this bill laid aside, its advocates would desert it as quickly as football players unscramble when the whistle of the referee is heard." On another occasion, after observing White make a series of trips downstairs to confer with Democrats in the reception room, Byrnes sneered: "Barkley can't do anything without talking to that nigger first." One Southern newspaper, enraged by talk of White's frequent meetings with the President and his wife, suggested that the NAACP executive had a secret tunnel from the Hay-Adams House direct to the White House. Connally accused the association of being "the parent organization of all these movements." Such references, and the selection of White for a *Time* cover story on the anti-lynching campaign, enormously boosted the NAACP's stature with liberals, and better enabled it to withstand the challenges to its leadership from black separatists and both extreme Negro conservatives and radicals.[52]

Finally, in the words of James Weldon Johnson, the anti-lynching campaign "dented the national conscience." The NAACP had skillfully used the revulsion of most Americans to the Claude Neal and Duck Hill lynchings to expose a wide range of racial injustice. No better issue than lynching existed on which to appeal to the morality of white America for racial reform. No other issue than the right to life itself proved more potent in strengthening the quest for federally sponsored interracial reform. The constant references to violence against Afro-Americans as a form of Nazi atrocity heightened the sense of shame and guilt the NAACP strived to instill in white America. The white response to that appeal, though not that of Congress and the White House, proved to blacks that they were not alone.[53]

12

A Culmination and a Beginning

The many changes in the status of civil rights produced during the New Deal era became most noticeable in 1940 and 1941. Blacks acted with a boldness and confidence that reflected the strength of their voting power and race betterment organizations. Negro spokesmen of all persuasions endorsed the goals of the civil rights groups. The increasingly urban, educated, and politically conscious blacks in the North mobilized in behalf of their aims. So did key white allies. From the start, numerous influential white leaders, organizations, and journals fought alongside blacks to end discrimination in the defense program. Together they pricked the consciences of whites by coupling Nazism with white supremacy and by emphasizing the hypocrisy of opposing fascism overseas while countenancing racism at home. Their rhetoric and actions made civil rights a major issue in American life. This, combined with the evidence of black militancy and white support, stimulated hope among Negroes. It was intensified by the black struggle in 1941 which secured for Afro-Americans the most significant official recognition of their aspirations since Reconstruction. Success whetted yet higher expectations.

Starting at the time of the Italian invasion of Ethiopia in 1935,

Afro-American spokesmen repeatedly stressed the connection between fighting fascism and opposing discrimination. Editorials in *The Crisis* and *Opportunity* amalgamated civil rights issues with their denunciations of Il Duce's actions. A. Philip Randolph associated the two matters in his plea to the AFL for their support of a resolution urging a boycott of Italy. And, according to many observers, the riotous celebration following Joe Louis's defeat of Primo Carnera signified more than just satisfaction for a black victory in the boxing ring.[1]

Nazi actions in the following years sharpened the focus of white Americans on their own racism. Adolf Hitler's deliberate snubbing of Jesse Owens and his black teammates at the 1936 Berlin Olympics provoked many articles and editorials on Nazi racist doctrines and a few on white supremacy in the United States. The number of the latter increased that year when Germany's Max Schmeling defeated Joe Louis for the heavyweight crown. Waving a congratulatory telegram from Joseph Goebbels, Schmeling laughingly lectured American reporters on the inferiority of his colored opponent. Two years later, Louis and Schmeling met again in a boxing match billed the "Battle of the Century." Writers on both sides of the Atlantic played up its ideological connotations. Hundreds of whites and blacks ringed Yankee Stadium with placards protesting against fascism abroad and racism at home. Louis knocked the "Aryan Knight" out of the fight in the first round, and numerous publications sang the praises of the Brown Bomber for inflicting a defeat on Nazi racism.[2]

Many white liberals related the poll tax and anti-lynching issues to Nazism and fascist dictatorships. Henry Wallace stressed the need to oppose both Nazi arms and Nazi racial ideas. At a dinner honoring Franz Boas, the secretary of agriculture bitterly lambasted Hitler's theories of race superiority. Attorney General Frank Murphy and Senator Robert Wagner compared white supremacy with German barbarism. So did Father John La Farge and the Federal Council of Churches. The president of Niagra University threatened to fire any professor teaching race superiority, because it smacked of Nazism. Southern liberals attacked Senators Bilbo and Reynolds for lauding the racial stands taken by Hitler and Mussolini. Labor leaders and Communists freely applied the epithet "fascist" to white supremacists.[3]

Despite the association of racism with Nazism, blacks in 1940 encountered rampant discrimination and segregation in the armed forces. While the Bigger Thomases wistfully watched white American pilots flying warplanes through the sky, the War Department refused Negroes admission to the Air and Signal Corps. The Army strictly limited the number of black enlistments and officers, and concentrated them in segregated service and labor battalions. The Navy Department would not accept Afro-Americans in the Marine Corps and Coast Guard. Blacks had the choice of serving as messmen or staying out of the Navy.[4]

In July 1940 the NAACP featured on the cover of *The Crisis* a picture of an airplane factory marked "For Whites Only." The caption read: "Warplanes—Negro Americans may not build them, repair them, or fly them, but they must help pay for them." It expressed the hurt caused by discrimination in defense industries to both the Negro's self-esteem and his quest for a decent life. Black workers constituted only 0.2 percent of the employees in the aircraft industry that year. The president of North American Aviation announced that "under no circumstances" would Afro-Americans "be employed as aircraft workers or mechanics, regardless of their training." Some jobs as janitors might be available, he added. Most employers and craft unions performing defense work stoutly held the color line. They justified their exclusion of blacks on the ground that they lacked proper training. At the same time, the United States Office of Education and other government agencies restricted the number of blacks allowed in their defense training programs because they claimed it would be a waste of time and taxes to teach workers who were almost sure to be denied employment.[5]

Negro leaders appealed to Roosevelt to lessen discrimination in the armed forces and the defense industries. The President temporized. Much as in the first years of his administration, the black struggle had to take a back seat to those matters Roosevelt considered pressing. Once again the President would not risk the alienation of Southern Democrats and others upon whom the success of his programs rested for the chance of racial reforms.[6]

The civil rights leadership of 1940, however, would no longer accept the President's promises of deferred assistance. The anti-lynching campaign had made its leaders confident and aware of the movement's potential power. They demanded immediate action. The discrimination and segregation in the armed forces and defense industries deeply embittered many blacks and any apathetic attitude by Negro leaders now would surely cause them to lose standing in the black community. "Democracy is never given. It must be taken," the *Defender* editorialized. Challenging New Dealers to organize a Committee to Defend America by Aiding in the Passage of the Anti-Lynch Bill and Abolish the Poll Tax Laws rather than supporting William Allen White's Committee to Defend America by Aiding the Allies, the *Defender* asked "Why die for democracy for some foreign country when we don't even have it here? . . . What democracy have we enjoyed since the last World War? Are our people not segregated? Are they not Jim-Crowed and lynched? Are their civil and constitutional rights respected?" George Schuyler used his weekly column in the *Courier* to reiterate: "Our war is not against Hitler in Europe, but against Hitler in America. Our war is not to defend democracy, but to get a democracy we have never had." Many black spokesmen agreed with Horace Cayton: "The greater the outside danger to the safety of this country, the more abundant the gains for Negroes will be likely to be." They were determined that the Axis threat to American security be used as a lever to end second-class citizenship. "Let the war spread," wrote Schuyler. "The dark world has nothing to lose but its chains, and a world to gain." The Communists, moreover, had highlighted the Jim Crow issue in their all-out battle against the President's defense program. The NAACP and Urban League could be no less critical of racism in their guarded support of the President.[7]

The major civil rights spokesmen feared that making joint cause with the isolationists would leave blacks open to charges of disloyalty, and they wanted Negroes to be able to serve their country, thereby bettering themselves economically and increasing the nation's sense of debt to Afro-Americans. Hence, they resolved to do everything necessary, short of opposition to the mobilization program, to extract the maximum gain from the defense emergency. Even many Southern conservative Negro leaders joined with civil rights spokesmen to lecture the government on the folly of expecting national unity while discrimination in the defense program persisted.[8]

In the spring of 1940 the NAACP amended its regular program to devote its full energies to eliminating Jim Crow in the armed forces. Following the pattern established in the anti-lynching campaign, the national office spurred its branches to deluge Washington with letters of protest and mobilized its white allies in Congress for support. Working alongside the association were new organizations like the Committee for the Participation of Negroes in the National Defense, begun by the *Courier* and headed by Rayford Logan. Established groups such as the National Negro Insurance Association and National Bar Association fought to open all branches of the military to blacks. The United Government Employees and National Association of Postal Employees lobbied for the admission of blacks into the Army Air Corps.[9]

The race betterment organizations first attempted to impel Congress to prohibit discrimination and segregation in the 1940 defense act. The amendment to the measure, introduced by Democratic Senators Sherman Minton of Indiana and Harry H. Schwartz of Wyoming, met the implacable opposition of the War Department and the solid phalanx of Southerners on the military and naval committees. They argued that any move toward integration would subvert military discipline and morale. Secretary of War Henry L. Stimson and Secretary of the Navy Frank Knox adamantly insisted that the efficiency of their services required

strict adherence to the tradition of segregation. The national crisis, they believed, precluded any reforms that might upset the
smooth workings of the defense machine. However, many Northern Senators, especially those from states with a large black population, demanded inclusion of some non-discrimination clause. To
break the impasse, Congress agreed to a mild non-discrimination
amendment written by the War Department in such a way as to
leave it free to continue its past practices.[10]

Congress also passed an anti-discrimination amendment to the
Selective Service Act in 1940. It too allowed the War Department
to administer the act as it saw fit. The compromises pleased
neither side. Yet, the leaders of interracial organizations found
cause for hope in the sensitivity of Northern Congressmen to racial issues.[11]

Since the upcoming election was expected to be close, the association hoped to make civil rights a major campaign issue. It
believed that both parties would be concerned about the votes of
the million blacks now living in Chicago, Philadelphia, and New
York City. Buoyed by the continued migration of Negroes to the
Northern industrial states with the largest number of electoral
votes, many Afro-American leaders joined with the NAACP to
threaten black defections to the Republican party unless Roosevelt acted against military discrimination.[12]

The Republicans, hungry for victory, welcomed the opportunity to capitalize on the civil rights issue. At their convention in
Philadelphia they wrote into the party platform the strongest
civil rights plank in the nation's history. The resurgence of Republican voting in 1938 had convinced party strategists that they
could win in 1940 if they recaptured the black vote. They vigorously supported federal anti-lynching legislation and protection
of the Afro-American's right to vote. The convention further
pledged "that our Americans of Negro descent shall be given a
square deal in the economic and political life of this country. Discrimination in the civil service, army, navy, and all other branches
of the government must cease." The Republicans also invited a

conspicuously large contingent of black delegates to the convention.[13]

Their nominee, Wendell Willkie, worked hard to gain the
backing of the civil rights leadership. He told a group of black
reporters at the end of the convention: "I want your support. I
need it. But irrespective of whether Negroes go down the line
with me or not, they can expect every consideration." During the
campaign, Willkie emphasized the necessity of federal anti-
lynching legislation. He also promised to end discrimination in
the armed forces and Jim Crow in the nation's capital.[14]

The Democrats proved more resistant to the appeals of black
spokesmen than did the Republicans. As in 1932 and 1936, Walter White unsuccessfully pleaded with the platform committee
for a civil rights plank. This time he urged the Democrats to condemn discrimination in the armed forces and industrial employment, endorse anti-lynching and anti-poll tax legislation, and end
all racial bias in the administration of federal aid. Firm Southern
opposition to any civil rights plank led the Democrats to scuttle
White's proposal. Nevertheless, the Democrats approved a platform statement reiterating the many benefits derived by blacks
from the New Deal. The growing political power of blacks and
the Republican challenge on civil rights had led the Democrats,
for the first time in their history, to mention the Negro by name
in its party platform. Though some Afro-American leaders seemed
gratified by this step, most denounced the Democratic evasion of
all the issues raised by White. The two largest Negro newspapers,
the *Courier* and the *Afro-American,* lambasted Roosevelt for his
cowardice and announced their support of Willkie. Throughout
the fall they published examples of Jim Crow in the Democratic
Administration and emphasized the differences between the two
parties on the issue of civil rights.[15]

The President moved cautiously to reassure Negro leaders of
his concern in order to stop a mass defection of black voters to
the GOP. In July he had the U.S. Office of Education announce a
nondiscriminatory policy for its defense training program. He ap-

pointed Robert Weaver to the National Defense Advisory Commission to develop plans to include blacks fully in defense employment. On August 31 the commission made public a new policy forbidding racial discrimination in industries engaged in defense production. Six weeks later, Roosevelt pointedly referred to that order in a special message to Congress.[16]

Still, rumors of the black vote going Republican persisted. The Black Cabinet and regular Negro Democratic leaders urged the White House to do something dramatic to counter Republican propaganda. "There is grave apprehension among Negroes," Mrs. Bethune warned the President, "lest the existing inadequate representation and training of colored persons may lead to the creation of labor battalions and other forms of discrimination against them in event of war."[17]

On September 5 Roosevelt directed the War Department to prepare a statement that "colored men will have equal opportunity with white men in all departments of the Army." A week later he informed the Cabinet that "he had been troubled by representations of the Negroes that their race under the draft was limited to labor battalions" and that they were denied a fair proportion of combat roles. The War Department agreed to give blacks "proportionate shares in all branches of the Army, in the proper ratio to their population—approximately 10 percent." Roosevelt ordered the department to publicize this as quickly as possible. On the same day that Congress approved the Selective Service Act, September 16, War Department officials announced that thirty-six thousand of the first four hundred thousand men drafted would be blacks and that "the creation of additional colored combat organizations is now under consideration." The following week the Roosevelt Administration released to the press details of a new Air Corps unit for blacks at Tuskegee. Some Afro-American spokesmen greeted these indications of an expanding role for the black soldier with hosannas, but most civil rights leaders demanded more. Encouraged by the President's actions, the NAACP and its allies hoped to keep the pressure on

Roosevelt right up until November. Separate but equal was not good enough, they informed the White House. There must be no compromise with Jim Crow in the military.[18]

In late September, Eleanor Roosevelt told her husband that the civil rights organizations' requests for a White House meeting necessitated "important and immediate action." The President conceded. He scheduled a conference with A. Philip Randolph, Walter White and T. Arnold Hill, NYA Negro adviser and acting head of the Urban League. The three blacks prepared a written memorandum for Roosevelt requesting the total desegregation of the armed forces as rapidly as possible. Although this proposal went considerably further than anything the President had been contemplating, recalled White, "he listened attentively and apparently sympathetically, and assured us that he would look into possible methods of lessening, if not destroying, discrimination and segregation against Negroes." But Secretary of the Navy Knox and Assistant Secretary of War Robert P. Patterson, sitting in for Stimson, vehemently rejected any move to desegregate. Knox insisted that the close living quarters on board ship required separating the races. Patterson would agree to nothing more than a vague promise to call up black reserve officers to active duty sometime in the future. Once again Roosevelt seemed to be caught in the middle. His apparent desire to hold the Negro vote pulled him one way; his wish to avoid an open rift at this time with Southern Democrats, the military establishment, and the Republicans in his unity Cabinet pushed him in an opposite direction. Above all, he feared any action that might impede defense preparations. Roosevelt announced that he would continue the discussion with additional government officials and then report back to the three blacks.[19]

He never kept that promise. After the meeting Knox threatened to resign if Roosevelt desegregated the Navy. Stimson flatly refused to countenance racial reforms for the Army. He was furious at the civil rights leadership for its "deliberate use of the war emergency to stir unrest and force new policies for which Negroes themselves were unprepared." The President was also concerned about the defense legislation pending before Congress. He chose not to oppose Knox, Stimson, and the Southern Democrats. On October 8 he initialed his "O.K." on a memorandum submitted by Patterson. Released to the press the next day, the policy statement on blacks in the armed forces merely publicized the War Department's 1937 plan "not to intermingle colored and white personnel in the same regimental organizations."[20]

Not only had the civil rights leaders failed to gain any concessions from their widely publicized meeting with the President, but White House Press Secretary Steve Early intimated to reporters that the blacks had approved the official policy. Incensed at this double-cross, Hill, Randolph and White immediately denied assenting to the 1937 policy. To counter allegations in the Negro press that they had "sold out" the race's interests, the three stepped up their attacks on Roosevelt's Jim Crow policies. They published the memorandum they had presented to the President calling for complete desegregation and issued a joint statement for all newspapers: "We are inexpressibly shocked that a President of the United States at a time of national peril should surrender so completely to enemies of democracy who would destroy national unity by advocating segregation. Official approval by the Commander-in-Chief of the Army and Navy is a stab in the back of democracy."[21]

Civil rights had become a factor in Democratic politics. The stinging rebuke to Roosevelt, especially the mocking use of his own famous phrase, created a sensation in the Negro press. Next John L. Lewis condemned the President for not abolishing discrimination in the armed forces. Shortly after, Steve Early kicked a black New York City policeman in the groin who had been assigned to protect the President at a campaign rally. Although Early, a Southerner, claimed it was accidental, the Republicans did all they could to publicize the rhubarb. They bought full-page advertisements in Afro-American newspapers throughout the country to reiterate denunciations of the President by prominent blacks. Virtually every major black leader now sided with the civil rights spokesmen in their controversy with the administration.[22]

White House officials hurriedly conferred with blacks to arrange a face-saving agreement. Negroes, both in and out of the government, suddenly found themselves deluged with requests for advice. "My telephone rang night and day," wrote White later, "with calls from friends of the President such as Governor Herbert H. Lehman of New York, Justice Felix Frankfurter, Anna Rosenberg of the War Manpower Commission, and others of lesser fame, who asked what could be done to repair the damage Early had done." Revealing to Will Alexander that Roosevelt feared losing the election, Harry Hopkins beseeched the close associate of the civil rights leadership for suggestions on how to keep the black vote Democratic. Alexander's recommendations, like those of White, Bethune, Randolph, Weaver, and various members of the Black Cabinet, all centered on Roosevelt's announcing a series of appointments that would demonstrate his desire to end discrimination in the military.[23]

In the two weeks prior to the election, Roosevelt moved down the path charted by the civil rights movement. He directed officials of the Office of Education, the Bureau of Employment Security, and the National Defense Advisory Commission to meet with black leaders and to announce their intention to include blacks in all phases of training and employment. The President ordered the War Department to publicize again its plans to establish new Afro-American combat and aviation units. Roosevelt also made public a letter to Hill, Randolph, and White apologizing for Early's misstatement of their position and declaring that his own stand on segregation in the Army had been "misunderstood." Press Secretary Early released his own public "correction" of earlier comments. Finally, just before the election, the Chief Executive notified the press of the promotion of Colonel Benjamin O. Davis—the only Afro-American of that rank in the Regular Army—to Brigadier General, the appointment of the

NAACP's William Hastie as Civilian Aide to the Secretary of War, and the creation of a special post of Negro Adviser to the Director of Selective Service, to be filled by Campbell O. Johnson.[24]

Although the President had carefully avoided publicly condemning Jim Crow in the defense program, his concessions to the Negro leadership accelerated the train of events propelling civil rights to the fore as a national issue. Never before had the movement been able to force the President to respond so directly to its demands. His concessions had proved both the potential of black voting power and the possibility of utilizing the White House as an agency for racial reforms, stimulating the hopes of Afro-American leaders for further steps by the Chief Executive toward their goal of ending discrimination. The results of the election gave blacks still more reason for optimism. With many middle-class whites and farmers returning to the Republican fold, Roosevelt's dependence on the urban coalition of liberals, labor, and blacks increased. His pre-election moves had aroused expectations but not stilled the movement's quest. This contributed to the growth of a new black militancy that would plague him throughout the first half of 1941.[25]

The pressures on Roosevelt to act for civil rights mounted. Black leaders grew more united and strident in their battle against bias. The glaring gap between America's preachments around the world and its practices at home became a major theme of Axis propaganda. Liberals publicized the crisis in black morale as evidence of the need for immediate and sweeping changes in the country's pattern of race relations. Dozens of Negro clergymen and politicians, never before involved in a protest movement, demanded an end to government discrimination and segregation. Prodded by aggressive young race leaders such as Adam Clayton Powell, Jr., in New York, Archibald Carey in Chicago, and a score of others who had first gained prominence in the CIO organizing drives, the Afro-American spokesmen derided Roosevelt's instructions to the Office of Production Management to establish a committee on industrial discrimination problems. They called for action, not more surveys. "Throughout the urban areas of the country," wrote Roi Ottley in the *New Republic,* "the Negro communities are seething with resentment, expressed in the utterances of ordinarily conservative Negro leaders, and in the Negro press and periodicals." Even the conservative New York *Amsterdam News* admitted: "While there was once tolerance and acceptance of a position believed to be gradually changing for the better, now the Negro is showing a 'democratic' upsurge of rebellion bordering on open hostility." The combination of the incessant militancy of the Negro press and the fear that Communists might capitalize on the mood of black discontent in their "The Yanks Are Not Coming" campaign led even Southern Negro college presidents to turn the occasion of the installation of a new president at Hampton Institute into a two-day conference on bias in the defense program. The black Southern conservatives issued a thirteen-point manifesto urging the full participation of blacks in the national defense program.[26]

Liberal whites supported the demand. On Lincoln's birthday, Max Lerner emphasized the contradiction of a Jim Crow Army fighting for democracy and Jonathan Daniels termed the process of whites taking jobs denied to blacks "lynching without bloodshed." The decision is simple, understood Brooks Atkinson, Americans must oppose fascism at home as well as abroad. Michigan Governor Murray Van Wagoner and New York Lieutenant Governor Charles Poletti took the lead among politicians in calling on all defense plants to cease excluding blacks. Vito Marcantonio of New York introduced a bill in the House of Representatives to provide stiff penalties for any defense contractor who refused jobs to blacks. The interventionist Fight for Freedom Committee demanded a fair employment code in defense production, a proposal seconded by most CIO leaders. In a single week in May, five New York City newspapers pleaded for equal employment opportunities for blacks. "A nation making an all-out effort cannot neglect any element in its population," stated the New York *Times*. "If it is engaged on the side of democracy it must leave open the doors of opportunity to all, regardless of race."[27]

More than a hundred leading industrialists and union officials, as well as members of the Federal Council of Churches, the Catholic Welfare Conference, and the Commission of the Central Conference of American Rabbis, signed the manifesto of the Committee on Negroes in Defense Industries. Written by Channing Tobias of the Young Men's Christian Association and Father John LaFarge, it declared that justice for blacks was the

> searching test of American democracy. Our concern for democracy in Europe or elsewhere lacks reality and sincerity if our plans and policies disregard the rights of minorities in our own country. . . . The country's immediate needs demand the cooperation of all willing, loyal, and competent workers. . . . Those, therefore, who raise unjust barriers at this critical period are responsible for obstructing the national defense and welfare. This is not time for Americans to compromise with race prejudice. . . . We maintain, therefore, that the time has come for the lasting repudiation of race prejudice as in influence in determining the policies of the Nation.[28]

Statements making the same point came from New York's Governor Herbert Lehman, Mayor Fiorello H. La Guardia, and City Council President Newbold Morris. Scores of prominent whites followed suit, adding their voices to the protest against racial discrimination in the defense program. Appeals to the government to act on behalf of blacks excluded from the defense program were issued by Pearl Buck; Marshall Field of Chicago; the Reverend Henry Sloane Coffin; James B. Carey, head of the electrical workers union; Wendell Willkie; University of Wisconsin Law School Dean Lloyd K. Garrison; and college presidents Harry Woodburn Chase of New York University, Frank Graham of the University of North Carolina, Homer P. Rainey of the University of Texas, and Charles Seymour of Yale University. "The nation cannot expect colored people to feel that the United States is worth defending," wrote Eleanor Roosevelt, "if the Negro continues to be treated as he is now."[29]

Each such statement, article, editorial, and speech by whites urging America to practice what is preached further augmented the civil rights movement. The legitimation of black aspirations by prominent whites spurred even more new recruits among Afro-Americans to become active in the fight for civil rights in 1941. At almost every turn, Northern urban blacks found both Negro and white spokesmen and organizations exhorting them to demand equality and join the movement: they were urged to attend rallies, support mail-ins, join committees, boycott, and picket. In many cities, black fraternal and business associations sponsored resolutions and letter-writing campaigns to protest discrimination. The NAACP, the Committee on the American Negro in Defense Industries, and the Committee for Participation of Negroes in the National Defense organized meetings to denounce White House inaction. In Kansas City, some fifty local black groups cooperated early in 1941 to stage a protest rally in the municipal auditorium. More than a hundred organizations, representing forty thousand St. Louis blacks, formed a Negro Committee on National Defense.[30]

The drive for civil rights had achieved respectability. Speaking for its eight hundred thousand members, the head of the African Methodist Episcopalian Church demanded that Roosevelt stop Jim Crow in government defense training programs. Negro women's clubs, fraternities, and sororities did the same. Adam Clayton Powell, Jr., established a Temporary National Protest Committee on Segregation, and John A. Davis set up a Citizens Non-Partisan Committee for Equal Rights in National Defense. While local organizations like the Chicago Council of Negro Organizations set up mass mailings, national groups like the Alpha Kappa Alpha sorority sponsored weekends in Washington to lobby against racial bias. The Urban League made its top priority for 1941 the cessation of exclusion of blacks from the national defense. "I am obliged to declare," said Lester Granger to the National Conference of Social Work, "that the greatest single subversive movement in the country today is to be found in the anti-Negro policies tolerated by the Federal Government and practiced directly through the military and naval arms of defense." Along with the NAACP, the Urban League joined with twenty-five of the largest black groups to establish the Conference of National Organizations. In its first public statement, the conference promised to remain militant until Roosevelt ended all discrimination in the defense program. When Roosevelt in mid-March asked every American "to put aside all personal differences until victory is won," his radio plea met an avalance of black criticism. Not a single Afro-American leader publicly defended the President. Rather, many applauded the historian Rayford Logan's bitter remark: "The one epitaph which I want on my tombstone is, 'The white man's distress is the black man's gain.'"[31]

The growing protest spirit in 1941 led to the establishment of some fifty new branches and a doubled membership for the NAACP. For the first time, membership topped one hundred thousand. The NAACP offered legal assistance to any black willing to challenge discrimination by the armed forces in the courts. It bemoaned the token number of Afro-Americans on draft boards and it attacked the War Department for stalling the induction of blacks. In the spring White delivered the commencement address at Fisk University. He insisted that all desires to temporize on civil rights be put aside. Prior to 1941 White's call for militancy would probably have been greeted with apprehension and skepticism by the Southern Negro leadership and press. In June, they welcomed it with widespread applause and editorial approval.[32]

Like the Urban League, the NAACP concentrated on racial bias in the defense program in 1941. It hoped to secure passage of Resolution 75, which would authorize the Senate to establish a special committee to investigate discrimination in defense industries. The association called on its branches to send protest letters and telegrams to Washington. Other civil rights groups were urged to organize "postcard blizzards" to the representatives from their states. Friendly legislators received fact-crammed surveys detailing the extent of bias, and the NAACP mailed every senator a reprint of White's *Saturday Evening Post* exposé, "It's Our Country, Too." In addition, the association sponsored National Defense Day protests in every major city on January 26 and directed its chapters to galvanize public opinion "through an organized campaign of militant action." Many locals picketed industrial plants holding government contracts that refused to hire blacks. Others started boycott campaigns to protest bias by employers and unions. The more the Senate stalled on Resolution 75, preferring to let Harry Truman's subcommittee on government contracts conduct such an inquiry, the more vitriolic Walter White's attacks on Jim Crow in government became and the more the NAACP participated in direct-action demonstrations. Indicative of the NAACP's militancy, that spring it announced its official support of the young movement called the March-on-Washington.[33]

The initial idea for a march on Washington grew out of a meeting in Chicago of several civil rights groups at the start of 1941 to discuss the exclusion of blacks from the defense program. "Mr. Chairman," a black woman angrily stated, "we ought to throw 50,000 Negroes around the White House, bring them from all over the country, in jalopies, in trains and any way they can get there, and throw them around the White House and keep them there until we can get some action from the White House." A. Philip Randolph seconded the proposal: "I agree with the sister. I will be very happy to throw [in] my organization's resources and offer myself as a leader of such a movement." Two weeks later the head of the Brotherhood of Sleeping Car Porters met with the civil rights leadership in New York to discuss the tactics of such a demonstration. Most thought they might draw five thousand blacks to Washington. Believing that such a puny figure would hardly attract attention, they agreed to issue a higher figure to the press and hope for the best. At the end of January, Randolph announced a nationwide mass demonstration of ten thousand Afro-Americans who would march on Washington to protest their exclusion from the national defense program. "The whole National Defense setup," charged the black labor leader, "reeks and stinks with race prejudice, hatred, discrimination." He called upon the black masses to march with him under the banner "We Loyal Colored Americans Demand the Right to Work and Fight For Our Country." Randolph asked them to put the lie to the charge that blacks were "scared and unorganizable." It was time, he concluded, to "wake up and shock official Washington as it has never been shocked before."[34]

Contrary to much that has been written about the supposed nationalism of the March-on-Washington Movement (MOWM) and its conflict with established civil rights organizations and beliefs, the leading proponents of desegregation in the Negro community agreed with the movement's goals and, in fact, endorsed the march. The idea of bringing pressure to bear on the government had been tried many times before by the NAACP and other groups. Randolph's emphasis on "power" and "pressure" reiterated the themes he first sounded as head of the National Negro Congress. Moreover, Randolph, much like most civil rights organizations in 1941, hoped to counteract Communist proselyting among blacks and to channel Negro "resentment, disillusionment, and desperation" into constructive political action. "It was apparent," Randolph later wrote, "that in order to avoid blind, reckless, and undisciplined outbursts of emotional indignation against discrimination upon defense jobs, that some unusual, bold and gigantic effort must be made to awaken the American people and the President of the Nation to the realization that the Negroes were the victims of sharp and unbearable oppression, and that the fires of resentment were flaming higher and higher." His nationalistic rhetoric in part was a tactic to avoid a Communist takeover of the MOWM, as white Communists had dominated the NNC.[35]

The MOWM fought for integration not separatism. It sought change by influencing the political system, not by supplanting it. The MOWM welcomed the assistance of "white liberals and labor" and "mixed organizations like the NAACP." And, much as the civil rights movement had worked in the thirties, it strived to arouse white America to the plight of blacks and to gain its support for the reform of traditional patterns of race relations.

Still, however traditional Randolph's goals and motives, his departure from the conventional rhetoric of civil rights spokesmen began to transform the character of the black protest movement. The radicalism of his appeal to the black masses appeared to capture the imagination of Afro-Americans previously indifferent to the struggle for civil rights. By utilizing ethnocentric and nationalistic themes in the fight against discrimination, he reached out to many of those unaffected by the activities of whites or groups like the NAACP. Thousands of them attended March rallies and sported buttons from the March-on-Washington Committee reading "Democracy Not Hypocrisy—Jobs Not Alms." In addition to broadening the base of the movement, Randolph's aggressiveness became the standard by which the black press judged other civil rights groups. His readiness to threaten rather than implore, to demonstrate rather than confer, became the model for others to follow. Everywhere that he established another MOWM chapter, Randolph forced other black organizations to act more militantly. The more strident they became, the more bellicose Randolph's preachings grew. Over and again he hammered home the necessity for conflict. He turned the campaign for inclusion in the defense program into a struggle for manhood: "We would rather die on our feet fighting for Negroes' rights," Randolph declared, "than to live on our knees as halfmen, as semi-citizens, begging for a pittance." More than any other single leader, organization, or event, Randolph's electrifying effort in behalf of the March-on-Washington catalyzed the supporters of civil rights into a mass movement that could not be ignored.[36]

Early in June, President Roosevelt vigorously moved to stop the proposed march. Randolph now was talking of a hundred thousand blacks descending on Washington and a "monster and huge" demonstration at the Lincoln Memorial after the march. The President feared the possibility of an outbreak of violence by Washington whites and police against the demonstrators. He wanted to avoid the embarrassment of a racial protest in the nation's capital. He worried that if he did not intervene the pressure on Congress to act might widen the fissure in the Democratic party at a time when he needed unity more than ever. So he agreed reluctantly to a series of meetings with black leaders. The civil rights spokesmen suddenly found themselves courted by administration officials and presidential aides. The President turned for advice more to Anna Rosenberg, Aubrey Williams, and Eleanor Roosevelt, who approved of the purpose of the MOWM, and less to McIntyre and Early, who scorned meeting with Negroes as "missionary work." He directed all government functionaries with any influence in the black community to beseech the civil rights heads to call off the march and rely on the President's good faith.[37]

The civil rights leadership, sensing the apprehension of the President, refused to cancel the march. In mid-June, Roosevelt asked Williams, La Guardia, and Mrs. Roosevelt to meet with Randolph and White in New York. Mrs. Roosevelt patiently explained that although she endorsed the goals of the MOWM she felt that the march would be bad at this time because of the tensions in Washington: "I feel that if any incident occurs as a result of this, it may engender so much bitterness that it will create in Congress even more solid opposition from certain groups than we have had in the past." Randolph interrupted: "I'm certain it will do some good. In fact, it has already done some good; for if you were not concerned about it you wouldn't be here now." The two blacks flatly rejected the appeal. The memory of the "sell-out" charges after their 1940 meeting with Roosevelt still rankled. Randolph and White would do nothing that smacked of timidity.

"We are busily engaged mobilizing our forces all over the nation for the march," Randolph concluded, "and could not think of calling it off unless we have accomplished our definite aim which is jobs not promises."[38]

Randolph and White also sought to strengthen their negotiating position by playing up accounts of Axis and Communist agents busily fishing in the troubled waters of black despair. Stories in the Negro press reported talk of a pro-Japanese Negro "fifth column." Articles stressed the apathy and cynicism of blacks, and their indifference to the war overseas. New York police arrested a Harlem doctor for driving in Manhattan with a large sign attached to his car that read: "Is There A Difference? Japs Brutally Beat American Reporters. Germans Brutally Beat Several Jews. American Crackers Beat Roland Hayes and Negro Soldiers." Walter White recounted the episode of a Southern black student telling him: "The Army jim-crows us. The Navy lets us serve only as messmen. The Red Cross refuses our blood. Employers and labor unions shut us out. Lynchings continue. We are disfranchised, jim-crowed, spat upon. What more can Hitler do than that."[39]

The Communists, meanwhile, hoped to utilize the march to discredit Roosevelt and disrupt defense production. They clamored even more loudly than Randolph and White for a mass offensive against all government-related discrimination. As soon as the news of meetings between government officials and the civil rights leadership appeared in the press, black Communists accused the bourgeois blacks of selling out. Articles by James Ford and Henry Winston attacked the slightest hint of concession. The *Daily Worker* editorialized: "Backsliding on the part of the initiators of the March is in the making. With bitterness and fear Roosevelt and his agents are getting alarmed. . . . The Negro people must continue their fight against the whole Jim Crow setup. They must not allow any backsliding and turncoating on the part of the initiators of the March on Washington." To good effect, the civil rights leaders used such comments to emphasize that they represented the "conservative" alternative to what might happen if Roosevelt spurned their demands.[40]

As the day of the march drew near, the black leadership increased its war of nerves by bombarding Washington with endorsements for the march. The *Defender* urged the movement to "intensify the struggle by militant action against a RAW DEAL." Black spokesmen ranging from Southern college officials to radicals aligned with Adam Clayton Powell, Jr., voiced their resolve that the march leaders not compromise their position. Many black fraternal, women's, and business groups issued similar public statements and more than a hundred Negro ministers urged their congregations to join the demonstration in Washington. The Negro press provided banner headlines proclaiming "March on Washington Draws Nationwide Response" and "100,000 In March To Capital." Many white church and liberal organizations, particularly the CIO unions, also offered pledges of support.[41]

Such an upsurge of black and white enthusiasm steeled the determination of the civil rights leaders not to approve administration overtures which failed to promise real change. In April they had criticized Hillman's letter urging defense contractors to end bias because it did not have "teeth in it." They demanded "something more punitive than a mere plea." They denounced as "too little, too late" Hillman's establishment of a Negro Employment and Training Branch under the direction of Robert Weaver and a Minority Groups Branch headed by Will Alexander. Meeting with Hillman early in May, the civil rights leadership insisted that Roosevelt personally take a public stand by approving an executive order prohibiting discrimination in defense industries. Not even the President's strongly worded memorandum to Hillman and Knudsen to end racial discrimination satisfied them. In his most forthright statement yet on bias, Roosevelt proclaimed that "our government cannot countenance continued discrimination against American citizens in defense production. . . . No nation combating the increasing threat of totalitarianism can afford arbitrarily to exclude large segments of its population from its defense industries." Words would not suffice. The March-on-Washington Committee ridiculed the President's message and again warned Roosevelt that he would soon see "the greatest demonstration of Negro mass power for our economic liberation ever conceived" if he did not issue an executive order specifically "abolishing discrimination in all government departments, army, navy, air corps, and national defense jobs."[42]

Friendly persuasion and intermediate concessions having failed, Roosevelt asked Randolph and White to meet with him on June 18. By the time of the conference, the President had already decided to give in on the issue of bias in employment but not on segregation in the armed forces. He knew he had to offer something tangible in exchange for ending the planned demonstration. Roosevelt guessed that most blacks and liberals were even more concerned about jobs than military desegregation. Equality of employment opportunity rather than integration of the armed services, moreover, would avoid an open break with Knox and Stimson and do less damage to his rapprochement with Southern lawmakers. Playing his diplomatic game consummately, Roosevelt gave White and Randolph all the time they wanted to state their case. He feigned ignorance of widely known facts of bias and twitted his OPM and military officials for doing so little for blacks. The President then rehashed all the reasons he thought a march at this time would be "bad and unintelligent." The civil rights leaders countered that "somber and responsible Negro citizens" now controlled the march committee but if they failed to get their demands the Communists might easily take over and use it to their own advantage. Finally, with apparent despair, Roosevelt turned to White: "Walter, how many people will really march?" "No less than one hundred thousand," the NAACP leader shot back. Fully savoring the moment, the President looked White straight in the eye and replied, "What do you want me to do?"[43]

Randolph handed the President a memorandum. It spelled out the civil rights leadership's demands for executive orders to forbid government contracts being awarded to firms not hiring blacks and to end racial bias in all departments and agencies of the federal government. In addition, the memorandum called on the President to end all discrimination and segregation in the armed forces and to request Congress to deny benefits of the National Labor Relations Act to unions excluding blacks. Roosevelt asked Randolph and White to go into the Cabinet Room to thrash out the details of the executive order with Knox, Patterson, Hillman, Knudsen, La Guardia, Rosenberg, and Williams, while he left to greet Princess Juliana. The Negro leaders immediately clashed with Knox and Knudsen. The head of General Motors angrily refused to consider any order telling industry whom it should hire. The navy secretary insisted that any attempt to utilize blacks other than as messmen would "provoke discord and demoralization."[44]

For six days the march leaders and presidential representatives battled over the contents of Roosevelt's executive order. The black spokesmen threatened to let the march proceed unless they won all their demands. The government officials refused to agree to anything more than a weak fair employment practices committee to act against discrimination in defense industries. Roosevelt's emissaries particularly objected to any mention of the armed forces or interference with the National Labor Relations Board. On June 24, with the march a week off, the civil rights leaders agreed to accept the order insisted upon by the White House if it included employment in the government as well as defense industries. The following day, Roosevelt issued Executive Order 8802. It stipulated that all employers, unions, and government agencies "concerned with vocational and training programs" must "provide for the full and equitable participation of all workers in defense agencies, without discrimination because of race, creed, color, or national origin." To administer the ruling, the President established a Committee on Fair Employment Practices (FEPC) in the OPM to "receive and investigate complaints," redress grievances and recommend to the government further measures if needed. The MOWM called off the march.[45]

The Negro press immediately hailed the order as a second emancipation proclamation. Black leaders termed it the greatest leap forward for Afro-Americans since the Civil War. The accounts of the negotiations emphasized that Randolph and White had forced Roosevelt to capitulate and that the order represented an uncompromised victory for black protest. They claimed a total rout of the forces of reaction in the government and never mentioned the discrepancy between the actual order and the demands they had submitted. In truth, the March on Washington ended in a split decision. Without the relentless pressure from the black leadership, supported by its key white allies, there would have been no FEPC. Roosevelt did all he could to avoid issuing Executive Order 8802. He resisted it for months. He tried to avoid it by making minor concessions and vague promises. He used whoever he could to dissuade the sponsors of the march. He capitulated as a last resort—but only partially. Roosevelt also had to contend with the forces of racial reaction, entrenched in his Cabinet and the Congress, in industry and the labor movement, and in the military. The President guarded his flank by minimizing the extent of his concessions to the blacks. He refused them even a promise of future action on Jim Crow in the armed services. The order remained mute on discrimination and segregation in government departments. Congress would not be asked to forbid the benefits of the National Labor Relations Act to unions denying membership to blacks. Moreover, Roosevelt snubbed White's request for a seat on the committee; he appointed Negro Councilman Earl B. Dickerson mainly as a favor to the Chicago Democratic organization, which wanted him out of its hair; and he selected as chairman of the President's Committee on Fair Employment not a black or Northern liberal like La Guardia, whom the civil rights spokesmen wanted, but Mark Ethridge, a white Mississippian who published the Louisville Courier-Journal.[46]

Nevertheless, black spokesmen dwelled only on the fact that they had forced a reluctant President to accede to their demands. Executive Order 8802 became a symbol of what black protest and determination could achieve. "The threat of the march on Washington proved one thing," Randolph claimed. "The Negro gets only what he has the power to take. Sure, we're a pressure group. In the March-on-Washington, we have the support of the two big Negro organizations, the NAACP and the National Urban League. But more important, we have the masses on the street behind us. And that gives us the power to make conferences produce something." Although the movement never actually had its strength tested, blacks repeated the shibboleths that power not pleas get you what you want and that a militant civil rights movement could indeed triumph where conciliation had failed.[47]

The establishment of the FEPC, and all the promise it implied, intensified the belligerence of the black community. The *Defender* heralded the death of "Uncle-Tomism" and the birth of a new age of mass protest. The NAACP spurred the lionization of Randolph by presenting him its Spingarn medal, and the prestige of all the Negro rights groups associated with the MOWM increased. Their new status served as a warning to black conservatives and moderates: join the black struggle or risk ostracism and isolation from the rank-and-file Negro. During the second half of 1941, all the major spokesmen and newspapers of Afro-America grew steadily more militant in their demands and denunciations of the government. "Why should colored Americans," announced the Reverend James H. Robinson of New York's Church of the Master, "hesitate to embarrass a country which has been embarrassing its colored citizens all along." Calling for a moratorium on conferences and meetings, the publisher of the *Courier* demanded: "Now is the time for action." Many black leaders who a year earlier had been willing to accept equality within the context of segregation now insisted on the complete integration of the armed forces. "This is no time to be conservative," exclaimed the editor of the Norfolk *Journal and Guide*. "There never was a time in the history of the United States," he wrote "when Negroes were more united concerning the impact of segregation on their lives." Less than a month before the bombing of Pearl Harbor, the *Defender* warned white America: "We are not exaggerating when we say that the American Negro is damned tired of spilling his blood for empty promises of better days." In its first editorial after American entry into the war, entitled "Awake White America, The Hour Is At Hand!" the *Defender* echoed the refrain of Negro newspapers all over the country: the United States must have unity if it is to win, and the price of unity is to "bomb the color line." "Prove to us," Walter White added, "that you are not hypocrites when you say this is a war for freedom. Prove it to us."[48]

On the day after Pearl Harbor, the NAACP announced its "two front" policy. "We shall not abate one iota our struggle for full citizenship rights here in the United States. We will fight," its board of directors stated, "but we demand the right to fight as equals in every branch of the military, naval, and aviation services." The fight against Hitlerism must begin in Washington, they believed. "Declarations of war do not lessen the obligation to preserve and extend civil liberties here while the fight is being made to restore freedom from dictatorship abroad. . . . A Jim Crow army cannot fight for a free world." The Negro press proclaimed the "time ripe for a new emancipation" and mobilized a "Double V" campaign to fight fascism and racism both abroad and at home. With a unanimity rare in the black community, church, labor, and political leaders called for "Democracy in Our Time!" By better than a two-to-one margin, seventy representatives of eighteen national black organizations meeting in New York supported a resolution authored by Judge William Hastie that unless Afro-Americans gained their full civil rights they would *not* fight "whole-heartedly, unselfishly, all-out in support of the present war effort." Instead of dismantling the MOWM, Randolph transformed it into a permanent organization. Jim

Crow, he proclaimed, "is a moral, spiritual, and intellectual insult to the soul of the Negro, and it must be erased from every corner of American life." The goals of the MOWM were now the complete elimination of "Jim Crow in education, in housing, in transportation, and in every other social, economic and political privilege; full enforcement of the Fourteenth and Fifteenth amendments; abolition of all suffrage restrictions and limitations; and of private and government discrimination in employment; and expansion of the role of Negro advisors in all administrative agencies." "We want," Randolph told a cheering rally in Detroit, "the full works of citizenship with no reservations. We will accept nothing less."[49]

Roosevelt had hoped to buy time with Executive Order 8802. He thought it would suffice to keep blacks quiescent during the war effort. Instead, his reactions helped unleash an even greater militancy that would accelerate the fight to bring civil rights to the fore as a major national concern.

13

Conclusion

The announcement by the Daughters of the American Revolution in March 1939 that it would not permit Howard University to use its Constitution Hall for a concert by Marian Anderson or any other black performer triggered a broad assault on white racism. Every major Negro organization and newspaper rushed to the attack. Tens of thousands of letters and telegrams poured into the offices of the DAR demanding that it reverse the decision. Such world-renowned musicians as Walter Damrosch, Leopold Stokowski, and Lawrence Tibbett decried the DAR's action. A New York *Times* editorial claimed that the DAR's bigotry warranted its losing the adjective "patriotic," and a petition from clergymen termed the DAR's policy "pagan." The announcement by the women's group so enraged the normally placid philanthropist Anson Phelps Stokes that he hurriedly wrote and published his own protest pamphlet, "Art and the Color Line." Justices of the Supreme Court, senators, congressmen, governors, and a majority of the nation's religious and labor organizations issued public statements condemning the Daughters. In her "My Day" column, Eleanor Roosevelt explained that she could no longer remain a member of the DAR. Over two-thirds of those questioned in a Gallup Poll approved of her resignation.[1]

The federal government worked hand in glove with the NAACP and other civil rights organizations on the matter. Assistant Secretary of the Interior Oscar Chapman grasped Walter White's suggestion that a free public concert be held at the Lincoln Memorial to focus on the bigotry of the DAR. Quickly, he secured the approval of Ickes, who convinced Roosevelt to endorse the plan. "Tell Oscar," the President replied to Ickes, "he has my permission to have Marian sing from the top of the Washington Monument if he wants it." With the assistance of New York Congresswoman Caroline O'Day and Eleanor Roosevelt, the NAACP arranged for dozens of diplomats, congressmen, Cabinet members, and Supreme Court justices, as well as representatives from the nation's leading cultural and educational institutions, to serve on the concert's sponsoring committee. On a cold, blustery Easter Sunday an interracial crowd of over seventy-five thousand stood in front of the memorial to the Emancipator to hear Marian Anderson sing the concert the DAR would not permit in Constitution Hall. From the opening bars of "America" to the closing notes of "Nobody Knows the Trouble I've Seen," the symbolism of a new deal for blacks suffused the musical performance. Two months later, after being the subject of a glowing *Time* cover story, Miss Anderson officially received the NAACP Spingarn Medal from the First Lady.[2]

Many proponents of civil rights believed that the Marian Anderson episode epitomized the changes that had occurred in the thirties. They contrasted it with the vastly dissimilar response of federal officials, and the almost total apathy of whites and blacks, to Herbert Hoover's decision at the start of the decade to segregate the Negro Gold Star Mothers sailing to France. They measured the advance toward equality by comparing the reports of the National Advisory Committees on Education promulgated during the Hoover and Roosevelt administrations. The second committee, appointed by FDR in 1937, called for specific guarantees that federal grants to states for education be spent equitably for black as well as white schooling. In 1930 that proposition was rejected by Hoover's committee. It appeared only in the minority report filed by three Negro members of the committee. In 1938 the minority opinion became the official majority recommendation, and the committee's words appeared verbatim in the Harrison-Thomas-Fletcher bill submitted to Congress. Similarly, they noted that Hoover's Commission on Law Enforcement had turned down flatly the NAACP's request that it consider lynching, peonage, disfranchisement, and discrimination in public accommodations, but that advocates of reform in all these matters had achieved some success in the three branches of government by the end of the depression decade. None who fought for civil rights considered these examples as substantive victories; rather, they were regarded as harbingers of a diminution of white hostility and black powerlessness. "Conditions were far from ideal," observed Paul Robeson when he returned to the United States in 1939, "they were not even so much changed in fact as they appeared to be, in the hopefulness of liberals and Negro leaders. But change was in the air," Robeson concluded, "and this was the best sign of all."[3]

Indeed, little had changed in the concrete aspects of life for most blacks. They remained a submerged caste, commonly discriminated against by industry, the labor movement, and government at all levels. Blacks continued to be mired in the ranks of menials, sharecroppers, unskilled laborers, and domestics. They were twice as likely to be unemployed as whites and earned only half the income of whites when they could find work. The advances made in educational opportunities, infant and maternal mortality rates, and occupational mobility served mainly to heighten black awareness of the disparities between Afro-Americans and whites that still existed. Blacks in the North overwhelmingly lived in ghettos that had turned into slums. In the South, where a majority of blacks endured, white supremacy and segregation remained the rule. The bulk of Afro-Americans could not vote. None could go to school with whites. All had to ride in the back of the bus. Every public toilet and drinking fountain in the region had signs lettered "White Only" or "Colored." In the heart of the nation's capital, blacks could not attend a movie, stay at a hotel, or buy a cup of coffee.

Those facts cannot be gainsaid. They stain the record of the Roosevelt Administration, as well as that of every individual and organization that should have done more to seek to alter the situation. The odds against their succeeding do not constitute a sufficient excuse for their timidity, half measures, and concessions. In moral terms, the horror of racism makes a mockery of lauding anyone as a humanitarian who compromised with its existence, as Roosevelt did repeatedly.

Historical judgment, however, requires attention to the nuances of context and to an awareness of limits. "Men make their own history," Karl Marx wrote in *The Eighteenth Brumaire*, "but they do not make it under circumstances chosen by themselves, but under circumstances directly encountered, given and transmitted from the past." Those intent upon reforming race relations in the 1930s had no *tabula rasa* upon which to work. They were in the midst of the worst depression in the nation's history. Voters wanted relief and recovery; they did not want government involvement in what they viewed as tangential matters that might hinder economic reconstruction. Those who desired a modification of traditional race relations had to operate in a political system better constructed to impede change than to promote innovation. The oppressing borough system, the poll tax and white primary, the variety of rules hampering the development of third parties— all aided in the defeat or dilution of desired reforms. So did traditions of decentralization, local control, and states' rights. The filibuster, seniority system, and the secrecy of committee proceedings bestowed upon the defenders of the status quo the advantage over those seeking reform in Congress. The desire for quick and fundamental change gave way to the Supreme Court's need to wait for cases to be brought before it, to take existing social relationships into account in its decision, and to depart slowly from the weight of precedents. The fact that less than 15 percent of Americans aged eighteen to twenty-one went beyond high school slowed the dissemination of ideas undermining racism. The control of the mass media by private corporations primarily concerned with profits restricted the expression of new or unpopular concepts.

For three centuries racism had infected the national mind as well as the body politic. No labor leader, no public official, could ignore the results. The majority of white Americans wanted no change in race relations. They favored neither desegregation nor equal opportunities for blacks. Millions remained enslaved by fear, ignorance, and prejudice, and their emancipation continued to be a dream deferred, as it did for most blacks. The majority of Afro-Americans stayed trapped in what Oscar Lewis would later call the "culture of poverty." Plagued by illiteracy, social disorganization, physical isolation, disfranchisement, and their "mark of oppression," most Negroes could not yet battle for full citizenship or rebel against the inequities destroying them.

It would take a quarter of a century of prosperity, a world war and a protracted cold war, the end of white colonialism in Africa, and a mass exodus of blacks from the South that would dwarf all such migration prior to 1940 before the basic conditions of life for blacks would change significantly. Those same developments would also make it possible for individuals, organizations, and movements to alter relations between the races to an extent not conceivable in the thirties. Even in the 1970s, moreover, racial equality would not be achieved. The goal of ending discrimination and racial injustice remained unfulfilled. To ignore this and to condemn those who assisted the black freedom struggle for failing to end racism in the 1930s is a judgment beyond history. Such an evaluation recapitulates the error of many liberals in the thirties who did not comprehend the persistence and depth of white supremacy. They believed it could be easily overcome. We should know better.

But something vital did begin in the thirties. Negro expectations rose; black powerlessness decreased; white hostility diminished. Together, these gave the proponents of civil rights hope, what the Philadelphia *Tribune* termed "the emergence of a new type of faith."[4]

Alongside the continuity of discrimination and segregation, the federal government aided blacks to an unprecedented extent, both substantively and symbolically. New Dealers joined with civil rights organizations to fight for equality of treatment for blacks in the relief and recovery programs and largely succeeded in the FSA, NYA, PWA, USHA, and FWA. The quota system instituted by Ickes became a model for the President's Committee on Fair Employment Practices and numerous other federal and state agencies to follow in their efforts to guarantee blacks a fair deal. The number of Afro-American federal employees tripled in the depression decade. Over a hundred Negroes were appointed to administrative posts by Roosevelt. The administration began the desegregation of federal restrooms, cafeterias, and secretarial pools. In addition, a host of government publications and conferences focused on "the Negro problem." They made explicit the federal government's responsibility for and recognition of issues of human rights. Never before, moreover, had a First Lady and so many high level government officials associated so closely with the civil rights movement. However half-heartedly, President Roosevelt also endorsed the campaigns for anti-poll tax and anti-lynching legislation. The most prominent whites in the nation had started to legitimate the aspirations of blacks on a wide variety of issues.

President Roosevelt's appointments further stimulated hope for racial changes. The presence of a Black Cabinet and such men as Will Alexander, Harry Hopkins, Harold Ickes, and Aubrey Williams helped to make civil rights a New Deal matter. "The worst fears of the unregenerate South are being realized," Hastie concluded at the end of the decade. "It seems that the U.S. Senate is the last stronghold of the Confederacy." With the exception of James Byrnes, Roosevelt's eight selections for the Supreme Court became pronounced partisans of civil rights. Indeed, what would culminate in the Warren Court clearly began in the Roosevelt Court. Its decisions in cases involving the exclusion of blacks from juries, the right to picket against discrimination in employment, inequality in interstate transportation, disfranchisement, racial restrictive covenants, and discrimination in the payment of Negro teachers and the admission of blacks to graduate education made the Afro-American less a *freedman* and more a *free man*. Equally important, the Court circumscribed the boundaries of permissible discrimination by its federalizing of the Bill of Rights and its expansion of the concept of state action. It signaled the demise of *Plessy* v. *Ferguson* by insisting on inquiring into the facts of segregation, rather than just the theory.[5]

The lessening of deference to Southern Democrats by Northern liberals on the race issue also buoyed the expectations of civil rights proponents. The prominence of Dixie Democrats in the conservative coalition and the decline of the power of the South within the Democratic party caused urban liberals to reevaluate their traditional support for their Southern colleagues in opposition to civil rights. The growth of the black vote in the North and the identification of racism with fascism, both at home and abroad, necessitated a switch. So did the endorsement of civil rights legislation by major Popular Front, labor, and liberal organizations. In 1922 only 8 Democrats broke party regularity to vote in favor of the Dyer anti-lynching bill. In 1937, however, when the House again voted on the issue, 171 of the 185 Northern and Western Democrats recorded deserted the South to vote aye.[6]

The hopefulness of black leaders that Robeson referred to similarly reflected the changes in the radical left and labor movements. Prior to the thirties, both had been indifferent or opposed to the Afro-American's quest for civil rights. By the end of the depression decade they were preaching the egalitarian gospel to millions of white Americans. The Communists and the CIO, in particular, became the loudest advocates of economic, political, and social equality for blacks, and the best-organized and financed proponents of Negro rights. In countless ways, they e phasized the need for interracial unity and proved it could work.

The politics of self-interest, far more than altruism or paternalism, had ended the isolation of blacks in their struggle for racial justice. As Malcolm Cowley witnessed: "Negroes no longer stand alone." Alongside them stood radicals pressing for class unity unhampered by racial divisions; labor leaders wanting strong unions; ethnic and political minorities desiring greater security for themselves from a strong central government that would protect constitutional rights; and liberals battling opponents of the New Deal. Civil rights became a stick with which to beat Southern conservatism.[7]

At the same time, the academic community provided the intellectual justifications for the changes in race relations supported by the coalition of blacks, leftists, unionists, and liberals. Biological and social scientists refuted the doctrines of inherent and irremediable racial differences and of the folly of governmental interference with folkways that had once been dogma. A new ideological consensus emerged, an American creed of treating all people alike, of judging each person as an individual and not as a member of an ethnic or racial group. It undermined racism by emphasizing environment rather than innate characteristics, by stressing the damage done to individuals by prejudice and the costs to the nation of discrimination, and by eroding the stereotype of the Negro as a contented buffoon. Intellectually, white supremacy went on the defensive. Its proponents could not deny the pervasiveness of racism nor make a respectable case that it was right. Symptomatically, most newspapers, journals, and publishing firms in the 1930s followed the lead of the New York *Times* in starting to spell Negro with a capital N.[8]

The civil rights movement benefited from these developments. Both black separatism and Negro conservatism lost ground. A new black leadership emerged. Aggressive advocates of racial equality and an end to segregation, such as Walter White, Lester Granger, A. Philip Randolph, and Adam Clayton Powell, Jr., be-

pokesmen for black America. They sought for
ghts, privileges, and opportunities enjoyed by
in conjunction with their new white allies, they
recedented amount of political punch, financial
access to the major institutions shaping public
olicy. A mounting number of blacks and whites,
consequ.... , began to listen to the movement and to respond.

Roosevelt's responses to the black demands of 1940 and 1941
indicated the extent of change in the civil rights movement since
the beginning of the depression. The views of the NAACP or of
Mary Bethune could no longer be ignored. Roosevelt believed
that he had to meet them halfway. His decision to establish the
President's Committee on Fair Employment Practices reflected
the intensification of Negro militancy as well as the importance
of the black vote in national elections. It also mirrored his awareness of the liberalization of attitudes toward the rights of blacks
that had occurred in the preceding decade. President Roosevelt's
Executive Order 8802 in 1941, the first such proclamation on Negro rights since Reconstruction, measured the distance traveled
by the movement. It symbolized a coming of age for civil rights.
Yet Roosevelt's actions also pointed to the limits of change. He
presented the proponents of racial reform with the weakest possible FEPC. He understood that however much black powerlessness had been diminished in the thirties, the advocates of racial
equality could not yet counter the strength of the forces arrayed
against change. White hostility had been dented, but not overcome.

Still, the hopes of blacks for a better tomorrow mounted. Many
believed along with Bethune that "we are on our way." Virtually every speech and article by the proponents of the black
struggle at the end of the New Deal era looked forward with
optimism. They saw in urbanization, in increasing education, in
involvement in the labor movement and politics, and in support
by white allies the social base for a growing civil rights movement. Most commented on the fact that blacks no longer ac-

cepted white superiority or their own plight. Some stressed the lessons learned through mass action about establishing networks of influence and information. All emphasized the awakening of Afro-Americans to the possibility of change, the belief that a new page in American history had been turned.[9]

The soil had been tilled. The seeds that would later bear fruit had been planted. They would continue to be nurtured by the legal and political developments, the ideas articulated, the alliances formed, and the expectations raised during the New Deal years. The sprouts of hope prepared the ground for the struggles to follow. Harvest time would come in the next generation.

Notes

CHAPTER 1

1. C. Vann Woodward, *The Strange Career of Jim Crow*, 2nd rev. ed. (New York, 1966), p. 70; and New York *Times*, June 1, 1876.
2. Paul Lewinson, *Race, Class, and Party: A History of Negro Suffrage and White Politics in the South* (New York, 1932), *passim;* and Woodward, *Strange Career of Jim Crow*, p. 74.
3. *Salughter-House Cases*, 16 Wallace 36 (1873); *United States* v. *Cruikshank*, 92 U.S. 542 (1876); and *United States* v. *Reese*, 92 U.S. 214 (1876).
4. *Civil Rights Cases*, 109 U.S. 3 (1883); *Hall* v. *De Cuir*, 95 U.S. 485 (1878); *Louisville, New Orleans, and Texas Railway* v. *Mississippi*, 133 U.S. 587 (1890); *Virginia* v. *Rives*, 100 U.S. 545 (1880); *Murray* v. *Louisiana*, 163 U.S. 101 (1896); *Cumming* v. *County Board of Education*, 175 U.S. 528 (1899); *Plessy* v. *Ferguson*, 163 U.S. 537 (1896); *Williams* v. *Mississippi*, 170 U.S. 213 (1897); and *Berea College* v. *Kentucky*, 211 U.S. 26 (1908).
5. William Gossett, *Race: The History of an Idea in America* (Dallas, 1963), ch. 7; I. A. Newby, *Jim Crow's Defense* (Baton Rouge, 1965), ch. 1; Claude H. Nolen, *The Negro's Image in the South* (Lexington, Ky., 1967), ch. 9; and William Graham Sumner, *The Challenge of Facts and Other Essays* (New York, 1914), pp. 302–3.
6. See the *Proceedings of the First National Conference on Race Betterment* (Battle Creek, Mich., 1914); and *Proceedings of the American Philosophical Society*, vol. LVI (1917), pp. 364–68.
7. James M. McPherson, "The Antislavery Legacy: From Reconstruction to the NAACP," in Barton J. Bernstein, ed., *Towards a New Past: Dis-*

337

senting Essays in American History (New York, 1968), especially pp. 131–40.

8. Beard quoted in George K. Hunton, *All of Which I Saw, Part of Which I Was* (New York, 1967), p. 25; Ray Stannard Baker, *Following the Color Line: An Account of Negro Citizenship in the American Democracy* (New York, 1908), p. 305; and New York *Times*, May 10, 1900.

9. Woodward, *Strange Career of Jim Crow*, p. 51; and Glass quoted in Lewinson, *Race, Class, and Party*, p. 86.

10. Lewinson, *Race, Class, and Party*, pp. 81, 214–20.

11. *Ibid.*, pp. 84–85.

12. Lerone Bennett, Jr., *The Negro Mood* (New York, 1964), p. 29; and Gunnar Myrdal et al., *An American Dilemma, The Negro Problem and Modern Democracy* (New York, 1944), pp. 529–43.

13. Woodward, *Strange Career of Jim Crow*, pp. 97–102; Hortense Powdermaker, *After Freedom: A Cultural Study in the Deep South* (New York, 1939), pp. 80–92; Baker, *Following the Color Line*, pp. 31–35; Booker T. Washington, *The Story of the Negro: The Rise of the Race from Slavery* (New York, 1909), p. 144; and Charles Wallace Collins, *The Fourteenth Amendment and the States* (Boston, 1912), pp. 77–78.

14. Baker, *Following the Color Line*, pp. 74–81; and Lerone Bennett, Jr., *Confrontation: Black and White* (Baltimore, 1965), pp. 79–83.

15. August Meier, "The Emergence of Negro Nationalism (A Study in Ideologies)," *Midwest Journal*, vol. IV (Summer 1952), pp. 95–111; Elsie M. Lewis, "The Political Mind of the Negro, 1865–1900," *Journal of Southern History*, vol. XXI (May 1955), pp. 189–202; and Clarence Bacote, "Negro Proscriptions, Protests, and Proposed Solutions in Georgia, 1880–1908," *ibid.*, vol. XXIX (Nov. 1959), pp. 471–98.

16. E. Davidson Washington, ed., *Selected Speeches of Booker T. Washington* (Garden City, 1932), pp. 3, 82–83, 243; and Booker T. Washington, *Up From Slavery* (New York, 1902), pp. 218–24.

17. August Meier, *Negro Thought in America, 1880–1915: Racial Ideologies in the Age of Booker T. Washington* (Ann Arbor, 1963), pp. 110–14.

18. Booker T. Washington, *My Larger Education* (New York, 1911), p. 178; and *idem.*, "My View of the Segregation Laws," *New Republic*, vol. V (Dec. 4, 1915), pp. 113–14.

19. Daniel Walden, "The Contemporary Opposition to the Political and Educational Ideals of Booker T. Washington," *Journal of Negro History*, vol. XLV (April 1960), pp. 103–15; and quote from the Niagara Movement's "Declaration of Principles."

20. James Weldon Johnson, *Along This Way* (New York, 1935), p. 203; and W.E.B. Du Bois, *The Souls of Black Folk: Essays and Sketches* (Chicago, 1903), especially pp. 51–59.

21. Elliot Rudwick, "The Niagara Movement," *Journal of Negro History*, vol. XLII (July 1957), pp. 177–200.

22. *Ibid.*; and W. E. B. Du Bois, *Dusk of Dawn* (New York, 1940), pp. 88–91.

23. Meier, *Negro Thought in America,* pp. 114–16, 178.
24. Dewey W. Grantham, "The Progressive Movement and the Negro," *South Atlantic Quarterly,* vol. LIV (Oct. 1955), pp. 461–77; and C. Vann Woodward, *Origins of the New South, 1877–1913* (Baton Rouge, 1951), ch. 14.
25. John R. Commons, *Races and Immigrants in America,* 2nd rev. ed. (New York, 1915), pp. 3–4.
26. Baker, *Following the Color Line.*
27. James L. Crouthamel, "The Springfield Race Riot of 1908," *Journal of Negro History,* vol. XLV (July 1960), pp. 164–81.
28. Mary White Ovington, *How the National Association for the Advancement of Colored People Began* (New York, 1914), pp. 1–3; and Mary White Ovington, *The Walls Came Tumbling Down* (New York, 1947), pp. 100–7.
29. Charles Flint Kellogg, "Villard and the NAACP," *The Nation,* vol. CLXXXVIII (Feb. 14, 1959), pp. 137–40; and Elliot M. Rudwick, "The National Negro Conference Committee of 1909," *Phylon,* vol. XVIII (Fourth Quarter, 1958), pp. 413–19.
30. Charles Flint Kellogg, *NAACP: A History of the National Association for the Advancement of Colored People, Vol. I: 1909–1920* (Baltimore, 1967), ch. 2; and M. A. DeWolfe Howe, *Portrait of an Independent: Moorfield Storey, 1845–1929* (Boston, 1932), pp. 252–54.
31. *Guinn v. United States,* 238 U.S. 347 (1915); *Buchanan v. Warley,* 245 U.S. 60 (1917); *McCabe v. Atchison, Topeka and Santa Fe Ry. Co.,* 235 U.S. 181 (1914); W.E.B. Du Bois, "Race Relations in the United States, 1917–1947," *Phylon,* vol. IX (Third Quarter, 1948), pp. 236–41; and Shillady quoted in Bennett, *Confrontation: Black and White,* p. 111.
32. Seth M. Scheiner, "President Theodore Roosevelt and the Negro, 1901–1908," *Journal of Negro History,* vol. XLVII (July 1962), pp. 169–82; and James A. Tinsley, "Roosevelt, Foraker, and the Brownsville Foray," *ibid.,* vol. XLI (Jan. 1965), pp. 43–65.
33. Du Bois, *Dusk of Dawn,* p. 23.
34. August Meier, "The Negro and the Democratic Party, 1875–1915," *Phylon,* vol. XVII (Summer 1956), pp. 173–91; and John B. Wiseman, "Racism in Democratic Politics, 1904–1912," *Mid-America,* vol. LI (Jan. 1969), pp. 38–58.
35. David A. Shannon, *The Socialist Party of America* (New York, 1955), pp. 50–52; R. Laurence Moore, "Flawed Fraternity—American Socialist Response to the Negro, 1901–1912," *Historian,* vol. XXXII (Nov. 1969), pp. 1–18; and Debs quoted in Ronald Radosh, ed., *Debs, Great Lives Observed* (Englewood Cliffs, N.J., 1971), p. 63.
36. George E. Mowry, "The South and the Progressive Lily White Party of 1912," *Journal of Southern History,* vol. VI (May 1940), pp. 237–47; and Arthur S. Link, "The Negro as a Factor in the Campaign of 1912," *Journal of Negro History,* vol. XXXII (Jan. 1947), pp. 81–99.
37. George C. Osborn, "The Problem of the Negro in Government: 1913,"

Historian, vol. XXIII (May 1961), pp. 330–47; Kathleen L. Wolgemuth, "Woodrow Wilson's Appointment Policy and the Negro," *Journal of Southern History*, vol. XXIV (Nov. 1958), pp. 457–71, and "Woodrow Wilson and Federal Segregation," *Journal of Negro History*, vol. XLIV (April 1959), pp. 158–73; Henry Blumenthal, "Woodrow Wilson and the Race Question," *ibid.*, vol. XLVIII (Jan. 1963), pp. 1–21; and Nancy J. Weiss, "The Negro and the New Freedom: Fighting Wilsonian Segregation," *Political Science Quarterly*, vol. LXXXIV (March 1969), pp. 61–79.

38. Arthur E. Barbeau and Florette Henri, *The Unknown Soldiers: Black American Troops in World War I* (Philadelphia, 1974), pp. 67, 30–39, 133, and general quoted from p. 86; Martha Gruening, "Houston: An N.A.A.C.P. Investigation," *Crisis*, vol. XV (Nov. 1917), pp. 14–19; W.E.B. Du Bois, "Documents of the War," *ibid.*, vol. XVIII (May 1919), pp. 16–21; and editorial, *ibid.*, vol. XX (Feb. 1920), p. 213.

39. Barbeau and Henri, *The Unknown Soldiers*, p. 175; George Edmund Haynes, "Race Riots in Relation to Democracy," *Survey*, vol. XLII (Aug. 9, 1919), pp. 697–98; and Herbert J. Seligmann, *The Negro Faces America* (New York, 1920), pp. 51–68, 141–49.

40. Robert T. Kerlin, *The Voices of the Negro, 1919* (New York, 1920); *Crisis*, vol. XVIII (May 1919), p. 14; and Theodore G. Vincent, *Voices of a Black Nation: Political Journalism in the Harlem Renaissance* (San Francisco, 1973), *passim*.

41. Edmund David Cronon, *Black Moses: The Story of Marcus Garvey and the Universal Negro Improvement Association* (Madison, 1955), pp. 183–95; Vincent, *Voices of a Black Nation*, pt. II; and Amy Jacques Garvey, ed., *Philosophy and Opinions of Marcus Garvey* (New York, 1925), pp. 37–39.

42. Ralph J. Bunche, "The Programs, Ideologies, Tactics, and Achievements of Negro Betterment and Interracial Organizations" (Unpublished manuscript prepared for the Carnegie-Myrdal study, 1940, Schomburg Branch, New York Public Library, hereafter cited "Programs and Ideologies"), pp. 444–560; and Donald Young, *American Minority Peoples* (New York, 1932), pp. 589–90.

43. L. Hollingsworth Wood, "The Urban League Movement," *Journal of Negro History*, vol. IX (April 1924), pp. 117–26; E. Franklin Frazier, "Social Work in Race Relations," *Crisis*, vol. XXVII (April 1924), p. 254; and William O. Brown, "Interracial Cooperation: Some of Its Problems," *Opportunity*, vol. XI (Sept. 1933), pp. 272–73.

44. Bunche, "Programs and Ideologies," pp. 218–71; and T. Arnold Hill, "Labor: Open Letter to Mr. William Green, American Federation of Labor," *Opportunity*, vol. VIII (Feb. 1930), pp. 56–57.

45. Walter White, "Solving America's Race Problem," *Nation*, vol. CXXVIII (Jan. 9, 1929), p. 42; Charles H. Wesley, *Negro Labor in the United States, 1850–1925* (New York, 1927), pp. 275–77; *Crisis*, vol. XXV (Feb. 1923), pp. 170–71; and Johnson, *Along This Way*, p. 371.

46. Vincent, *Voices of a Black Nation*, pts. II and III; W.E.B. Du Bois, "Marcus Garvey," *Crisis*, vol. XXI (Jan. 1921), p. 114; and Du Bois, *ibid.*, vol. XL (April 1933), p. 93.

47. Ralph J. Bunche, "The Political Status of the Negro" (Unpublished manuscript prepared for the Carnegie-Myrdal Study, 1940, Schomburg Branch, New York Public Library), pp. 1335–56; NAACP, Minutes of the Board of Directors, Feb. 9, 1920, July 14, 1924; NAACP Papers, Library of Congress, Washington, D.C.; and Elbert L. Tatum, *The Changed Political Thought of the Negro, 1915–1940* (New York, 1951), pp. 100–101.

48. NAACP, *Annual Report: 1921* (New York, 1921), pp. 8–10; Will Winton Alexander, "Reminiscences," Oral History Collection, Butler Library, Columbia University (Hereafter cited "COHC"), pp. 303–7; and speech in New York *Times*, Oct. 27, 1921.

49. *Crisis*, vol. XXVI (Oct. 1923), p. 248; Walter White to Calvin Coolidge, Aug. 23, 1923, and White to Ernest Gruening, Sept. 17, 1924, NAACP Papers; NAACP, *Annual Report: 1924* (New York, 1924), pp. 46–48; and *Crisis*, vol. XXVIII (July 1924), p. 104, and (Oct. 1924), p. 247.

50. Alpheus T. Mason, *William Howard Taft: Chief Justice* (New York, 1964), p. 152; Walter White, *A Man Called White* (New York, 1948), pp. 106–10; and W.E.B. Du Bois, "Postscript," *Crisis*, XXXIX (Nov. 1932), pp. 262–63.

51. Noel P. Gist, "The Negro in the Daily Press," *Social Forces*, vol. X (March 1932), pp. 405–11; Roi Ottley, *Lonely Warrior: The Life and Times of Robert S. Abbott* (Chicago, 1955), p. 132; Thomas R. Cripps, "The Myth of the Southern Box Office," in James Curtis and Lewis Gould, eds., *The Black Experience in America* (Austin, 1970), p. 133; and Erik Barnouw, *A Tower in Babel, A History of Broadcasting in the United States to 1933* (New York, 1966), pp. 225–30.

52. Gossett, *Race*, pp. 370–408; and "The Negro," *Encyclopedia Britannica* (New York, 1926), vol. XIX, pp. 344–49.

53. Gossett, *Race*, pp. 368–69; and Carl C. Brigham, *A Study of American Intelligence* (Princeton, 1923), especially pp. 209–10.

54. Guy B. Johnson, "The Negro Migration and Its Consequences," *Journal of Social Forces*, vol. II (March 1924), pp. 404–08. All statistics on population, education, health, and income in this study, unless otherwise noted, come from the Decennial Census and *Historical Statistics of the United States, Colonial Times to 1957* (U.S. Bureau of the Census, Washington, D.C., 1960).

55. Bunche, "Political Status of the Negro," vol. 6.

56. W.E.B. Du Bois, "Criteria for Negro Art," *Crisis*, vol. XXXII (Oct. 1926), pp. 290–97; James Weldon Johnson, "Race Prejudice and the Negro Artist," *Harper's*, vol. CLVII (Nov. 1928), pp. 769–776; V. F. Calverton, "The Negro's New Belligerent Attitude," *Current History*, vol. XXX (Sept. 1929), pp. 1081–88; and Langston Hughes, "The Negro

Artist and the Racial Mountain," *Nation*, vol. CXXII (June 23, 1926), p. 692.

57. E. Franklin Frazier, "Garvey: A Mass Leader," *Nation*, vol. CXXIII (Aug. 18, 1926), pp. 147–48; and *idem.*, "Marcus Garvey," *Journal of Negro History*, vol. XXV (Oct. 1940), pp. 590–92.

58. Richard Kluger, *Simple Justice* (New York, 1976), pp. 116, 123; and *idem.*, "Black and Gold Stars," *Nation*, vol. CXXXI (July 23, 1930), p. 86.

CHAPTER 2

1. "Negroes Out of Work," *Nation*, vol. CXXXII (April 22, 1931), pp. 441–42; Gordon Parks, *A Choice of Weapons* (New York, 1965), p. 55; Charles S. Johnson, "Incidence Upon the Negroes," *American Journal of Sociology*, vol. XL (May 1935), pp. 737–45; and Hill quoted in New York *Times*, April 5, 1931.

2. Three classic studies of Southern agriculture and rural blacks during the depression are Arthur F. Raper, *Preface to Peasantry* (Chapel Hill, 1936); Charles S. Johnson, *Shadow of the Plantation* (Chicago, 1934); and Thomas J. Woofter, "The Negro and Agricultural Policy" (Unpublished memorandum prepared for the Carnegie-Myrdal study, 1940, Schomburg Branch, New York Public Library).

3. T. Arnold Hill, "The Present Status of Negro Labor," *Opportunity*, vol. VII (May 1929), p. 145; *idem.*, "Briefs from the South," *ibid.*, vol. XI (Feb. 1933), p. 55; and Hilton Butler, "Lynch Law in Action," *New Republic*, vol. LXVII (July 22, 1931), p. 257.

4. National Urban League, *The Forgotten Tenth: An Analysis of Unemployment Among Negroes and Its Social Costs, 1932–1933* (New York, 1933); and Richard Sterner, *The Negro's Share* (New York, 1943), pp. 233–36.

5. Clyde Kiser, "Diminishing Family Income in Harlem," *Opportunity*, vol. XIII (June 1935), pp. 173–74; E. Franklin Frazier, "Some Effects of the Depression on the Negro in Northern Cities," *Science and Society*, vol. II (Fall 1938), p. 489; and Miller quoted in Norfolk *Journal and Guide*, Dec. 24, 1932.

6. Alba M. Edwards, *Social-Economic Grouping of the Gainful Workers of the United States in 1930* (Washington, 1938), pp. 46–59; and Newell D. Eason, "Attitudes of Negro Families on Relief," *Opportunity*, vol. XIII (Dec. 1935), pp. 367–69.

7. The Mayor's Commission on Conditions in Harlem, *The Negro in Harlem: A Report on Social and Economic Conditions Responsible for the Outbreak of March 19, 1935* (New York, 1935), pp. 19–34.

8. Roi Ottley, *New World A-Coming* (New York, 1943), p. 154; Anna Arnold Hedgeman, *The Trumpet Sounds* (New York, 1964), p. 56; and *Opportunity*, vol. IX (Feb. 1931), p. 57.

9. *Courier*, May 28, Nov. 5, 1932; Report of the Secretary, July 7, 1932, NAACP Papers; White quoted in NAACP Press Release, June 17, 1932, NAACP Papers, and New York *Times*, May 23, 1932; John R. Hawkins, "Why the Negro Should Vote for Mr. Hoover," *Crisis*, XXXIX (Oct. 1932), pp. 313–14; and Simmons quote and editorial in *Defender*, Oct. 28, 21, 1932.

10. New York *Times*, Aug. 19, 1920; Frank Freidel, *Franklin D. Roosevelt: The Ordeal* (Boston, 1954), pp. 30, 193–98, and *ibid. Franklin D. Roosevelt: The Triumph* (Boston, 1956), p. 276; editorial in *Defender*, Oct. 14, 1932; editorial in Cleveland *Gazette*, Sept. 17, 1932; and Walter White to Roosevelt, Sept. 28, 1932, President's Personal File 1336 (hereafter cited "PPF"), Franklin D. Roosevelt Papers, Roosevelt Library, Hyde Park.

11. Norfolk *Journal and Guide*, May 26, July 9, 1932; Cleveland *Gazette*, Sept. 17, 1932; Joseph P. Lash, *Eleanor and Franklin, The Story of Their Relationship Based on Eleanor Roosevelt's Private Papers* (New York, 1971), p. 512; and NAACP, *Annual Report: 1932* (New York, 1932), pp. 31–32.

12. Harold F. Gosnell, "The Negro Vote in Northern Cities," *National Municipal Review*, vol. XXX (May 1941), pp. 264–67, 278; Edward H. Litchfield, "A Case Study of Negro Political Behavior in Detroit," *Public Opinion Quarterly*, vol. V (1941), p. 271; and Samuel Lubell, *White and Black: Test of a Nation* (New York, 1964), p. 25.

13. Minutes of the Board of Directors, Nov. 14, 1932; March 13, 1933, NAACP Papers; and editorials in *Defender*, Dec. 31, 1932; March 18, 1933.

14. Patrick Anderson, *The President's Men* (Garden City, 1968), pp. 13–17; and Eleanor Roosevelt, *This I Remember* (New York, 1949), p. 164.

15. Eleanor Roosevelt to Stephen Early, Aug. 8, 1935, and Early to Walter White, June 15, 1937, PPF 1336, Roosevelt Papers; White to Eleanor Roosevelt, Feb. 4, 1936, Eleanor Roosevelt to White, Feb. 10, 1936, and Marvin McIntyre to William Hassett, June 23, 1938, Eleanor Roosevelt Papers, Roosevelt Library; and Minutes of the Board of Directors, March 13, 1933, NAACP Papers.

16. Stephen Early to Malvina Scheider, Aug. 5, 1935, Eleanor Roosevelt Papers; and E. Roosevelt, *This I Remember*, 164.

17. Stephen Early to Charles Michelson, June 21, 1935, PPF 1336, Roosevelt Papers; Eleanor Roosevelt to Walter White, Nov. 23, 1934, and White from memorandum of conference with the attorney general, Jan. 16, 1936, NAACP Papers; Will Alexander, Oral History Collection, Butler Library, Columbia University, pp. 606–08; *Afro-American*, June 24, 1939; and Lash, *Eleanor and Franklin*, 514, 521.

18. Roy Wilkins, COHC, pp. 98–99; Frank Freidel, *FDR and the South* (Baton Rouge, 1965), p. 36; and E. Roosevelt, *This I Remember*, p. 162.

19. Edwin R. Embree to Walter White, April 16, 1935, NAACP Papers; *Washington Post*, March 14, 1934; and *Courier*, July 28, 1934.

20. John Salmond, "'Aubrey Williams Remembers': A Note on Franklin D. Roosevelt's Attitude Toward Negro Rights," *Alabama Review*, vol. XXV (Jan. 1972), pp. 68–69. The most authoritative account of the relationship between Roosevelt and the Southern-dominated Congress is James T. Patterson, *Congressional Conservatism and the New Deal* (Lexington, 1967).

21. Walter White, *A Man Called White* (New York, 1948), pp. 169–70.

22. Henry Lee Moon, "Racial Aspects of the Federal Public Relations Programs," *Phylon*, vol. IV (First Quarter, 1943), p. 69.

23. Harold Ickes, *The Secret Diary of Harold L. Ickes*, 5 vols. (New York, 1953), 1:680; Minutes of the Interdepartmental Group Concerned with the Special Problems of Negroes, Feb. 7, March 2, 30, April 28, June 1, 1934, Record Group 48, and Robert Weaver to Lawrence Oxley, June 22, 1937, Record Group 183, National Archives; and William Hastie to Walter White, Feb. 11, 1939, NAACP Papers.

24. Black powerlessness in the recovery program is treated excellently by Raymond Wolters, *Negroes and the Great Depression: The Problem of Economic Recovery* (Westport, 1970), pp. 3–215.

25. Ralph J. Bunche, "The Political Status of the Negro," pp. 1414–15; Robert C. Weaver, "Federal Aid, Local Control, and Negro Participation," *Journal of Negro Education*, vol. XI (Jan. 1942), pp. 47–59; Clark Foreman, "What Hope for Rural Negro?" *Opportunity*, vol. XII (April 1934), pp. 105–6; and Mark Ethridge, *America's Obligation to Its Negro Citizens* (Atlanta, 1937), p. 8.

26. Arthur Raper to Charles Houston, May 14, 1937, Forrester B. Washington to Walter White, Dec. 11, 1934, and Roy Wilkins to Aubrey Williams, Jan. 28, 1935, NAACP Papers; Donald S. Howard, *The WPA and Federal Relief Policy* (New York, 1943), pp. 285–86, 290, 296; and Ruth Durant, "Home Rule in the WPA," *Survey*, vol. LXXV (Sept. 1939), pp. 274–75.

27. Jesse O. Thomas, "The Negro Looks at the Alphabet," *Opportunity*, vol. XII (Jan. 1934), p. 12; official quoted in John P. Davis, "NRA Codifies Wage Slavery," *Crisis*, vol. XLI (Oct. 1934), p. 300; editorial in *ibid.* (Nov. 1934), p. 333; Edward Lewis, "The Negro on Relief," *Journal of Negro Education*, vol. V (Jan. 1936), pp. 73–78; and *Opportunity*, vol. XII (Dec. 1934), p. 360.

28. Major Philip Fleming of the Corps of Engineers to Nannie Burroughs, Aug. 4, 1933, and Commissioner of Education John Studebaker to Charles Houston, May 19, 1937, NAACP Papers; Robert C. Weaver, *The Negro Ghetto* (New York, 1948), pp. 70–92; and John P. Murchison to Clarence Pickett, Oct. 23, 1934, and "Memorandum Prepared by the NAACP Concerning the Present Discrimination Policies of the Federal Housing Administration," Oct. 28, 1944, NAACP Papers.

29. TVA Chairman Arthur Morgan to Eleanor Roosevelt, Oct. 19, 1934, Eleanor Roosevelt Papers; Charles H. Houston and John P. Davis, "TVA: Lily-White Reconstruction," *Crisis*, vol. XLI (Oct. 1934), pp.

290–91; Cranston Clayton, "The TVA and the Race Problem," *Opportunity*, vol. XII (April 1934), pp. 111–12; and John P. Davis, "The Plight of the Negro in the Tennessee Valley," *Crisis*, vol. XLII (Oct. 1935), pp. 294, 315.

30. John P. Davis, "A Black Inventory of the New Deal," *Crisis*, vol. XLII (May 1935), pp. 141–42; Walter White to Roosevelt, July 30, 1935, NAACP Papers; and Raper, *Preface to Peasantry*, p. 263.

31. Thurgood Marshall, "Memorandum on Discrimination Against Negroes in Certain Federal Agencies," Jan. 30, 1939, NAACP Papers. Much supporting material is found in Stetson Kennedy, *Southern Exposure* (Garden City, 1946); Wilma Dykeman and James Stokely, *Seeds of Southern Change: The Life of Will Alexander* (Chicago, 1962); and George B. Tindall, *The Emergence of the New South, 1913–1945* (Baton Rouge, 1967).

32. Bonita Golda Harrison, "Social Security: What Does It Mean for the Negro," *Opportunity*, vol. XIV (June 1936), pp. 171–73; and George Edmund Haynes, "Lily-White Social Security," *Crisis*, vol. XLII (March 1935), pp. 85–86.

33. Minutes of the Board of Directors, March 11, 1935, NAACP Papers; and Keyserling quoted in Wolters, *Negroes and the Great Depression*, p. 185.

34. William Anderson, "The New Deal for the Sharecroppers," *Nation*, vol. CXL (Feb. 13, 1935), pp. 185–86; Harold Hoffsommer, "The AAA and and the Sharecropper," *Social Forces*, vol. XIII (May 1935), pp. 494–502; Sterner, *The Negro's Share*, pp. 11–16; and Norman Thomas, *Plight of the Sharecroppers* (New York, 1934), pp. 19–25.

35. Walter White to Roosevelt, Feb. 16, 1935, and Roy Wilkins to Henry Wallace, March 8, 1935, NAACP Papers; E. E. Lewis, "Black Cotton Farmers and the AAA," *Opportunity*, vol. XIII (March 1935), pp. 72–74; Raper, *Preface to Peasantry*, p. 56; Woofter, "The Negro and Agricultural Policy," pp. 56–57; and Davis, "A Black Inventory of the New Deal," pp. 141–2.

36. "Negro Complaints Against Codes," *Christian Century*, vol. LI (March 28, 1934), p. 434; John P. Davis, "Blue Eagles and Black Workers," *New Republic*, vol. LXXXI (Nov. 14, 1934), pp. 7–9; memorandum from Lucy Randolph Mason to Roosevelt, "Objections to Minimum Wage Discrimination Against Negro Workers," PPF 1820, Roosevelt Papers; John P. Davis's statement before the Complaint Hearing of the National Recovery Administration, Feb. 28, 1934, Donald Richberg to Eleanor Roosevelt, Oct. 23, 1934, and Walter White to Roosevelt, May 21, 1935, NAACP Papers; and *Journal and Guide* quoted from Leslie H. Fishel, Jr., "The Negro in the New Deal Era," *Wisconsin Magazine of History*, vol. XLVIII (Winter 1964), p. 114.

37. These articles, as well as numerous others critical of the New Deal, appear in the monthly issues of *Crisis* and *Opportunity*, 1933 to 1935. The Davis quotes are in "What Price National Recovery," *Crisis*, vol. XL (Oct. 1934), pp. 271–72; "A Survey of Problems of the Negro Under

the New Deal," *Journal of Negro Education,* vol. V (Jan. 1936), pp. 10–11; and Davis, "A Black Inventory of the New Deal," pp. 141–2.

38. Eleanor Ryan, "Toward a National Negro Congress," *New Masses,* vol. IV (June 1935), pp. 14–15; and speeches made at conference quoted in the *Journal of Negro Education,* vol. V (Jan. 1936).

39. *Defender,* June 8, 1935.

CHAPTER 3

1. Fishel, "The Negro in the New Deal Era," pp. 111–26; and Myrdal, *An American Dilemma,* p. 74.

2. Roy Wilkins, COHC, pp. 98–100; Eleanor Roosevelt, "Some of My Best Friends are Negroes," *Ebony,* vol. VIII (Feb. 1953), pp. 17–18; and *Crisis,* vol. XL (July 1933), p. 160.

3. E. Roosevelt, *This I Remember,* p. 174; and Lash, *Eleanor and Franklin,* p. 513.

4. Minutes of the Board of Directors, March 13, 1933, NAACP Papers; and P.L.S. to Stephen Early, May 10, 1934, OF 93, and Eleanor Roosevelt to Stephen Early, Aug. 8, 1935, PPF 1336, Roosevelt Papers.

5. Grace Tully, *F. D. R., My Boss* (New York, 1949), p. 107; Robert E. Sherwood, *Roosevelt and Hopkins* (New York, 1948), p. 831; Raymond Clapper, "The Ten Most Powerful People in Washington," *Reader's Digest,* vol. XXXIII (May 1941), p. 48; Frank Freidel, *Franklin D. Roosevelt: Launching the New Deal* (Boston, 1973), ch. 17; James Mac-Gregor Burns, *Roosevelt: The Lion and the Fox* (New York, 1956), pp. 27, 173; William Leuchtenburg, *Franklin D. Roosevelt and the New Deal* (New York, 1963), p. 192; Lash, *Eleanor and Franklin;* and Tamara K. Hareven, *Eleanor Roosevelt, An American Conscience* (Chicago, 1968).

6. White, *A Man Called White,* pp. 168–69; editorials in *Opportunity,* vol. XIV (Jan. 1936), p. 5, and *Crisis,* vol. XLVII (Nov. 1940), p. 343; and Rexford Tugwell, *The Democratic Roosevelt* (Garden City, 1957), pp. 527–29.

7. Eli Ginzberg and Alfred S. Eichner, *The Troublesome Presence, American Democracy and the Negro* (Glencoe, 1964), p. 293; *The Public Papers of Franklin D. Roosevelt* (New York, 1938), 5:538; *Courier,* Nov. 17, 1934; and Ovington, *Walls Came Tumbling Down,* p. 257.

8. *Crisis,* vol. XLI (Jan. 1934), p. 20.

9. Joseph Lash, *Eleanor Roosevelt: A Friend's Memoir* (New York, 1964), pp. 168–69; *Opportunity,* vol. XII (June 1934), p. 167; "My Day" column of Feb. 28, 1939, in Eleanor Roosevelt Papers; and column in *Ladies' Home Journal,* vol. LVIII (Sept. 1941), p. 21.

10. *Opportunity,* vol. XIV (Jan. 1936), p. 5. Also see editorials in *Crisis,* vol. XLVI (Sept. 1939), p. 265, and *Afro-American,* May 23, 1936; and

T. Arnold Hill To Eleanor Roosevelt, Dec. 18, 1935, Eleanor Roosevelt Papers.

11. New York *Times*, Oct. 23, Dec. 19, 1937; Feb. 11, April 22, 1938; Jan. 13, 1939; *Courier*, Dec. 3, 1938, Jan. 21, 1939; *Crisis*, vol. LVI (Feb. 1939), p. 54; Eleanor Roosevelt to Walter White, Jan. 23, 1936, Eleanor Roosevelt Papers; and Lucy Randolph Mason to Clark Foreman, Feb. 29, 1940, and Clark Foreman to Frank Graham, March 18, 1940, Southern Conference on Human Welfare Papers, Atlanta University.

12. Philadelphia *Independent*, Feb. 20, 1938.

13. Columns by Floyd J. Calvin, *Courier*, Oct. 13, 1934, and by David W. Howe, *Defender*, Feb. 3, 1940; Walter White to Rexford Tugwell, July 26, 1935, NAACP Papers; Frank Tannenbaum to Edwin Embree, Jan. 11, 1935, Charles S. Johnson Papers, Dillard University, New Orleans; and editorial in *Defender*, Oct. 13, 1934.

14. Editorial, *Opportunity*, vol. XV (March 1937), p. 69; Mary McLeod Bethune, "I'll Never Turn Back No More!" *ibid.*, vol. XVI (Nov. 1938), pp. 324–26; William Hastie to Roosevelt, Feb. 11, 1939, NAACP Papers; Frank Murphy to Roosevelt, July 7, 1939, Frank Murphy Papers, Michigan Historical Collection, University of Michigan; and Hastie to Walter White, Jan. 4, 1939, NAACP Papers. Initially, the impetus and pressure to create a Civil Rights Section came from organized labor, not blacks. Soon after it was established, however, most of its attention focused on matters of Negro rights. See John T. Elliff, "Aspects of Federal Civil Rights Enforcement: The Justice Department and the FBI, 1939–1964," *Perspectives in American History*, vol. V (1971).

15. Harold Ickes, "My Twelve Years with F. D. R.," *Saturday Evening Post*, vol. CCXX (June 26, 1948), pp. 79–81, and "The Negro as a Citizen," *Crisis*, vol. XLIII (Aug. 1936), pp. 230–31; *idem.* 1:199–200, 680; 2: 105–6, 115; 3:641; W. J. Trent, Jr., "Federal Sanctions Directed Against Racial Discrimination," *Phylon*, vol. III (Second Quarter, 1942), pp. 177–79; and Robert C. Weaver, "An Experiment in Negro Labor," *Opportunity*, vol. XIV (Oct. 1936), pp. 295–98, and "Racial Policy in Public Housing," *Phylon*, vol. I (Second Quarter, 1940), pp. 153–54.

16. Robert C. Weaver, *The Negro Ghetto* (New York, 1948), pp. 73–74, *idem.*, "Negroes Need Housing," *Crisis*, vol. XLVII (May 1940), pp. 138–39, and *idem.*, "Racial Employment Trends in National Defense," *Phylon*, vol. II (Fourth Quarter, 1941), p. 347; and Myrdal, *An American Dilemma*, p. 350.

17. Robert C. Weaver, "The Public Works Administration School Building—Aid Program and Separate Negro Schools," *Journal of Negro Education*, vol. VII (July 1938), pp. 366–74; and Charles S. Johnson, "The Negro," *American Journal of Sociology*, vol. XLVII (May 1942), p. 857.

18. Weaver, "An Experiment in Negro Labor," Herbert Northrup, *Organized Labor and the Negro* (New York, 1944), p. 29; and Robert C. Weaver, "The Value of Federal Employment to Negroes," *Opportunity*, XV (April 1937), p. 107.

19. Trent, "Federal Sanctions Directed Against Racial Discrimination," pp. 171–82; Charles S. Johnson, "The Present Status of Race Relations in the South," *Social Forces*, vol. XXIII (Oct. 1945), pp. 27–28; T.R.B., "Washington Notes," *New Republic*, vol. XCIX (Jan. 15, 1940), p. 83; and Robert C. Weaver, "The New Deal and the Negro," *Opportunity*, vol. XIII (July 1935), p. 202.

20. Howard, *WPA and Federal Relief Policy*, pp. 285–86, 290; Weaver, "New Deal and the Negro," p. 200; *Crisis*, vol. XLIII (Nov. 1936), p. 337; and Studs Terkel, *Hard Times, An Oral History of the Great Depression* (New York, 1970), p. 115.

21. Sterner, *The Negro's Share*, pp. 239–49.

22. Gustav A. Stumpf, "Harlem Tops New York WPA Classes," *Crisis*, vol. XLV (Jan. 1938), pp. 10–11; Levi C. Hubert, "Harlem WPA Sings Opera," *ibid.*, vol. XLIII (July 1936), pp. 203, 214; James H. Baker, Jr., "Art Comes to the People of Harlem," *ibid.*, vol. XLVI (March 1939), pp. 78–80; and Hallie Flanagan, *Arena* (New York, 1940), pp. 74–75, 81–84, 136–37, 144–48.

23. Flanagan, *Arena*, 253–54, 318–19, 390–93; Jerre Mangione, *The Dream and the Deal, The Federal Writers' Project, 1935–1943* (Boston, 1972), pp. 253–72; and *Opportunity*, vol. XVII (Feb. 1939), p. 34.

24. Walter Daniel and Carroll Miller, "The Participation of the Negro in the National Youth Administration," *Journal of Negro Education*, vol. VII (July 1938), p. 361; Marian Thompson Wright, "Negro Youth and Federal Emergency Programs: CCC and NYA," *ibid.*, vol. IX (July 1940), pp. 402–5; and Ira DeA. Reid, *In a Minor Key, Negro Youth in Story and Fact* (Washington, 1940), p. 70.

25. Will Alexander, COHC, pp. 388–90, 454–55; Will Alexander to Frank Tannenbaum, Feb. 18, 1935, and Charles Johnson to Alexander, April 15, 1935, Charles S. Johnson Papers; and various articles in *The Crisis* on the FSA, 1938–1940.

26. "The New Social Security Act," *Crisis*, vol. XLVII (Feb. 1940), pp. 42–43, 59; Wright, "Negro Youth and Federal Emergency Programs: CCC and NYA," pp. 399–400, 405; and the overall account, John A. Salmond, "The Civilian Conservation Corps and the Negro," *Journal of American History*, vol. LII (June 1965), pp. 75–88.

27. Myrdal, *An American Dilemma*, p. 299; Johnson, "The Negro," p. 862; and W.E.B. Du Bois, "Race Relations in the United States, 1917–1947," *Phylon*, vol. IX (Third Quarter, 1948), pp. 240–41.

28. Virginius Dabney, *Below the Potomac, A Book About the New South* (New York, 1942), pp. 205–06; and U.S. Bureau of the Census, *Vital Statistics—Special Reports: 1940* (Washington, 1941), vol. XIV, p. 9.

29. Laurence J. W. Hayes, *The Negro Federal Government Worker* (Washington, 1941), pp. 73, 153; Fishel, "The Negro in the New Deal Era," pp. 115–16; Roy Wilkins, COHC, pp. 68–69; Myrdal, *An American Dilemma*, p. 503; *Courier*, Oct. 13, 1934; and Bunche, "Political Status of the Negro," p. 1361.

30. William Birnie, "Black Brain Trust," *American Magazine*, vol. CXXXV (Jan. 1943), pp. 36–37, 94–95; and Tindall, *The Emergence of the New South, 1913–1945*, p. 556.

31. Edwin Embree to Will Alexander, April 4, 1934, and Embree to Charles Johnson, April 18, 1934, Charles S. Johnson Papers; Will Alexander, COHC, pp. 370–71; editorials in *Afro-American*, Sept. 13, 1933, *Courier*, Sept. 6, 1933, and *Defender*, Sept. 16, 1933; Roy Wilkins to Harold Ickes, Aug. 22, 1933, NAACP Papers; Ickes to Wilkins, Aug. 31, 1933, PPF 93, Roosevelt Papers; and editorials in *Courier*, Nov. 25, 1933, and *Opportunity*, vol. XI (Nov. 1933), p. 327.

32. Harold Ickes to Clark Foreman, Oct. 16, 1933, and Minutes of the Interdepartmental Group Concerned with the Special Problems of Negroes, Feb. 7, March 20, April 28, June 1, 1934, Record Group 48, National Archives.

33. Birnie, "Black Brain Trust."

34. Rackham Holt, *Mary McLeod Bethune* (Garden City, 1964), pp. 190–98; Will Alexander, COHC, p. 369; and Moon, "Racial Aspects of Federal Public Relations Programs," pp. 66–72.

35. Wilson episode in Robert A. Lowe, "Racial Segregation in Indiana, 1920–1950" (Unpublished Ph.D. dissertation, Ball State University, 1965), p. 69; and Jane Motz, "The Black Cabinet" (Unpublished M.A. essay, University of Delaware, 1964), especially pp. 34–36.

36. Holt, *Mary McLeod Bethune*, pp. 181, 190–94.

37. Eleanor Roosevelt to Jim Farley, July 16, 1936, Eleanor Roosevelt Papers; and Chuck Stone, *Black Political Power in America* (Indianapolis, 1968), p. 87.

38. Holt, *Mary McLeod Bethune*, pp. 243–47; Bethune to Aubrey Williams, Oct. 17, 1939, OF 93, Roosevelt Papers; *Afro-American*, Aug. 12, Dec. 9, 1939; and Roi Ottley, "The Big Ten Who Rule Negro America," *Negro Digest*, vol. VI (May 1948).

39. Bethune to Eleanor Roosevelt, Dec. 1, 8, 1936, Eleanor Roosevelt Papers; Minutes of the Executive Committee of the Julius Rosenwald Fund, Dec. 19, 1940, Julius Rosenwald Papers, Dillard University; and materials from the Office of Education about conferences on the Negro, PPF 30, Roosevelt Papers.

40. Bethune to Eleanor Roosevelt, Jan. 4, 13, 1937, Eleanor Roosevelt Papers; materials on the conference, PPF 4266, Roosevelt Papers; and Holt, *Mary McLeod Bethune*, p. 199.

41. Lerone Bennett, Jr., *Confrontation: Black and White*, p. 132; Myrdal, *An American Dilemma*, p. 74; Ralph Bunche, "The Negro in the Political Life of the United States," *Journal of Negro Education*, vol. X (July 1941), p. 580; Philadelphia *Tribune*, Oct. 27, 1938; and *Opportunity*, vol. XVII (Sept. 1939), p. 278.

CHAPTER 4

1. Eleanor Roosevelt to Jim Farley, July 16, 1936, and Eleanor Roosevelt to Sam Rayburn, July 19, 1936, Eleanor Roosevelt Papers; and Eugene Kinckle Jones, "The Negro and the Economic World," address delivered on Oct. 19, 1935, National Urban League Papers, Library of Congress.
2. Report of the Acting Secretary, April, May, June, 1930, NAACP Papers; Walter White, "The Negro and the Supreme Court," Harper's, vol. CLXII (Jan. 1931), p. 241; Bennett, Confrontation: Black and White, p. 132; Richard L. Watson, Jr., "The Defeat of Judge Parker: A Study in Pressure Groups and Politics," Mississippi Valley Historical Review, vol. L (Sept. 1963), pp. 213–34; and New York Times, May 8, 1930.
3. Crisis, vol. XXXVII (July 1930), p. 244, and (Dec. 1930), p. 425; Roy Wilkins to Walter White, July 1, 1930, and Oscar DePriest to White, Sept. 11, 1930, NAACP Papers; Walter White, "The Test in Ohio," Crisis, vol. XXXVII (Nov. 1930), p. 374; William Pickens to White, May 9, 1931, and Robert L. Vann to White, Nov. 5, 1931, NAACP Papers: New York Times, May 23, 1932; and White, "The Negro and the Supreme Court," op. cit., 238–40.
4. Report of the Secretary, July 7, 1932, NAACP Papers; and Donald R. McCoy, Landon of Kansas (Lincoln, 1966), pp. 45, 104–5.
5. Editorials in Courier, Sept. 11, 1932, Afro-American, May 1, 1932, and New York Amsterdam News, Oct. 4, 1932; Bishop Reverdy C. Ransom, "Why Vote for Roosevelt," Crisis, vol. XXXIX (Nov. 1932), p. 343; Lester Walton, "Vote for Roosevelt," ibid.; Walter White to Claude A. Barnett, June 28, 1932, NAACP Papers; and Arthur Krock, "Did the Negro Revolt?" Opportunity, vol. XI (Jan. 1933), p. 19.
6. U.S. Congress, Congressional Record, 73rd Cong., 2nd sess., pp. 11848–49; "They Stand Out From the Crowd," Literary Digest, vol. CXVIII (Dec. 8, 1934), p. 10; and Gosnell, Negro Politicians, pp. 90–91.
7. James Reichley, The Art of Government (New York, 1959), p. 69; and Miller quote in Courier, Nov. 17, 1934.
8. Bunche, "Political Status of the Negro," p. 1059; Litchfield, "A Case Study of Negro Political Behavior in Detroit," p. 268; and Harold F. Gosnell, "The Chicago 'Black Belt' as a Political Battleground," American Journal of Sociology, vol. XXXIX (Nov. 1933), pp. 329–30.
9. Bureau of the Census, Historical Statistics of the United States, pp. 44–47; and "Black Game," Time, vol. XXVIII (Aug. 17, 1936), p. 10.
10. "Black Game," Time, vol. XXVIII (Aug. 17, 1936), pp. 10–11, "Wooing the Negro Vote," Nation, vol. CXLIII (Aug. 1, 1936), p. 119; NAACP, Minutes of the Board of Directors, Feb. 10, 1936, Roy Wilkins to Walter White, March 2, 1936, White to Raymond Clapper, March 25, 1936, and White to Robert Vann, April 18, 1936, NAACP Papers; Crisis, vol. XLVIII (Jan. 1936), p. 17, and (Oct. 1936), p. 305; and Afro-American, Oct. 17, 1936.

11. NAACP, Report of the Secretary, Aug. 31, 1936, and Robert Weaver to Walter White, Oct. 19, 1936, NAACP Papers; New York *Times*, June 7, 11, 1936; and *Newsweek*, vol. VIII (Sept. 12, 1936), pp. 18–19.

12. Roy Garvin, "Alf Landon as I Know Him," *Crisis*, vol. XLVIII (May 1936), p. 139; Frances Rivers, "The Negro Should Support Landon," *ibid.* (Oct. 1936), p. 296; advertisement of the Republican National Committee, *ibid.*; and McCoy, *Landon of Kansas*, pp. 240, 312, 333.

13. "Black Game," *Time;* "Jesse Owens Dashes to G.O.P. in Colored Vote Race," *Newsweek*, vol. VIII (Sept. 12, 1936), p. 18.

14. New York *Times*, June 25, 1936; *Defender*, July 4, 1936; Allan A. Michie and Frank Ryhlick, *Dixie Demagogues* (New York, 1939), pp. 266, 281; Heywood Broun, "Roosevelt Comes Up Swinging," *Nation*, vol. CXLIII (July 4, 1936), p. 9; and *Afro-American*, July 4, 1936.

15. "Black Game," *Time;* Ickes, *Secret Diary*, 1:680; *Congressional Record*, 74th Cong., 2nd sess., pp. 10288, 10839–40; advertisement of the Democratic National Committee, *Crisis*, vol. XLIII (Oct. 1936); Terkel, *Hard Times*, pp. 115, 502; and William E. Leuchtenburg, "Election of 1936," in Arthur M. Schlesinger, Jr., and Fred L. Israel, eds., *History of American Presidential Elections* (New York, 1971), 3:2848–49.

16. Paul Ward, "Washington Weekly," *Nation*, vol. CXLIII (Aug. 1, 1936), pp. 119–20; Walter White to Eleanor Roosevelt, July 7, 1936, Eleanor Roosevelt Papers; New York *Times*, Sept. 3, 1936; New York *Age*, Sept. 26, 1936; and *Courier*, Oct. 29, 1936.

17. Leuchtenburg, "Election of 1936," p. 2848; Rita Werner Gordon, "The Change in the Political Alignment of Chicago's Negroes During the New Deal," *Journal of American History*, vol. LVI (Dec. 1969), pp. 584–603; William W. Griffin, "The Negro in Ohio, 1914–1939" (Unpublished Ph.D. dissertation, Ohio State University, 1968), pp. 420–21; Larry Grothaus, "The Negro in Missouri Politics, 1890–1941" (Unpublished Ph.D. dissertation, University of Missouri, 1970), pp. 151–52; and H. Viscount Nelson, Jr., "Race and Class Consciousness of Philadelphia Negroes with Special Emphasis on the Years Between 1927 and 1940" (unpublished Ph.D. dissertation, University of Pennsylvania, 1969), pp. 206–31.

18. Elmer W. Henderson, "Political Changes Among Negroes in Chicago During the Depression," *Social Forces*, vol. XIX (May 1941), pp. 338–46; Litchfield, "A Case Study of Negro Political Behavior in Detroit," p. 271; Nelson, "Race and Class Consciousness of Philadelphia Negroes," p. 229; and Harold F. Gosnell, "The Negro Vote in Northern Cities," *National Municipal Review*, vol. XXX (May 1941), p. 267.

19. Kelly Miller, "Why the Negro Should Vote for President Roosevelt," *Courier*, Oct. 5, 12, 19, 26, 1936; Joel Spingarn to Roosevelt, Oct. 12, 1936, OF 93, Roosevelt Papers; undated press release, "President of NAACP to Make Eight Speeches—Has Not Endorsed Any Political Candidate for Twenty Years," NAACP Papers; and *Crisis*, XLIII (Dec. 1936), p. 369.

20. Editorials in *Courier*, Nov. 7, 1936, Norfolk *Journal and Guide*, Nov. 7, 1936, and St. Louis *Post-Dispatch*, April 7, 1937; Earl Brown, "How the Negro Voted in the Presidential Election," *Opportunity*, vol. XIV (Dec. 1936), p. 359; James H. Brewer, "Robert Lee Vann, Democrat or Republican: An Exponent of Loose-Leaf Politics," *Negro History Bulletin*, vol. XXI (Feb. 1958), pp. 100–3; Stanley High, *Roosevelt—And Then?* (New York, 1937), p. 211; and Charlestown *News and Courier*, Feb. 10, 1940.

21. Ralph J. Bunche, *The Political Status of the Negro in the Age of FDR*, ed. Dewey W. Grantham (Chicago, 1973), pp. 390, 206, 433, 413, 389; and Myrdal, *An American Dilemma*, p. 488.

22. Bennett, *Confrontation: Black and White*, pp. 137–38; Raleigh *News and Observer*, April 7, 1935; and Bunche, *Political Status of the Negro in the Age of FDR*, pp. 315–17, 448.

23. Bunche, *Political Status of the Negro in the Age of FDR*, pp. 300–1, 307–11, 325–26, 444–46.

24. *Ibid.*, pp. 319, 422–24, 254–55; Lee Collier, "The Solid South Cracks," *New Republic*, vol. XCVII (March 23, 1938), pp. 185–86.

25. Nelson, "Race and Class Consciousness of Philadelphia Negroes," p. 218; Griffln, "The Negro in Ohio," p. 316; and James L. Sundquist, *Dynamics of the Party System* (Washington, 1973), p. 258.

26. Ickes, *Secret Diary*, 2:94–95, 131, 153; Roosevelt to Bishop R. R. Wright, Jr., Nov. 14, 1936, PPF 4120, Roosevelt Papers; Rufus Clement to Walter White, May 11, 1938, Senator Elmer Thomas to White, May 4, 1938, Senator Josh Lee to White, July 8, 1938, and White to Roy Wilkins, Oct. 11, 1938, NAACP Papers; Joseph Gelders to A. T. Oliphant, March 20, 1940, Southern Conference on Human Welfare Papers; J. Finley Wilson to Mary Church Terrell, July 13, 1939, Mary Church Terrell Papers, Library of Congress; and *Nation*, vol. CXLVI (Feb. 26, 1938), p. 258.

CHAPTER 5

1. Norman Beasley and Rixey Smith, *Carter Glass* (New York, 1939), p. 324; Freidel, *FDR and the South*, pp. 36, 55; Joe Starnes to Marvin McIntyre, Dec. 1, 1935, OF 300, Roosevelt Papers; and George E. Mowry, *Another Look at the Twentieth-Century South* (Baton Rouge, 1973), p. 66.

2. Freidel, *FDR and the South*, 47, 61, 75; Glass quoted in Beasley and Smith, *Carter Glass*, pp. 362–63; Russell quoted in George Wolfskill, *Happy Days Are Here Again! A Short Interpretative History of the New Deal* (Hinsdale, Ill., 1974), p. 120; and Talmadge quoted in Dabney, *Below the Potomac*, p. 52.

3. Patterson, *Congressional Conservatism*, ch. II; and New York *Times*, June 12, 29, 1935.

4. Norman R. Phillips, "The Question of Southern Conservatism," *South Atlantic Quarterly*, vol. LIV (Winter 1955), p. 3; John Temple Graves, *The Fighting South* (New York, 1943), p. 126; and Alexander Heard, *A Two-Party South* (Chapel Hill, 1952), pp. 153–54.

5. Fletcher Green, "Resurgent Southern Sectionalism, 1933–1955," *North Carolina Historical Review*, vol. XXXIII (April 1956), p. 225; Kennedy, *Southern Exposure*, pp. 128–29; and New York *Times*, Jan. 30, 31, 1936.

6. *Afro-American*, May 23, 1936; New York *World-Telegram*, April 17, 1936; editorial in *Crisis*, vol. XLVII (Nov. 1940), p. 343; and Reinhard H. Luthin, *American Demagogues, Twentieth Century* (Boston, 1954), p. 193.

7. Josiah Bailey to James Farley, July 21, 1936, OF 300, Roosevelt Papers; and Glass quoted in Patterson, *Congressional Conservatism*, p. 98.

8. James F. Byrnes, *All In One Lifetime* (New York, 1958), p. 95.

9. Stanley High, "Whose Party Is It?" *Saturday Evening Post*, vol. CCIX (Feb. 6, 1937), p. 11; and article by William Allen White, New York *Times*, Aug. 15, 1937.

10. Jasper B. Shannon, "Presidential Politics in the South," *Journal of Politics*, vol. I (April 1939), pp. 146–70 (August 1939), pp. 278–300; Marian D. Irish, "The Proletarian South," *ibid.*, vol. II (Aug. 1940), pp. 231–58; Hugh Johnson, "Third Term????" *Saturday Evening Post*, vol. CCXI (Dec. 17, 1938), p. 56; and New York *Times*, April 7, 1940.

11. Smith quoted in Michie and Ryhlick, *Dixie Demagogues*, pp. 267, 281; Glass and Bailey quoted in Patterson, *Congressional Conservatism*, pp. 99, 257, 285, 292, Freidel, *FDR and the South*, pp. 91–92, and Mowry, *Another Look at the Twentieth-Century South*, pp. 52–53.

12. New York *Times*, July 13, 1938; Byrnes quoted in Mowry, *Another Look at the Twentieth-Century South*, pp. 69–70; and Graves, *Fighting South*, p. 245.

13. Heard, *A Two-Party South*, pp. 18, 117.

14. David M. Potter, *The South and the Concurrent Majority* (Baton Rouge, 1972), pp. 68–69.

15. Raymond Clapper, "Leadership in Congress," *Review of Reviews*, vol. XCV (Jan. 1937), pp. 47–51; and William Allen White, *Selected Letters*, ed. Walter Johnson (New York, 1947), p. 370.

16. Patterson, *Congressional Conservatism*, ch. 3.

17. Raymond Clapper, "Roosevelt Tries the Primaries," *Current History*, vol. IL (Oct. 1938), p. 19; and Robert S. Allen, "The New Deal Fights for Its Life," and "Roosevelt Fights Back," *Nation*, CXLV (July 10, Aug. 21, 1937), 35–36, 187–88.

18. U.S. Congress, Senate, *Congressional Record*, 75th Cong., 1st sess., pp. 3136, 8196; U.S. Congress, House of Representatives, *Congressional Record*, 75th Cong., 1st sess., pp. 3301, 5227, 9294, and *ibid.*, 75th Cong., 2nd sess., p. 1828; and New York *Times*, April 6, June 20, Aug. 8, 1937 and July 17, 1938.

19. Josiah W. Bailey, "The Supreme Court, the Constitution, and the Peo-

ple," *Vital Speeches of the Day*, III (March 1, 1937), pp. 290–95; and Carter Glass's speech quoted in Smith and Beasley, *Carter Glass*, pp. 496–510.

20. Howard Odum to Charles S. Johnson, Sept. 21, 1938, Charles Johnson Papers; and W. J. Cash, "The South Hides Its Eyes," Charlotte *News*, Oct. 2, 1938.

21. *Public Papers and Addresses of Franklin D. Roosevelt*, 7:399; and Ickes, *Secret Diary*, 2:466, 475.

22. *Public Papers and Addresses of Franklin D. Roosevelt*, 7:167–68; Walter White to Eleanor Roosevelt, June 24, 1938, Eleanor Roosevelt Papers; Lucy Randolph Mason to Franklin D. Roosevelt, March 25, 1938, Lucy Randolph Mason Papers, Duke University, Durham, North Carolina; Bunche, *Political Status of the Negro in the Age of FDR*, p. 206; and "New Deal Round Up," *Nation*, vol. CXLVII (Aug. 13, 1938), p. 139.

23. Leonard N. Plummer, "Ellison Durant Smith," in *Public Men In And Out Of Office*, ed. J. T. Salter (Chapel Hill, 1946), pp. 348–49; Harry Ashmore, *An Epitaph for Dixie* (New York, 1957), 100–101; Turner Catledge, New York *Times*, Aug. 23, 1938; and Charleston *News and Courier*, Aug. 31, 1938.

24. Robert C. Brooks, "One of the Four Hundred and Thirty-Five: Maury Maverick, of Texas," in *The American Politician*, ed. J. T. Salter (Chapel Hill, 1938), p. 157; and Roman J. Zorn, "Theodore G. Bilbo," in *Public Men In And Out Of Office*, ed. Salter, p. 277.

25. *Congressional Record*, 75th Cong., 3rd sess., pp. 873–74, 7348; and *Time*, vol. XXXI (Jan. 24, 1938), p. 9.

26. *Congressional Record*, 76th Cong., 1st sess., pp. 4649–73; and Theodore Bilbo, "An African Home For Our Negroes," *Living Age*, June 1940, pp. 327–35.

27. NAACP, Report of the Secretary, April 4, May 6, 1935; Feb. 8, March 9, April 7, 1938, NAACP Papers; William Seagle, "How Not to Stop Lynching," *Nation*, vol. CXL (May 1, 1935), p. 626; and Lee Coller, "Roosevelt and the South," *New Masses*, vol. XXVII (April 26, 1938), pp. 15–16.

28. *Congressional Record*, 75th Cong., 1st sess., pp. 3692–94; and Martin Dies, *The Martin Dies Story* (New York, 1963), pp. 124–38.

29. William Gellerman, *Martin Dies* (New York, 1944), pp. 188, 191–94, 287; Martin Dies, *The Trojan Horse in America* (New York, 1940), pp. 118–29; and, on opposition to Dies, *Congressional Record*, 76th Cong., 3rd sess., pp. 572–605.

30. *Congressional Record*, 76th Cong., 3rd sess., pp. 572–605; Walter Goodman, *The Committee, The Extraordinary Career of the House Committee on Un-American Activities* (New York, 1968), p. 64; and *Social Justice*, Sept. 1938.

31. Michie and Rhylick, *Dixie Demagogues*, pp. 7, 65, 227–31.

32. Harold Ickes, "Nations in Nightshirts," *Vital Speeches*, vol. IV (Jan. 1, 1938), pp. 180–81; Owen Blaine, "Night Ride in Birmingham," *New*

Republic, vol. LXXXIV (Aug. 28, 1935), pp. 65–67; and Herman Wolf, "And Southern Death," *Common Sense*, vol. V (Feb. 1936), pp. 12–14.

33. Ralph McGill, *The South and the Southerner* (Boston, 1964), pp. 142–43; Kennedy, *Southern Exposure*, pp. 182–86; Louis Cochran, "Mussolini of Mississippi," *The Outlook*, vol. XXVII (June 17, 1938), pp. 203–5; Walter Davenport, "The Fuehrer of Sugar Creek," *Collier's*, vol. XC (Dec. 6, 1941), p. 17; Hamilton Basso, "Our Gene," *New Republic*, LXXXVI (Feb. 19, 1936), 35–37; T. R. B., "Washington Notes," *ibid.*, vol. LXXXVIII (Dec. 8, 1937), p. 44; Joseph L. Morrison, *W. J. Cash: Southern Prophet* (New York, 1967), p. 73; Harold Martin, "About Ralph McGill," *New South*, vol. XXVIII (Spring 1973), p. 25; Clarence Cason, *90° in the Shade* (Chapel Hill, 1935), p. 106; Michie and Rhylick, *Dixie Demagogues*, p. 16; and Couch quoted in Kennedy, *Southern Exposure*, p. 85.

34. Lucy Randolph Mason to Eleanor Roosevelt, Feb. 11, 1938, Eleanor Roosevelt Papers; Thomas L. Stokes, *Chip off my Shoulder* (Princeton, 1940), pp. 398–99, 488–89, 529–30; and Virginius Dabney, "Paternalism in Race Relations is Outmoded," *Southern Frontier*, vol. III (July 1942), p. 4.

35. Clark Foreman, "The Decade of Hope," *Phylon*, vol. XII (Second Quarter, 1951), pp. 137–50; and McGill, *The South and the Southerner*, p. 159.

36. McGill, *The South and the Southerner*, p. 170; H. C. Nixon, "The New Deal and the South," *Virginia Quarterly Review*, vol. XIX (Summer 1943), pp. 321–33; John R. Skates, "From Enchantment to Disillusionment: A Southern Editor Views the New Deal," *Southern Quarterly*, vol. V (July 1967), pp. 363–80; and Maury Maverick to Eleanor Roosevelt, April 19, 1940, Eleanor Roosevelt Papers.

37. McGill, *The South and the Southerner*, pp. 190–92.

38. Francis P. Locke, "Claude D. Pepper," *Public Men in and Out of Office*, ed. Salter, pp. 257–76; *Congressional Record*, 76th Cong., 1st sess., pp. 11165–68; and Bailey quoted in Patterson, *Congressional Conservatism*, p. 326.

39. Morrison, *W. J. Cash*, chs. 3 and 4; and W. J. Cash, *The Mind of the South* (New York, 1941), especially pp. 343–429.

40. Howard Odum to Mark Ethridge, Dec. 6, 1938, and "Memorandum Adopted at a Meeting of the Southern Policy Conference in Atlanta, April 25–28, 1935," Frank Graham Papers, Southern History Collection, University of North Carolina, Chapel Hill; article by Virginius Dabney in New York *Times*, May 17, 1936; Virginius Dabney, "Dixie Rejects Lynching," *Nation*, vol. CXLV (Nov. 27, 1937), pp. 579–80, and "Shall the Poll Tax Go?" *New York Times Magazine*, Feb. 12, 1939; Virginius Dabney, *Below the Potomac, A Book About the New South* (New York, 1942), p. 185; and Lillian Smith, "One More Sigh for the Good Old South," *Pseudopodia*, vol. I (Fall 1936), pp. 6, 15.

41. Joseph Gelders to Frank Graham, Oct. 8, 1938, Frank Graham Papers;

Joseph Gelders to Franklin Roosevelt, July 10, 1940, OF 1113, Roosevelt Papers; Joseph Gelders to Virginia Durr, July 30, 1938, Southern Conference on Human Welfare Papers, Atlanta University; Clark Foreman to Jonathan Daniels, June 8, 1948, Southern Conference on Human Welfare Papers; Clark Foreman to Gay Morenus, Nov. 24, 1948, SCHW Papers; and Clark Foreman Oral History Interview, Southern Historical Collection, UNC, pp. 39–43.

42. Franklin Roosevelt to Lowell Mellett, June 22, 1938, Mellett to Roosevelt, July 25, 1938, and Mellett to Clifford Durr, Aug. 12, 1938, SCHW Papers; Frank Graham to Henry Foscue, July 28, 1938, Frank Graham Papers; National Emergency Council, *Report on Economic Conditions of the South* (Washington, 1938); editorials in Richmond *Times-Dispatch*, July 10, 1938, and Atlanta *Journal*, Jan. 17, 1939; "The Kiplinger Washington Letter," Aug. 13, 1938; and Dabney, *Below the Potomac*, pp. 6, 22.

43. Mark Ethridge to Frank Graham, Nov. 30, 1938, and Graham to Francis Miller, Feb. 15, 1939, Frank Graham Papers; and Mark Ethridge to Howard Odum, Oct. 24, 1938, and Odum to Will Alexander, Nov. 30, 1938, Howard Odum Papers, Southern Historical Collection, UNC.

44. Foreman, "Decade of Hope"; Dabney, *Below the Potomac*, pp. 306–8; and Charles S. Johnson to Howard Odum, Sept. 6, 1938, Howard Odum Papers.

45. *Report of the Proceedings of the Southern Conference on Human Welfare* (Birmingham, Alabama, Nov. 20–23, 1938), and Franklin D. Roosevelt to Louise O. Charlton, Nov. 19, 1938, SCHW Papers; and Thomas A. Krueger, *And Promises To Keep, The Southern Conference for Human Welfare, 1938–1948* (Nashville, 1967), pp. 16–17.

46. Charles S. Johnson, "More Southerners Discover the South," *Crisis*, vol. XLI (Jan. 1939), pp. 14–15; Sterling A. Brown, "South on the Move," *Opportunity*, vol. XVI (Dec. 1938), pp. 366–68; *Defender*, Nov. 27, 1938; Lillian Smith, "Southern Conference," *North Georgia Review*, vol. V (Spring 1940), p. 23; and speaker quoted in Fletcher Green, "Resurgent Southern Sectionalism, 1933–1955," *North Carolina Historical Review*, vol. XXXIII (April 1956), p. 227.

47. Report of Joseph Gelders to Second Meeting of the Southern Conference on Human Welfare, April 16, 1940, and Gelders to Frank Graham, Sept. 20, 1939, SCHW Papers; Frederick D. Ogden, *The Poll Tax in the South* (University, Alabama, 1958), pp. 250–51; Lee Geyer to W. C. Hueston, Feb. 27, 1940, and Roy Wilkins to Joseph Gelders, March 13, 1940, SCHW Papers; and National Committee to Abolish the Poll Tax, *Meet the National Committee to Abolish the Poll Tax* (Washington, 1942).

48. George Stoney to Clark Foreman, Sept. 6, 13, 19, 26, 1939, SCHW Papers; Alabama industrialist quoted in Kennedy, *Southern Exposure*, 101–2; *News* quoted in Bunche, *The Political Status of the Negro in the Age of FDR*, p. 337; V. O. Key, Jr., *Southern Politics in State and Nation* (New York, 1949), pp. 657–60; judge quoted in American Council

on Public Affairs, *The Poll Tax* (Washington, 1940), p. 22; and registrar quoted in Bunche, *The Political Status of the Negro in the Age of FDR*, p. 401.

49. Roosevelt quoted in Kennedy, *Southern Exposure*, p. 359, Freidel, *FDR and the South*, p. 98, and New York *Times*, Sept. 10, 1938; Joseph Gelders to Lincoln Kirstein, Feb. 27, 1940, SCHW Papers; and Harrison quoted in Bunche, *The Political Status of the Negro in the Age of FDR*, p. 380.

50. Ogden, *Poll Tax in the South*, pp. 186–87; Stokes, *Chip off my Shoulder*, pp. 529–30; Janet Marshall, "The Ring Around the Ballot Box," *New Republic*, vol. XCVII (Sept. 28, 1938), pp. 207–9; Allen Fletcher, "Poll Tax Politics," *ibid.*, vol. XCIX (March 20, 1940), pp. 664–66; Maury Maverick to Eleanor Roosevelt, April 19, 1940, Eleanor Roosevelt Papers; and Maury Maverick, "Let's Join the United States," *Nation*, vol. CXLX (May 11, 1940), pp. 592–94.

51. Gessner McCorvey to E. Ray Scott, Oct. 2, 1942, Box 1, Democratic National Committee Files, Roosevelt Papers; and *Congressional Record*, 77th Cong., 2nd sess., p. 8174.

52. Joseph Gelders to Ethel Clyde, Feb. 27, 1940, SCHW Papers.

53. Francis Miller to Frank Graham, Dec. 21, 1938, and Congressman Luther Patrick to Graham, Jan. 11, 1939, Frank Graham Papers; Barry Bingham to Virginia Durr, May 27, 1940, SCHW Papers; and Virginius Dabney Oral History Interview, Southern Historical Collection, UNC, p. 77.

54. Dewey W. Grantham, *The Democratic South* (New York, 1965), pp. 74, 96.

CHAPTER 6

1. Terkel, *Hard Times*, p. 532; Dorothy Stafford to Howard Lee, April 18, 1940, and George Stoney to Clark Foreman, Sept. 19, 26, Oct. 4, 1939, SCHW Papers; and Walter White to P. A. Stephens, April 20, 1931, NAACP Papers.

2. Several recent studies that emphasize some of these points include: Paul Buhle, "Marxism in the United States, 1900–1940" (Unpublished Ph.D. dissertation, University of Wisconsin, 1975); Mark Naison, "The Communist Party in Harlem, 1928–1936," (Unpublished Ph.D. dissertation, Columbia University, 1976); and Mark Solomon, "Red and Black: Negroes and Communism, 1929–1932" (Unpublished Ph.D. dissertation, Harvard University, 1972).

3. Labor Research Department of the Rand School of Social Science, *The American Labor Year Book, 1927* (New York, 1927), p. 123, and *The American Labor Year Book, 1929* (New York, 1929), p. 152; and *Courier*, March 16, 1929.

4. James S. Allen, *The Negro Question in the United States* (New York, 1936), pp. 3–5; Robert Minor, "The First Negro Workers' Congress,"

Workers Monthly, vol. V (Dec. 1925), pp. 70–73; and *Defender*, Oct. 31, 1925, Dec. 24, 1927.

5. "Resolution of the Communist International," *The Communist Position on the Negro Question* (New York, 1931), p. 50; and Benjamin Gitlow, *I Confess* (New York, 1940), pp. 480–81.

6. "Resolution on the Negro Question in the United States," *The Communist*, vol. X (Feb. 1931), p. 157.

7. *Daily Worker*, Dec. 30, 1929; George B. Charney, *A Long Journey* (New York, 1968), p. 74; "Draft Program for the Negro Laborers in the Southern States," *The Communist*, vol. IX (April 1930), pp. 246–47; Beal, *Proletarian Journey*, pp. 139–40; Cyril V. Briggs, "The Negro Question in the Southern Textile Strikes," *The Communist*, vol. VIII (June 1929), p. 325; Harry Haywood, "The Crisis of Jim-Crow Nationalism of the Negro Bourgeoisie," *ibid.*, vol. X (April 1931), pp. 330–38; and various articles in *Negro Worker*, 1930–1931.

8. Cyril V. Briggs, "Our Negro Work," *The Communist*, vol. VIII (Sept. 1929), pp. 494–500; Horace Cayton and George Mitchell, *Black Workers and the New Unions* (Chapel Hill, 1939), p. 340; Nathan Glazer, *The Social Basis of American Communism* (New York, 1961), p. 174; and *Courier*, Nov. 10, 1928.

9. *Afro-American*, Aug. 11, 1922; and *Daily Worker*, March 9, 1931.

10. The most recent and best account is Dan T. Carter, *Scottsboro: A Tragedy of the American South* (Baton Rouge, 1969).

11. *Daily Worker*, April 10, 11, 12, 17, 18, 25, 1931; Saunders Redding, *They Came in Chains* (Philadelphia, 1950), 278; and Harry Haywood, "The Scottsboro Decision," *The Communist*, vol. XI (Dec. 1932), p. 1075.

12. Gosnell, *Negro Politicians*, p. 328; New York *Times*, May 17, 1931; *Afro-American*, May 13, 27, 1933; *Daily Worker*, Sept. 24, Oct. 4, 1932; and Carter, *Scottsboro*, p. 144.

13. Various stories in *Daily Worker* and New York *Times*, June and July, 1931; Carter, *Scottsboro*, pp. 146, 167; and Angelo Herndon, *You Cannot Kill the Working Class* (New York, 1934).

14. See special issue on Scottsboro, *Labor Defender*, vol. XI (April 1937); New York *Times*, Jan. 22, 23, 24, May 28, Oct. 11, Nov. 8, 1932; and Papers of Charles E. Hughes, Box 157, Library of Congress.

15. Haywood, "The Scottsboro Decision," p. 1068; and *Powell v. Alabama*, 287 U.S. 45 (1932).

16. *Daily Worker*, Nov. 26, 1934; Adam Clayton Powell, Jr., *Marching Blacks* (New York, 1945), p. 64; and James W. Ford, "The United Front in the Field of Negro Work," *The Communist*, vol. XIV (April 1935), p. 166.

17. "The Offensive of Fascism and the Tasks of the Communist International in the Fight for the Unity of the Working-Class Against Fascism," *The Communist*, vol. XIV (Sept. 1935), pp. 928–29; Earl Browder, "The United Front—The Key to Our New Tactical Orientation," *ibid.*

(Nov. 1935), p. 1105; *Daily Worker*, Dec. 31, 1935; Memorandum of Agreement Between Organizations Cooperating in the Scottsboro Defense, Dec. 19, 1935, NAACP Papers; editorial, New York *Times*, April 2, 1935; and Minutes of the Board of Directors, Dec. 16, 1935, and John Haynes Holmes to Walter White, Nov. 21, 1935, NAACP Papers.

18. Special issue of *Labor Defender*, vol. XI (Nov. 1937); Walter Wilson, "Georgia Suppresses Insurrection," *Nation*, vol. CXXXIX (Aug. 1, 1934), pp. 127–28; and Benjamin J. Davis, *Communist Councilman From Harlem, Autobiographical Notes Written in a Federal Penitentiary* (New York, 1969), p. 75, and "Why I Am A Communist," *Phylon*, vol. VIII (2nd Quart. 1947), p. 109.

19. Editorials in *New Masses*, vol. X (March 27, 1934), p. 4, and *ibid.*, vol. XI (June 5, 1934), pp. 5–6; Claude Nelson to Frank Graham, Oct. 5, 1935, Frank Graham Papers; and Davis, *Communist Councilman*, p. 83.

20. Cruse, *Crisis of the Negro Intellectual*, p. 149; and "It's Herndon Day over the Nation," *Daily Worker*, Nov. 30, 1936.

21. *Herndon v. Georgia*, 295 U.S. 441 (1935), and *Herndon v. Lowry*, 301 U.S. 242, pp. 264–70; and comments of Earl Browder quoted in *Daily Worker*, July 29, 1935.

22. Paul Hutchinson, "Hunger on the March," *Christian Century*, XL (Nov. 9, 1932), pp. 1377–78; *Defender*, Nov. 5, 1932, March 11, 1933; *Daily Worker*, Feb. 10, 1930; B. K. Gebert, "How the St. Louis Unemployed Victory Was Won," *The Communist*, vol. XI (Sept. 1932), pp. 786–91; and St. Louis *Post-Dispatch*, March 7, 1930, Jan. 18, 1931, July 9, 11, 1932.

23. Bernard Karsh and Phillips J. Gorman, "The Impact of the Political Left," in *Labor and the New Deal*, eds. Milton Derber and Edwin Young (Madison, 1957), pp. 86–93; and *Defender*, March 20, 1937.

24. Drake and Cayton, *Black Metropolis*, p. 87; columns by Cyril V. Briggs, *Harlem Liberator*, May 20, 27, July 22, 1933; and Harold D. Lasswell and Dorothy Blumenstock, *World Revolutionary Propaganda* (New York, 1939), pp. 78, 280.

25. *Defender*, Aug. 1, 8, 1931; Lasswell and Blumenstock, *World Revolutionary Propaganda*, pp. 196–204; and *Daily Worker*, Aug. 6, 7, 8, 1931.

26. Drake and Cayton, *Black Metropolis*, pp. 87, 734–37; Gosnell, *Negro Politicians*, pp. 330–31; Len De Caux, *Labor Radical* (Boston, 1970), p. 172; Angelo Herndon, *Let Me Live* (New York, 1937, reprinted 1969), pp. 73–75, 290–93, 315–22; and editorials in *Defender*, Aug. 29, 1931, Jan. 13, 1933.

27. Symposium of Negro Editors, "Communism and the Negro," *Crisis*, vol. XXXIX (April-May, 1932), pp. 117–19, 154–56.

28. Drake and Cayton, *Black Metropolis*, p. 736; Asbury Smith, "What Can the Negro Expect from Communism," *Opportunity*, vol. XI (Nov. 1933), p. 211; Johnson quoted in New York *Age*, May 27, 1933; and editorial in *Crisis*, vol. XLII (Dec. 1935), p. 369.

29. Gitlow, *I Confess*, pp. 479–80; Herndon, *Let Me Live*, pp. 88–89; Mike

Gold, "Mr. Civil Rights," *The Mike Gold Reader* (New York, 1954), pp. 164–175; John Williamson, *Dangerous Scot: The Life and Work of an American "Undesirable"* (New York, 1969), pp. 81, 95–96; Melech Epstein, *The Jew and Communism, 1919–1941* (New York, 1959), p. 246; and Myra Page, "Inter-Racial Relations among Southern Workers," *The Communist,* vol. IX (March 1930), p. 164.

30. *Daily Worker,* Feb. 19, 1931; Drake and Cayton, *Black Metropolis,* pp. 132, 137, 139, 146, 148; Elizabeth Dilling, *The Roosevelt Red Record and Its Background* (Chicago, 1936), pp. 222–23; and Dies, *Trojan Horse in America,* pp. 119–20.

31. Claude McKay, *Harlem, Negro Metropolis* (New York, 1940), pp. 232–37; and Cruse, *Crisis of the Negro Intellectual,* pp. 150–51, 158, 167.

32. De Caux, *Labor Radical,* p. 174; Communist Party, *Race Hatred on Trial: The Yokinen Case* (New York, 1931); and New York *Times,* March 1, 2, 1931.

33. Gosnell, *Negro Politicians,* pp. 324, 341; Cruse, *Crisis of the Negro Intellectual,* p. 146; *Defender,* Jan. 13, 1933; and *Harlem Liberator,* Dec. 23, 1933, April 28, 1934.

34. Sidney and Beatrice Webb, *Soviet Communism: A New Civilization?* (New York, 1938), pp. 139–58; Richard Wright quoted in Richard Crossman, ed., *The God That Failed* (New York, 1965), p. 117; Freeman reprinted in *Common Ground,* vol. IV (1944), p. 87; and Langston Hughes, "Minority Peoples in Two Worlds," *New Masses,* vol. XIV (Feb. 12, 1935), pp. 18–20.

35. Editorial, *Nation,* vol. CXXXVIII (Dec. 19, 1934), p. 696; article by Ted Poston, New York *Amsterdam News,* May 10, 1933; editorial, *Common Sense,* vol. I (Feb. 16, 1933), p. 6; Richard Dicter, "Jim-Crow Education," *ibid.,* p. 16; Covington Hall, "Triumphant 'White Supremacy,'" *ibid.,* vol. IV (March 1935), p. 24; editorial, *The New Industrial Unionist,* vol. I (May 1939), p. 10; and A. Ziegler, "The Negro Problem," *ibid.,* pp. 9–10.

36. *Defender,* Feb. 9, Aug. 24, Oct. 5, 1929, Jan. 11, 1930.

37. Ernest Doerfler, "Socialism and the Negro Problem," *American Socialist Quarterly,* vol. II (Summer 1933), pp. 23–36; and Margaret I. Lamont, "Negro's Stake in Socialism," *ibid.,* vol. IV (March 1935), pp. 41–51.

38. League for Industrial Democracy press release, May 6, 1933, and Edward Levison to Walter White, May 12, 1933, NAACP Papers; and *New Republic,* vol. LXXV (May 31, 1933), p. 75.

39. Norman Thomas, "Can America Go Fascist?" *Crisis,* vol. XLI (Jan. 1934), pp. 9–10, *Human Exploitation in the United States* (New York, 1934), pp. 258–83, *The Choice Before Us: Mankind at the Crossroads* (New York, 1934), pp. 99–100, and "The Socialists' Way Out for the Negro," *Journal of Negro Education,* vol. V (Jan. 1936), pp. 100–4; Norman Thomas to Walter White, June 13, 1935, and Thomas's speech to 1936 NAACP convention, NAACP Papers; and Bertram D. Wolfe,

"Marxism and the Negro," *Race*, vol. I (Winter 1935–1936), pp. 37–40, 49.

40. Paul Robeson, *Here I Stand* (New York, 1958), pp. 56–60.

41. Cruse, *Crisis of the Negro Intellectual*, pp. 158–63, 169; H. L. Mitchell, COHC, pp. 80–84; Ernest R. McKinney, COHC, pp. 62–73; New York *Times*, Oct. 17, 1937; and *Courier*, Dec. 4, 1937.

42. David Clendenin to Richard Rovere, April 9, 1940, and Rovere to Clendenin, May 6, 1940, Richard Rovere Papers, Wisconsin Historical Society, Madison, Wisconsin.

43. Materials in Workers Defense League Folder, Socialist Party Papers, Duke University.

44. *Student Advocate*, vol. III (March 1938), p. 30; Vivian Liebman, "The American Student Union Meets at Vassar," *ibid.*, p. 8; editorial, *ibid.*, vol. I (Feb. 1936), p. 5; James Lee Johnson, "I Was Railroaded From Annapolis," *ibid.* (April 1937), pp. 21–22; "Do You Sanction Murder?" *ibid.*, vol. II (May 1937), p. 20; and Richard Collins, "Liberalism and Negroes," *ibid.*, vol. I (Feb. 1937), p. 8.

45. Daily Worker, July 10, 1935; American Youth Congress, *Joint Session Congress of Youth, Fourth Session, Milwaukee, July 2–5, 1937* (New York, 1937), pp. 25–40; *Journal of Negro Education*, vol. V (Oct. 1936), pp. 651–52; and Abbot Simon to Franklin Roosevelt, March 5, 1938, PPF 2282, Roosevelt Papers.

46. Editorials in *New Masses*, vol. XXXI (May 10, 1939), p. 6, and *Afro-American*, May 24, 1941; and Arthur Raper, "The South Strains Toward Decency," *North American Review*, vol. CCXLIII (Spring 1937), p. 112.

CHAPTER 7

1. Sterling D. Spero and Abram L. Harris, *The Black Worker, The Negro and the Labor Movement* (New York, 1931), pp. 56, 85–115, 128–46; T. Arnold Hill, "An Open Letter to Mr. William Green, President of the American Federation of Labor," *Opportunity*, vol. VIII (Feb. 1930), pp. 56–59; Will Alexander, "Negroes and Organized Labor in the South," *ibid.* (April 1930), pp. 109–11; and W.E.B. Du Bois, "The A. F. of L.," *Crisis*, vol. XL (Dec. 1933), p. 292.

2. "The Negro and Organized Labor," *Opportunity*, vol. VII (Nov. 1929), pp. 335–36; Ira De A. Reid, "Lily White Labor," *ibid.*, vol. VIII (June 1930), p. 170; Kelly Miller, "The Negro as a Workingman," *American Mercury*, vol. VI (Nov. 1925), pp. 310–13; and *Crisis*, vol. XXVIII (May 1924), p. 34.

3. Hosea Hudson, *Black Worker in the Deep South, A Personal Account* (New York, 1972), pp. 34–36; John Howard Lawson, "In Dixieland We Take Our Stand," *New Masses*, vol. XI (May 29, 1934), pp. 8–10; James S. Allen, "Sharecropping as a Remnant of Chattel Slavery," *The*

Communist, vol. XIII (Dec. 1934), pp. 1241–53; Robert Wood, "The I. L. D. in Dixie," *Labor Defender*, vol. XI (June 1935), p. 24; Albert Jackson, "Alabama's Blood-Smeared Cotton," *New Masses*, vol. XVI (Sept. 24, 1935), p. 13; Will Herberg, "Shall the Negro Turn to Labor or to Capital," *Crisis*, vol. XXXVIII (July 1931), pp. 227–28; and editorial in *Opportunity*, vol. IX (Aug. 1931), p. 234.

4. Howard Mitchell, COHC, pp. 1, 19–25, 80–84; Howard Kester, *Revolt Among the Sharecroppers* (New York, 1936), pp. 55–57, 66–69; (March 23, 1935), p. 1; and Ward Rogers, "Sharecroppers Drop Color Line," *Crisis*, vol. XLII (June 1935), pp. 168–69, 178.

5. Mitchell, COHC, pp. 1–3, 40–41, 90; Kester, *Revolt Among the Sharecroppers*, pp. 60–69; and Cedric Belfrage, *A Faith to Free the People* (New York, 1944), pp 43–44, 57–59, 148–51.

6. Alexander, COHC, pp. 372–82; C. T. Carpenter, "King Cotton's Slaves: The Fate of the Share-Cropper Becomes a National Issue," *Scribner's*, vol. XCVIII (Oct. 1935), pp. 193–99; H. L. Mitchell to Clarence Senior, April 5, 10, 1935, May 21, 1936, Socialist Party Papers; and Harold Preece, "Epic of the Black Belt," *Crisis*, vol. XLIII (March 1936), pp. 75, 92.

7. Jacob Potofsky, COHC, p. 673; and John Brophy, COHC, p. 542.

8. Bruce B. Minton and John Stuart, *Men Who Lead Labor* (New York, 1937), pp. 149–51.

9. Brailsford R. Brazeal, *The Brotherhood of Sleeping Car Porters: Its Origin and Development* (New York, 1946), pp. 221–22; Minton and Stuart, *Men Who Lead Labor*, p. 149; and Terkel, *Hard Times*, p. 145.

10. Spero and Harris, *The Black Worker*, pp. 459–60.

11. Jervis Anderson, *A. Philip Randolph, A Biographical Portrait* (New York, 1972), p. 216; A. Philip Randolph, "Pullman Porters Vote for Organization They Want," *American Federationist*, vol. XLII (July 1935), pp. 727–29; and Randolph to White, June 16, 1935, NAACP Papers.

12. *Report of the Proceedings of the Fifty-fourth Annual Convention of the American Federation of Labor* (Washington, 1934, hereafter cited *AFL Proceedings*, with date), pp. 330–34; John Brophy, *A Miner's Life* (Madison, 1964), p. 246; and William Green to Walter White, July 29, 1935, NAACP Papers.

13. Lester Granger, "Old Guard vs. A. F. of L.," *Race*, vol. I (Winter 1935–1936), pp. 46–47; *AFL Proceedings, 1935*, p. 809; and Minutes of the Board of Directors, Sept. 4, 1935, and NAACP press release, Nov. 15, 1935, NAACP Papers.

14. *AFL Proceedings, 1935*, pp. 808–19.

15. *Crisis*, vol. XLI (Nov. 1934), p. 342, and XLIII (July 1936), 209; and Minton and Stuart, *Men Who Lead Labor*, 143–44.

16. Brazeal, *Brotherhood of Sleeping Car Porters*, pp. 151–70; and *Courier*, Sept. 3, 1938, April 15, Sept. 23, 1939.

17. Herbert Northrup, *Organized Labor and the Negro* (New York, 1944), p. 3.

18. A. Philip Randolph, "The Crisis of Negro Railroad Workers," *American Federationist*, vol. XLVI (Aug. 1939), pp. 807–21; and *AFL Proceedings, 1938*, pp. 21–22, 353–57, 360, *AFL Proceedings, 1939*, pp. 456–60, 546, and *AFL Proceedings, 1940*, pp. 511–12.

19. Herbert Northrup, "The Negro and the United Mine Workers of America," *Southern Economic Journal*, vol. IX (1942–1943), pp. 213–26; and Horace Cayton and George Mitchell, *Black Workers and the New Unions* (Chapel Hill, 1939), pp. 314–68.

20. *Afro-American*, June 3, 1934; and Max D. Danish, *The World of David Dubinsky* (Cleveland, 1957), pp. 81–82.

21. Spero and Harris, *The Black Worker*, p. 355; and Walter White to John L. Lewis, Nov. 27, 1935, NAACP Papers.

22. Lucy Randolph Mason, *To Win These Rights, A Personal Story of the CIO in the South* (New York, 1952), pp. 16–17, 19, 147–56, 164; Myles Horton Oral History, pp. 8–11, Southern Historical Collection, UNC; Frank Cormier and William Eaton, *Reuther* (Englewood Cliffs, 1970), pp. 17–18; Brophy, *A Miner's Life*, p. 19; Hudson, *Black Worker in the Deep South*, p. 79; Wyndam Mortimer, *Organize! My Life as a Union Man* (Boston, 1971), p. 3; L. H. Whittemore, *The Man Who Ran the Subways, The Story of Mike Quill* (New York, 1968), p. 18; and J. D. Tate, "Philip Murray" (Unpublished Ph.D. dissertation, New York University, 1967), pp. 132–35.

23. Minton and Stuart, *Men Who Lead Labor*, pp. 110, 139, 162–63, 168, 196, 245; De Caux, *Labor Radical*, pp. 240, 423–25; and Mortimer, *Organize!*, pp. 157–58.

24. Whittemore, *The Man Who Ran the Subways*, pp. 24–26, 34, 78; and Philip S. Foner, *The Fur and Leather Workers, A Story of Dramatic Struggles and Achievements*, pp. 486–87, 453.

25. Alice and Staughton Lynd, eds., *Rank and File, Personal Histories by Working-Class Organizers* (Boston, 1973), pp. 97–105; and Whittemore, *The Man Who Ran the Subways*, pp. 131–32.

26. Ernest R. McKinney, COHC, p. 29; Philip Murray, "The Problem Before the SWOC," June 17, 1936, Katherine Pollack Papers, Pennsylvania Historical Collections, Pennsylvania State University; "The Organization of Steel Workers and Its Importance to Negro Labor," Aug. 7, 1936, CIO 1936 File, Amalgamated Clothing Workers of America Papers, New York City; John P. Davis, "Organization Drive of the Steel Workers Organizing Committee," July 10, 1936, and John P. Davis to John L. Lewis, Aug. 13, 1937, CIO Central Office Correspondence, Alpha File, Box 16, CIO Papers, Catholic University, Washington; and "Blood for the Cause," *Crisis*, vol. XLIV (July 1937), p. 209.

27. *Packing House News*, Jan. 2, March 20, April 3, 1939, Feb. 17, May 12, 1941; *CIO News*, July 17, 1939; John P. Davis to John L. Lewis, Oct.

24, 1939, CIO Papers; editorial, *Courier*, July 18, 1936; and "Industrial Unions and the Negro Worker," *Crisis*, vol. XLIII (Sept. 1936), p. 273.

28. Lloyd H. Bailer, "The Negro Automobile Worker," *Journal of Political Economy*, vol. LI (Oct. 1943), pp. 416–17.

29. *Courier*, Sept. 2, 1937; and "Report of UAW National Coordinating Committee on Race Relations," March 4, 1939, Brown Collection, Labor History Archives, Wayne State University.

30. *Courier*, July 6, 1940; George S. Schuyler, "Reflections on Negro Leadership," *Crisis*, vol. LXIV (Nov. 1937), pp. 327–28; Horace White, "Who Owns the Negro Church," *Christian Century*, vol. LV (Feb. 9, 1938), pp. 176–77; and White, *A Man Called White*, pp. 212–15.

31. United Auto Workers press releases, March 19, April 18, 1938, Brown Collection, Labor History Archives; *UAW Worker*, Dec. 17, 1938, Nov. 29, Dec. 6, 1939, Feb. 21, 1940; NAACP, Minutes of the Board of Directors, April 14, 1941, NAACP Papers; and editorials in *Crisis*, vol. XLVIII (May 1941), p. 161, and *Courier*, April 19, 1941, and *Defender*, April 19, 1941.

32. Adam Clayton Powell, Jr., "Soap Box," New York *Amsterdam News*, April 30, 1938; and editorial, New York *Age*, April 12, 1941.

33. Edward L. Strong to John L. Lewis, March 13, 1939, CIO Papers; and Alton Laurence to John T. Jones, June 3, 1941, and Bernard Borah to Virginia Foster Durr, Sept. 20, 1940, SCHW Papers; and *CIO News*, Jan. 29, July 2, 16, Oct. 15, Nov. 28, Dec. 5, 26, 1938; Jan. 30, Feb. 6, 13, April 17, Dec. 4, 1939; Jan. 22, Feb. 26, 1940.

34. *CIO News*, March 26, Nov. 21, 1938; April 3, 1939; Feb. 19, March 4, 1940.

35. NAACP, Minutes of the Board of Directors, March 11, April 8, Dec. 9, 1940, NAACP Papers; *CIO News*, Sept. 17, 1938; Nov. 20, 1939; Walter White to John L. Lewis, May 31, 1940, CIO Papers; and John H. Sengstacke column, *Defender*, Dec. 7, 1940.

36. Charles S. Johnson et al., *Into the Mainstream, A Survey of Best Practices in Race Relations in the South* (Chapel Hill, 1947), p. 115; Hudson, *Black Worker in the Deep South*, p. 72; and Du Bois, "Race Relations in the United States," p. 236.

37. Johnson et al., *Into the Mainstream*, p. 88.

CHAPTER 8

1. Will Alexander, "The Negro as a Human Person," *Missionary Review of the World*, vol. LIX (June 1936), pp. 292–93.

2. Franz Boas, "Race," *Encyclopedia of the Social Sciences*, vol. XIII, pp. 25–34; Melville J. Herskovits, "Race Mixture," *ibid.*, pp. 41–43; J. B. S. Haldane, *Heredity and Politics* (New York, 1938); Ashley Montagu, *Man's Most Dangerous Myth: The Fallacy of Race* (New York, 1945),

and "The Concept of Race in the Human Species in the Light of Genetics," *Journal of Heredity*, vol. XXIII (1941), pp. 243–47; J. S. Huxley, "The Concept of Race," *Man Stands Alone* (New York, 1941), pp. 106–26; and Herbert J. Muller, *Out of the Night: A Biologists' View of the Future* (New York, 1935), p. ix.

3. Franz Boas, *The Mind of Primitive Man*, rev. ed. (New York, 1938); Lancelot Hogben, "The Concept of Race," *Genetic Principles in Medicine and Social Science* (New York, 1931), pp. 122–44, and *idem.*, "Race and Prejudice," *Dangerous Thoughts* (New York, 1940), pp. 44–58; Theodore Dobzhansky, *Genetics and the Origin of Species* (New York, 1937); S. J. Holmes, *The Negro's Struggle for Survival* (Berkeley, 1937); and Julian H. Lewis, *The Biology of the Negro* (Chicago, 1942).

4. Harry L. Shapiro, *The Heritage of the Bounty* (New York, 1936); W. E. Castle, "Race Mixture and Physical Disharmonies," *Science*, vol. LXXI (1930), pp. 603–6; and Herskovits, "Race Mixture."

5. Franz Boas, "An Anthropologist's Credo," *Nation*, vol. CXLVII (Aug. 27, 1938), pp. 201–4, and "History and Science in Anthropology: A Reply," *American Anthropologist*, vol. XXXVIII (1936), p. 140; Ruth Benedict, *Patterns of Culture* (Boston, 1934); and Margaret Mead, *Growing Up in New Guinea* (New York, 1930), and *idem. The Changing Culture of an Indian Tribe* (New York, 1932).

6. Paul Radin, "Boas and 'The Mind of Primitive Man,'" *Books That Changed Our Minds* ed. Malcolm Cowley and Bernard Smith (New York, 1938), pp. 129–42.

7. Robert M. Yerkes, "Psychological Examining in the United States Army," *National Academy of Science, Memoir*, vol. XV (1921), especially p. 870.

8. Otto Klineberg, *Negro Intelligence and Selective Migration* (New York, 1935), and *idem.*, *Race Differences* (New York, 1935), quoted on p. 189; Thomas R. Garth, *Race Psychology: A Study of Racial Mental Differences* (New York, 1931), p. 211; and C. C. Brigham, "Intelligence Tests of Immigrant Groups," *Psychological Review*, vol. XXXVII (1930), p. 165.

9. Editorial, *Crisis*, vol. XLII (March 1935), p. 81; and "Psychologists Protest 'Racial' Psychology," *Bulletin of the Society for the Psychological Study of Social Issues*, vol. X (1939), pp. 302–4.

10. Ruth Benedict, *Race: Science and Politics* (New York, 1940), pp. 259–66; Lothrop Stoddard, *Into the Darkness* (New York, 1940); Jacques Barzan, *Race, A Study in Modern Superstition* (New York, 1937); Newby, *Jim Crow's Defense*, p. 33; and *Courier*, Oct. 28, 1939.

11. Franz Boas, *Aryans and Non-Aryans* (New York, 1934); Ruth Benedict, "Franz Boas: An Obituary," *Nation*, vol. CLVI (Jan. 2, 1943), pp. 15–16; and Marvin Harris, *The Rise of Anthropological Theory, a History of Theories of Culture* (New York, 1968), p. 292.

12. Kurt Lewin, "Psycho-Sociological Problems of a Minority Group," *Character and Personality*, vol. III (1935), pp. 175–87, and "Patterns of

Aggressive Behavior in Experimentally Created 'Social Climates,'" *Journal of Social Psychology*, vol. X (1939), pp. 271–99; John Dollard, *Frustration and Aggression* (New Haven, 1939); and Ben Hecht, *A Guide for the Bedeviled* (New York, 1944), p. 31.

13. Frank H. Hankins, "Social Discrimination," *Encyclopedia of the Social Sciences*, vol. XIV, pp. 131–34; Emory S. Bogardus, "Causes of Race Antagonism," *Sociology and Social Research*, XXIV (Nov. 1939), pp. 166–70; Mapheus Smith, "A Study of Change of Attitudes toward the Negro," *Journal of Negro Education*, vol. VIII (Jan. 1939), pp. 64–70; E. L. Horowitz, "The Development of Attitude toward the Negro," *Archives of Psychology*, vol. XXVIII (Jan. 1936), pp. 5–36.

14. Sterling Brown, "Negro Character as Seen by White Authors," *Journal of Negro Education*, vol. IV (Jan. 1933), pp. 180–201; quote from Lewis C. Copeland, "The Negro as a Contrast Conception," *Race Relations and the Race Problem*, ed. Edgar T. Thompson (Durham, 1939), pp. 152–79; and W. O. Brown, "Race Prejudice as a Factor in the Status of the Negro," *Journal of Negro Education*, vol. VIII (July 1939), pp. 349–58.

15. Bruno Lasker, *Race Attitudes in Children* (New York, 1929); Henry A. Davidson, "The Anatomy of Prejudice," *Common Ground*, vol. I (Winter 1941), pp. 3–12; Robert E. Park and Ernest W. Burgess, *Introduction to the Science of Sociology* (Chicago, 1924), p. 578; and Robert E. Park, "The Nature of Race Relations," *Race Relations and the Race Problem*, ed. Thompson, pp. 3–45.

16. John Dollard, *Caste and Class in a Southern Town* (New Haven, 1937), p. 33, and *idem.*, *Children of Bondage: The Personality Development of Negro Youth in the Urban South* (Washington, 1940); Kenneth B. and Mamie P. Clark, "The Development of Consciousness of Self and the Emergence of Racial Identification in Negro Preschool Children," *Journal of Social Psychology*, vol. X (1939), pp. 591–99, and *idem.*, "Skin Color as a Factor in Racial Identification of Negro Preschool Children," *ibid.*, vol. XI (1940), pp. 159–69; and a series done for the American Youth Commission in 1940, published by the American Council on Education.

17. L. L. Bernard, "The Teaching of Sociology in the United States in the Last Fifty Years," *American Journal of Sociology*, vol. L (Jan. 1945), p. 546; Brewton Berry, "The Concept of Race in Sociology Textbooks," *Social Forces*, vol. XVIII (1940), pp. 411–15; Hugh Carter, "Research Interests of American Sociologists," *ibid.*, vol. VI (1927), pp. 209–12; and Howard Odum, "The Errors of Sociology," *ibid.*, vol. XV (1937), pp. 327–42.

18. E. Franklin Frazier, "Race Contacts and the Social Structure," *American Sociological Review*, vol. XIV (Feb. 1949), pp. 1–11, and "Sociological Theory and Race Relations," *ibid.*, vol. XII (June 1947), pp. 265–71.

19. R. B. Eleazer, "School Books and Racial Antagonism," *The High School Journal*, vol. XVIII (Oct. 1935), p. 197; Lawrence D. Reddick, "A New Interpretation for Negro History," *Journal of Negro History*, vol. XXII

(Jan. 1937), pp. 17–28; and Merl R. Eppse, *The Negro, Too, in American History* (Chicago, 1939).

20. Dykeman and Stokely, *Seeds of Southern Change,* p. 155; and "The Needs of Negro Education in the United States," *Journal of Negro Education,* vol. III (Jan. 1934), p. 11, and (Oct. 1934), pp. 650–60.

21. E. B. Reuter, "Racial Theory," *American Journal of Sociology,* vol. L (May 1945), pp. 452–61.

22. Du Bois, "Race Relations in the United States."

23. Charles R. Drew, "Negro Scholars in Scientific Research," *Journal of Negro History,* vol. XXXV (April 1950), pp. 135–49; and Maud Cuney-Hare, *Negro Musicians and Their Music* (Washington, 1936).

24. Erik Barnouw, *The Golden Web, A History of Broadcasting in the United States* (New York, 1968), pp. 111, 120–21; and materials in Box 1532, Eleanor Roosevelt Papers.

25. Cripps, "Myth of the Southern Box Office," pp. 119, 133; Edgar Dale, "The Movies and Race Relations," *Crisis,* vol. XLIV (Oct. 1937), p. 294.

26. Donald Bogle, *Toms, Coons, Mulattoes, Mamies and Bucks* (New York, 1973), pp. 131–38; and *Time,* vol. XXII (Sept. 25, 1933), p. 13.

27. Loren Miller, "Hollywood's New Negro Films," *Crisis,* vol. XLV (Jan. 1938), pp. 8–9; Dale, "Movies and Race Relations," pp. 294–96, 315; Ella Winter, "Hollywood Wakes Up," *New Republic,* vol. XCVII (Jan. 12, 1938), pp. 276–78; and Thomas Cripps, *Slow Fade to Black, The Negro in American Film, 1900–1942* (New York, 1977), p. 388.

28. *Variety,* April 24, 1934, and Nov. 17, 1940.

29. Loften Mitchell, *Black Drama* (New York, 1967), pp. 96–105; and Doris Abramson, *Negro Playwrights in the American Theatre, 1925–1959* (New York, 1969), p. 83.

30. Anne Powell, "The Negro and the Federal Theatre," *Crisis,* vol. XLIII (Nov. 1936), pp. 340–41; Clarence J. Wittler, *Some Social Trends in WPA Drama* (Washington, 1939), pp. 103–11; and Howard, *WPA and Federal Relief,* pp. 294–95.

31. James Farrell, "The End of a Literary Decade," *American Mercury,* vol. XLVIII (Dec. 1939), p. 413; "Call for an American Writers' Congress," *New Masses,* vol. XIV (Jan. 22, 1935), p. 20; and "Call for an American Artists' Congress," *ibid.* (Oct. 1, 1935), p. 33.

32. Oscar Cargill, *Intellectual America* (New York, 1941), p. 396.

33. Record, *Negro and the Communist Party,* p. 110; "Like Lindbergh's Baby," *Mike Gold Reader,* pp. 97–99; and Walter I. Daykin, "Negro Types in American White Fiction," *Sociology and Social Research,* vol. XX (1936), pp. 98–105.

34. Sterling A. Brown, "The American Race Problem as Reflected in American Literature," *Journal of Negro Education,* vol. VIII (April 1939), pp. 275–90.

35. Richard Wright, "Blueprint for Negro Writing," *New Challenge,* vol. II (Fall 1937), pp. 53–65; Langston Hughes, "To Negro Writers," *American Writers Congress* (New York, 1935), pp. 139–41; Ralph Ellison,

"Recent Negro Fiction," *New Masses*, vol. XL (Aug. 5, 1941), pp. 22–25; and Eugene C. Holmes, "Problems Facing the Negro Writer Today," *New Challenge*, vol. II (Fall 1937), pp. 69–75.

36. Langston Hughes, "Harlem Literati in the Twenties," *Saturday Review of Literature*, vol. XXII (June 22, 1940), pp. 13–14, and *idem.*, "My Adventures as a Social Poet," *Phylon*, vol. VIII (Fourth Quarter, 1947), pp. 205–12; Norman MacLeod, "The Poetry and Argument of Langston Hughes," *Crisis*, vol. XLV (Dec. 1938), pp. 358–59; and Verna Arvey, "Langston Hughes, Crusader," *Opportunity*, vol. XVIII (Dec. 1940), 363–64.

37. Harlan Hatcher, *American Mirror* (New York, 1940), pp. 78–80; and Edward Margolies, *Native Sons* (Philadelphia, 1968), pp. 47–64.

38. Irving Howe, "Black Boys and Native Sons," *Dissent*, vol. X (Fall 1963), pp. 353–68; and Constance Webb, *Richard Wright, A Biography* (New York, 1968).

39. Malcolm Cowley, "Long Black Song," *New Republic*, vol. XCVIII (April 6, 1938), p. 280; and Richard Wright, "How 'Bigger' Was Born," *Saturday Review of Literature*, vol. XXII (June 1, 1940), p. 19.

40. Burton Rascoe, "Negro Novel and White Reviewers: Richard Wright's *Native Son*," *American Mercury*, vol. L (May 1940), pp. 113–17; and Hugh M. Gloster, "Richard Wright: Interpreter of Racial and Economic Maladjustments," *Opportunity*, vol. XIX (Dec. 1941), pp. 361–65.

41. Howe, "Black Boys and Native Sons."

42. Dorothy Canfield Fisher, "Introduction," in Richard Wright, *Native Son* (New York, 1940).

43. "Conclusion," Richard Wright, *12 Million Black Voices* (New York, 1941).

CHAPTER 9

1. Du Bois, "Race Relations in the United States," p. 235.

2. William E. Leuchtenburg, "The Constitutional Revolution of 1937," *The Great Depression*, ed. Victor Hoar (Vancouver, 1969), p. 64; and Bernard H. Nelson, *The Fourteenth Amendment and the Negro Since 1920* (New York, 1946), p. 162.

3. *Crisis*, vol. IX (Jan. 1915), pp. 133–34; Brandeis cited in Oliver Allen, "Chief Counsel for Equality," *Life*, vol. XXXVIII (June 13, 1955), p. 141; and William H. Hastie, "Toward an Equalitarian Legal Order, 1930–1950," *Annals*, vol. 407 (May 1973), 21.

4. Richard Kluger, *Simple Justice* (New York, 1976), pp. 126–29; August Meier and Elliot Rudwick, "Attorneys Black and White: A Case Study of Race Relations within the NAACP," *Journal of American History*, vol. XLI (March 1976), pp. 933–34; and Charles Houston, "To the Officers

and Delegates of the 26th Annual Conference," June 24, 1935, NAACP Papers.

5. Johnson, *Along This Way*, pp. 385–86; Committee on Negro Work, "Memorandum for the American Fund for Public Service," in AFPS folder, Johnson Collection; and Roger Baldwin to L. H. Wood, Oct. 21, 1929, and Report of the Committee on Negro Work, Oct. 18, 1929, AFPS Records, New York Public Library.

6. Nathan Margold, "Preliminary Report to the Joint Committee Supervising the Expenditure of the 1930 Appropriation by the American Fund for Public Service to the NAACP," and NAACP, Minutes of the Board of Directors, Oct. 13, 1931, NAACP Papers.

7. *Yick Wo v. Hopkins*, 118 U.S. 356 (1886), especially pp. 373–74; and Margold Report, *op. cit.*, esp. 3–14.

8. NAACP, Minutes of the Board of Directors, July 10, 1933, NAACP Papers; and *AFPS Report, 1930–1934*, AFPS Records.

9. NAACP, Minutes of the Board of Directors, May 14, Nov. 9, 1934, Walter White to Nathan Margold, May 22, 1934, White to Charles Houston, Aug. 10, 1934, NAACP Papers; and NAACP *Annual Report, 1934*, p. 22.

10. Charles Houston to Walter White, Sept. 17, 1936, NAACP Papers; and Loran Miller, *The Petitioners, The Story of the Supreme Court of the United States and the Negro* (Cleveland, 1967), pp. 259–62.

11. Charles Houston to Thurgood Marshall, Nov. 22, 1934, NAACP Papers; Charles Houston, "Cracking Closed University Doors," *Crisis*, vol. XLII (Dec. 1935), p. 364; Marshall quoted in Alfred H. Kelly, "The School Desegregation Case," *Quarrels That Have Shaped the Constitution*, ed. John A. Garraty (New York, 1964), p. 254; and Charles Houston, "Educational Inequalities Must Go!" *Crisis*, vol. XLII (Oct. 1935), pp. 300–1.

12. Raleigh *News and Observer*, March 29 and April 1, 1933; and NAACP, Report of the Secretary, April 6, 1933, NAACP Papers.

13. *Pearson v. Murray*, 169 Md. 478 (1936); and Charles Houston, "Memorandum for the Joint Committee of the NAACP and AFPS," July 24, 1936, NAACP Papers.

14. *Powell v. State*, 224 Ala. 553 (1932); and New York *Times*, Jan. 23, June 1, 1932.

15. *Powell v. Alabama*, 287 U.S. 45 (1932), especially pp. 57–58, 75–77.

16. *Daily Worker*, Nov. 8, 1932; Morris Ernst, "Dissenting Opinion," *Nation*, vol. CXXXV (Dec. 7, 1932), p. 559; Hays in New York *Times*, Nov. 8, 1932; "Scottsboro," *Opportunity*, vol. XI (May 1933), p. 134; and Frankfurter in New York *Times*, Nov. 13, 1932.

17. New York *Times*, June 29, 1934, Feb. 16, 1935; *Lee v. State*, 161 Atl. 284 (1932); *Hale v. Crawford*, 65 Fed. (2d) 739; Walter White, "George Crawford—Symbol," *Crisis*, vol. XL (Jan. 1934), p. 15; *Hollins v. State of Oklahoma*, 295 U.S. 394 (1935); Scovel Richardson, "Changing Concepts of the Supreme Court as They Affect the Legal Status of

Negroes," 1 *National Bar Journal*, p. 117; and David Fellman, "Constitutional Right to Counsel," 30 *Nebraska Law Review*, p. 559.

18. *Norris* v. *Alabama*, 294 U.S. 587; and *Patterson* v. *Alabama*, 294 U.S. 600.

19. *Nixon* v. *Herndon*, 273 U.S. 45 (1927); and *Nixon* v. *Condon*, 286 U.S. 73 (1932).

20. William Pickens, "The Supreme Court Blesses and Damns," Norfolk *Journal and Guide*, April 13, 1935; *Grovey* v. *Townsend*, 295 U.S. 45 (1935); lawyer quote in 20 *Michigan Law Review*, p. 673; and Andrew G. McLaughlin, *A Constitutional History of the United States* (New York, 1935), p. 727.

21. John Dewey, "Liberalism and Civil Liberties," *Social Frontier*, vol. II (Feb. 1936); and Wesley McCune, *The Nine Young Men* (New York, 1947).

22. *Carolene Products Company* v. *United States*, 304 U.S. 144, 152 n. 4 (1938); and Louis Lusky, "Minority Rights and Public Interest," 52 *Yale Law Journal*.

23. *Johnson* v. *Zerbst*, 304 U.S. 458 (1938); *Hale* v. *Kentucky*, 303 U.S. 613 (1938); *Pierre* v. *Louisiana*, 306 U.S. 354 (1939); and *Smith* v. *Texas*, 311 U.S. 128 (1940).

24. *State* v. *Brown*, 173 Miss. 563; and *Brown* v. *Mississippi*, 297 U.S. 278 (1936).

25. *Crisis*, vol. XLVII (March 1940), p. 84; *Chambers* v. *Florida*, 309 U.S. 227 (1940); *White* v. *Texas*, 310 U.S. 530 (1940); *Lomax* v. *Texas*, 313 U.S. 544 (1941); and *Vernon* v. *Alabama*, 313 U.S. 547 (1941).

26. *New Negro Alliance* v. *Sanitary Grocery Co.*, 303 U.S. 552 (1938); and John A. Davis, "We Win the Right to Fight for Jobs," *Opportunity*, vol. XVI (Aug. 1938), pp. 230–37.

27. *Hansberry* v. *Lee*, 311 U.S. 32 (1940); *Corrigan* v. *Buckley*, 271 U.S. 323, 330 (1926); Ernest E. Johnson, "Supreme Court 1940," *Crisis*, vol. XLVIII (July 1941), pp. 220–22; and Drake and Cayton, *Black Metropolis*, pp. 182–90.

28. *Defender*, May 15, 1937, March 5, 1938, April 22, 1939, Nov. 23, 1940.

29. *Mitchell* v. *United States*, 313 U.S. 80 (1941); "Federal Intervention in Private Actions Involving the Public Interest," 65 *Harvard Law Review*, p. 319; "Comment on Recent Decisions," 26 *Washington University Law Quarterly*, p. 561; and Hubert Aultman, "Constitutional Law—Commerce Clause—Unjust Discrimination," 4 *Georgia Bar Journal*, p. 56.

30. Pete Daniel, *The Shadow of Slavery: Peonage in the South, 1901–1969* (Urbana, 1972), p. 181; and *Taylor* v. *Georgia*, 315 U.S. 25 (1942).

31. *United States* v. *Classic*, 313 U.S. 299 (1941), especially pp. 314, 318; NAACP, Minutes of the Board of Directors, Nov. 10, 1941, NAACP Papers; and Conference Notes, No. 51, Frank Murphy Papers.

32. *Lane* v. *Wilson*, 307 U.S. 268 (1939).

33. Thurgood Marshall to William Hastie, July 21, 1939, Minutes of the

Legal Committee of the NAACP, Aug. 18, 1939, and NAACP, Minutes of the Board of Directors, Sept. 11, 1939, NAACP Papers.

34. "Maryland, Inequalities of Teachers' Salaries," *Crisis*, vol. XLIV (Jan. 1937), p. 53; NAACP, Minutes of the Board of Directors, Sept. 13, 1937, and Report of the Secretary, Oct. 5, 1939, NAACP Papers; and *Mills* v. *Board of Education of Anne Arundel County*, 30 F.S. 245 (1939).

35. *Alston* v. *Board of Education of the City of Norfolk*, 112 F.S. 992 (1940); NAACP, Minutes of the Board of Directors, June 20, 1940, NAACP Papers; and *Crisis*, vol. XLVII (Dec. 1940), pp. 390–91, and vol. XLVIII (May 1941), p. 164.

36. Editorial, *Opportunity*, vol. XVIII (Jan. 1940), p. 3.

37. Walter White to Garland Fund, Jan. 7, 1936, and NAACP, Minutes of the Board of Directors, Sept. 14, 1936, NAACP Papers; and "Lloyd Gaines Case vs the University of Missouri," *Crisis*, vol. XLV (Dec. 1938), p. 398.

38. *Missouri ex rel Gaines* v. *Canada*, 305 U.S. 337 (1938); and "University of Missouri Case Won," *Crisis*, vol. XLVI (Jan. 1939), p. 10.

39. "Press Comment on the Gaines Case," *Crisis*, vol. XLVI (Feb. 1939), pp. 52–53, 61; editorial, *Opportunity*, vol. XVII (Jan. 1939), pp. 2–3; Raymond Pace Alexander, "The Upgrading of the Negro's Status by Supreme Court Decisions," *Journal of Negro History*, vol. XXX (April 1945), p. 137; William Pickens, "Educating Negroes for Democracy," *Opportunity*, vol. XVII (June 1939), pp. 164–65; and Robert J. Harris, *The Quest For Equality, The Constitution, Congress and the Supreme Court* (Baton Rouge, 1960), p. 131.

40. *Plessy* v. *Ferguson*, 163 U.S. 537 (1896).

41. *Gong Lum* v. *Rice*, 275 U.S. 78 (1927); and Bernard Nelson, "The Negro Before the Supreme Court," *Phylon*, vol. VIII (1st Quart. 1947), pp. 34–38.

42. Editorial, *Norfolk Journal and Guide*, Jan. 7, 1939; and NAACP, Report of the Department of Branches, June 12, 1939, NAACP Papers.

43. Moton, *What the Negro Thinks*, p. 140; *Opportunity*, vol. XV (Aug. 1937), p. 228; *Courier*, Jan. 28, 1939; Dabney, *Below the Potomac*, 223; and Glenn Hutchinson, "Jim Crow Challenged in Southern Universities," *Crisis*, vol. XLVI (April 1939), pp. 103–5.

44. Morroe Berger, "The Supreme Court and Group Discrimination Since 1937," 49 *Columbia Law Review*, p. 201; and Milton R. Konvitz, "A Nation Within a Nation—the Negro and the Supreme Court," *American Scholar*, vol. XI (Jan. 1941), pp. 69–78.

45. Will Alexander, COHC, p. 258.

CHAPTER 10

1. NAACP, Minutes of the Board of Directors, March 9, Dec. 21, 1931, Memorandum from Walter White to Roy Wilkins, William Pickens and

Arthur Spingarn, Aug. 17, 1932, and Report of the Secretary, Dec. 8, 1932, NAACP Papers; T. A. Hill, "The National Urban League," *Southern Workman* (May 1936), p. 138; Strickland, *History of the Chicago Urban League*, pp. 105–6; and Will Alexander to J. E. Clark, Jan. 4, 1933, George Fort Milton Papers, Library of Congress.

2. Walter White to William Rosenwald, Feb. 17, 1932, White to Herbert H. Lehman, March 16, 1933, and NAACP, Report of the Secretary, Jan. 4, 1933, NAACP Papers; Eugene Kinckle Jones to Jessie O. Thomas, Dec. 19, 1932, National Urban League Papers; J. E. Clark to James Burton, Dec. 30, 1932, George Fort Milton Papers; and Mary White Ovington to Arthur B. Spingarn, July 22, 1934, Arthur Spingarn Papers, Library of Congress.

3. NAACP, Report of the Secretary, Sept., Oct., Nov., 1933, and Minutes of the Board of Directors, Sept. 11, 1933, June 11, Oct. 4, Nov. 9, 1934, NAACP Papers.

4. T. A. Hill to Eugene Kinckle Jones, Dec. 29, 1930, and Hill to Executive Secretaries of Affiliated Branches, May 21, 1935, National Urban League Papers; Lester B. Granger, COHC, p. 85; Carl Murphy to Charles S. Johnson, Dec. 1, 6, 1934, March 18, 1935, Charles S. Johnson Papers; and Roy Wilkins, COHC, 65–75.

5. Nancy J. Weiss, *The National Urban League, 1910–1940* (New York, 1974), pp. 265–80; Strickland, *History of the Chicago Urban League*, pp. 121, 135; "Urban League in Action," *Opportunity*, vol. XIII (June 1935), p. 190; and *Annual Report for 1935*, National Urban League Papers.

6. Press release, Aug. 12, 1933, National Urban League Papers; Frank Crosswaith, "Sound Principle and Unsound Policy," *Opportunity*, vol. XII (Nov. 1934), p. 340; Lester Granger, "The Urban League in Action: Emergency Advisory Councils," *ibid.*, vol. XIII (May 1935), p. 158; and Guichard Parris and Lester Brooks, *Blacks in the City: A History of the National Urban League* (Boston, 1971), pp. 242–43.

7. T. A. Hill, "Building New Roads," *Opportunity*, vol. XII (Dec. 1934), p. 376; Hill, "Memorandum on Proposed Labor Plan," March 8, 1934, Lester Granger, "What Objectives Shall the League Set for the Next Five Year Period in the Field of Organization in Industry," Nov. 27, 1935, and Granger to John L. Lewis, Dec. 3, 1935, National Urban League Papers; and Granger, "The Negro—Friend or Foe of Organized Labor," *Opportunity*, vol. XIII (May 1935), pp. 142–44.

8. Weiss, *National Urban League*, pp. 272–76, 292–97; Strickland, *History of the Chicago Urban League*, pp. 130–32; William Jones, "Trade Boycotts," *Opportunity*, vol. XVIII (Aug. 1940), p. 240; and *Opportunity*, vol. XIX (July 1941).

9. Walter White to Joseph A. Gavagan, March 2, 1935, "Application of the National Association for the Advancement of Colored People to the Christian Social Justice Fund," Jan. 15, 1936, and Walter White,

"Memorandum to the Branches," Sept. 22, 1939, NAACP Papers; and William H. Hastie, "A Look at the NAACP," *Crisis*, vol. XLVI (Sept. 1939), pp. 263–64, 274.

10. Charles Houston to Walter White, Jan. 1, 23, 1935, Roy Wilkins to Joel Spingarn, May 23, 1935, and White to P. L. Prattis, June 4, 1935, NAACP Papers; Du Bois, *Dusk of Dawn*, pp. 288–97; and Bunche, "Programs and Ideologies," pp. 168–202.

11. Bunche, "Programs and Ideologies," pp. 144–45; and Walter White to George S. Schuyler, July 15, 1932, NAACP Papers.

12. "Findings: Second Amenia Conference, Aug. 18–21, 1933," NAACP Papers; and "Youth and Age at Amenia," *Crisis*, vol. XL (Oct. 1933), p. 226.

13. Du Bois' views appear in *Crisis*, vol. XLI (Jan. 1934), p. 20; (Feb. 1934), pp. 52–53; (March 1934), p. 85; (April 1934), pp. 115–16; (May 1934), pp. 134, 147; (June 1934), p. 183; (July 1934), pp. 245–46; and in "A Negro Nation Within the Nation," *Current History*, vol. XLII (June 1935), pp. 265–70.

14. "Segregation—A Symposium," *Crisis*, vol. XLI (March 1934), pp. 79–81; James Weldon Johnson, *Negro Americans, What Now?* (New York, 1934), pp. 5–11, 87–89, 98–99; Francis J. Grimke, "Segregation," *Crisis*, vol. XLI (June 1934), pp. 173–74; and Ferdinand Q. Morton, "Segregation," *ibid.* (Aug. 1934), pp. 244–45.

15. Claude McKay to James Weldon Johnson, May 16, 1935, NAACP Papers; E. Franklin Frazier, "The Du Bois Program in the Present Crisis," *Race*, vol. I (Winter 1935–36), pp. 12–13; George Streator, "In Search of Leadership," *ibid.*, p. 15; Lester Granger to James Weldon Johnson, March 30, 1936, NAACP Papers; photograph and editorial in *Defender*, March 24, 31, 1934; and A. N. Fields, "I Heard Dr. Du Bois," *Defender*, March 24, 1934.

16. NAACP, Minutes of the Board of Directors, April 12, May 14, 1934, NAACP Papers.

17. Charles Houston to Roy Wilkins, May 22, 1935, and Wilkins to Joel Spingarn, May 23, 1935, NAACP Papers; and Loren Miller, "How Left is the NAACP?" *New Masses*, vol. XVI (July 16, 1935), pp. 12–13.

18. NAACP, Minutes of the Board of Directors, July 9, 1934, Walter White to Joel Spingarn, Aug. 22, 1934, "Preliminary Report of the Committee on Future Plan and Program of the NAACP," Sept. 1934, "Report of the Committee on Future Plan and Program of the NAACP" as revised by the Board of Directors, June 14, 1935, and Charles Houston to Walter White, Feb. 9, 1935, NAACP Papers.

19. Abram Harris to W.E.B. Du Bois, Jan. 6, 1934, quoted in Wolters, *Negroes and the Great Depression*, pp. 317–18; Du Bois to George Streator, June 26, 1934, *ibid.*, p. 340; and Charles E. Russell to Walter White, June 14, 1935, NAACP Papers.

20. NAACP, Minutes of the Board of Directors, June 10, 1935, NAACP Pa-

pers; Bunche, "Programs and Ideologies," p. 167; Howard Kester to Walter White, July 30, 1935, and White to Roy Ellis, Aug. 14, 1935, NAACP Papers.

21. Walter White, "Proposed Congressional Investigation of Economic Status of the Negro under the New Deal," March 11, 1935, NAACP, Minutes of the Board of Directors, April 11, Dec. 12, 1938, March 13, April 10, May 8, Sept. 11, 1939, and Report of the Secretary issued each September for the resolutions passed by the annual NAACP conferences, NAACP Papers; and *Courier*, Jan. 1, Feb. 12, 1938, May 6, 1939.

22. NAACP, Minutes of the Board of Directors, April 19, 1937, Report of the Secretary, June 13, 1938, Charles Houston to James Byrnes, April 25, 1938, NAACP Papers; *Crisis*, vol. XLVIII (May 1941), pp. 161, 171; and *UAW Worker*, Dec. 17, 1938; Nov. 29, Dec. 6, 1939; Feb. 21, 1940.

23. William Pickens to Walter White, June 12, 1933, White to Harry E. Davies, Jan. 27, 1936, Charles Houston to White, Jan. 31, 1936, NAACP Papers; *Crisis*, vol. XLII (Jan. 1935), p. 26, vol. XLIV (March 1937), p. 89, vol. XL (Jan. 1933), p. 17, vol. XLVIII (May 1941), p. 165, and vol. XLVIII (July 1941), p. 226; and Record, *Race and Radicalism*, pp. 88–92.

24. Bunche, "Programs and Ideologies," pp. 319–20; John P. Davis, *Let Us Build a National Negro Congress* (Washington, 1935), especially pp. 29–30; Cayton and Mitchell, *Black Workers and the New Unions*, pp. 415–24; "Toward Negro Unity," *Nation*, vol. CXLIII (March 11, 1936), p. 302; and Bunche, "Triumph?–or Fiasco?" *Race*, vol. I (Summer 1936), pp. 93–96.

25. Bunche, "Programs and Ideologies," p. 353; and NNC, official resolutions and copies of *National Negro Congress News* in National Negro Congress Manuscripts, Schomburg Collection, New York Public Library.

26. New York *Times*, April 3, 1938; John P. Davis, "Report of the National Secretary, Cleveland, Ohio, June 19–20, 1936," and *idem.*, "The Negro Vote and the New Deal" (1939) in National Negro Congress Manuscripts; *Defender*, July 8, 1939; New York *Amsterdam News*, April 5, 12, 26, 1941; A. Philip Randolph to Walter White, June 22, 1937, and John P. Davis to White, March 31, 1938, NAACP Papers; Davis to Roosevelt, Oct. 18, 1938, PPF 4266, Roosevelt Papers; and Lawrence S. Wittner, "The National Negro Congress: A Reassessment," *American Quarterly*, vol. XXII (Winter 1970), pp. 883–901.

27. "Draft Call to the Southern Negro Youth Conference," NAACP Papers; *Souvenir Bulletin of the Southern Negro Youth Congress* (1937), National Negro Congress Manuscripts; *Afro-American*, May 6, 1939; and editorial, *New Masses*, vol. XXXI (May 10, 1939), p. 6.

28. *Afro-American* and *Courier*, Dec. 3, 1938; Aubrey Williams to David Conrad, June 30, 1959, Aubrey Williams Papers, Box 30, Franklin D. Roosevelt Library; Myrdal, *An American Dilemma*, p. 469; and Sterling

Brown, "South on the Move," *Opportunity*, vol. XVI (Dec. 1938), pp. 366-68.

29. Mary M. Bethune, "I'll Never Turn Back No More!" *Opportunity*, vol. XVI (Nov. 1938), pp. 324-26; Walter White to Daisy Lampkin, June 23, 1938, NAACP Papers; James McClendon to Mayor Richard Reading, Oct. 11, July 12, 1938, and Snow Grigsby to Reading, Feb. 1, 1938, Mayor's Papers, Burton Collection, Detroit Public Library; Drake and Cayton, *Black Metropolis*, pp. 737-39; Charles H. Loeb, *The Future is Yours: The History of the Future Outlook League* (Cleveland, 1947), *passim;* Charles C. Webber, "Sweet Land of Liberty," *Christian Century*, vol. LV (May 18, 1938), pp. 624-25; *Courier*, Jan. 15, March 19, 1938; Dec. 20, 1939; *Afro-American*, Aug. 12, 1939; and Norfolk *Journal and Guide*, Feb. 19, 1938; Sept. 2, 1939.

30. August Meier and Elliot Rudwick, "The Origins of Nonviolent Direct Action in Afro-American Protest: A Note on Historical Discontinuities," in *Along the Color Line, Explorations in the Black Experience* (Urbana, 1976), pp. 312-44, quote on p. 314; and Bunche quoted in Bennett, *Confrontation: Black and White*, p. 142.

31. Dollard, *Caste and Class in a Southern Town*, p. 68; Virginius Dabney, *Liberalism in the South* (Chapel Hill, 1936), pp. 262-64; and Myrdal, *An American Dilemma*, p. 1022.

32. Du Bois, *Souls of Black Folk*, p. 53.

33. *Courier*, Dec. 4, 1937; Oct. 15, 1938; Feb. 11, May 6, Aug. 12, 1939; Dec. 21, 1940; *Civil Liberties Quarterly*, vol. XV (Jan. 1935), p. 1; *Civil Rights News*, vol. IV (July 1940), p. 1; George G. Battle to Frank Graham, June 27, 1940, Frank Graham Papers; *Defender*, March 6, Dec. 4, 1937; La Guardia and Benson in *Courier*, Oct. 7, 1939 and Sept. 24, 1938; New York *Times*, Sept. 17, 1940; NAACP, Minutes of the Board of Directors, April 10, 1939, NAACP Papers; and Benedict, *Race: Science and Politics*, pp. 249-66.

34. *Courier*, Jan. 22, Feb. 12, April 16, July 30, 1938, April 15, Dec. 16, 1939; "Johns Hopkins Loses," *New Republic*, vol. XCVIII (June 7, 1939), pp. 115-16; Richard Collins, "Liberalism and Negroes," *Student Advocate*, vol. II (Feb. 1937), p. 8; and editorials, *ibid.*, vol. I (Feb. 1936), vol. II (May 1937), and vol. III (March 1938).

35. George L. Lunberg, "The Social Position of the Protestant Clergy," *Journal of Social Issues*, vol. VIII (1944), pp. 16-33; Hubert C. Herring, "Congregationalists and Race Discrimination," *Christian Century*, vol. XLVIII (June 17, 1931), p. 814; *Courier*, Feb. 19, July 16, 1938; July 29, 1939; editorial, *Crisis*, vol. XLIV (Nov. 1937), p. 337; and Benjamin E. Mays, "World Churchmen Score Prejudice," *ibid.*, pp. 340-41, 347.

36. Robert W. Miller, "The Attitudes of American Protestantism toward the Negro, 1919-1939," *Journal of Negro History*, vol. XLI (1956), pp. 224-25; Dykeman and Stokeley, *Seeds of Southern Change*, pp. 280-81;

George Edmund Haynes, "Changing Racial Attitudes and Customs," *Phylon*, vol. II (First Quarter, 1941), pp. 28–43; and newsletters and pamphlets in Fellowship of Southern Churchmen Papers, Southern Historical Collection, UNC.

37. George K. Hunton, as told to Gary MacEoin, *All of Which I Saw, Part of Which I Was* (Garden City, 1967), pp. 14–20, 57–61, 64–69, 74, 86, 96; Reverend John M. Cooper, "Religion and the Race Problem," *Crisis*, vol. XLII (June 1935), pp. 170, 178; "Catholic Students Ask Square Deal for Negro," *ibid.*, vol. XLIV (Sept. 1937), p. 277; Floyd J. Calvin, "Catholic Interracial Promotion," *Interracial Review*, vol. XII (Jan. 1939), pp. 9–10; and *Courier*, Nov. 4, 25, 1939.

38. David Reimers, *White Protestantism and the Negro* (New York, 1965), pp. 95–96, 108.

39. Malcolm Cowley, "Two Books About the Negro," *New Republic*, vol. XCV (May 13, 1936), p. 22; and Holt, *Mary McLeod Bethune*, p. 182.

CHAPTER 11

1. *Opportunity*, vol. XI (April 1933), p. 104; *Nation*, vol. CXXXI (Nov. 26, 1930); *Congressional Record*, 71st Cong., 2nd sess., 3239; and James Weldon Johnson to Walter White, Oct. 30, 1933, James Weldon Johnson Collection, Yale University.

2. Commission on Interracial Cooperation, *The Interracial Front, A Brief Report of Recent Activities* (Atlanta, 1939), quoted from p. 2.

3. *New York Times*, Jan. 12, 1930; Alexander, COHC, pp. 247–48; and Dykman and Stokeley, *Seeds of Southern Change*, pp. 136–37, 141.

4. Alexander, COHC, pp. 248–50; Southern Commission on the Study of Lynching, *Lynchings and What They Mean* (Atlanta, 1931), especially pp. 5–7; George Fort Milton, "The Impeachment of Judge Lynch," *Virginia Quarterly Review*, vol. VIII (1932), pp. 247–56; and Minutes of the Meeting of the Southern Commission on the Study of Lynching, Sept. 5, Dec. 22, 1930, Commission on Interracial Cooperation Papers, Atlanta University.

5. Arthur Raper Oral History Interview, Southern Historical Collection, UNC, pp. 7–8; and Dykeman and Stokeley, *Seeds of Southern Change*, pp. 140–41.

6. George Fort Milton to Walter White, Jan. 30, 1934, Milton Papers; Dabney, *Below the Potomac*, p. 184; and Dykeman and Stokeley, *Seeds of Southern Change*, p. 193.

7. "Reminiscences of Jessie Daniel Ames: 'I Really Do Like a Good Fight,'" *New South*, vol. XXVII (Spring 1972), p. 35; Alexander, COHC, pp. 240–44; and Willie Snow Ethridge, "Southern Women Attack Lynching," *Nation*, vol. CXXXI (Dec. 10, 1930), pp. 647–50.

8. Association of Southern Women for the Prevention of Lynching (here-

after cited ASWPL), *Beginning of the Movement* (Atlanta, 1932); and Jessie Daniel Ames, *Southern Women Look at Lynching* (Atlanta, 1937), especially pp. 4–5.

9. Jessie Daniel Ames, *Southern Women and Lynching* (Atlanta, 1936).

10. Lewis T. Nordyke, "Ladies and Lynching," *Survey Graphic*, vol. XVIII (Nov. 1939), pp. 683–86; ASWPL, *Organizations Committed to a Program of Education to Prevent Lynching* (Atlanta, 1940); "Reminiscences of Jessie Daniel Ames," *op. cit.;* and Ames, *Southern Women Look at Lynching.*

11. "Reminiscences of Jessie Daniel Ames," p. 39; resolution adopted by ASWPL, Atlanta, Jan. 9, 1934; in Jessie Daniel Ames Papers, Southern Historical Collection, UNC; and Jessie Daniel Ames to George Foster Peabody, Nov. 21, 1934, ASWPL Papers, Atlanta University.

12. Report of Jessie Daniel Ames to ASWPL, Jan. 10, 1935, letters from Ames to council members, April 18, 1935; Oct. 18, 1937, and Minutes of Executive Sessions, Jan. 26, 27, 1939, ASWPL Papers.

13. Editorial, Norfolk *Journal and Guide*, Feb. 17, 1940; Margaret Long, "Mrs. Dorothy Tilly: A Memoir," *New South*, vol. XXV (Spring 1970), pp. 43–45; Jessie Daniel Ames to Doris Loraine, March 5, 1935, ASWPL Papers; Jessie Daniel Ames and Bertha Payne Newell, *"Repairers of the Breach,"* A *Story of Interracial Cooperation Between Southern Women, 1935–1940* (Atlanta, 1940); and Edwin L. Clarke, *White Women in a Biracial Society* (Atlanta, 1942).

14. Materials in George Fort Milton Papers, Box 88.

15. Materials in Boxes C-194 and C-195, NAACP Papers.

16. Walter White to Herbert Stockton, April 19, 1933, and Lucille Milner to White, April 17, 1933; James Weldon Johnson to White, Oct. 30, 1933, Johnson Collection; White to Frank Murphy, Dec. 9, 1933; July 25, 1934, Frank Murphy Papers; and NAACP, Report of the Secretary, Dec. 7, 1933, and Minutes of the Board of Directors, Jan. 8, 1934, NAACP Papers.

17. Herbert Seligman, William Pickens, Robert Bagnall, and Roy Wilkins, "To the Board of Directors," Dec. 21, 1931, NAACP, Minutes of the Board of Directors, Jan. 4, Feb. 8, March 14, April 11, May 9, 1932, and J. E. Spingarn to the Board of Directors, March 6, 1933, NAACP Papers.

18. E. J. Kahn, Jr., "Profile," *New Yorker*, vol. XXIV (Sept. 4, 11, 1948), pp. 28–32, 38–40; Roger Baldwin, COHC, vol. I, pp. 317–18; and Will Alexander, COHC, p. 259.

19. Walter White to James Weldon Johnson, July 12, 1934, Johnson Collection; and Alex B. Spence, "Lynching and the Nation," *Commonweal*, vol. XV (April 13, 1932), pp. 658–59.

20. New York *Times*, Nov. 21, 24, 28, 1933.

21. Walter White to Edward Costigan, Nov. 27, 1933, NAACP Papers; New York *Times*, Nov. 29, 30, Dec. 7, 1933; and *Crisis*, vol. XLI (Jan. 1934), p. 5.

22. NAACP, Report of the Secretary, Feb. 9, March 8, April 5, May 9, 1934, Emmanuel Cellar to Walter White, Dec. 4, 1933, and White to Celler, Dec. 13, 1933, NAACP Papers.

23. Minutes of Meeting of Federal Anti-Lynching Legislation Committee, Jan. 15, 1934, NAACP Papers; and New York Times, June 4, 1934.

24. Minutes of Meeting of Federal Anti-Lynching Legislation Committee, Jan. 15, 1934, NAACP Papers.

25. NAACP Minutes of the Board of Directors, Feb. 9, April 5, 1934, NAACP Papers; and Hearings on S. 1978, To Assure to Persons Within the Jurisdiction of Every State the Equal Protection of the Law by Discouraging, Preventing, and Punishing the Crime of Lynching, 73rd Cong., 2nd sess., 1934.

26. Walter White to Felix Frankfurter, Jan. 18, 1934, and H. L. Mencken to White, Feb. 6, 1934, NAACP Papers; Opportunity, vol. XII (June 1934), p. 181; editorial, Courier, Jan. 13, 1934; and Eleanor Roosevelt to White, May 2, 1934, NAACP Papers.

27. Walter White to Edward Costigan, May 8, 1934, and NAACP Report of the Secretary, June 6, 1934, NAACP Papers.

28. Walter White to Eleanor Roosevelt, May 29, 1934, Eleanor Roosevelt Papers; and Transcript of the Presidential Press Conference, May 23, 1934, Roosevelt Papers.

29. NAACP, Report of the Secretary, June 6, Sept. 5, Nov. 9, 1934, NAACP Papers; White to Roosevelt, June 13, 1934, OF 93A, Roosevelt Papers; Congressional Record, 73rd Cong., 2nd sess., p. 1819; and New York Times, July 5, Oct. 29, 1934.

30. White to Roosevelt, Dec. 27, 1934, OF 93A, Roosevelt Papers; Eleanor Roosevelt to White, Nov. 23, 1934, Jan. 22, 1935, Eleanor Roosevelt Papers; 26th Annual Report for 1935 (New York, 1935), 19–26; and Crisis, vol. XLII (Jan. 1935), pp. 6–7, 10–11, 14, 22, 26, 29.

31. Fred Greenbaum, "The Anti-Lynching Bill of 1935: The Irony of 'Equal Justice—Under Law,'" Journal of Human Relations, vol. XV (Third Quarter 1967), p. 78; and Congressional Record, 74th Cong., 1st sess., p. 2167.

32. New York Times, Feb. 12, 1935; NAACP, Minutes of the Board of Directors, Feb. 11, 1935, NAACP Papers; "An Art Exhibit Against Lynching," Crisis, vol. XLII (April 1935), quote on p. 106; and New Masses, vol. XIV (March 19, 1935), p. 29.

33. Howard Kester Oral History Interview, pp. 42–43, Southern Historical Collection, UNC; NAACP, The Lynching of Claude Neal (New York, 1934); Crisis, vol. XLII (Jan. 1935), p. 18; Nation, vol. CXL (Jan. 30, 1935), p. 13; and Defender, Feb. 19, 1935.

34. NAACP, Report of the Secretary, April 4, May 6, 1935, NAACP Papers.

35. Congressional Record, 74th Cong., 1st sess., pp. 6, 290–95.

36. Ibid., pp. 6, 351–687.

37. Charles Houston to White, July 3, 1935, and NAACP, Report of the

Secretary, Sept. 6, 1935, NAACP Papers; Walter White, "United States Department of (White) Justice," *Crisis*, vol. XLII (Oct. 1935), p. 238; White to Eleanor Roosevelt, Sept. 12, 1935, NAACP Papers; Oswald Garrison Villard, "The President's Worst Failure," *Nation*, vol. CXL (June 5, 1935), p. 647; and William Seagle, "How Not to Stop Lynching," *ibid.* (May 1, 1935), p. 626.

38. White to Eleanor Roosevelt, Nov. 13, 1935, NAACP, Minutes of the Board of Directors, Dec. 9, 1935, and Memorandum of the Interview of the Secretary of the NAACP with the President at the White House, Jan. 2, 1936, NAACP Papers; and White to Roosevelt, June 2, 1936, OF 93A, Roosevelt Papers.

39. White to Roger Baldwin, Nov. 23, 1936, and materials in Box C-241, NAACP Papers; editorials, *Crisis*, vol. XLIV (Jan., Dec. 1937), pp. 17, 369, and *Opportunity*, vol. XV (June 1937), p. 165; Richmond *Times-Dispatch*, Feb. 2, 1937; *New Republic*, vol. XCVII (Dec. 1, 1937), pp. 86–87; and NAACP, Minutes of the Board of Directors, March 8, 1937, and "Quotations From Letters of Senators to the N.A.A.C.P. Stating Their Position on Anti-Lynching Legislation," Jan. 1937, NAACP Papers.

40. *Congressional Record*, 75th Cong., 1st sess., pp. 3856–57, 3252–53, 3386.

41. *Congressional Record*, 75th Cong., 1st sess., pp. 3560–64; *Crisis*, vol. XLIV (April 1937), p. 113; *Opportunity*, vol. XV (May 1937), p. 155; and White to Eleanor Roosevelt, May 21, 1937, Eleanor Roosevelt Papers.

42. NAACP, Report of the Secretary, Aug. 24, 1937, and Charles Houston to Roger Baldwin, Dec. 13, 1937, NAACP Papers; editorials in *Crisis*, vol. XLIV (July 1937), p. 209, and (Sept. 1937), p. 273; and Josiah Bailey to Clara Cox, Oct. 21, 1937, ASWPL Papers.

43. *Courier*, Jan. 11, 1938; and White to Theodore Green, Jan. 4, 1938, Arthur Spingarn to White, Jan. 16, 1938, and NAACP, Report of the Secretary, Feb. 8, 1938, NAACP Papers.

44. *Newsweek*, vol. XI (Jan. 31, 1938), p. 13; "Lynch Filibuster Must Be Halted," *Equal Justice*, vol. XII (Feb. 1938), p. 4; *Courier*, Jan. 22, 29, Feb. 11, 1939; editorials in *Opportunity*, vol. XVI (March 1938), p. 69, *CIO News*, Jan. 29, 1938, *New Masses*, vol. XXVI (Jan. 25, 1938), p. 9, and (Feb. 1, 1938), p. 10; John P. Davis to Roosevelt, March 16, 1938, PPF 4266, Roosevelt Papers; and White to Roy Wilkins, March 10, 1938, White to Leon Ransom, March 14, 1938, NAACP, Report of the Secretary, April 7, 1938, NAACP Papers.

45. *Congressional Record*, 75th Cong., 3rd sess. (Jan. 7 to Feb. 17, 1938), especially pp. 138–61, 253–75, 493–511, 610–32, 813–35, 964–1001, 1098–1138, 1385–1407.

46. *Congressional Record*, 75th Cong., 3rd sess., pp. 1490–97, 1532–62, 1623–43, 2022–37, 2090–118.

47. Huthmacher, *Senator Robert F. Wagner*, pp. 240–42.
48. *Congressional Record*, 75th Cong., 3rd sess., pp. 1166, 1887–88, 2007; and NAACP, Report of the Secretary, March 9, 1938, NAACP Papers.
49. NAACP, *29th Annual Report for 1938* (New York, 1938), 5; NAACP, Report of the Secretary, March 9, May 5, 1939, and White to Frances Williams, Jan. 16, 1939, NAACP Papers; and *Courier*, May 28, 1938; July 22, Aug. 5, Dec. 4, 1939.
50. Memorandum Re the Conference with President Roosevelt, April 12, 1939, NAACP Papers; and *Congressional Record*, 76th Cong., 2nd sess., pp. 253–54.
51. *Southern Frontier*, vol. I (Jan. 1940), p. 1; *Courier*, Feb. 26, April 9, 1938, April 8, 1939; Henry A. Schweinhaut, "The Civil Liberties Section of the Department of Justice," *Bill of Rights Review*, vol. I (1940–41), 206–7; American Civil Liberties Union Press Bulletin #809, March 25, 1938, in Socialist Party Papers; Jessie Daniel Ames to Lillian Smith, Dec. 30, 1941, Jessie Daniel Ames Papers; and Roy Wilkins, COHC, pp. 43–44, 70, 75–76, 101–02.
52. Kahn, "Profile," pp. 35–37; Moore, *Senator Josiah W. Bailey*, p. 115; *Congressional Record*, 75th Cong., 2nd sess., pp. 68, 3rd sess., p. 310, and 76th Cong., 1st sess., pp. 559–60; and cover story of *Time*, XXXI (Jan. 24, 1938).
53. James Weldon Johnson to White, March 8, 1938, NAACP Papers; White to Eleanor Roosevelt, Dec. 23, 1938, Eleanor Roosevelt Papers; Roy Wilkins, COHC, p. 71; and Walter White, "End Lynching," *Equality*, vol. II (Jan. 1940), pp. 5–7.

CHAPTER 12

1. W.E.B. Du Bois, "Inter-Racial Implications of the Ethiopian Crisis," *Foreign Affairs*, vol. XIV (Oct. 1935), pp. 82–92; NAACP, Report of the Secretary, June 7, July 5, Aug. 2, 1935, NAACP Papers; *Crisis*, vol. XLII (July 1935), pp. 214, and (Aug. 1935), p. 241; and Saunders Redding, *They Came in Chains* (Philadelphia, 1950), pp. 290–91.
2. Ottley, *New World A-Coming*, pp. 194–97; editorials, *Courier*, Dec. 3, 10, 1938; Sept. 23, 1939; and *Afro-American*, Nov. 26, Dec. 10, 1938; July 15, 22, Sept. 2, 1939.
3. Editorials, *Defender*, July 6, 1939, and *Afro-American*, Feb. 17, 1940; New York *Times*, Feb. 13, 1939; and *Courier*, Nov. 25, Oct. 7, 1939; July 2, Dec. 17, Jan. 15, Oct. 8, 1938.
4. Ulysses G. Lee, Jr., *United States Army in World War II, Special Studies, The Employment of Negro Troops* (Washington, 1966), chs. II–III; and "The Negro in the United States Navy," *Crisis*, XLVII (July 1940), pp. 200–201.
5. *Crisis*, vol. XLVII (July 1940); quote in *Afro-American*, March 29,

1941; and Robert C. Weaver, "Racial Employment Trends in National Defense," *Phylon*, vol. II (Fourth Quarter, 1941), pp. 337–58.

6. Edwin Watson to Walter White, Oct. 17, 1939, and remarks of Roosevelt at Presidential Press Conference, June 5, 1940, Roosevelt Papers.

7. Editorials, *Defender*, July 22, Aug. 19, 1939; June 22, 29, July 6, Aug. 10, Sept. 7, 1940; quotes from April 20, 27, May 18, 1940 issues; columns by George Schuyler, *Courier*, Oct. 5, Dec. 21, 28, 1940; Cayton quoted in Redding, *They Came in Chains*, p. 291; 1940 pamphlets of the NNC, *Negro People Speak Out Against Jim Crow*, *A Negro Looks at the War*, *Jim Crow in Uniform*, *Old Jim Crow Has Got to Go*, and NBC broadcast script by John P. Davis, "The N.N.C. Reports to the People," April 28, 1940, National Negro Congress Papers; and editorials, *Afro-American*, July 15, 22, Sept. 2, 16, 1939; Feb. 17, Sept. 14, 1940.

8. NAACP press release, Aug. 1, 1940, NAACP Papers; Dr. John W. Davis, quoted in *Afro-American*, Nov. 30, 1940; and voluminous correspondence in Roosevelt Papers, OF 93, particularly Collier Anderson to Roosevelt, Sept. 15, 1939, and Harlem Youth Congress to Roosevelt, May 30, 1940.

9. NAACP, *Annual Report, 1940*, p. 6; Minutes of the Board of Directors, June 10, Sept. 9, 1940, and press release, Aug. 9, 1940, NAACP Papers; Robert L. Vann to Roosevelt, Jan. 19, 1939; June 13, 1940, OF 335, Roosevelt Papers; and Benjamin McLaurin, COHC, pp. 64–65, 295–96.

10. James Middletown to Roosevelt, June 13, 1940, Roosevelt Papers, OF 93; *Afro-American*, June 22, 1940; and Diary of Henry L. Stimson hereafter cited Stimson Diary), Sept. 30, 1940, Yale University.

11. Charles H. Thompson, "The American Negro and the National Defense," *Journal of Negro Education*, vol. IX (Oct. 1940), pp. 541–42; and *Selective Service in Peacetime, First Report of the Director of Selective Service, 1940–1941* (Washington, 1942), pp. 323–335.

12. *Crisis*, vol. XLVII (Feb. 1940), p. 54; Walter White speech reported in *Afro-American*, June 29, 1940; NAACP, Minutes of the Board of Directors, June 20, Oct. 14, 1940, NAACP Papers; and White to Eleanor Roosevelt, Sept. 17, 1940, Eleanor Roosevelt Papers.

13. *Courier*, June 29, 1940, and *Defender*, July 6, 1940.

14. Moon, *Balance of Power*, p. 32; William Pickens to Walter White, Sept. 20, 1940, NAACP Papers; and "Colored Citizens Committee for Willkie" advertisement, *Courier*, Sept. 28, 1940.

15. *Courier*, July 13, 20, 1940; and editorials in *Afro-American*, July 27, Sept. 14, Oct. 12, 19, 26, Nov. 2, 1940, and *Courier*, Sept. 28, Oct. 12, 26, Nov. 2, 1940.

16. *Courier*, July 27, Sept. 7, Oct. 19, 1940.

17. Charles C. Diggs to Stephen Early, July 1, 1940, OF 93, White House Memorandum on views of Congressman Arthur Mitchell, Aug. 8, 1940, PPF 2289, Roosevelt Papers; and Bethune to Roosevelt, July 12, 1940, Eleanor Roosevelt Papers.

18. Lee, *Employment of Negro Troops*, pp. 75-76; and *Courier*, Sept. 14, 21, 1940.
19. Stephen Early to Edwin Watson, Sept. 19, 1940, OF 2538, Roosevelt Papers; Walter White to Eleanor Roosevelt, Oct. 3, 1940, Eleanor Roosevelt Papers; and NAACP press release, Oct. 5, 1940, NAACP Papers.
20. Stimson Diary, Sept. 27, 1940; Stephen Early to Charles Michelson, Oct. 9, 1940, OF 93, Roosevelt Papers; NAACP, *Annual Report, 1940*, pp. 4–5; and "White House Blesses Jim Crow," *Crisis*, vol. XLVII (Nov. 1940), pp. 350–51, 357.
21. White, Randolph, and Hill to Early, Oct. 10, 1940, Early to Roosevelt, Oct. 14, 1940, and Roosevelt to Early, Oct. 14, 1940, OF 93, Roosevelt Papers; White to Early, Oct. 21, 1940, Eleanor Roosevelt Papers; and NAACP press releases, Oct. 5, 11, 1940, NAACP Papers.
22. *Courier*, Sept. 21, 28, 1940; and "The Problem," *Time*, vol. XXXIV (Oct. 28, 1940), p. 19.
23. Stimson Diary, Oct. 22, 23, 1940; White, *A Man Called White*, p. 180; Alexander, COHC, pp. 358–60, 685; and Mary McLeod Bethune to Eleanor Roosevelt, OF 93, and James Rowe to Roosevelt, OF 2538, Roosevelt Papers.
24. New York *Times*, Oct. 16, 1940; *Defender*, Oct. 19, 26, 1940; Stimson Diary, Oct. 25, 1940; Stephen Early to White, Oct. 25, 1940, and Roosevelt to White, Randolph, and Hill, Oct. 25, 1940, OF 93, Roosevelt Papers; and *Defender*, Nov. 2, 1940.
25. Hill and Randolph to Roosevelt, Nov. 1, 1940, OF 93, and White to Roosevelt, Nov. 4, 1940, PPF 1336, Roosevelt Papers; column by George Schuyler, *Courier*, Nov. 30, 1940; and editorials, Norfolk *Journal and Guide*, Nov. 2, 1940, *Afro-American*, Nov. 3, 30, 1940, and *Defender*, Dec. 7, 1940.
26. "Negro Organizations and the War Effort," Report from Special Service Division, April 28, 1942, RG 228, National Archives; Roy Wilkins, COHC, pp. 83–88; Roi Ottley, "Negro Morale," *New Republic*, vol. CV (Nov. 10, 1941), p. 613; and *idem.*, *Black Odyssey*, p. 283; NAACP, Minutes of the Board of Directors, Dec. 9, 1940, NAACP Papers; *Crisis*, vol. XLVII (Dec. 1940), p. 375, and XLVIII (Jan. 1941), pp. 22–23; materials in Roosevelt Papers, OF 335-H; and *Afro-American*, Dec. 7, 1940, and *Courier*, Dec. 14, 1940.
27. Max Lerner, "I Thought of Lincoln," *New Republic*, vol. CIV (Feb. 10, 1941), p. 177; Jonathan Daniels, "Native at Large," *Nation*, vol. CLIV (Feb. 9, 1941), p. 156; Brooks Atkinson, "The Decision Is Simple," *ibid.* (March 1, 1941), pp. 262–65; *Courier*, Dec. 28, 1940, Jan. 4, 25, Feb. 8, March 8, 15, 1941; editorials in *Defender*, May 17, 1941, and New York *Times*, May 7, 1941.
28. Phelps-Stokes Fund to Roosevelt, April 22, 28, 1941, OF 93, Roosevelt Papers; and New York *Times*, May 6, 7, 1941.
29. Editorial, New York *Times*, May 9, 1941; Pearl Buck to Roosevelt, Jan.

10, 1941, PPF 7339, Roosevelt Papers; *Afro-American,* April 19, May 10, 1941; and *Defender,* May 17, 1941.

30. Alexander, COHC, pp. 674–75; front page editorial, *Afro-American,* May 3, 1941; St. Louis *Post-Dispatch,* Feb. 9, 1941; and St. Louis *Argus,* Feb. 28, 1941.

31. Myrdal, *An American Dilemma,* p. 816; NAACP letter to *Courier,* July 5, 1941; *Afro-American,* March 1, 1941; materials in OF 93, Roosevelt Papers; "Where Democracy Fails" and "American Nazism," *Opportunity,* vol. XIX (Jan. 1941), p. 3, and (Feb. 1941), p. 35; Lester Granger, "The Negro and Economic Opportunity," *Proceedings of the National Conference on Social Work, 1941,* p. 76; editorials in *Defender,* April 5, 1941, *Crisis,* vol. XLVIII (April 1941), and *Opportunity,* vol. XIX (April 1941); and *Afro-American,* March 29, 1941.

32. NAACP, Report of the Department of Branches, 1941, NAACP Papers; and *Afro-American,* Jan. 4, 18, 25, June 7, 1941.

33. NAACP, Minutes of the Board of Directors, Feb. 10, 1941, and NAACP Press Releases, Jan. 17, Feb. 2, 7, 14, April 1, 4, 25, May 2, 8, 13, 1941, NAACP Papers; Walter White, "It's Our Country, Too: The Negro Demands the Right to Fight For It," *Saturday Evening Post,* vol. CCXIII (Dec. 14, 1940), 63 ff.; and *Afro-American,* Jan. 4, 25, April 9, May 10, 17, 1941.

34. Lester B. Granger, COHC, p. 304; Benjamin McLaurin, COHC, pp. 295–96; and *Afro-American* and *Courier,* Jan. 25, 1941.

35. Randolph, "The Negro March on Washington," *The Black Worker,* July 1941; Benjamin McLaurin, COHC, p. 299; and column by John Sengstacke in *Defender,* Jan. 18, 1941.

36. Benjamin McLaurin, COHC, p. 36; *Defender,* Feb. 15, 22, 29, 1941; A. Philip Randolph, *idem.,* "Let the Negro Masses Speak," *Black Worker,* March 1941, *idem.,* "Call to Negro America to March on Washington for Jobs and Equal Participation in National Defense," *ibid.,* May 1941, and *idem.,* "The Call to the March on Washington," *ibid.,* July 1941; and Randolph to Eleanor Roosevelt, June 3, 1941, Eleanor Roosevelt Papers.

37. Eleanor Roosevelt to Robert Patterson, June 10, 1941, Eleanor Roosevelt Papers; Benjamin McLaurin, COHC, p. 300; Stephen Early to Wayne Coy, June 6, 1941, OF 10B, Roosevelt Papers; *Afro-American,* June 7, 1941; Salmond, " 'Aubrey Williams Remembers,' " pp. 73–75; and P.L.F. to M. Thompson, May 27, 1941, Eleanor Roosevelt Papers.

38. Randolph to Roosevelt, May 29, 1941, OF 93, Roosevelt Papers; White, *A Man Called White,* pp. 189–92; and New York *Amsterdam News* June 21, 1941, and *Afro-American,* June 21, 1941.

39. Editorials, *Crisis,* vol. XLVIII (March 1941), p. 71, *Opportunity,* vol. XIX (Feb. 1941), p. 35, *Defender,* June 21, 1941, *Courier,* June 28, 1941; Ottley, *New World A-Coming,* 306–7; and Walter White, "What the Negro Thinks of the Army," *Annals,* vol. CCXXIII (Sept. 1942), p. 67.

40. Editorials, *Daily Worker,* Feb. 10, March 3, June 17, 1941; articles by

James Ford and Henry Winston, *ibid.*, June 11, 16, 1941; and Walter White to John T. Graves, July 14, 1941, in Graves, *The Fighting South*, pp. 129-30.

41. Edwin Watson to Roosevelt, June 14, 1941, and Wayne Coy to Roosevelt, June 16, 1941, OF 391, Roosevelt Papers; *Defender*, June 21, 1941; *Courier* and New York *Amsterdam News*, June 7, 14, 21, 1941; and New York Governor Herbert Lehman to Roosevelt, June 9, 1941, OF 93, Roosevelt Papers.

42. Will Alexander, COHC, pp. 669–73; *Afro-American*, April 9, 1941; Sidney Hillman to Eleanor Roosevelt, May 23, 1941, Eleanor Roosevelt Papers; New York *Times*, May 11, June 12, 13, 14, 16, 1941; *Defender*, June 21, 1941.

43. Roosevelt to Edwin Watson, June 14, OF 391, Roosevelt Papers; Stimson Diary, June 18, 1941; New York *Amsterdam News*, June 28, 1941; Benjamin McLaurin, COHC, pp. 301–5; and White, *A Man Called White*, pp. 191–92.

44. Memorandum "Proposals of the Negro March-on-Washington Committee to President Roosevelt for Urgent Consideration," Roosevelt Papers, OF 391; White, *A Man Called White*, p. 192; and Lawrence D. Reddick, "The Negro in the Navy in World War II," *Journal of Negro History*, vol. XXXII (April 1947), p. 202.

45. Louis Ruchames, *Race, Jobs, and Politics* (New York, 1953), pp. 19–21; NAACP, Minutes of the Board of Directors, June 26, 1941, NAACP Papers; and March-on-Washington Committee press release "Why and How the March Was Postponed," March-on-Washington Movement Pamphlet File, Schomburg Collection, New York Public Library.

46. Editorials, *Afro-American, Courier, Defender*, and New York *Amsterdam News*, July 5, 1941; NAACP, Minutes of the Board of Directors, June 26, 1941, NAACP Papers; Mary McLeod Bethune to Eleanor Roosevelt, July 10, 1941, and Randolph to Roosevelt, June 30, 1941, Eleanor Roosevelt Papers; Channing Tobias to Roosevelt, July 3, 1941, Randolph to Roosevelt, July 7, 1941, and White to Roosevelt, July 8, 1941, OF 4245-G, Roosevelt Papers; and Mark Ethridge to Stephen Early, Aug. 20, 1941, OF 391, Roosevelt Papers.

47. Editorials, *Afro-American*, Aug. 2, 1941, *Defender*, Oct. 11, Nov. 8, 1941; column by Roy Wilkins, New York *Amsterdam News*, July 5, 1941; and Randolph, "The Negro March on Washington."

48. *Defender*, June 28, 1941; editorials, New York *Amsterdam News*, July 12, 1941, *Afro-American*, Nov. 1, 29, 1941, *Defender*, Oct. 11, 1941; Robinson quoted in *Afro-American*, Nov. 8, 1941; *Courier*, Nov. 1, 1941; *Defender*, Dec. 13, 1941; and Walter White, "The Negro and National Defense," in Harry W. Laidler, ed., *The Role of the Negro in Our Future Civilization* (New York, 1942), p. 40.

49. NAACP, Minutes of the Board of Directors, Dec. 8, 1941, and Memorandum to NAACP State Branches, Dec. 12, 1941, NAACP Papers; *Crisis*, vol. XLIX (Jan. 1942), p. 7; *Defender*, Dec. 13, 1941, and

Courier, Feb. 14, 1942; New York *Times*, Jan. 10, 11, 1942; and A. Philip Randolph, "Government Sets Pattern of Jim-Crow," *Interracial Review*, vol. XV (July 1942), pp. 101–2, "Why Should We March?" *Survey Graphic*, vol. XXXI (Nov. 1942), p. 489, and "Keynote Address to the Policy Conference of the March-on-Washington Movement" (Sept. 26, 1942), March-on-Washington Movement Pamphlet File.

CHAPTER 13

1. NAACP, Report of the Secretary, March 9, April 7, 1939, and Minutes of the Board of Directors, March 13, April 14, 1939, NAACP Papers; New York *Times*, March 1, 12, 19, 23, April 5, 19, 1939; Stokes to Frank Murphy, Nov. 4, 1939, Frank Murphy Papers; "My Day" column of Feb. 28, 1939, Eleanor Roosevelt Papers; and *Crisis*, vol. XLVI (April 1939), p. 115.
2. Walter White to Eleanor Roosevelt, Feb. 29, 1939, Eleanor Roosevelt Papers; Ickes, *Secret Diary*, 2:612–17; Roosevelt quoted in column by Harry McAlphin, *Defender*, Jan. 30, 1943; Walter White to Daisy Lampkin, Feb. 17, 1939, NAACP Papers; *Afro-American*, March 4, April 8, 15, 1939; and Eleanor Roosevelt, "Presentation of Spingarn Medal to Marian Anderson," *Crisis*, vol. XLVI (Sept. 1939), p. 285.
3. Editorials in New York *Evening Post*, April 10, 1939, and *Defender*, July 8, 1939; Walter White to Eleanor Roosevelt, June 13, 1939; David A. Lane, Jr., "The Development of the Present Relationship of the Federal Government to Negro Education," *Journal of Negro Education*, vol. VII (July 1938), pp. 278–80; and Hoyt, *Paul Robeson*, p. 97.
4. Philadelphia *Tribune*, Oct. 27, 1938.
5. William Hastie to Walter White, Jan. 4, 1939, NAACP Papers; and Miller, *The Petitioners*, pp. 432–33.
6. New York *Times*, Jan. 26, 1922, April 16, 1937.
7. Cowley, "Two Books About the Negro."
8. Editorial, New York *Times*, March 7, 1930.
9. Holt, *Mary McLeod Bethune*, p. 182; and Powell, *Marching Blacks*, pp. 116–18.

Index